Also by James Kotsilibas-Davis

Great Times, Good Times:
The Odyssey of Maurice Barrymore

The Barrymores:
The Royal Family in Hollywood

MYRNA LOY

Being and Becoming

MYRNA LOY

Being and Becoming

*by James Kotsilibas-Davis
and Myrna Loy*

Alfred A. Knopf · New York

1987

This Is a Borzoi Book
Published by Alfred A. Knopf, Inc.

Copyright © 1987 by James Kotsilibas-Davis and Myrna Loy
All rights reserved under International and Pan-American Copyright
Conventions. Published in the United States by Alfred A. Knopf, Inc.,
New York, and simultaneously in Canada by Random House of Canada
Limited, Toronto. Distributed by Random House, Inc., New York.

All photographs, except those listed below, are from the private collection of Myrna Loy: PRODUCTION STILLS (Section #3): Courtesy of
the Academy of Motion Picture Arts and Sciences: page 1 (bottom).
Courtesy of the Douglas Whitney Collection: pages 6 (bottom); 7 (middle); 8 (both); 11 (middle); 14 (bottom); 16 (top & middle). Courtesy of
the John Kobal Collection: pages 9 (bottom); 11 (bottom). PUBLICITY
SHOTS (Section #4): Courtesy of the Douglas Whitney Collection: pages
4 (top); 12 (top); 13 (top); 14 (both); 16 (bottom). PRIVATE PURSUITS
(Section #5): Courtesy of the Douglas Whitney Collection: pages 6
(both); 7 (bottom). Courtesy of David McGough: page 16.

Library of Congress Cataloging-in-Publication Data

Kotsilibas-Davis, James.
Myrna Loy : being and becoming.
Includes index.
1. Loy, Myrna, [date]   . 2. Actors—United States—Biography.
I. Loy, Myrna, [date]   . II. Title.
PN2287.L67K68   1987   791.43'028'0924 [B]   87-45237
ISBN 0-394-55593-7 *BIO*
LOY

Manufactured in the United States of America

FIRST EDITION

Designed by Peter A. Andersen

MEMO FROM

MYRNA LOY

*Life is not a having
and a getting; but a
being and a becoming.*
— Matthew Arnold,

---

* An interpretation of "Not a having and a resting, but a growing and a becoming is the character
of perfection as culture perceives it"—Matthew Arnold

PREFACE

January 15, 1985: a hairdresser and a makeup man follow Myrna Loy around her Manhattan penthouse, preparing the seventy-nine-year-old star to be honored at Carnegie Hall tonight. I'm relieved that experts are in tow. When Myrna does her own hair and makeup, she adds twenty years to features relatively unscathed by the rigors of eight decades. Such things were done for her for so long she just never developed the knack.

She is obviously excited as the final hour approaches, although her enthusiasm has been guarded until now. "It's about time!" she snapped privately when the Academy of Motion Picture Arts and Sciences announced its tribute. She was not ungrateful. She was not bowled over, either. After all, the woman whom *The New York Times* two days ago called "the most modern actress of her generation" has never even been nominated for the Academy's Oscar. She always made acting look too easy. "I don't know any other actress who has the wit that Myrna Loy has," George Cukor told me, "the kind of wit that amuses me—underplayed, suggested, very, very subtle. The whole look of her is witty and wise, but beneath all this there's a kind of humanity and tenderness. She has something in that lovely face, something about her that touches your heart."

Having repeatedly overlooked these qualities, the Academy is making amends—sort of. It is throwing this big all-star gala to honor Myrna Loy and raise money for itself. It is not, however, presenting her with a coveted Special Oscar before the vast millions who will view the televised Academy Awards ceremony in March. Such subtleties escape Myrna, who must be the least aggressive, most unpremeditative person to achieve major stardom within the Hollywood studio system. She is pleased that the proceeds of her tribute will benefit the Academy Foundation's education and film-preservation programs. She has agreed to appear, although recovering from illness, mainly because she considers them good causes.

This is typical of Myrna Loy. She does not see the world as a vehicle for herself. She seldom asks for favors, seldom makes demands of anyone but herself. I once asked her why, during her Metro-Goldwyn-Mayer heyday, she had never stipulated that Adrian design all of her clothes, as Crawford, Shearer, and Garbo had. "Dolly Tree was better for me," she replied. "Besides, I wasn't in a position to make such demands." As a matter of fact, she was the studio's top female star at the time, the only one of those ladies consistently making the top ten box-office lists in the late thirties. No other actress touched post-Depression Americans the way she did. "There ought to be a law against any man who doesn't marry Myrna Loy," declared young Jimmy Stewart in 1937. Every man wanted to marry her. Every woman wanted to be her.

Not that Myrna is a Pollyanna. She knows her way around. She will not allow herself to be compromised. Joseph L. Mankiewicz must be recalling all the scripts she resolutely returned to him when he observes at Carnegie Hall: "Myrna Loy has a smile that automatically changes the subject."

Robert Mitchum, who flew in from Hollywood for the tribute, recalls her pragmatism during an ill-conceived shoot for *The Red Pony*: "She told me not to worry. She had contract right of approval over every publicity shot. Myrna just said, 'If the studio wants to waste all that money, let them,' and killed every picture in that twenty-thousand-dollar shoot."

She has always been aware of a star's prerogatives, but belaboring them seems trivial to the daughter of pioneer cattlemen and legislators. Something basic, something involving courage and decency and modesty, is ingrained from a childhood spent in the sprawling Montana valley settled by her Welsh grandparents. Her battles are not fought merely for herself. Her accomplishments are not measured by outward shows. Self-interest and ostentation embarrass her.

During a visit to Hollywood in preparation for this book, we made a side trip to Montana. She had a bad cold on the day of our departure, and regretted leaving her heavy clothing back in New York. I reminded her of the opulent mink coat she had just received for doing that "What becomes a legend most?" ad. The sender, to avoid the New York tax, had mailed it to her Los Angeles address. Well, my innocent reminder elicited the look of scornful incredulity Myrna usually reserves for bigots or rabid conservatives. How could her biographer, after years of friendship and months of intensive interviews, imagine that Myrna Loy would return to Montana flaunting thirty thousand dollars' worth of Blackglama pelts? She wore instead an inadequate raccoon jacket, and borrowed a heavy cloth coat from her cousin's wife against the cold Montana spring. "She's not a movie queen, you know," George Cukor admonished when I started this book. "She's not that. She's a *real* personality."

At Carnegie Hall, two hours of film clips and tributes from sixty years apprise a full house of her infinite variety as an actress and a woman. Her effervescent Nora Charles makes its expected impact. Her brittle Lady Esketh in *The Rains Came*, her quintessential postwar wife in *The Best Years of Our Lives*, her alcoholic mother in *From the Terrace* astound those who think she is limited to comedy. Versatile evocations of characters from Steinbeck, Sherwood, and Hammett, Nathanael West, Philip Barry, and John O'Hara highlight clips representing a mere twenty-two of her hundred and twenty-four films. Only Lionel Barrymore and a few busy character actors can approach that number.

Burt Reynolds appears to lament the fact that he was born too late to join the likes of Tracy, Gable, and Powell as a Loy leading man, but had to content himself with playing her son in *The End*.

Sidney Lumet, who in 1981 directed *Just Tell Me What You Want*, her last feature to date, observes: "Myrna is like all the great ones. She has enormous reserves of power as an actress, so you can feel ten things she's not showing you for the one detail you can see. Both as a woman and as a performer, she has an incredible personal dignity."

Lena Horne elaborates: "I remember her both as a great star and a woman of accomplishment. She has pursued an extraordinary public career and along with it, quietly, without fanfare, she lived a useful, purposeful life. She interrupted her career during World War II to work with the Red Cross. From the very beginning, she was a member of the American Association for the United Nations, a colleague of Mrs. Roosevelt, and a delegate to UNESCO. She was active in the National Committee Against Discrimination in Housing with my uncle Frank Horne, who admired her commitment. She is dedicated, compassionate. To look like that and be like that—well, that's a great woman. I salute you, Madam."

They all salute her, lining the stage beneath those celluloid shades of her departed colleagues, lifting their arms and hearts to her: Sidney Lumet, Teresa Wright, Harold Russell, Sylvia Sidney, Tony Randall, Maureen O'Sullivan, Robert Mitchum, Lauren Bacall, Burt Reynolds, Lena Horne, Maureen Stapleton, Joseph L. Mankiewicz, Lillian Gish. The audience, three thousand friends and fans and strangers, stand and turn to applaud a radiant blur of bronze beads and copper hair in the dress circle. The honoree rises to acknowledge the sustained ovation, holding up a bouquet of long-stemmed red roses as if to shield herself from adulation she considers excessive.

Modesty and hothouse flowers recall the fragrant wild roses she loved that grew along the fences of her grandfather's Crow Creek Valley cattle ranch. Those roses she remembers were long gone when we returned there. But the split-log ranch buildings, the valley itself, still lay like perpetual offerings to the Big Belt and Bitterroot Ranges. Despite their awesome omnipresence, these soaring extensions of the Northern Rockies remain comforting, perhaps because the vast, unbroken sky dwarfs them.

Sky—there is more of it in Montana, somehow—dominates the mountains. While, far below, the ornate granite monument to Myrna Loy's paternal grandparents dominates the valley's blunt, straw-tufted graveyard. This cut and polished slab was intended to crown a family plot, but the family scattered. Only infants who predeceased their parents, marked by five small stones, attend them here. Just as David T. and Ann Williams abandoned Welsh valleys for a new world, their progeny left the Crow Creek Valley. Most of them went no farther than the mountainsides of Helena forty miles away, yet each cleared a place and made a stand. And one of them, this red-haired granddaughter withstanding tribute at Carnegie Hall, took courage from her pioneer past and strength from valley earth, and reached for the sky.

MYRNA LOY

Being and Becoming

PIONEER
STRAINS

In a business that thrives on public exposure, I've managed to get away
with being a very private person. How is that possible? Well, for one
thing, I kept my mouth shut, which wasn't as easy as it sounds. Louella
Parsons and that bunch were always sniffing around, but they gave me
the willies. I wouldn't let them in my house. It didn't stop there. During the so-called Golden Age of Hollywood, interviews resembled Presidential press conferences and studios required daily sacrifices of time
and privacy for the sake of almighty publicity. Liaison men from Metro-
Goldwyn-Mayer's vast publicity department handled each star, and Larry
Barbier, poor soul, had two of the toughest charges: Spencer Tracy and
me . . . if you don't think that was a load! To avoid dreaded interviews
and studio schemes, Spence went on bats and I just went, leaving poor
Larry to cover for us.

As you pass eighty, however, preserving your privacy becomes far
less urgent than sharing your experience. So I stopped resisting and
agreed to do this book. All the digging was rather like intense psycho-
analysis, but I wanted it to be complete and candid. It can be, you
know, without being one of those bed-to-bed marathons that keep appearing. Not that those things don't occasionally offer a valid aspect of
Hollywood, but it's only one aspect. Any business involving so many
beautiful and high-strung people working together on such intense and

intimate terms is bound to breed a kind of easy promiscuity. God knows, I've fended off my share of amorous men—attractive, desirable men.

John Barrymore in all his glory stayed in hot pursuit during my early years at Warner Brothers. That was by no means a singular honor. He also pursued every other pretty young thing on the lot, and just because he felt like a little redhead now and then didn't incline me to join the club. I sent Clark Gable flying off my back porch into the bushes one night, and, boy, did he punish me for that! Keeping ahead of Spencer Tracy wasn't easy, either. He chased me for years, then sulked adorably when I married someone else. Leslie Howard wanted to whisk me off to the South Seas, and, believe me, that was tempting. But he happened to be married at the time—they all were—and that sort of thing never appealed to me. Besides, I was usually married or about to be myself, so extracurricular activities didn't interest me. No one has ever been able to make me understand how you can love one man and sleep with another at the same time.

These days you're made to feel dull and defensive if you weren't the Whore of Babylon. Well, succumbing isn't the only interesting aspect of a relationship, is it? And relationships are not the only compelling part of life. Most of those sensation-oriented biographies, written by people who go to Hollywood for three or four weeks and come back and tell the "inside story," eliminate the vital details that constitute life—in my case a life that began in Montana with the mingling of several pioneer strains. You see, my grandparents were adventurers. I mean, they were all young people from Wales and Scotland and Sweden. It's incredible when you think of it—whether they came for gold or land, for freedom or a better life—going out to this wild, woolly West.

My paternal grandfather, David Thomas Williams, came from Neith, a little stretch of valley eleven miles from Swansea in South Wales. His parents and their parents and theirs before them were farmers, but the land didn't hold young David. In 1856, before his twenty-first birthday, he sailed from Liverpool to Philadelphia. He went directly to Miners Mills, where they were hiring immigrants in the mines, but higher wages lured him to mines in Johnstown, then Mason City, Virginia. It took two years to accumulate enough capital for the long westward journey to the goldfields of Monte Cristo, California.

A moderate strike didn't keep him in Monte Cristo. The richer possibilities of the country's deep interior diverted him. He joined the stampede to newly discovered goldfields near Austin, Nevada, where he found gold and something he hadn't bargained for. I mean, he met my future grandmother, Ann Morgan Davis, who had come over from Glamorganshire, Wales, with her parents in the Family Immigration of 1851. To appease Annie's skeptical father, David established himself in business, purchasing two four-horse teams for hauling freight to and from Salt Lake City. With a prophetic stroke of showmanship, he hired "Martin the Wizard," an itinerant magician, to entertain at forts and settlements en route. They accepted everything from rabbit skins to pumpkins in payment for tickets, later selling the accumulation profitably in Salt Lake City. After a lucrative week in Tooele, Utah—what my grandfather called "a clean-up"—he married Annie in September, 1865.

The following spring, leaving his pregnant bride safe in Salt Lake City, he started for Elk City, Idaho, with teams carrying full complements of freight. Six more teams joined him at the Snake River for the trek through Indian country. Evading or fighting hostile Indians became commonplace during his early years on the plains, but one encounter impressed him. "At Campbell's Creek," he recorded, "we met a band of Indians who gave us no trouble, but showed us a large number of white man's scalps, which they exhibited on long poles." Undaunted, he made two more profitable hauls to Salt Lake City and back, before settling in Idaho with Annie to raise horses and cattle. That didn't hold him for long. When a better opportunity appeared in the Montana Territory, he sold the Idaho spread, retaining only some breeding stock.

Driving two well-supplied wagons pulled by bull teams, my grandparents started across the Bitterroot Range into Montana. God knows, those pioneer women had spunk: *Progressive Men of Montana* gives a full account of Grandfather, but there's nothing about Annie other than that he married her. As a matter of fact, they both drove wagons to Montana, as they had from Utah to Idaho. He drove one. She drove the other—while pregnant and tending their two children, her blind mother, her gooseberry and blueberry bushes, and her apple-tree seedlings. The orchard she planted thrived for a century. I played there as a child. Only a few scattered, gnarled trees remain, but when I visited recently, they were blossoming.

When they reached Radersburg, in 1870, it was still a booming gold-rush town, but gold hadn't lured the restless Welshman. The advantageous topography of Crow Creek Valley, four miles below town, brought him there. Smooth foothills of the Northern Rockies made the valley a fertile bowl—they still do—and Crow Creek still irrigates it, winding into the source of the Missouri. My grandfather, at the age of thirty-five, purchased a hundred and sixty acres, added fences and sturdy split-log buildings, planted and harvested, and began raising stock. By 1876, he had entered another two hundred acres under the Desert Act.

There were still hazardous times, let me tell you. That same year, less than two hundred miles from the Crow Creek Valley, Sitting Bull dispatched Custer at Little Bighorn. The new ranch was all fenced in and under cultivation when the devastating winter of '86 nearly wiped out the stockmen. Grandfather endured and prospered. When in 1889 the Montana Territory won statehood, most of the valley's twelve square miles were his.

They paid the price. Of ten children born to my grandmother between 1866 and 1890, only five survived. Three boys and two girls were lost to scarlet fever and climate in that virile valley. The deaths of his older brothers left my father, David Franklin Williams, born in 1879, the eldest boy. He was attending grammar school in Radersburg when he first encountered Della Mae Johnson, the girl who would be my mother. She was born there, a year after he had been, to a Scottish mother and a Swedish father, who were every bit as enterprising as my Welsh grandparents.

Scots are adventurous people, you know, they really are. You find them firmly entrenched everywhere in the world. My maternal grandmother, Isabel Giles, sailed from Scotland with a Kennedy aunt around 1860. She hadn't planned to stay in America, but the thirty-five-day passage made her so seasick she would never return home, although her mother wrote begging for her "lost bairn." There's a story about her ancestry that I've always suspected a little bit, because it resembles the plot of *The Swan*, a very old, very romantic tale. Cousins of mine have documentation—papers, crests, and things—so this one could be true. Supposedly we're descended from the ancient Kennedy clan, which dates back to the Picts. They were reputedly a fierce brood, who once roasted a local abbot on a spit at Culzean Castle, the family seat in Ayrshire. Several generations later, my grandmother's grandmother eloped from the castle with her tutor. They settled west of Glasgow in the city of

6

Largs, where he became a prominent citizen while his aristocratic bride made lace and bore thirteen children.

Whatever her antecedents, my maternal grandmother settled in the little Scottish community of Ohio, Illinois, after her uncomfortable crossing. She married before turning eighteen; but soon after the birth of their only child, her husband died. The adventurous widow took her son, her French china, and her cut glass—some of which I still have—and crossed the plains with a wagon train. They've always been heroic figures to me, my two grandmothers, coming from protected childhoods in Wales and Scotland to a strange new land, fighting like hell to make civilized environments for their men and children. I longed to play women like them in the movies, but it never happened.

My grandmother reached Radersburg in 1867, at the height of its gold rush. That same year, after crossing from Göteborg to Canada, and settling for a time in Chicago, my Swedish grandfather, John Johnson, came up the Missouri on a river steamer with his friend A. W. Sederburg. They walked a hundred and fifty miles from the Fort Benton landing to Radersburg, allowing some ladies who had sailed with them to take the only available stage. Free-milling gold ore and the district's biggest hard-rock mine had lured the young Swedes; but their placer mines came later. Cabinetmakers by trade, they first established a shop in a two-story log building that housed the local Masonic Temple upstairs. According to their sign, Johnson & Sederburg made everything from cradles to coffins.

The Scottish widow and the Swedish cabinetmaker met, married, and settled in Radersburg. My mother, the youngest of their three children, remembered accompanying her father to the diggings during the summer mining season. It was rich mining country then; they took thousands of dollars out. Mother used to pick gold nuggets out of the races. At clean-up time, the nuggets were right on the bedrock. The miners didn't pay much attention, she said, because they were after the gold dust. Grandmother Johnson, a great entertainer in the summer, always gave her departing houseguests souvenir nuggets.

As children, my parents shared the thriving social and cultural life of Radersburg: Fourth of July picnics, where someone always recited the Declaration of Independence; church services on the second floor of the school building whenever Brother Van rode into town on his beautiful white horse; exclusive dancing parties, with armed chaperones at the door to remove roughnecks with guns under their belt or liquor on their breath. Even in a three-saloon mining town, the amenities could be observed.

It was the women who perpetuated culture in what was left of pioneer society. Now it's interesting to find that women are the ones who are keeping culture alive. Today on Broadway, for instance, it's women's parties that keep a show going. Men seem to have become victims of televised sports.

"Our Literary Society meetings were regular Saturday evening parties," Mother boasted. "There was no electric light, but we had powder that we put on for the tableaux. Once we had Hattie McKay clinging to the cross with all these colored lights on her. It was just beautiful." Mother always cherished those times. In fact, years later I had a log house built for her on the ranch so she could spend summers there.

There were also sad memories. Her father died young, leaving her mother to carry on in the mines for several years with Mr. Sederburg. After finally selling out, Grandmother Johnson bought a lovely house in Helena and devoted time to cultivating her three children and her English garden. Following her graduation from Helena High School, my mother studied at the American Conservatory of Music in Chicago.

When my parents connected again, in Helena, he was the privileged son of a reputedly kind and indulgent father. Grandfather Williams could afford to be. By 1900, his Crow Creek Valley "estate," as locals called it, covered more than a thousand acres, where he wintered fifteen hundred head of cattle and numerous horses. The Helena *Independent* judged him "one of the richest men in Broadwater County."

His eldest son avoided ranching after attending the state agricultural college. Gregarious and expansive, he became popular with a lively circle in the capital. He used to tell me about Charles Russell, the Western painter, and Frank Linderman, creator of the popular *Indian Why Stories*. They were bound not only by conviviality but also by concern for the plight of the landless Indians, which led eventually to the creation of the Rocky Boys Indian Reservation. At twenty-three, my father represented Broadwater County at the Eighth Session of the Montana House of Representatives, becoming known as "Honest Dave" after his successful campaign. I have a copy of the House Register, which indicates just how honest he must have been. In the space designated for religion, he boldly scrawled "None"—hardly a politic move for a congressman in 1903.

My mother, great-eyed and spirited, fresh from musical studies in Chicago, proved to be a match for him. He began spending considerable time at the Johnson house, chaperoned by Grandmother and Old Sederburg. They decided to marry and settle in Helena, where "Honest Dave" could pursue his political career.

Toward the end of 1903, Grandfather Williams, at the age of sixty-eight, was stricken by what doctors called a "compilation of diseases." My father returned to Crow Creek Valley. He had already dabbled in cattle-raising after receiving a piece of the ranch; now he was expected to forget politics and run the entire operation. His brother Arthur was still in college, while Elmer was cutting adolescent capers around Radersburg.

On April 13, 1904, nearly half a century after leaving his stretch of Welsh valley, my grandfather died. "Broadwater County can ill afford to lose such men as D. T. Williams," eulogized the Townsend *Star*. "His business force and foresight was needed to guide the helm of progress, while policies of government are being more substantially established. . . . The gentle dews and bright sunlight of well spent life will kiss into existence the many hued flowers to deck the grave of such a man."

Six months later to the day, Annie Davis Williams died at the age of sixty. She was laid to rest beside her husband on the windswept rise that shields the valley they had tamed. I went back there recently and time has stood still. Radersburg is virtually a ghost town now, but the graveyard, the proud Williams stone, and the ranging mountain sentinels stand as I remembered them.

That summer, my parents married and returned to the valley of their birth. Away from the friends and pastimes of the capital—the lives they had made for themselves—they attempted ranch life. One of my father's duties was taking the cattle to market in Chicago, traveling in stock cars, sleeping in the caboose. I was on the way in 1905 when he happened to stop near Broken Bow, Nebraska, on the Burlington Railroad. It wasn't a proper station, really, just a whistle-stop where you got water or fuel for the coal-burning engines. Sometimes they had classical names left by itinerant scholars, and this one was called "Myrna." The expectant father decided then and there, if the child was a girl, that would be her name.

When I was born, on August 2nd, there were great battles between him and my mother and grandmother. The ladies wanted Annabel, a composite of my grandmothers' names, but for once my father held out against the strong women of the family. He gained considerable leverage from the appearance of my mother on the cover of *Field and Stream*. During his absence, while nearly seven months pregnant with me, she had become the first woman to pack through the highest point of the Tetons in the Southern Rockies. My father supposedly blew his stack when he saw it.

So they named me Myrna Adele Williams, because my father liked the sound of it. The Welsh in him probably thought Myrna was a pretty name. All Welshmen are like that, you know, they have a certain amount of poetry in them.

I

THE DÉBUTANTE
1905–1918

Miss Myrna Williams, charming daughter of Mr. and Mrs. David Williams of this city, gave the feature, "The Bluebird Dance," in the Rose Dream Operetta, presented at the Marlow Theater last week. Miss Williams, who is much admired for her grace and beauty, has received many compliments upon her interpretation of the dance.

—*Montana* Record-Herald, 1917

W e call them ranches in Montana, but they are farms as well. We grow everything. The ranch was a wonderful place for a small child. Wild roses with their soft fragrance climbed all over the fence in front. Bitterroot, a kind of cactus with beautiful purplish blossoms, dotted the foothills, but they were a nuisance if your horse stepped on them. Grandmother Williams hadn't planted flowers; this was plains country. Her apple trees were still out back, of course, and my grandfather had planted cottonwood trees around the house. They're very pretty, cottonwood, and they taste good, too. I used to taste everything, all the leaves and flowers.

My baby lambs used to butt me around and, according to Mother, I kept falling asleep in my high chair all over Timothy and Alfalfa, my cats. My father had named them after the grasses they gave to the cattle for fodder. These were precious things to a rancher. My dear old dobbin, Dolly, was so big my legs hardly got over her. I still rode her, though, without a saddle, just a bridle, wearing a ten-gallon hat bigger than I was.

There were no radios or phonographs or touring orchestras in those days, but there was always music. Mother and her sister Lulu Belle, my Aunt Lou, both played piano and violin, Uncle Fred played the guitar, and we had a ranch hand from Germany who was an accomplished violinist. Gathered around the piano in the parlor with other musical friends and relatives, they would play me to sleep with the Berceuse from *Jocelyn* and Brahms's Lullaby way out in Montana where there's not supposed to be any culture.

We had two working ranches then: one for livestock, one for wheat. But my father never really took to ranching again after his days in the capital. He became discouraged with the idea, so we moved back to Helena when I was five. He didn't return to politics, for some reason, but went into real estate, became the director of a bank, and dabbled in stocks and bonds. He was just incredible, a Santa Claus type of man, who never came down the hill without his arms full of presents. He made a big fuss about holidays, particularly Christmas, which was fantastic; its festivity engulfed him—the stories, the decorations, the gifts, and the food. He always cooked holiday dinners, because Mother loathed cooking. He was darn good at it, too, having learned over a campfire at roundup time. In fact, he became quite a gourmet for a cowboy; he even imported cracked crab on ice all the way from Chicago for us. What a dear man he was—a *giving* kind of person.

We lived high off the hog on Fifth Avenue, which was not, of course, Fifth Avenue, New York. It was just a nice middle-class neighborhood. Most of the richer families were building on the opposite mountainside. Helena is a spacious city, climbing up Mount Ascension and Mount Helena from Last Chance Gulch, so we had wonderful, steep streets. When it snowed, you could slide past Judge Cooper's house all the way to the railroad station in the valley part of town. The Coopers lived just below us in a fairly elegant house with an iron fence around it. My parents knew them, but I didn't see much of their son Gary, who was four years older and spent some time at school in England. Later, in Hollywood, we used to laugh about living on the wrong side of town, but, curiously, we seldom talked about our Helena days. That didn't keep him from talking to others about them. According to Edith Goetz, Louis B. Mayer's daughter, Gary would cheerfully describe me "belly bustin' hell-bent for election" down the street past his house.

Gary Cooper confided she had bright red hair in braids, great big freckles, and a turned-up nose, revealed Myrna's erstwhile co-star, William Powell, after the three converged in Hollywood. She wasn't what a boy might call beautiful, but there was some-

thing about her that got to him. He was shy and she was shy, and the most pleasure he got out of the romance was leaning on the Williamses' picket fence listening to Myrna play "The Wedding of the Winds."

The only time he ever spoke to her in those Helena days was one afternoon when he went to the Williamses' house on an errand for his mother. Mrs. Williams, the soul of Montana hospitality, sent Myrna down to the cellar for a glass of apple jelly. Now, back of the furnace down there was a dark hole that had become a phobia with Myrna. She went down the steps bravely enough, carefully made her way to the jelly shelf, but visions horrible and dank rose from the black hole. "Yo-oo-oow!" shrieked Myrna, falling up the cellar steps, bruising her knees and tearing her stockings.

"You," remarked Master Cooper, "are a sissy," probably the only ungallant thing Gary Cooper ever said to a lady. Certainly there have been no complaints since. Myrna, completely mortified, chose to forget the entire episode, including Judge Cooper's little boy, as quickly as possible. They met eventually in Hollywood, but by that time Gary had his hands full with the temperamental Lupe Velez, and Myrna was already far gone into the bizarre. Nothing ever came of the Loy-Cooper romance.

My first beau was another neighbor—John G. Brown, Jr. Actually, he wasn't really my beau. I had a terrible crush on him, but he had no time for me. He would let my girlfriend Ruth Rae ride on the back of his tricycle, while I just trailed along, very disturbed by the whole thing. On Saturday afternoons, Ruth would ask me to call him up for her, and I like a fool would do it. This went on and on, but he never paid any attention to me at all.

Years later, when I started at Warner Brothers, who should send me my first fan letter? Johnny Brown! I had played only a few parts, probably the Orientals, but he wanted pictures of me for his room at college. He claimed the whole college wanted to know about me. Well, I thought, this is my revenge for all those years he ignored me.

Much of my childhood was spent at Grandmother Johnson's house in the valley part of town, where she had the most beautiful gardens— pansy beds, peonies, and tiger lilies taller than I was. In her front-hall settle I discovered programs from the touring companies that played the Marlow with stars like Mrs. Fiske and John Drew. They fascinated me for some reason. I would always get them out and pore over them.

When something appropriate played, Grandmother would take me to the theater—she in her sweet little hat with the velvet pansies. Oh, she was a great lady. There was always great taste in her, and in my mother as well. One play from those days, Maeterlinck's *The Blue Bird*, really stands out—even to what I wore. My dress was China silk, as they called it then, blue China silk, very, very delicate. There were barrettes in my hair I wasn't too crazy about, but Mother had bought me a blue feather fan, my own little fan. Well, this play, a real extravaganza, absolutely *stunned* me. It was the most wonderful thing I'd ever seen in my life. *The Blue Bird* is what did it, I'm sure; the one that finally got me.

We had done a few things in school. I remember being some kind of angel once in a ridiculous outfit in the gymnasium. But my piano and drawing lessons had taken precedence. In fact, contact with my art teacher, a nun at the local Catholic convent, and with my aunts, who were avid Methodists and Presbyterians, had left me rather religious. I passed through the usual self-sacrificing stage, longing to be a nun or a nurse and spend my life doing good to others. After *The Blue Bird*, however, anything but being on stage seemed inconceivable. It wasn't nearly so noble as being a nun, but it *was* attractive. The world and the flesh won out, but it took a long time to reconcile myself to the idea of not being noble.

I began doing plays in our cellar—not on the furnace side with the coal chutes and the dark place that Gary remembered; on the other side, away from imaginary creatures, where Mother kept jellies and preserves. I rigged a curtain and announced *Sleeping Beauty*, no less, as my first production, making up all the lines, but resisting the temptation to cast myself in the title role. A carrot-topped, freckle-faced kid they used to torment with "Redhead, gingerbread, five cents a loaf!" just wasn't beautiful enough for Sleeping Beauty. I gave the role to a girl up the street who had big blond bologna curls, and contented myself with the part of the prince. I made tights from Mother's black stockings, wore my black bloomers over them, and fashioned a collar like Sir Walter Raleigh's from paper. The highlight of my ensemble was this perfectly beautiful gray-and-black feather of Mother's, a very expensive ostrich plume, which I stuck in one of my father's hats. I invited relatives, friends, and, bound to impress him, Johnny Brown to the performance—which was really quite courageous for a basically shy little girl. During my entrance, Mother cried, "Oh, my God! There's my feather!" Stunned, I pulled the curtain and ended the show. *That* was my theatrical début.

During the winter of 1912, my mother nearly died of pneumonia. There were empty tanks of oxygen everywhere in the house, and everyone seemed to have given up; then her nurse came in with a full tank and pulled her through. In order to spare her the rest of the winter in Montana, my father sent us off to La Jolla, California, a beach town near San Diego, which became a dream place for me. We took a house across the road from a steep, rocky cove. At high tide waves reached the road, but when the tide was out I could climb down rough-hewn steps in the cliff to gather specimens with my best friend, Mr. Kline, who ran the local aquarium. Imagine a six-year-old having such a wonderful guide to the brimming marine life of Hell's Bottom!

Mother loved Southern California and saw great opportunity there. When my father, the real-estate man, came down for my seventh birthday, she urged him to buy, among other properties, the corner on Sunset Boulevard where Charlie Chaplin later built his studio. There was nothing on it then. My father could have made a mint, but he was "a Montana boy, by God!" *He* wasn't going to California. Finally, he said, "Enough!"—and we all went home. There was a good deal of trouble about that. I realize now that Mother was experiencing the frustrations of a capable woman who wants to do something and is trapped. She was involved with her music and active in local politics—she was a staunch liberal Democrat; he was a Teddy Roosevelt Republican—yet anything beyond that probably threatened my father's standing as head of the family. Mother wasn't the rambunctious type that pressured others, but she fought every kind of provincialism and bigotry. There was no snobbery in her, no prejudice.

I remember when the first black family moved into our neighborhood. There were very few blacks in Helena in 1912, and our other neighbors were wary or worse. Mother made no distinction at all. She welcomed them and encouraged us to play with their children. "Myrna, come look at this," she called from the front porch one Sunday morning. "Isn't that marvelous?" My little brother David, a towhead, all done up for church in his starched linen suit, was sitting on the curb beside Bubby, the little black boy from across the street, who was in his play clothes. The contrast and the closeness of those two little boys left a fond memory I've carried with me all my life.

Considerable strain persisted between my parents. My father wanted his family in Montana. My mother wanted to be in California. She needed a hysterectomy, and argued that it would be safer to have it done in Los Angeles. He finally gave in, so mother, David, and I took off again. While mother convalesced, we stayed in Ocean Park, on Hart Avenue, with her friend Viva McLaughlin, then moved across the street into a house of our own. Like all the houses on Hart Avenue, ours had two stories, shingles, a sun porch with a swing, and trellises covered with little pink Cécile Brunner roses. Everywhere there was honeysuckle. Ocean Park was a peaceful little corner of the world. People made friends easily in that beachfront community and there seemed to be little harshness or crime to speak of. Well, we did have one scandal. Two boys were arrested for playing marbles for keeps and released to the custody of their parents.

Hart Avenue led to the ocean, and three blocks over stood the Nat C. Goodwin Pier, with its festive café and syncopated orchestra. This was before World War I, when the first jazz was being played. Mother went there with Ocean Park neighbors or friends from Montana, who always seemed to be visiting. This part of life appealed to her—parties and nightclubs, champagne and music. She was a very gay lady with a great love of living.

I preferred the things that went on under the pier—barnacles and creatures that cling to the pilings. My explorations led to a private beach beside the pier and my first movie stars. They wore wonderful bathing costumes with all that Valeska Suratt business of the hair wrapped up in turbans. Of course, in those days everybody had to wear stockings and sort of bloomers for swimming, but the movie people just seemed more glamorous. I thought they were something, really classy. We would sneak under the pier to spy on them and they would chase us away. I had a closer look at movie people during a tour of Universal Studios, where they were making a Western. Even to this day, I look up at that hill and remember the blue lights—they didn't use white light then— and William Farnum shootin' it up with some wranglers. The whole thing fascinated me, but I had no intention of forsaking the theater.

When a cold or something kept me in bed for a few days, the girl next door, whom I hadn't met, sent over a balloon. Her name was Louella Bamberger—MacFarlane after she married—and she is still one of my dearest friends.

I was walking home from school a few days after sending the balloon, relates Lou MacFarlane, *when from behind me came a lovely, lilting voice, which she had even then, saying, "Excuse me, aren't you the girl who sent me the balloon?" I turned around and saw what to me was a goddess. She was three feet taller than I was, at least. Myrna got her full height very young—she was eleven when we met; I was eight—so she looked like a young lady to me, and I was so embarrassed about sending the balloon.*

We both had younger brothers, so we started taking them to the beach and building sand castles and making up stories about what went on in the castles. There were two boys on the next street we had crushes on. Well, I was at the age when it didn't matter to me, but Myrna had an eye for the boys. If Myrna wanted to have a crush on whatever the older boy's name was— he was Russian, very elegant, very handsome—that was fine; I'd have a crush on the other, slightly rougher one. We were too young to interest them, anyway, so we made them the heroes of our sand-castle stories, which were strongly influenced by the Satur-day serials.

We went to the movies every Saturday, but The Perils of Pauline *is all I ever remember seeing. Afterward, we would go to the ballroom at the Ocean Park pier, where they had Saturday-afternoon dancing for children. I had never danced, but Myrna said, "It's easy; I'll teach you." So, we would go to the ballroom and Myrna led and I followed and she taught me how to dance.*

Dancing kind of got to me. I wreathed Cécile Brunner roses in my hair and around my ankles and began imitating what I'd seen on stage. How I carried on! Lessons didn't start until we got back to Montana, but I was a natural dancer. Around that time, my father put his foot down again and said, "You're coming home!"

Europe was at war, leaving America equivocating about interven-tion, and the Williams family battling over Presidential candidates. Mother pushed for Woodrow Wilson and peace; my father tended toward Charles Evans Hughes and intervention. I learned politics early from my family—several points of view. To be an American means speaking one's mind; I wasn't brought up to be intimidated. They believed that you were supposed to be involved, that it was your right. Father and Uncle Arthur both served in the Montana legislature. Mother participated vigorously in Democratic organizations and Aunt Lou served as Treasurer of Broadwater County. Wilson's efforts for a League of Nations, for "peace without victory" appealed to me in 1916. On those issues, Mother and I convinced my father to vote for Wilson over Hughes.

I faced more mundane problems with my grammar-school teacher, an old, set-in-her-ways woman who had also taught my mother. Mathematics, her specialty—her passion, really—happened to be my worst subject, but I was determined to pass her big test. I went to Uncle Len Qualls, a schoolteacher who had married my father's sister Nettie, and he helped me to study for it. When I passed, that woman accused me of cheating. *Well*, honesty was fundamental in our family; they used to call my father "Honest Dave," for God's sake! Cheating was unthinkable. I walked out of that classroom, reported that teacher to the principal, and went home. And I wouldn't go back until she apologized!

At least there were dancing lessons to counteract the hazards of grammar school. I had started ballet classes with Miss Alice Thompson, who chose me to perform in the Rose Dream Operetta at the Marlow Theater. A man named Jansen used to get up these things in various cities and share profits with local groups like the Elks. It was a big event in Helena. I choreographed my own dance piece—based on *The Blue Bird*, of course—and designed a beautiful diaphanous blue costume. I only wish Grandmother Johnson could have seen it; she had died the previous year, leaving a terrible void in my life. Anyway, Mother was excited and proud, but my father went out of town on business the day of the performance. He may have purposely planned it that way, because he disapproved of my theatrical ambitions. All theater was burlesque to him. He must have seen the big picture of me in costume that ran in the local paper, though that, along with my first review, was on the society page.

Despite Wilson's election, we entered "the war to end all wars." My father contemplated enlisting. I think he must have been in pain. He

BEGINNINGS

LEFT: Myrna's Welsh grandparents, David
Thomas Willams and Ann Davis Williams,
immigrated to America in the 1850s and tamed a
Montana valley. BELOW: This portrait of Della
Mae Johnson was taken in 1904 at the time of
her engagement to David Franklin Williams.
BOTTOM: Della, who became Myrna's mother,
is seated at the feet of her sister, Lou, and
her mother, Isabel Giles Johnson, in their
Helena parlor.

Unmistakably Myrna: Her first photograph, taken in 1905; a jaunty pose three years later; and a portrait with her younger brother, David, in 1915. OPPOSITE ABOVE: Myrna already commands the camera in this 1911 sitting with her parents in Helena. OPPOSITE BELOW: At a genteel family gathering in the wilds of Montana, Myrna shares a table with cousin Laura Belle, while her mother, father, Aunt Lou, and grandmother sit with assorted relatives at Grandmother Johnson's house.

The Williams family posed with a stuffed ostrich at Colston's Ostrich Farm, Pasadena, when they wintered in California in 1912.

RIGHT: Coquette in a tree: Myrna in
Helena around 1910. BELOW: Myrna,
at far left, and Louella Bamberger
MacFarlane, second from left, have
remained friends all their lives. The
occasion pictured here, Lou's ninth
birthday in Ocean Park, California, also
included Myrna's brother, David, tight-
lipped and towheaded, at right.

Myrna made her stage debut in 1916 in the Rose Dream Operetta at the Marlow Theater, Helena, choreographing her own dance—based on *The Blue Bird*—and designing her own diaphanous blue costume.

LEFT: While attending Venice High School, Myrna posed as "Aspiration" for a sculpture group by her art teacher, Henry Fielding Winebreiner, which still stands in front of the school. BELOW: In Culver City, Myrna, at fifteen, posed dramatically with her friend Jean Chessler. The Goldwyn lot, where they often played, can be seen in the background. BOTTOM: They sit in front of the Williams house on Delmas Terrace.

During her teenage years, Myrna flitted about Culver City fulfilling her ambition to be a danseuse in the Ruth St. Denis tradition.

ABOVE: The danseuse left school and obtained her first job as a performer at Grauman's Egyptian Theatre on Hollywood Boulevard. She is the second kneeling dancer on the Pharaoh's right in the spectacular prologue for De Mille's first *Ten Commandments* in 1923. OPPOSITE RIGHT: Myrna is costumed for a nautch dance in Grauman's prologue for Douglas Fairbanks' *Thief of Bagdad*. OPPOSITE LEFT: Henry Waxman's publicity shots of Myrna and Lillian Butterfield for the *Ten Commandments* prologue impressed Rudolph Valentino and won Myrna her first screen test.

This striking fifteenth-birthday portrait was taken in August, 1920. (Montana Historical Society)

Myrna posed with her mother, her brother,
and his sculptures in their Beverly Hills home
in 1930.

was having problems, probably some I didn't know about, but chiefly the continuing friction between him and Mother had taken its toll. Sometimes, looking back on it now, I think he was probably going through some kind of breakdown. The idea of his going to war at thirty-nine was almost suicidal.

We were sitting out on the back porch one balmy autumn evening when he told me he definitely planned to enlist. "You're my little soldier," he said. I was wearing a child's military outfit, a jacket that resembled a soldier's, a little cap. "When I go, I'm leaving you to take care of things. Maybe it won't last long. Maybe it will. But your dad's going to depend on you. If I don't come back, you'll always take care of your mother and your brother, won't you?"

That was in the fall of 1918, just before Spanish influenza struck Helena. It devastated the town. You couldn't get nurses. You couldn't get doctors; I mean, you got them to stop in and then they would disappear into the night. People walked the streets with makeshift surgical masks over their mouths. Mother and David came down with it. My father and I nursed them. When they were half recovered, it struck me. I couldn't be upstairs with the others, so my father made up a couch for me in the dining room. He took care of me; he took care of all of us. He used to come and wrap me in sheets every night, frozen sheets, trying to get my temperature down. That man sat there—I can remember him sitting right over me—and he went through the agony with me, afraid that I was going to die.

Finally, I passed the crisis, and Mother and David recovered. One night, while I was still sleeping downstairs, I heard terrible noises, an awful sound from my father's room upstairs. He was hemorrhaging. He had this disease—probably a long time before it showed itself, because he'd been so busy taking care of everybody else. And particularly taking care of me. Well, I became hysterical. To get me out of the way, they took me across town to one of my mother's friends, a woman who had stayed with us in California. She had a huge house with three or four stories. I just wandered around from room to room.

There's an old Swedish saying that when a bird hits a window, someone is going to die. Well, while I was wandering around that house, I walked into the parlor and a bird hit one of the windows. A few minutes later, the telephone rang and I took off up the stairs, running up and up and up as far as I could go. They started calling for me, but I wouldn't answer. When I finally went down, Mother's friend was on her bed crying. I knew my father was dead.

Ironically, he died on the day of the false armistice—newspapers announced it before the Germans actually signed—so the whole town was celebrating. We buried him on November 11, 1918, the day of the true armistice, outside of town at Forestvale. Helena was in an uproar when we rode back. People stood in the streets cheering. Sirens wailed and firecrackers blasted. That night a torchlight procession twisted through town. The celebration went on for two days, echoing up the hill to our house of mourning.

I worshipped him, you see, worshipped him. I coped with his loss by accepting the responsibility for my mother and brother he had entrusted to me. I didn't realize for years how much damage this had done. It turned me into this person who had to take care of them. As a matter of fact, too much so, for too long a time. I didn't marry until I was past thirty. Years later, when I told an analyst about it, she said, "What a terrible burden to place on a child!"

"But I wasn't a child," I protested. "I was already an adult." Which, of course, wasn't the case at all. I had just turned thirteen.

2

THE
BACCHANTE
1918–1925

There's a great buzzing and roaring in our ears: It's the thousands upon thousands of readers asking, "Who . . . is . . . she? Who is she? Whoisshe?" Well, she's what Mrs. Rudolph Valentino says is going to be the 1926 Flapper model. You don't know whether she is innocent or sophisticated; but you do know that she is very, very young, and very, very fascinating.
— Motion Picture *magazine, 1925*

Mother loved Montana, but she didn't love those winters. After my father died, she contemplated returning to California. Her Ocean Park friend Viva McLaughlin had moved to Culver City. "Well, if you come," she wrote, "why not come to Culver City?" So we did. We moved to California, and, of course, I thought it was fabulous—it always is when you come upon it.

We bought a house on Delmas Terrace in Culver City, a hamlet between Hollywood and the Pacific Ocean. In our garden there were little orange trees, a peach tree, and an apricot tree that bore fruit. Trellises arched over the driveway laden with roses four or five times bigger than the wild ones in Montana. We kept a goat out in the back. My brother had a touch of TB, and goat's milk was prescribed. The TB didn't last very long; it disappeared—apparently the goat's milk worked.

When we first arrived, I taught Sunday school at the Presbyterian church. One day I missed the answer to some Biblical question from Mr. O'Connell, the minister. He breathed fire and brimstone all over me. I never went back. Mother worried afterward that he might see me dancing between the two tall palm trees in the front yard. I staged dance recitals there with Jean Vandyke, a girl from Mississippi whose brother was in the movies, and Lou MacFarlane, my Ocean Park cohort. We wore makeshift Grecian tunics and did Ruth St. Denis poses like "The Water Lily" all over the front lawn.

Metro-Goldwyn-Mayer was in Culver City; I mean, later on—at that time it was just Goldwyn. There were quite a few studios there. Thomas H. Ince's resembled a Southern mansion—they even had a liveried black butler receiving authorized visitors at the door. Hal Roach had his studio there for years. There may have been other little fly-by-night places, but those were the principal studios. You weren't allowed anywhere near them unless you had official business, but we would climb over the fence into the Goldwyn back lot. We'd take pictures of one another doing dances on top of the fence and striking poses on the standing sets. We had great plans. I was going to be Ruth St. Denis with the studio and the dance company, and Lou would write the plays for us to choreograph. Even as a kid, she made up the stories that we furtively played out together on the Goldwyn back lot. I would return there later under very different circumstances.

My mother put me in the Westlake School for Girls in Los Angeles. That had been decided in Helena, because some people she knew, rich brewers named Kessler, were sending their two daughters. She chose that very exclusive school not for its exclusivity—Mother was in no way ever a snob—but for its promise of an atmosphere that would foster my artistic pursuits. She didn't have a lot of money. My father's legacy would have sufficed in Montana, perhaps, but not in California, not with Mother's tastes. To supplement her income, she gave private music lessons and helped in a friend's dress shop. She used to get clothes for me there. Although far from the richest girl at Westlake, I was certainly the best dressed.

I commuted on the Venice Short Line, which went from Western Avenue all the way to the beach. We had wonderful streetcars—I wish we had them now. I would get off on Western Avenue, walk a few blocks to Westmoreland, and there was Westlake. My experience there began agreeably with an adored language teacher and a special music teacher, who came in to give me piano lessons. I could also dance at their May Festival. Privately, I studied ballet in downtown Los Angeles at Mme. Matildita's École de Choreographie Classicet. I loved those afternoons in town. After class, I would go to the public library, take out an armful of classics, and devour them on the Venice Short Line going home.

Mme. Matildita, a former star ballerina at La Scala, adhered to traditional European methods, teaching all the positions, all in French, swatting you if you moved incorrectly. She revealed my tragedy as far as ballet is concerned: I couldn't dance on my toes. They were too long. You really should have short toes, rather stubby, so they will bend under. As it is, dancers go through hell with their feet, but mine were just hopeless. "Never, never will you dance on those toes!" Madame decreed. But the lessons were an enriching experience, a base for everything that I did later.

Classes met on the top floor of the Majestic Building, in a sort of ballroom surrounded by big windows. One day during class, the whole room suddenly shook and the building swayed. I stood stock-still— stopped—which is often my reaction to such things. Others ran helter-skelter, trying frantically to go down in the elevators, which had stopped. But Madame had been in the San Francisco earthquake. She stood in the doorway, where there's likely to be a steel girder to grab if the walls go. The walls didn't go. The center hit Long Beach, I believe, so Los Angeles escaped severe damage. It was quite a jolt, though, my first earthquake. When I finally made it home, my two wonderful palm trees in the front yard were uprooted. There were aftershocks all night long in Culver City. They went on and on. I peered out the window, just repeating, "Oh, my God, this will never end. . . ."

We had gathered quite a ménage on Delmas Terrace. Old Sederburg, Grandfather Johnson's partner from Radersburg, stayed with us. A bachelor, he had always lived with our family in Radersburg, then with Grandmother in Helena, and, after her death, with my aunt or with us. When he died, his considerable estate went to a girlfriend he'd kept stashed somewhere.

My aunt and my cousin came to live with us—Aunt Lou Wilder, Mother's sister, whose late husband had been a dentist in Townsend. Her daughter Laura Belle, while walking along the street one day, suddenly fell, just fell, and from then on could never walk without help. She had one of those diseases of muscle deterioration, I'm sure, which now can be treated. We might have helped her if they had known then, but we could only comfort her as she grew weaker.

Culver City was a haven for Aunt Lou, and having her there relieved my mother of the housekeeping duties she despised. Mother was clever—she always managed to have someone around to do the cook-

27

ing. She had some specialties, and did them well, but basically she hated to cook. My aunt happened to be a fine cook, and enjoyed it, besides. Having Aunt Lou there benefited me on several levels. I was very close to her. She supplied me with many of the homely things that my mother didn't.

Mother was a busy lady, a prime mover of the Culver City Women's Club, of which she became president, and actively devoted to the arts. She and her great friend Bessie Zuckerman, another lively lady, were instrumental in starting the Hollywood Bowl. They were very much involved with L. E. Behymer, the impresario of the Philharmonic, who brought all the touring productions and concert artists to Los Angeles. He was another of Mother's musical friends. She surrounded herself with artistic people, and I was very fortunate to be able to participate.

At one of Bessie's receptions, later on, I met two English actors— Barry Jones and Maurice Colbourne. They were touring with a Shaw repertory company, and begged me to join them. "We are going to kidnap you," they threatened. "You are the perfect Shaw woman." That was the atmosphere in which I lived, and my mother was very much a part of it. To a great extent, I think, the fact that she never used her music frustrated her. She probably would have been a concert pianist if she hadn't lived when she did and had two children. I don't know. It's hard to say.

During my second year at Westlake, the ladies in charge, the Misses Vance and Delaguna, called me into the office. "We understand that you are taking dancing lessons downtown," they began rather accusingly.

"Yes, of course," I answered. "Haven't I been dancing at your festivals?"

"Oh, yes . . . yes . . . of course." They were struggling with this thing, you see. "Well, what do you plan to do with it?"

"I plan to do it as a professional," I told them. "I plan to be a dancer, a great dancer."

"Well! Well, this is terrible!" They were horrified. What went on afterward escapes me, except the realization, as young as I was, that this was an *attitude* toward the theater. In those days, you see, such schools were just set up to make "ladies" out of us. Well, I'd learned all that at home—table manners, all those things. I didn't have to learn them at school.

We not only mingled with artistic people at home, but we had season tickets to the Philharmonic Auditorium, where Mr. Behymer brought great actors and concert artists. I saw Duse. I heard Chaliapin, Gigli, Galli-Curci, even Paderewski. I saw Pavlova there when I was a young girl. She did *The Dying Swan*—not *Swan Lake*, but a special piece that Fokine, I believe, choreographed. She's been hit by an arrow—as I remember, they had little spatters of blood on the feathers—and she dies. Her death was the most touching and beautiful thing I had ever seen. I've watched others do it over the years and wondered, What's wrong? Something is missing. What did she do? Then I realized what it was: the heartbeat. Pavlova indicated the heartbeat with a hand over her breast, a slight but terribly touching gesture. It beat a little bit slower and a little bit slower until she died.

So, you see, this Westlake attitude stunned me. I didn't ask, "What am I supposed to do?" of those two ladies. I just said, "Thank you very much," and walked out of the office.

I went home and repeated the whole encounter to my mother. "This is awful," I told her. "I don't want to go there anymore." And she said, "Yes, it is awful, and you don't have to go there."

Now the Westlake School for Girls is smack in the middle of Bel-Air, and its existence depends on the children of the very people they sneered at. It's humorous when you think of it. They were so uppity! In fact, all of Los Angeles was for many years, and still is to a certain extent. They always sort of look down on the picture business until they want money for a music center. I was invited to social things in Los Angeles, perhaps because of my mother's associations, I don't know. In any case, I was invited and so was Irene Dunne. We were the only two actresses asked to anything down there. I guess they thought we were "ladies"—whatever *that* is.

I switched from Westlake to Venice High School, toward the beach from us. Ironically, its level of cultural activity surpassed that of Westlake. Concerts were brought down from Los Angeles, and notable people from every creative field came to meet with us. My English teacher, W. H. Head—"Old Pop Head," we called him—taught us never to use a flat "a" or too broad an "a," but something in between. That remains one of my great lessons. Although my grandparents came from Wales and Scotland, none of their children affected British accents. Nor did they affect this so-called "Western twang"—much of that is put on.

They spoke good English. Pop Head reaffirmed that. He also elected that I should play Ophelia in the senior class play—*if* the senior already cast broke her leg. The senior didn't break her leg, but it gave me a great opportunity to study Shakespeare. (I was touched and honored thirty years later when Venice High named its annual speech and drama awards "Myrnas," after me.)

Venice High had a great art teacher, Harry Fielding Winebreiner, so I began sculpting. Actually, I wasn't very good, not good enough to go on with it, but something rather special came out of it. The administration decided to decorate the fountain in a large lily pond in front of the school. Mr. Winebreiner, commissioned to create an appropriate sculpture group, chose a typically symbolic motif of that period: a girl reading a book, a young male athlete, and, towering above them, a figure symbolizing youthful aspiration. He chose me as the model for "Aspiration."

The ambitious statue, arms extended, head uplifted, required hours of rigid posing. He draped my body with wet cloth and gauze to get the flowing effect of the draperies. When it was finally finished, a local promoter, Bert Lennon, who later fathered the Lennon sisters, worked it into the city's Memorial Day pageant. A plaster cast of the statue and I were hauled aboard the U.S.S. *Nevada* anchored a half mile off Venice. Swathed in drapery beside my plaster likeness, I came to life on deck under the direction of Thomas H. Ince, no less, Culver City's pioneer filmmaker. They expected me to strew flowers from the prow of the battleship during the rest of the ceremony. Lord! The whole thing was a mess as far as I was concerned, but it attracted a lot of favorable comment.

The impressive sculpture group survived for fifty years, becoming something of a landmark. Of course, "Aspiration," in her gauzy drapery, has tormented the young men. After football games in Santa Monica, they would march to Venice and put rubber tires around her neck and arms. They were always doing one thing or another to the statue, but nothing crucial. Recently, however, the vandals have got to it. It's barbaric! They actually knocked off *my* head!

During my time at Venice High, I taught dancing at the Ritter School of Expression in Culver City. My pupils were tiny tots—babies, practically—who didn't do much dancing, but we did manage to teach them something. My salary, forty dollars a month, went directly from Mrs.

Ritter to my mother. I also filled in for a friend as a splicer at the Hal Roach Studio. The film had already been cut, and all I did was put the pieces into a machine and pull a lever to splice them. I don't remember the picture—there was a dog in it, I think. My paycheck was more memorable, because it was the first paid directly to me. It seemed like such a lot of money, something like eighteen dollars for the week.

Mother frequently traveled back to Montana during that time; she always kept close ties there. I was usually too busy to accompany her, so it happened that we were separated on my eighteenth birthday. I still have the telegram she sent from Helena. It is so characteristic of her: MISS MYRNA. TODAY YOU REACH YOUR MATURITY. SUPPOSE YOU FEEL GROWN UP. WHAT A CELEBRATION THERE WOULD BE WERE I THERE. WILL HAVE ONE WHEN I GET HOME. BROTHER AUNTIE UNCLES AND COUSINS JOIN IN LOVE AND BEST WISHES. MOTHER.

I continued dance and music lessons, becoming obsessed with the idea of dancing, if not on my toes, then in the modern styles of St. Denis and Duncan. I filled notebooks with lists titled "Emotional Qualities to be Expressed in Terpsichorean Form" and "Literary Characters to be Interpreted in Dance." I listed favorite poets and composers— Rupert Brooke, Rachmaninoff, Rabindranath Tagore—adapting them for recitals at the Ebell Club and other cultural groups, getting Lou MacFarlane and Betty Black to cut classes and perform with me. When I think of what I did! I don't know how I ever did it, but that whole time, that time of my life, was very good. . . . Most of my life has been very good.

I'd kept up with Lou, and through her met Betty Berger, who is now Betty Black. She and Lou were great friends, and she became one of my greatest friends. It's a wonderful thing, you know, being able to keep people on. Some you can keep, some you can't keep—it's often hard to hang on to people. Later, when I got into films, Betty and Lou had to be very patient with me. But they hung in there. They've had to put up with a lot, because when you're working in films, you just don't do anything else—at least, I don't. I prize those friendships.

One day Lou and I came out of junior high, which was next to the high school in Venice, Betty Black remembers. This tall girl was waiting there for a streetcar. She and Lou greeted each other effusively, and Lou said, "Betty, this is Myrna Williams that I

*was telling you about." I was very happy to finally meet her. She
was standing in the sun on the side of an incline and we were
below her. I looked up and saw this bright red hair and turned-
up nose with the freckles on it. As she spoke to Lou, I was impressed by her pretty voice, a very soft voice, and by her long
fingers, which moved so gracefully. I was taken by this girl with
the little turned-up nose.*

*When her mother invited Myrna's young friends over, she in-
cluded Lou and me. Their house became a gathering place for
artistic Culver City teenagers, with Myrna as sort of the hub of
the wheel. She had become a campus celebrity at Venice High.
Mr. Winebreiner had done her statue and she had been elected
most beautiful and talented girl at school, sort of Queen of the
May, for May Day exercises that year.*

*Most of us who came to the house became interested in dance
under Myrna's influence, so she started a little dancing school,
teaching us modern dance and pantomime, and writing pieces for
us to perform. Her cousin Laura Belle would wait all day for us
to arrive so that she could sit up and watch the dancing. I thought
Laura Belle was very beautiful. But I thought anything about
Myrna was beautiful. When we finished dancing, Myrna's mother
would fix something special called "shrimp wiggle." She actually
cooked at that time, because Auntie was preoccupied with Laura
Belle. Della really did everything to make this the center for her
daughter and her son, who was also artistic. She entered into
what they were trying to achieve, wanting them to have everything of the finest, which, she felt, included the friends.*

*About that time, summer of 1923, Myrna began looking for
a real job. We heard that there were some openings at Grauman's
Egyptian Theatre in Hollywood. She applied for the chorus of the
live prologues that they used to have before the pictures. Hundreds
of girls were applying, so we all waited and waited by the phone
to hear if Myrna made it.*

I left school at the age of eighteen. I had to. Not being able to graduate
was a big tragedy at the time, but money was running low and I had
to work, that's all. Nobody said, "Myrna, go to work!" I suppose it
was that sense of responsibility instilled by my father. I don't mean to

play the martyr—the chance to get on with my dancing probably delighted me.

I went down to some hall in Los Angeles to audition for Fanchon and Marco. They were a dance team, sister and brother, who became very successful doing prologues for national theater circuits. They hired me for thirty-five dollars a week, darn good money in those days. It certainly helped the coffers at home.

The Egyptian was a movie house but a very elegant one, every bit as beautiful as the Chinese that Sid Grauman built later. Grauman, the first person really to exhibit movies with style, had created this live prologue concept. His prologues were famous, and he was already something of a Hollywood legend. I didn't know him when I worked there. He was a god; everybody important is a god when you're starting out. You don't know your producer if you're a punk. We were just dancers.

I saw him in a different light twelve years later, when he asked Bill Powell and me to put our footprints in the forecourt of his Chinese Theatre. Sid was reputedly a great practical joker, so Bill and I decided to have a little fun. We arrived for the ceremony wearing enormous clown's shoes at least a foot long. Well, I'll never forget Sid Grauman's face. We almost broke his heart. He took that ritual very seriously, and couldn't bear the idea that we were deriding it. We had a terrible time convincing him that it was just a prank. When I finally made my impression in the cement, I wrote: "To Sid, who gave me my first job," which somewhat reassured him.

I started at the Egyptian in the prologue for De Mille's first *Ten Commandments*. Fanchon and Marco were marvelous dancers and hard taskmasters. Everything had to be very strict, according to form. The dance was supposed to be Egyptian to complement the picture's Biblical sequences, so we rehearsed all those square movements associated with ancient Egypt. We wore little pants and sort of Egyptian halters and headdresses. It was very interesting and apparently quite beautiful, I was told.

No terrible trauma comes to mind surrounding my professional début. We must all have been very scared but for some reason I don't remember. Mother came to see me, of course, and thought it was all right. She didn't think it was great; it wasn't—it couldn't compare to the kind of dance she was accustomed to—but she approved of my participation in every aspect of the arts, because she was a great fan herself.

She still made sure that I received tickets to the productions that Mr. Behymer imported.

I took Lillian Butterfield, who danced with me, to see Duse. Because of our matinées at Grauman's, we could only see the last acts of her three plays. We had everything placed in our dressing room so that we could change and catch the streetcar to the Philharmonic downtown. On one occasion, as we hurried into the auditorium, the second act of *Thy Will Be Done* was ending. Duse let out this piercing scream, which absolutely stunned me. Her son had renounced her, and although she only spoke Italian, that heartrending scream said it all.

The place was packed. We climbed way, way up to the second balcony, the only seats that Mother could get. But we had a wonderful view of the entire stage, which this sixty-five-year-old woman, small and gray-haired, dominated—incredible . . . *incredible* . . . She never wore any makeup, even when she played a young woman, but she was absolutely fascinating. The interesting thing, which is something that I must have remembered always, was her control. Unlike Bernhardt, who apparently overacted and showed off, Duse was very sparse in the things that she did—except at high moments, of course, like the scream.

As we stood weeping during Duse's curtain calls, a woman turned to Lillian, who had dark, Mediterranean looks, and said, "Oh, *I'm* not even Italian like you, but I cried, too." She never understood a word, neither did we, but we had all been moved to tears. And there Duse stood, I will never forget it as long as I live, a little woman with gray hair surrounded by banks of red roses.

She continued her tour, two months later reaching Pittsburgh, where, one rainy night, she couldn't get into the theater. I know what that feeling is. It's happened to me many, many times. You try to find a stage door and you go crazy because nothing seems to work, you can't get in. Well, apparently she got drenched and she caught a chill and died. Eleonora Duse died, during that tour, in Pittsburgh.

I made several close friends at Grauman's—Lillian, Melva Lockman, Helen Virgil. We had two shows a day, matinée and evening, so we'd go out for dinner between shows on Hollywood Boulevard. That's when it was still quite nice. Hollywood was just a little town. It still is, except it's terribly rundown now. It was brighter then, with an easier quality about it, more like a little Spanish town. There were farmlands

and open fields where you'd see pepper trees and wild California pop-
pies, all those things that smelled good. The business section around
the Egyptian comprised about six blocks of low buildings, mostly painted
yellow and white. There were nice restaurants among them where we'd
have our meals—Henry's, The Blue Front, Frank's Café.

Tired of commuting between Culver City and Hollywood four times
a day, I rented a house near the theater with Melva, Lillian, and Helen.
It was the first time that I'd ever lived separately from my mother. She
was not terribly pleased about it—she had made up her mind to keep
her brood close to the nest—but the house with the girls didn't work
out. It got so that I was the mother and doing all the cooking and
housekeeping, so I left and went back to Culver City. But those girls
remained my friends through the years.

*When Myrna moved back to Culver City, I would spend week-
ends there, Betty Black relates. One time, just to illustrate the
kind of relationship we shared, I was taking the streetcar to her
house after school. I was about sixteen and green as grass, just
sitting there with my books and long dark curls, when a woman
next to me said, "You're certainly a pretty young lady." She moved
closer and started questioning me. "I'm going to Hollywood," she
said, patting my leg. "Why don't you come into Hollywood with
me?" She became insistent and continued to pat my leg. Even if
she was a woman, it scared me. I grabbed my books—she was
sort of holding me a bit—jumped off the streetcar, and ran all
the way to Myrna's.*

*Myrna came home rather late from Grauman's, and had an
early rehearsal call in the morning, so we went to bed early. I
could hardly wait to tell her of my peculiar encounter. I told the
story and said, "Myrna, wasn't it silly of me to be so scared? She
was only trying to be nice, to take me to tea. I just didn't like
the way she moved closer and closer to me."*

*"Well, Betty, you knew instinctively that something was
wrong," Myrna explained. "You have to be careful at your age.
You see, it isn't only men that can have affairs with you. Women
can have affairs with other women, too."*

"But how could they do it? What do they do?"

"Well, I don't know all the techniques of it, but at Grau-

man's we've talked a little about it. And since you're not inclined toward that sort of thing, you were very wise to do what you did."

My people were all strict Orthodox Jews, and my mother had not told me any of the facts of life. I would go to Myrna, until the day I married, whenever anything worried me, didn't seem kosher or quite right. I thought that others would only laugh at me; but she would explain. Even as a teenager—she was eighteen at that particular time—she always explained it very carefully. We would lie awake nights, when a group of girls were together, and discuss different issues. Even then, she was concerned about world problems and politics, things that other kids considered kind of peculiar to worry about. She had no use for prudishness. The prudish girls in our school, the girls who were very practical in their thinking, those girls didn't interest her at all. She always wanted people who were delving into something. She considered repressive moral attitudes and mores old-hat Victorian, even in those days. We say that now. Well, Myrna was saying that at fifteen and sixteen. Her outlook was way ahead of her time.

When Bob Black proposed to me, I felt guilty and confused, because a rabbi had made me swear on my father's grave that I would never marry a gentile. Myrna knew we were in love and she liked Bob, saw a big future for him. "Your father had just died and they played on your emotions," she explained. "You can't reproach yourself for that promise. If you want to marry Bob, if you think it's right for you, forget superstitions." She bought me a beautiful nightgown—my big trousseau—and I eloped with Bob. She has had an influence on me from the time I was thirteen until . . . even now, sixty years later.

My second prologue, preceding Douglas Fairbanks's *Thief of Bagdad*, featured an East Indian nautch dance. We were barefoot, with skirts that whirled around and bells on our ankles. That was my stuff. That's what I liked. Actually, we were probably belly dancers, but we didn't know it then. It was fun to do, anyway, in your bare feet, and all those lovely movements. I would be in my bare feet a lot during my first years in Hollywood.

Producers occasionally used the Fanchon and Marco ballets in their pictures. They hired the *Thief of Bagdad* ensemble for an orgy scene in

The Wanderer, a Raoul Walsh picture based on the Prodigal Son parable. So we all went over to Paramount to be bacchantes. That comes
to mind because I was acting my head off, drinking and hanging over
this couch with a wine goblet, trying to do what they told me to do.
Otherwise, I wasn't too impressed with moviemaking. With all the studios in Culver City, movies were no novelty. Lots of movie people lived
there: those who worked in the studios; hopefuls who came from all
over to try. James Flood, a director at Warner Brothers, lived just across
the street from us. Several Metro technicians and players were neighbors. Jean Vandyke's brother Truman, who starred in Selig-Roark serials, was sort of a beau of mine—he used to take me tea dancing at the
Montmartre on Hollywood Boulevard, where a lot of stars went. But
the movies didn't interest me then. *I* was a danseuse.

Those shows ran for months at the Egyptian. When *The Thief of
Bagdad* box office thinned a bit, they decided to put some pictures of
the dancers in the courtyard. Our stage manager announced that Henry
Waxman, a noted portrait photographer, was coming to choose girls for
the pictures. He chose Melva, Helen, and me. At his studio on Sunset,
he photographed the other girls first. Then he started on me. He went
crazy. He just kept shooting pictures—long shots, close-ups, portraits,
art studies—all through the night. During the matinée the next day, I
was too exhausted to move.

Henry blew up several of my pictures and had them around his
studio when Rudolph Valentino came for a sitting. "Who's that girl?"
Valentino asked. "She's a little girl from Grauman's I found the other
night," Henry said. "Isn't she incredible?" I'm photogenic, you see, and
this is what had Henry so excited. Valentino apparently agreed. "Could
she come over to the studio?" he asked. "I want my wife to see her."

His wife, Natacha Rambova, had sort of moved into his business.
They were looking for a leading lady for *Cobra,* their first independent
production. I met her at Paramount, where their Ritz-Carlton Productions had offices. She was absolutely beautiful, the most beautiful woman
I had ever seen. Her real name, Winifred Shaunessy, later became
Hudnut when her mother married the perfume manufacturer. But her
own creation, Natacha Rambova, better suited her. She always wore
turbans and long, very stark dresses, usually velvet or brocade of the
same golden brown as her eyes. She was breathtaking and I was scared.

"I know they call me everything from Messalina to a dope fiend," she disclosed to calm me, "but I really don't eat little dancers for break-fast." She wanted to make a test, and, assuming I was a poor little kid, she offered to bring some of her clothes for me to wear. When I fretted about a little separation between my front teeth, she dismissed my anxiety: "Oh, that can be taken care of. We can simply put caps on them."

I didn't make the test with Valentino, but he was hanging around all the time. He was marvelous-looking, more like some sleek jungle creature, a panther, than a man. I was just out of my mind. Imagine! I was a kid, and he was the *big* star, yet he wasn't on the make ever, which pleased me, because I was very young. I found him a very gentle person, a sweet man, charming and seemingly well bred, far less flamboyant than his wife. There was never any of that "sheik" stuff with him, any more than there was "exotica" with me later on. Valentino was a nice Italian man who liked fixing cars. That's how the "Great Lover" spent his time, puttering around with the custom-made cars he collected.

Rudy lent me his portable dressing room to get ready for my test. As I was preparing, he appeared with a rabbit's foot, used in those days instead of a sable brush to wipe off powder. "I thought maybe you could use this," he said, and stood there chatting a bit, trying to put me at ease before the test. "Have you got everything you need?" he asked; then, as he was leaving, he turned and said, "You look perfectly lovely." What a dear man!

It was easy to see why Natacha took charge of his career. He was like a trusting child who wanted to be liked, agreeing to everything, then expecting her to get him out of it. Everyone knew Rudy was sweet and agreeable; therefore, his wife became the villain. "I was a fool," she maintained after they separated, "young and optimistic and full of fight. I didn't realize the uselessness. Studios don't care about your ideas or you. They want to crowd as many pictures into as little time as possible to collect on you as quickly as they can. What happens to the star is of no concern." It would be a while before I saw the truth of her words firsthand.

I didn't do very much in the test—just took some books, walked across the set, and put them on a shelf, something like that. It was that kind of test, just to get different angles. We didn't have sound yet, you see. I took Henry Waxman to a screening that the Valentinos had arranged for me. Just the two of us attended. This was the first time that

I ever saw myself on the screen. Oh, it was unbelievable! It looked like one of those old wound-up movies, with me going all over the place with the books, rushing here, rushing there like the Keystone Kops. Oh, it was just awful. I didn't understand. I didn't move that fast. Henry was baffled, too. He didn't know anything about movie projectors either. I went home absolutely brokenhearted.

It turned out that the operator had very carelessly shown the film at the wrong speed. I hadn't the sense to realize that, being unaware of such things then. In any case, that was the end of *Cobra* so far as my involvement was concerned. The Valentinos didn't call me back; they decided against using me, and wisely, too. Everyone blamed it on Natacha, saying, "Mrs. Valentino didn't like you," but I never would have been able to do it without any training. I was just too young, still a skinny kid. They used Gertrude Olmstead, a girl from M-G-M.

Dancing remained my goal, but the Valentino experience aroused an enormous interest in films. Those prologues went on for months and months, and despite my discipline, I would get bored. I understood the necessity of being strict about everything, of moving with the other girls, but occasionally I would do something a little extra. During rehearsals of the new prologue for Lillian Gish's *Romola*, Fanchon said, "Myrna, you ought to be in the movies. You're always trying to do something different."

When I decided to leave—this is a curious thing with me—when I decided to leave the Egyptian Theatre, nothing was ahead for me at all. Nothing. But the realization had struck that I was getting nowhere— and that was not where I wanted to go. I wanted to get out and accomplish something, maybe go to New York. That decision to leave stands out very definitely. Everybody was shocked. The girls all asked, "What are you going to do?"

Well, I danced at functions, doing more of that Denishawn stuff— very spiritual. I won a medallion, Gothic-style, from the Norse Studio, and received a rapturous poem, "To a Danseuse," from a retired U.S. Army major! I haunted the Metro-Goldwyn-Mayer casting office, which stood just outside the studio's main gate in Culver City. I used to walk over and sit day after day on a wooden bench in that office. "I don't know how she does it," Aunt Lou would say. "I'd go mad. I would not have the patience to do what she is doing."

One day late in 1924, "the god in the grille"—the casting director,

Bob McIntyre—spotted me. "You all right?" he asked. "You got enough to eat?" And, of course, I lived just around the corner where we had plenty to eat, but I looked so forlorn he gave me a job: "Look, we're making a test of Kathleen Key's costume, the leper costume, for *Ben-Hur*. Don't bother with makeup. Just get the dress and go over to stage so-and-so."

My first chance to crash the gates of M-G-M. I was elated. I went up, put on a heavy theater makeup, then rushed down to the set in the leper costume. Lillian Rosine, the makeup woman, took one look at me and said, "My God! Where did you get that makeup?" She grabbed me and, without asking anybody's permission, took me back up and put a decent makeup on. (She was always like that with all of us; she treated us like children.) By the time she brought me down again, I'd attracted a little attention. Christy Cabanne, who was directing one of the *Ben-Hur* units, approached me.

"Are you under contract here?" he asked.

"Under contract? *No!* I just got in. I've been trying to get in this place for a long time." I didn't know what he was driving at, but at the end of the day, after they took the costume test, he came back.

"I'd like to make a test of you," he told me, "for the Virgin Mary in *Ben-Hur*. We're looking around and we can't find anyone." He called Rosine over and said, "Get her a wonderful blond wig."

The next day, they made a test of me, which I understand was a *fabulous* test. They had it around there for years and used to get it out and show it at Christmastime—I never could figure out why; it must have been awfully spiritual—but, anyway, it started a big rumpus between two studio factions: Was the girl who played the part to be well known or a nobody? They considered the risk of using an unknown who would suddenly turn out to have a "reputation." It was all stupid and silly. I thought they were going to look up my sex life—not that I had very much at that time; I was still very young. These factions pulled one against the other: the people who wanted me and the people who wanted a name.

In the meantime, Bob McIntyre gave me a $7.50-a-day extra job. Rosine covered my red hair with a long black wig dripping with pearls, and I played one of many mistresses surrounding a Roman senator in his box at the races—a far cry from the Virgin Mary. They shot that famous chariot race on the back lot where they had built the enormous

Circus Maximus set. I was in the box waiting for them to start when I saw a black limousine drive up and out got this little blonde with several people hovering around her. I didn't know who she was at the time, but I soon found out. It was Betty Bronson, who had just played Peter Pan at Paramount, and they signed her for the Virgin Mary. I guess they figured they were safe with Peter Pan.

Bob McIntyre gave me a consolation prize, a job in *Pretty Ladies*. That's when I met Joan Crawford. We were both chorus girls in this thing, which starred ZaSu Pitts and Tom Moore and featured Norma Shearer, Conrad Nagel, and a lot of people impersonating Ziegfeld Follies stars. It's amazing to think that Norma, Joan, and I would all become rather important to M-G-M in later years. And here we were, Joan and I, these two little extras, as part of a human chandelier. They had us hanging on to this thing with our toes out, all these girls going in different directions. It was a riot.

Joan had just been signed to a contract, and she was living on nothing but black coffee to slim down for the camera. She was still Lucille Le Sueur then. They ran a contest after *Pretty Ladies* to find her a new name. Oh, she was wonderful! She was learning all the new dances, Black Bottom, Charleston, and urging me to go down to the Ambassador and do them with her. Being such a snob about dance, of course, I wouldn't have any part of it. But that's what made her a star, later on, in *Our Dancing Daughters*.

One day, Joan came into the dressing room looking very unhappy. She fell into my lap—we were snowflakes covered with marabou that kept getting into our mouths—and she began to cry. Joan always worried terribly. I did, too, but never showed it. Apparently, Harry Rapf, the producer who discovered her, had chased her around the desk the night before. She was having a terrible time. She had such a beautiful body that they were all after her. I didn't have quite that much trouble—my sort of snooty attitude put them off a bit.

Joan and I became friends and stayed friends, which is the most that came out of my first M-G-M experience. They didn't sign me. Despite *Pretty Ladies* and all the excitement over my *Ben-Hur* test, nobody did anything about keeping me. I went back later, and practically spent the rest of my *life* there. But they didn't grab me then.

Natacha Rambova came to the rescue. Henry Waxman called to say that she wanted me at the studio, so I hurried over. Lou and Betty waited by the phone until I called home with the news that Natacha had hired me for a small but showy part in *What Price Beauty?* Mother made a midnight supper and Lillian Butterfield and Melva Lockman, my friends from Grauman's, joined us for a celebration. They all stayed overnight, five of us crosswise in one double bed, chattering away, planning brilliant futures for ourselves.

What Price Beauty? had a dreadful script, a variation on the country-girl-in-the-big-city theme, but done with the Rambova touch. She'd found a young designer named Adrian Greenberg—that's where M-G-M's Adrian started. His big test, and my only scene, was a futuristic dream sequence depicting various types of womankind. Natacha dubbed me "the intellectual type of vampire without race or creed or country." Adrian designed an extraordinary red velvet pajama outfit for me, with a short blond wig that came to little points on my forehead, very, very snaky. This bizarre film wasn't released for three years, but Henry Waxman took pictures of me in that outfit. They appeared in a fan magazine captioned "Who is she?" and eventually led to my first contract.

I traveled with a sort of artistic avant-garde at that time—writers and would-be writers, painters, sculptors—young people in the arts who would have lived in Greenwich Village if we'd been in New York. Some of them decided that the name Williams was too ordinary for a performer. I resisted. I considered it a perfectly good name. They mentioned Earle Williams, Kathlyn Williams, and several other actors of that name, and started tossing around variations, awful combinations, really absurd. Someone even suggested "Myrna Lisa," playing on the Mona Lisa, which I found embarrassing. Then Peter Rurick, a wild Russian writer of free verse, suddenly came up with "Myrna Loy." And I said, "What's that?" It sounded all right, but I still wasn't convinced about changing my name.

My Welsh friends, of course, have never been convinced. After all my years as Loy, Richard Burton would never introduce me by that name. Whenever we went anywhere, he always said, "Do you know Miss Williams?" The same thing with Emlyn Williams. They considered my changing it a major crime. Well, I guess it is, but in 1925 I wrote "Myrna Loy" on the back of those *What Price Beauty?* pictures that Henry Waxman had taken. That marvelous man, who was always

selling me, brought them over to Minna Wallis, a power behind the
throne at Warner Brothers.

My windows in the old Warners building looked out across Sun-
set at a little business block where Henry Waxman had his stu-
dio, Minna Wallis related. He came over one day with some pho-
tographs of a girl he wanted me to see. Well, those pictures were
absolutely out of this world they were so beautiful. He said, "Why
don't you give her a test?" Well, tests are rather difficult. You're
never yourself. You're always terrified. It was a good time to get
her in—Warner Brothers had just begun building up a stock com-
pany—but I wanted to present her properly.

My office was next to Jack Warner's, and just outside was a
water cooler where all of them, Mike Curtiz, Darryl Zanuck,
Ernst Lubitsch, Henry Blanke, used to stop for a drink and a
chat before going upstairs. Those chats and my job as Jack's as-
sistant kept me informed on production. I knew we were doing a
Lowell Sherman picture with a big banquet scene. I decided to
put this girl beside Lowell, so that during his close-ups she would
be visible. I called and told her that I wanted to use her in a
small part instead of making a test. She came to the studio and
they shot the scene.

A couple of days later, when the rushes were ready, I went
down to the projection room with Jack Warner and my brother
Hal Wallis, who then ran the publicity department. When the
close-up of Lowell came on, they both noticed the girl.

"Who's that next to Sherman?" Jack asked.

"It's a girl I'd like to put under contract," I told him.

"Sign her," he said. "Fast!"

3

THE VAMP!
1925-1931

This is the best picture from Warner Bros. studio that we have seen in quite a while. . . . Monte Blue does his hero nicely. Jane Winton makes a nice Kentucky girl. But this here Myrna Loy is the star player and the memorable one of the cast; she is the subject of a thousand poems and stories of the orient.

—CARL SANDBURG, 1926*

* Review of *Across the Pacific*, Chicago *Daily News*.

Minna Wallis pulled it off. The picture she used as my test, titled *Satan in Sables*, of all things, happened to be directed by Jimmy Flood, my neighbor. He gave me, I suspect, a particularly showy bit, crowning Lowell Sherman with my shoe or something. I can't remember what the fuss was about, but it convinced Jack Warner to offer one of those typical long-term contracts. They signed me on July 13, 1925, for seven years, starting at seventy-five dollars a week. Every six months, if I was still delivering, they renewed it and added twenty-five dollars. It was exploitative, of course, slave labor, but it seemed like a big chance and a lot of money to me.

My apprenticeship began in the imposing old Warners building on Sunset (now a television studio). They put me into one part after another in rapid succession. It's a production before you even reach the set, you know, because you're up at five-thirty, at the studio by seven. Your hair has to be done, which meant spending hours under the dryer in those days. Your makeup has to be applied, not only to your face. If you had bare arms or legs, as I did in most of those early roles, they used body makeup. Those makeup people were always your friends—Ernie Westmore, who headed the department, and all the others. They got you first thing in the morning, scolding and chattering: "What were *you* doing last night? You look *awful!*" You took a lot of punishment

47

from them, but it was all in fun, and they really saved you on bad days. When they had finished, you put on your costume, your jewels, and reported to the set by nine o'clock. I've done that all my working life.

Between my dozen or so pictures that first year at Warner Brothers, I usually romped on beaches with beach balls and fellow contract players for the publicity department. I even did some picture layouts with Rin Tin Tin, the studio's canine star, serenading him with a banjo while he howled an accompaniment. Newspapers and magazines featured me in outlandish turbans and slinky gowns as "Warner Brothers' version of the 1926 vampire type" and "the Oriental type" or in sarongs and bathing suits displaying "the most beautiful figure at Warner studio"—with my thick legs and knees! I was a dancer and could slink, so they fostered this exotic sexy image.

My childhood ambition had been stage acting; then, dancing predominated. The movies changed all that. What an opportunity! What a bonanza Warner Brothers had in European directors like Ernst Lubitsch, Michael Curtiz, Lewis Milestone, or the great journeymen Archie Mayo, Roy Del Ruth, Lloyd Bacon, who knew pictures from the ground up. I worked with all of them in those early years. The studio was a great training ground. I didn't come there with the kind of serious background that one might have acquired in New York—somebody with preconceptions taking everything so seriously, as they do, taking the joy out of what you are doing. Oh, I hoped, we all hope it's leading somewhere. Of course I was ambitious, but it didn't seem that I was pushing that hard at first. It all seemed exciting and wonderful. Maybe my work was lousy, but it was getting better. And, whatever it was, I was having a ball.

Lubitsch used me in *So This Is Paris* as Patsy Ruth Miller's maid. I was supposed to wake her in one scene by knocking on her boudoir door. I knocked in the usual way, overhand. "No, no, this way," Lubitsch directed, turning his palm upward. "Turn your hand over and rap lightly with your knuckles. It is more *gentle* waking her up that way." Talk about the "Lubitsch touch"! He made it frightfully complicated for actors, even in a tiny part like mine, but the results justified his means. Unfortunately, although we became friends later on, I never worked with him again.

I did three bits for Michael Curtiz, who gave me a lot of encouragement. In fact, he wanted to do *Madame Bovary* with me. He fought and fought, but Warners wouldn't film the novel—they were afraid of its adulterous theme. They were afraid of everything about that idea.

One morning, John Barrymore swept past me in the long hall of the Warners building. I turned to watch this legend pass, and he was giving me an over-the-shoulder look, really taking me in with that inimitable Barrymore leer. Soon after that, Minna sent me over to the *Sea Beast* set with a note for him. There he sat as old Ahab, surrounded by all these dress-extra sailors. I don't know what that note was all about— perhaps Mr. B. just wanted to take another look at me. I was scared to death of him, but nothing came of it then.

Not long after that first meeting, somebody got the crazy idea of casting me as Lucrezia Borgia to his Don Juan. I was a wraith, for God's sake, a skinny kid without the bust or anything to play that formidable lady. Perhaps Barrymore himself had suggested it, because after they padded me for the test, he came strolling onto the set looking dissatisfied. He can't stand it, you see, so he sends for the seamstress. "She hasn't got enough padding on," he tells her. "Where are your pins?" Then that devil starts sticking pins into me. "You see," he says, jabbing away, "there's nothing there, nothing here; you've got to fill her out!" He keeps this up interminably, teasing me, ragging me. And there I am, my life on the line, because, bust or not, I want this part.

Well, Estelle Taylor played Lucrezia Borgia, and they cast me as her lady-in-waiting. I used to joke about being her chief poisoner, but mostly I just tagged along looking seductive during her assignations with Don Juan. During one of these, Alan Crosland, our director, wanted an overhead shot. He gave us our instructions before going way up on the scaffolding to supervise. Jack—we all called him that—decided to change Alan's blocking, merely the trivial matter of when to lower the masks we wore. Never quite sure whether Jack was serious or just teasing me, I followed Alan's instructions. Jack went wild. He started berating me, swearing a blue streak. I looked at him, turned around, and walked off the set.

I wasn't important. They could have replaced me in a minute. But *Miss* Williams wasn't having any of that, thank you! I went down to my friends in the makeup department, who were absolutely flabbergasted. You just didn't do this kind of thing. Production was stopped. Eventually, the production assistants—there must have been at least six of them—found me and coaxed me back to the set. Jack was conciliatory, but I gave him the nose in the air, refusing to speak to him.

A few days into this silent treatment, he was sitting near me in one of those studio chairs. I heard a tentative "Ahem," followed by "Myrna, you must forgive me. I was in agony the other day. My damned boots were too tight." A charming apology, but I remained unappeased.

"No one's ever sworn at me like that," I railed, rather unsportingly, "and they're not starting now." He bore it patiently, eventually cajoling me out of my pique.

Despite his bravado, Jack had a gentle side, but he seldom showed it to me. He usually tortured me during that early period at Warners, making a serious play for me on and off the set. He used to call in the middle of the night from some Culver City night spot. "This is the ham what am," he would intone in that matchless voice, urging me to join him or wanting to join me. God knows he was attractive, but he was really a rascal and I knew it. Actually, there was more to it than that. I sensed something going wrong in him, and it frightened me.

Between Barrymore and Lowell Sherman, you had to be on your guard at the studio. You'd walk onto the stage and one of those devils would materialize from behind a curtain, coming right at you. He'd grab you; you'd scream. Well, *I* would scream. Perhaps some of the others wouldn't. "Look out for Stage One," the Costello sisters warned me. "Those two are always behind the curtain."

"You don't have to tell me," I said. "I've had enough trouble with them." The Costellos warned me, and what finally happened? Dolores married Jack, and Helene married Lowell. "Thanks a lot," I told them. "I got the warnings, and you got the husbands." But it was probably just as well, as things turned out. Well, I think it was . . . who knows? I probably would have fallen madly in love with Jack and had my heart broken.

Mary Astor did. She and Jack had been lovers while filming *Beau Brummel*, but during *The Sea Beast* he had ditched her for Dolores. And here was poor Mary in *Don Juan*, working with him again. While doing retakes at Vitagraph, I blundered into a dressing room Dolores had used for another picture, expecting to find her there. I walked in, and there sat Mary weeping bitterly, surrounded by Dolores's pictures of Jack. It was awful, just awful, a very sad day. Mary had been very young when she first met him—seventeen, I think. It really broke her heart.

My next Barrymore picture, *When a Man Loves*, was based on *Manon Lescaut*. Dolores played the title role, so Jack was on his good behavior. My part amounted to no more than an extra bit as one of the prostitutes deported from France to populate Louisiana. I didn't recall working with Dolores, which a mutual friend told her years later. "What do you mean she doesn't remember?" Dolores boomed. "We were chained together for two weeks!" Well, that brought back the agony we shared up there on Sunset North at Vitagraph. We shot at night, sprawled on the deck of a ship in rags, absolutely freezing, with a crew of tough-looking sailors eyeing us. All these girls, a whole gang of us, were trying to keep warm by drinking gin. It was a very funny time—funny but agonizing. That was my contribution to *When a Man Loves*; you never saw me again, so Dolores and I didn't have much of an exchange. *The Sea Beast* had catapulted her to stardom, and Jack was after her. In any case, she was a very shy girl. But, my gosh, what beauty—like a flower, more like an orchid than a woman.

My first substantial role—at least, the first that impressed me—was *Across the Pacific*, with Monte Blue. He was a big Warner Brothers star then, a very nice man, part Cherokee, who had started as a Griffith stuntman. I thought he was terrific and got a big crush on him. He cured it by taking me home for dinner to meet his wife.

I'd moved to Beverly Hills by that time to eliminate commuting from Culver City at those early hours. In fact, I could walk to the studio from my new apartment, but Monte used to pick me up and drive out to Malibu, where we shot most of *Across the Pacific* on location. The Malibu colony is there now, but then it was nothing but beautiful untouched beach. To simulate a tropical setting, they stuck palm trees into the sand. (Actually, they were eucalyptus trees clayed and painted to resemble palms.) And there I was, just about as real, wearing a sarong and a long black wig, playing my first native girl, a Philippine spy. That role proved to be a turning point in my career. It garnered a lot of critical praise, amazingly enough, and led to years of exotica. You see, Darryl F. Zanuck had written the script, and when he gained power at the studio later on, he could only see me in that kind of role.

Oh, there were other roles, too. There were bound to be when you did so many pictures, often two or three at the same time. We had no union then, and they worked us to death. But those exotics started to predominate. My bit as a mulatto in *The Heart of Maryland* led to a role that I'm very much ashamed of. Zanuck wrote *Ham and Eggs at the Front*, a blackface parody of *What Price Glory?*, casting me as a spy. How could I ever have put on blackface? When I think of it now, it horrifies me. Well, our awareness broadens, thank God! It was a tasteless slapstick comedy that I mercifully recall very little about.

Fox borrowed me and expanded my capacity for exotica. I played my first Chinese part, under the direction of Howard Hawks, in *A Girl in Every Port*. With the structure around my eyes, it turned out, makeup could make me look Oriental. It seems strange of a redhead from Montana, but that part of my face, at least, is easily adapted. They just whitened my upper lids, accented the natural line, and I got away with it. So what do they do back at Warners? They cast me as a Chinese in *The Crimson City*, with Anna May Wong. Up against her, of course, I looked about as Chinese as Raggedy Ann.

Interviewers often assume that I had a miserable time playing all those evil creatures, all those women with knives in their teeth. Not at all. I can't say that things came easily—it took a long, long time to find my real niche—but those roles were fun to play, despite their unreality. The characters were always so nefarious that they had to die at the end. In *The Crimson City*, I commit suicide by jumping off a ship. We shot it in the middle of the night off Santa Barbara. Something went wrong and I nearly drowned. They almost lost me on that one.

My few scenes in *The Jazz Singer* were silent, but I heard Al Jolson. Stars, extras—all of us left our own sets to watch that first talking sequence being shot. It must have been a very costly day. We all stood on the sidelines just listening to him sing. He was really magnetic, one of those rare entertainers that reach out to you with their voice, their eyes, their arms, everything. We knew they were recording his voice, and there was a certain excitement about it, of course, but we were mainly just pleased to have some time off and hear Al Jolson sing. Nobody realized that we had entered a whole new age.

The Jazz Singer put Hollywood into an uproar. Oh, heavens, the arguments that went on! The establishment for the most part cried: "No, no talkies! The great form is the silent picture." The major studios, afraid of tampering with success, hesitated to let their big stars talk. But Warner Brothers had Vitaphone, and they were bound to use it to place themselves firmly with the majors. I went through that whole agonizing transition.

Conrad Nagel and I were shooting *State Street Sadie*, a silent picture, when Jack Warner invaded the set. "Com'ere," he said, leading us off the stage to a velvet cyclorama surrounding what turned out to be a *microphone*. Bringing us right up to this strange device, he ordered: "Say something!" Can you imagine? Say *what*? I was terrified, unable to get a word out. Fortunately, Conrad, who had been in the theater, was a little more at ease with this voice thing. He started a conversation, I answered him, and we got something out—enough for a voice test.

State Street Sadie was one of several pictures casting me as a moll opposite Conrad's gangster, which, if you knew him, seemed ridiculous. He was so reserved, a devout Christian Scientist, good-looking, well spoken, and a fine actor. He was very patient with me, because I hardly knew my way around then. We were in the midst of a scene, sitting in a car, when someone came over: "We're going to put sound on the last half of this piece." That's how we learned the omnipotent voice experts had determined we could "talk." So we tagged a dialogue sequence onto *State Street Sadie*. I made several pictures like that—silents with a little dialogue added to exploit the talkie craze, although the studio was still hedging its bets. "You'll see pantomime combined with sound," promised the *State Street Sadie* ads. "Two arts intensifying the thrills of this dramatic story." Sound, of course, won.

We had a terrible time making those half-talkies. The process was extremely awkward, even for those of us who could "talk." Cameras were still very noisy then. You could hear the constant *rrrrr* of the reels turning, so they enclosed them in soundproof boxes with windows. This hampered the cameras' mobility and ours, compounding the fact that we were terribly conscious of the microphones hidden all over the set— in the flowers, under the furniture, everywhere. Many people that I'd supported in my first years couldn't make the jump. Stars were falling like leaves in that studio. Marie Prevost, a beautiful little comedienne, Patsy Ruth Miller—so many of them just seemed to disappear. The studio never gave those poor girls a chance. They didn't yet have voice coaches, who would have said, "Can you get your voice down a bit? It's too high, too light." Having studied with a voice teacher in Los Angeles while I was still at school, I had something to go on when sound came crashing in, despite my low, soft sort of voice. The sound men had to open it up all the way. But I learned to use it effectively and it worked for me.

> *Myrna used to take me in her car to Warner Brothers when the talkies were just in,* Betty Black recalls. *She was the first of us to get a driving license. Della, who handled all Myrna's money, doled it out as needed. She started her on a Buick, then worked up to a Franklin. There weren't enough sound stages for all the companies during the day, so Myrna worked all night sometimes. She was very interested in this new phase of motion pictures. In fact, she had everyone's lines memorized, and worried as much about the stars' voices coming across as she did about her own. Every aspect of picture-making concerned her. She was always helpful around the set. I think that's why she moved forward.*
>
> *In those days, a lot of girls I knew were sleeping their way to the top. Myrna was never interested in getting a part that way. Naturally, as a young girl, she had many offers of desirable parts if she'd sleep with somebody. But no, Myrna wanted a part because she had earned it. In other words, she wasn't interested in* whom *she could get to further her career, but in* what *she could do by working at it. People realized that around the studio. She was no prude. She had many men interested in her, but they knew if they approached her it had to be in the way of art for art's sake instead of the other way.*

People always ask about the giddy social life of Hollywood in the twenties. Well, the hours were so terrible that everyone just worked, as far as I could tell. You avoided too much nightlife because you had to be up so early every workday looking your best. Mother always arranged to have tickets for me at the Philharmonic, and because of her involvement with the Grand Opera Association, I was one of the few picture people attending the opening of the opera season. Occasionally I'd endure those studio-organized premières, but never submitted to publicity "dates" with my fellow contract players. There were beaus, of course, but they were mostly people I just saw a couple of times. Barry Norton, a sort of perpetual male ingénue of the silents, was one of my more serious flings. He looked like the archetypal all-American boy but happened to be a cultured Argentinean—an irresistible combination to me, although I didn't usually date actors. A lot of those guys, those so-called heartthrobs, were boring, just plain dull.

I moved back with Mother when she sold the Culver City house and bought one in Beverly Hills—not in that great big rich section, but on Elm between Wilshire and Santa Monica. It became a meeting place for my old friends and new studio friends, young people starting out as I was. My Fisher radio-phonograph was one of the first around, so we would listen to music and dance to the latest records. There were always pads and pencils for the word games I liked to play. We did the things that young people do. Now that I look back on it, Mother most likely had us there all the time to maintain her relationship as mother hen. She was a very strong woman, an extraordinary person, who gave us a tremendous amount; but she was possessive. After a beau of hers proposed, I asked if she planned to accept. "No, I'm not going to marry him," she said. "I'm going to devote my time to my children." It might have been better if she had remarried. Women like Mother, who are full of spunk, must get into things. She had so much energy and talent, but early conditioning held her back. I'm sure she suffered because of it. Women still do. Look at the battle we're having for equal rights. Imagine! In this day and age. So Mother started interfering with her children's lives; she controlled them for a long time.

I wanted to send my brother to France to study at the Sorbonne, but that was before I moved back home, and Mother was fit to be tied. The thought of also losing her son was too much. She didn't realize that I was grown up and David was beginning to be. He'd finished high school, but didn't want college. He didn't know what he wanted. He was a talented artist—I still have some of his fine sculptures. It seemed for a while that he'd go in that direction, but for some reason or other he never developed it. Probably one of the reasons was Mother's spoiling him, giving him money, keeping him so close even after he married. David said, "Oh, well, I just wasn't talented enough." But who knows? You never know. He remained as independent as was possible with a famous sister and an overindulgent mother, eventually working for Howard Hughes at the aircraft company. He was with the company for many years, using his art doing mechanical renderings. Our relationship was a loving one until his untimely death in 1982. He had a wonderful sense of humor, very funny, and we always had a grand time together.

In addition to her civic and cultural pursuits in Los Angeles, my mother remained active in the Society of Sons and Daughters of Montana Pioneers and in the politics of our home state. When the Anaconda Copper interests started buying votes from immigrant workers, she returned to Montana to campaign against their candidates. She never lost her taste for politics or civic duty, but she wouldn't have been caught dead in that club for the mothers of stars—Motion Picture Mothers, Inc., they called it. Mother wanted to feel independent. Dolly Cooper, Gary's mother, was always pestering her to join. Dolly was a real go-getter—I'd see her at nightclubs selling tickets to their various social functions. She transplanted the poor judge from Montana to Hollywood, where he always seemed lost and lonely. I used to invite him, later on, for tea and comfort by the big fireplace in my Hidden Valley house.

Gary would occasionally appear at my mother's house for affection and attention during his stormy affair with Lupe Velez. After one of his bouts with the "Mexican Spitfire," he turned up depressed and tipsy. "Yes, dear, yes . . . I know," I consoled him, before leaving the sitting room to make some coffee. He was gone when I returned, which, considering his condition, worried me. I finally found him slumped in a chair on the sun porch, staring into space. He looked so forlorn and vulnerable, utterly touching, with that long body sort of crumpled, those fine eyes clouded. I spontaneously laid my hands on his shoulders. He stirred, murmuring like a lost child, "Mother?"

It occurs to me that I somehow managed to appear in all of Warners' landmark films during that innovative period. *Don Juan* had the first recorded background music. *The Jazz Singer* was the first feature with dialogue. *The Desert Song* was the first all-talking, all-singing musical. This last landmark almost occurred without my participation, thanks to Darryl Zanuck, who'd risen from writer to head of production under Jack Warner. I'd been under contract nearly four years, talked in several pictures, yet Darryl made me test for the role of Azuri. You see, *I* wasn't from New York. Except for the comics, everybody in *The Desert Song* came from the stage. That's how terrified they still were of sound in 1929—scared to death.

It was a tough test. I not only had to dance and talk but create my own dialect as well. We still didn't have coaches, so I was left on my own to determine how a North African native spoke. Having studied a little French in school, I used that as a base to create an incredible accent. For years afterward, friends would approach me with a strange look and mimic one of my lines: "Vere ees Pierrre?"

I sat with Darryl in the projection room when he screened my test. Despite the fake accent and the nut-brown makeup with my light eyes, it looked relatively convincing to me. "I don't know, you're pretty nervous," observed Darryl, who always enjoyed needling me.

"Yeah, I guess so." I'd perspired a pool during the dance. "So would you be if you were in that spot."

"Well, I'm not sure you can handle this," he continued. "If I put you in the part and then have to give you the hook, that won't be good for your career. It would be better not to put you in at all. But you've got to make the decision."

I remember sitting in that room, thinking, Sister, there's a bridge, and if you don't cross it, if you don't say yes and risk being pulled out, this will be the end for you. I said to Zanuck: "I'll take the chance."

That's how I went to work on *The Desert Song*, with that threat hanging over me. The first day out, someone mentioned that John Barrymore wasn't working on his set because his stars weren't right. That's what Jack claimed; he probably had a hangover. Anyway, I thought, Oh, boy, what if my stars aren't right? My big scene was scheduled that day, a dance number with a huge backup chorus and dozens of extras tossing money at me, all shot in sound and Technicolor. Well, my stars must have been right; they didn't give me the hook.

The Desert Song's success sort of solidified my exotic non-American image. Fox, supposedly at John Ford's behest, borrowed me for *The Black Watch*, based on *King of the Khyber Rifles*. I played an Indian princess, but they made her a descendant of Alexander the Great to establish her Aryan credentials, so she could get the British officer, Victor McLaglen. Isn't that incredible? Talk about racism! As it turned out, the precaution was unnecessary: trying to shoot love scenes with Victor was hilarious. He would not *give*. He forgot that he was an actor, I guess, and resisted playing a lover. "Myrna, she's just a child," he kept telling Jack Ford. Jack finally took me aside and sort of stage-whispered, "Let's get off the set and try it in Victor's dressing room." We tried everything, but he never responded. I think Jack finally gave up on the love scenes.

John Ford had *tremendous* sensitivity, but we seldom see the gentle things he did. It makes me quite angry that his retrospectives concentrate on the macho stuff. When you first discover my exotic character in *The Black Watch*, she's asleep surrounded by yards of mosquito netting. A servant comes to wake her, saying, "Sahiba," gradually pulling away the netting as this beautiful creature emerges—God! It took a lot of doing to achieve that quality. Jack knew how to do it, but they never show such things. There are lots of those moments in his films. We worked together only twice, but I remember several of his pictures with that certain gentle quality.

He asked me to a party at his house after we finished shooting. When Mary, his wife, opened the door, she looked bewildered. "Mr. Ford invited me to his party," I said. "I'm Myrna Loy." She took me into the library where Jack sat surrounded by that old gang of his. That son of a gun was having a stag party, and he'd invited me. What a terrible thing to do to a girl, particularly one as shy as I was in those days. He was always up to his tricks; for years he played these strange, funny little pranks because he had this thing about me. He liked me— very much, I think. "Wouldn't you know," he once complained, "the kid they pick to play tramps is the only good girl in Hollywood?" But, anyway, I stayed and had a wonderful time with the boys. John Wayne was there, young and handsome and just out of college, as shy as I was. He was a property man on the picture; at least, he'd been around on the set all the time. Jack was grooming him.

My ultimate vamp came in *The Squall*. We shot that out at First National, in Burbank, which Warners had just taken over. Everybody seems to disown that picture, but everybody remembers it, even Alexander Korda, who directed it before going on to greater achievements. We made that thing at night. They only had sound equipment for one company, and Corinne Griffith, their big star, used it during the day. (She didn't use it for long—talkies pretty much finished her career.) My God! It was freezing! I ran around barefoot all night as the gypsy girl— Oh, what was her name? . . . Nubi, that's it: "Nubi, she be geepsy, she do dis, she do dat, she do dee other ting." She was a real heller, that one.

Loretta Young was the ingénue. What a sweet little thing! She seemed like a baby to me, yet poor Loretta had eloped with Grant Withers, then left him, and had that pressure to contend with during filming.

There are certain personalities that you meet in your life that you want to know better, Loretta Young *discloses. I thank God that I did get to know Myrna better, because when we first met, I had that kind of stay-away feeling from her. There was an aloofness about her, I thought, heightened by that upturned nose of hers— it's the only one like it in the world that I've ever seen, and beautiful . . . beautiful. It could almost have been "Miss Loy." She wasn't old enough for that, but in* The Squall *and the other two pictures we made together she played gorgeous, glamorous femme fatales to my simpering ingénues. At sixteen or seventeen, those roles seemed real to me, and I was in awe of her.*

Nubi, this seductive creature in The Squall, *goes through all the men in the house, the husband, the father, the sweethearts, the male servants, the gardeners, everybody, and the women can't wait to get rid of her. Finally, they catch her red-handed, and throw her out, bolting the big wooden gates behind her. I'll never forget the preview of that picture, because everything was going along fine until that point—the sound worked and everybody was thrilled. Then there's a shot of Myrna banging on the gates, yelling, "It's Nubi . . . it's Nubi. . . . Let me in!" and they cut to all the women inside leaning on those huge gates, as if this one poor girl could break them down. They keep cutting back and forth between the women inside, Nubi outside, and the gypsies coming over the hill in a wagon to take her. All the while she's pleading, "It's Nubi. . . . Let me in . . . let me in. . . ." Finally someone in the back of the theater shouts, "For God's sake, let her in!"*

That broke up the audience. It was near the end of the picture and the whole mood was destroyed. I was horrified, but all they did was go back to the cutting room, take out a few "Let me in"s, and it played beautifully. That's what previews are for. In fact, if they had more previews now, you wouldn't have these Heaven's Gate *disasters. There's hardly a picture that cutting can't improve.*

I continued my succession of international vamps at Warners—Burmese, Chinese, a South Seas Islander, a couple of Mexicans, and, on loan to Fox, a Creole. They had a hard time casting me, because Darryl Zanuck still couldn't see me in a straight part. He never shook that, even when I did *The Rains Came* for him at Fox ten years later. I always had trouble with him, which puzzled me. I never could figure it out. I opened the wrong door at the studio once, and caught a sort of half-star at Warners, sitting on his lap. I quickly closed the door, but maybe he never forgave me for that. I used to tease him about it, which didn't help matters. He had enough trouble on that score; his wife, Virginia, used to invade his office wielding a pistol. She wasn't letting him fool around in those days.

Soon after the stock market crash, Darryl sent for me. "We don't have enough of those parts to keep you under contract," he announced. "We can't afford you. There aren't enough wenches for you to play." Obviously, he'd already made up his mind that they weren't going to make a star out of me. Well, in those things how could they? So Zanuck fired me. He never forgave me for it—I mean, for *him* firing me.

I was devastated. I went to Bill Koenig, an executive who'd always been helpful: "What am I going to do?" He said, "Why don't you go see Minna Wallis? She's in the agency business now, you know." That's exactly what I did, and Minna signed me up. Her influence throughout my whole career has been incalculable. She was an amazing person, devoted to the picture business and to her clients. Clark Gable adored her. She discovered him and, among others, Errol Flynn and George Brent. They used to be called "Minna's boys." She had a terrific lot to do with my career and the careers of so many others.

We were falling into the Great Depression, but Minna kept me working as a free-lance from studio to studio, picture to picture. I was a suicidal waif tormented by Joseph Schildkraut in *Cock o' the Walk*, which read better in script form than it played. I did it mainly to work with Schildkraut, whom I'd admired on stage. He turned out to be a bit of a masher, but interesting, full of stories about Max Reinhardt and the European theater in which he and his famous father had acted. In *Bride of the Regiment*, I wore heavenly costumes, danced on a banquet table, and played wonderful scenes with Lupino Lane, who was a darling. For *Rogue of the Rio Grande*, a minor Sono Art Western, Eduardo Cansino, Rita Hayworth's father, coached me in a Spanish dance.

We shot *The Last of the Duanes*, a George O'Brien Western, in the fabulous red-rock country of northern Arizona. We had a ball staying in a closed boys' school near Sedona, where the crew's discovery of great quantities of saltpeter in the kitchen prompted great jokes and mischief. During my time off, they let me have a horse. I rode along the rims of hills and into Oak Creek Canyon, where the red rocks seemed like Babylonian cities that had melted.

What comes to mind about *Renegades* is the desert location and all that sand in my teeth. I sprawled on my belly for days with a machine gun, shootin' up the Legion, until one of them finally shot me. We had a wonderful company headed by Victor Fleming and Warner Baxter. Victor, a man's man and a master of his craft, would later direct me more auspiciously at M-G-M. And I have fond memories of Warner, a good actor and a charming man, because we did several pictures together. *Renegades* was a happy film because of them.

I can remember always being surprised at how modest Myrna was about her own looks, her own ability, observes Lou MacFarlane. *That to me has always been the striking thing about her. She has changed somewhat now, has more understanding of herself and her worth, but in those days she thought of herself as freckled and too bony and not very attractive. She was the only woman in* Renegades, *and just gorgeous, so beautiful that everyone on the set was in love with her. She had a good time, as any woman would, being the favorite of all these men. When the picture ended, Myrna was the only woman invited to their party.*

I went shopping with her and helped choose this beautiful dress, crushed gold cloth, heavily beaded, but it was short and low-cut. Myrna fretted about it because she never liked her legs or neck, and they'd enhanced her bosom and hips a bit in the picture, so she was afraid to face them without her padding. "You know, when I walk in there," she said at the last minute, "all those men are just going to die they'll be so disappointed." I couldn't convince her that she was beautiful, that the bones in her neck, everything, looked beautiful. I actually had to force her out of that house to the party. Well, of course, when she got home she'd had a marvelous time. Nobody had been the least disappointed.

I wasn't as much of a social being then as I became during my years with Arthur Hornblow, but I was beginning to get around. One of my first forays into the so-called inner circle was a party at Ira and Lee Gershwin's house. When I walked, a little shyly, into their celebrity-filled drawing room, Oscar Levant, a stranger to me then, was at the piano. There were long-stemmed red roses in a vase nearby, and as I passed, he reached out, handed me one, and went right on playing. I've always cherished that graceful welcome to Hollywood society.

Arthur Hornblow came into my life because he was Sam Goldwyn's production supervisor. Minna sent me over to see him about a role in *The Devil to Pay*. He seemed surprised when I entered his office: "What is this? You're not a stuffed China doll. You don't look anything like those silly parts they've been giving you." That struck me as rather nice. He gave me the part, and continued to treat me very well during filming, never indicating then that he might be interested in me. He was still married to Juliette Crosby, who frequently visited the set, since George Fitzmaurice directed the picture, Ronald Colman starred, and they were all very chummy.

These people exemplified the kind of élite company that Goldwyn always assembled. Working for him was considered something special, even in those days, because quality was his byword. My role, a sophisticated English actress with a sense of humor, provided a welcome departure from my usual fare. It also presented a challenge. Ronald Colman, sensing this, soothed and encouraged me. At one point I became nervous about a scene we were doing. "Courage, my sweet," he kept saying in that beautiful voice of his. "Courage, my sweet." I liked him very much then, and later on, when we used to see quite a bit of him socially. But he was an *Englishman*, you know, in every sense of the word.

That graceful respite proved to be short-lived. On the strength of *Renegades*, Fox gave me a long-term contract in October, 1930, returning me to vamp status. Very few of those pictures stand out. I remember menacing Elissa Landi in a couple of her starring vehicles; she was lean and bright, with wonderful humor, and we became friends to a certain extent. She asked me to some of her cocktail parties, where she always had worldly, interesting people, whose conversation ranged way beyond the picture business.

A Connecticut Yankee is memorable because of Will Rogers, another of those rascals who liked to tease me. I don't know why. Perhaps men need that as an excuse for contact, particularly shy men like Will;

even little boys do it. He'd drive past me on the street and make a big fuss, waving and hollering, just to get a rise out of me. Around the studio, he'd always engage me in that innocent kind of corny way of his. But on the set, like Victor McLaglen, he became extremely shy. Of course, he's supposed to be. When I, as Morgan le Fay, try to seduce him, they tinted the scene somehow so that he blushed. His face actually turned red on the screen. This was Will Rogers as far as I was concerned, very much the Connecticut Yankee, very much that character.

William Farnum, whom I'd seen shootin' it up on that Universal tour years before, played King Arthur. He was still a very good-looking man. And, of course, Maureen O'Sullivan was the ingénue. Fox brought her from Ireland with John McCormack, the great tenor. They built a thatched Irish cottage on the lot as his dressing room—they even put shamrocks in the garden. Years later, when I made *The Rains Came* there, they turned that cottage over to me; McCormack and the shamrocks were long gone. Maureen was lovely. I've always loved her warm exuberance, and still see her in New York. She mentioned recently that I was the first movie star she saw on the Fox lot. She'd seen some of my exotica in Ireland, so when we met on the way to her first voice lesson, it amazed her. She remembers thinking, Well, if they can make this freckle-faced redhead into all those sloe-eyed creatures, maybe there's hope for me. She was nineteen, a newcomer, and didn't know yet what the camera could do.

The highlight of my Fox contract, *Transatlantic*, gave me a straight part and a wonderful director, William K. Howard. I admired his meticulous methods, and his films retain an original quality derived from them. He had respect for me and my work, which pleased me no end. I was never unhappy, but it was kind of rough being pushed around from picture to picture. It was nice occasionally to meet someone you respected, who respected you for your craft. Fox greeted my departure from exotica with publicity handouts labeled "Revamped Vamp," then thrust me back into a series of bad-girl parts. Facing the same kind of typing that had limited me at Warners, I said, "I want out!" And Fox released me.

Free-lancing again, I heard that Edward H. Griffith wanted someone who could convincingly take a beau away from Ina Claire in *Rebound*. Minna sent me over to make a test. Hedda Hopper, who appeared in the picture, attended the screening of my test. She remembered Ina scoffing, "You don't think 'Sunbonnet Sue' there could take a man away from *me*, do you?"

"I don't know," Ned Griffith told her, "but this is Friday—we start Monday. Unless you come up with someone better, we'll have to take a chance. That's an order from the front office."

While always polite and never blatantly upstaging me, Ina certainly didn't help "Sunbonnet Sue." I think she was becoming very conscious of her age, and I was no slouch in those days either. Not that I was any threat to Ina, a great star and a great actress, but I can understand how she felt. Several years ago, I was doing a television show out at Universal, and the first day Jill St. John, who played my daughter, came onto the set I saw this ravishingly beautiful girl and thought, Oh, brother! But that didn't keep me from working closely with Jill or becoming friends with her during the Eugene McCarthy campaign.

I admired Ina to the extent of sneaking onto her closed set to watch her work. It was a lovers' scene, a high point in the story, where she had to do a lot of tricks. She did them brilliantly. When she came off the set, she spotted me. "Really," I said, "it was a beautiful scene."

"Delsarte," she explained with a sweeping gesture. "Pure Delsarte."

I waited for that scene at the screening and, curiously, it never happened. I mean, it didn't come across the way I'd heard it. It would have been an effective thing on stage, but there is something mysterious about film—it's got to come from inside, it can't be technical. I thought to myself, My God, that *was* technique she was using.

Thirty years later, when I finally went on the stage, that incident came back to me. One of my directors, during a long run, said, "Every day it's as though you were doing it for the first time. I think your film work has made it possible for you to keep this part fresh."

"Well, we had to do that," I replied. "If we didn't, it showed." So, with a nod to Miss Claire, I probably developed a technique without knowing it, although technique is a word that scares me. It's never used correctly.

You know, when Myrna first was signed to pictures, Lou Mac-Farlane relates, *someone said to Betty Black and me, "What a shame, you three girls have been so close, and this is bound to make a difference." Betty and I, very annoyed, denied that this would happen. And it didn't happen. Myrna's very loyal to her friends, very generous to people who need help—beyond the point of friendship, sometimes. My job in pictures came about through her. I'd wanted to learn motion-picture writing since we saw our first* Perils of Pauline, *back in Ocean Park, but you couldn't get in. It was still Depression time and hard to get any job, to say nothing of jobs in the picture business. So Myrna took me with her to the studios, introducing me as her secretary.*

I was with her on several pictures, two directed by Ned Griffith, who really got her started with the kind of thing that made her a big star. Myrna was learning, and I was learning right along with her. In Rebound, *she had a wonderful scene with Ina Claire, which Myrna and I rehearsed repeatedly at a certain speed. When they ran through it on the set, Claire let her go with it, and Ned was thrilled. Claire, of course, the great lady of the stage, had very little to do with anybody at all, but she knew her craft. The minute Ned said "Action!" she started out in a staccato voice, and Myrna couldn't even interrupt. Myrna, just a novice, simply couldn't beat down this old actress who really knew how to cut out everybody. She really ruined the scene for Myrna. Ned tried it a few more times to see if she could get through, but he didn't do much about it. Claire was the star. He couldn't risk having her walk off the set.*

They looked down on movie people, those stage stars Myrna worked with in the early years of talkies. Later, on The Animal Kingdom, *Ann Harding, much like Claire, was very much of the stage, condescending to do a part in a picture. She did it well, but kept herself apart from everything. Even Leslie Howard, who adored Myrna and treated me pleasantly, seemed a bit patronizing. On any of these pictures, I can tell you, Myrna was much more popular with the rest of the cast and crew than any of the stars were. She always behaved decently toward everybody, which is more than I can say for some of the others.*

It wasn't always so easy to be pleasant. Those were pre-union days, and we worked long, hard hours. We got up very early in the morning, and Myrna would have makeup applied to her for hours, and she would stand sometimes, because she couldn't sit in those costumes. We worked until eight, nine, ten o'clock at night. Nobody got overtime. Some of the crafts might have, but certainly not any of the actors or office staff. People worked very, very hard. I remember one "poverty-row" quickie she did in ten days. You'd get up at four in the morning and work until four the next morning, sometimes. And we were doing Vanity Fair— *Thackeray in ten days! And it wasn't bad! Myrna made a good Becky Sharp, even though it was rushed through without any rehearsal.*

In order to have lived through that particular period in Hollywood, to have survived the pace, you needed more than just talent and personality and good looks and that photographic quality that comes out on the screen. You also had to have a boundless energy. Myrna was endowed with that. She always did have it and always will have it. I've never heard her say, "I can't." It's a great quality.

Knowledge was the harvest of those frantic, free-lance years: Lou learned, and eventually wrote such original screenplays as *The Mating of Millie* and *The Guilt of Janet Ames* for Columbia; and I kept learning. On *Consolation Marriage*, Pat O'Brien, another import from Broadway, shared his experience. "Stop acting with your neck!" he admonished. "Relax!" I should have known better by then, but I was showing emotion with my neck muscles, rather than being tensed up internally. Pat and I were laughing about that nearly—ye gods!—fifty years later, when we played Burt Reynolds's parents in *The End*. "You'll never know how much you taught me in *Consolation Marriage*," I told him.

Minna sent me back to Goldwyn for *Arrowsmith*, Sidney Howard's adaptation of the Sinclair Lewis novel, which influenced so many of the "message pictures." John Ford directed that beautifully, with more of his wonderful soft touches. There's an epidemic on a West Indian island, and Dr. Arrowsmith, played by Ronald Colman, is inoculating the natives. We see their arms being injected, one by one; then, when he reaches me, the fair Englishwoman, Ford just takes the camera right up my arm to my face. That's how he introduces me to Arrowsmith and to the picture.

That was Jack Ford again, with his special thing for me—it wasn't overt, but I knew it was there. You can tell when a man has a yen. There's always banter and teasing, little jokes. It was particularly funny on *Arrowsmith*, as it turned out, because Arthur Hornblow's interest was also emerging by that time. Nothing came of it until his wife left him, but he was making eyes at me.

At the end of the picture, Jack bolted after a fight with Sam Goldwyn, leaving retakes unfinished. They weren't sure what to do, because Jack got into the bottle from time to time, and then would reappear. After a few days, when they were getting frantic, I received a wire from someplace—God knows where—in the South Pacific, something like: HAVING A WONDERFUL TIME. WISH YOU WERE HERE. JACK. You know, just to put me on the spot; everybody's looking for him and I'm the only one who knows where he is. Whether or not I told them escapes me now, but that typified the kind of prank he liked to play on me. Oh, it was really a harmless little flirtation, although he carried it on for years. And, ironically, when I married Gene Markey, Jack had to give me away.

I don't think I sent Myrna anywhere they didn't take her, attested Minna Wallis. I must say, everybody who saw her wanted to use her; you didn't have to force her down their throats. You said, "Myrna Loy," she'd go out to see them—sometimes I just ran a film of her—and she'd be hired. "She had an authority," my brother Hal says. "She was different from all those little blond girls." No matter how small the part, she got noticed, but I felt she needed a strong studio behind her. At that time, autumn of '31, Metro-Goldwyn-Mayer was emerging as the prestige studio with a knack for developing female stars. Irving Thalberg, Louis B. Mayer's second in command, supervised all production at their Culver City studio. I was very close to Irving through his wife, Norma Shearer, a good friend of mine. I told him about Myrna and suggested he see a clip of her. He said, "Let me see it before you show it around." So I sent part of Skyline, I think, one of her last under the Fox contract. He saw the film, and he signed her. Irving Thalberg liked her, which was like getting gold.

All that comes to mind about *Skyline*, curiously, is that I played Thomas Meighan's mistress in a blond wig. Yet supposedly Metro signed me on the strength of it. So much went through my head as I drove onto the M-G-M lot again. Having been there once before, for *Ben-Hur* and *Pretty Ladies,* when they did nothing about me, I was determined that this time something important would happen. I remember saying to myself: "I'm gonna beat this place yet!"

4

THE
PERFECT WIFE

1931–1935

There had been romantic couples before, but Loy and Powell were something new and original. They actually made marital comedy palatable. I remember Bill Powell when he started out as a melodramatic actor. Then, by some alchemy, he suddenly became comic. But Myrna gave the wit to the whole thing. They hit that wonderful note because he always did a wee bit too much and she underdid it, creating a grace, a charm, a chemistry. —GEORGE CUKOR, 1983

No one person really discovered me. I was discovered over and over again, every time some director or producer saw a quality he could bring out that I usually didn't even know I had. I wasn't aware at first that Irving Thalberg had brought me to M-G-M. But even he, it turned out, wanted me for a very strange role: the ruthless trapeze star in *Freaks*, who marries a midget for his money, then poisons him. God Almighty! Even Thalberg! That's how difficult it was to shake that image.

Well, fate saved me from *Freaks*. Baclanova got that; but the alternative was no better. Metro started me out with a string of relatively normal, definitely minor ingénues. After six years and sixty pictures, it didn't seem like progress to be playing a spoiled snot who ill-treats Marie Dressler. My disappointment must have showed. "Get your chin up, kid," Marie advised. "You've got the whole world ahead of you." *Emma* was fun because of her. She was a delight, a lovely woman, high-spirited and caring. I was crazy about her. She inspired awe, too, with her robust presence and extraordinary achievements. In her sixties she'd returned from near oblivion to become the movies' biggest box-office draw, beloved as few stars ever have been. It seemed that she'd go on forever.

They had me running from set to set, making three pictures at once. After completing a scene for *Emma*, I'd put on a blond wig and do a scene for *The Wet Parade* with Jimmy Durante. "Moyna," he'd ask, "where'd you get that schnozzola?" My nose always fascinated Jimmy. Then I'd remove the wig for a scene in *New Morals for Old* with Robert Young. We laughed again about one of his lines from the movie when I ran into him out at Universal recently. "Remember that line I had to say to you?" Bob asked. " 'I want to walk barefoot through your hair'?"

Rouben Mamoulian rescued me, borrowing me for *Love Me Tonight*, his musical spoof of Lubitsch. I knew Rouben—he was one of my beaus. We weren't involved in anything important, but we were good friends and used to date once in a while. "Now listen, Myrna," he said, "this is what's happening. Paramount's adamant about eliminating the role of Countess Valentine, but she's very important to my concept for the film. I know what I plan to do with her, but she won't be in the script. I'll send you your lines separately until they see it my way." Well, I had confidence in Rouben: "Sure, I'll try anything!" Every few days, he'd send little pieces of blue interoffice-memo paper with four or five lines typed on them. This was my part. I don't know how Rouben managed it, but when the men in the front office saw my first scenes, they said, "Oh, yes, keep her."

Myrna delivered those lines in that lovely offhand manner that made them excruciatingly funny, says Lou MacFarlane. As small as that role was, she stood out, and Jeanette MacDonald inadvertently made her even more prominent. MacDonald came on the set for a masquerade sequence looking very lovely, and Myrna came on looking even lovelier, in a gown which really wasn't that much different, but Miss MacDonald said, "I want that dress." I guess Mamoulian didn't want any trouble, because they gave her Myrna's dress.

Myrna and I rushed down to the wardrobe department to find another one. We had a terrible time looking through yards of costumes, but finally we came across a perfectly plain black velvet dress, a musty old thing, probably worn a thousand times. It looked like nothing, but when Myrna put it on, took a tuck in here and there, she looked gorgeous. She walked back on the set in that black dress and a powdered wig, and you didn't see anyone else in that scene. You see, all the others wore pastels—whites, pinks, things like that. And what's-her-name—I have trouble re-

*membering it, she was such a nasty lady on that picture—was
really livid. She couldn't very well say, "I want that dress!" I've
never seen anyone so angry in my life. So if Myrna had worn the
pink dress that MacDonald appropriated, she might never have
made such an impact and become a star. Who knows?*

Love Me Tonight was actually a vehicle for Maurice Chevalier, Paramount's big musical star. His car would pick me up and take me out
to the San Fernando Valley, where we shot some hunt sequences. I
remember driving with him through the mornings and never getting to
know him at all. Having seen his exuberant screen performances, I expected a dynamic man. But he was one of those people, a little bit like
Hank Fonda, with tremendous reserve. He remained an enigma to me,
Chevalier, a very, very strange man, keeping completely to himself.
And then he would walk onto the set, the lights would go on, and this
thing would happen—this marvelous thing that everybody adored.

I never really saw it until we met on the summer circuit, nearly
forty years later. Since my *Barefoot in the Park* company was rehearsing
during the day and he performed at night, I sent word that I could
attend his last show. "Ladies and gentlemen," he announced, "an old
friend of mine is in the audience tonight, and I am going to sing a song
in her honor from a picture we made together a long, long time ago."
He sang "Mimi," then asked me to join him on stage. He kissed me,
and the house went wild; I mean, they yelled and screamed, while
Maurice absolutely radiated warmth and charm. The next day, in all
the little shops around Cohasset, the talk was that Maurice Chevalier
had kissed me. The ladies were aflutter. And this was the personality I'd
always expected from him, and finally saw when he was well into his
seventies.

We posed for pictures together before he left and I asked him to
send me one autographed, something I seldom did during my long career. When you're working with people, you don't think of those things.
Maurice said he'd send one if I'd do the same. So we exchanged autographed pictures.

"I'm going around the world one more time," he told me that day;
"one last tour and then I'll take it easy."

"I don't believe it," I said. But he did retire after that tour, and not
long afterward died. Performing was his life.

Oh, the riches in *Love Me Tonight!* Can you imagine what we had in that film? Charlie Ruggles and Charlie Butterworth punctuating that witty script, Maurice and Jeanette MacDonald singing those wonderful Rodgers and Hart songs: "Isn't It Romantic?," "Lover," and "Mimi," of which even I had a verse—the only time I've sung in the movies. Richard Rodgers and I became friends on that picture. He loved teasing me about Arthur Hornblow. That was when my romance with Arthur really started. His wife had left him, taken off with their son, when we met one night in the Beverly-Wilshire drugstore. We hadn't seen each other since *Arrowsmith*, the year before. The next day, a fabulous array of roses arrived with an invitation to dinner enclosed. Oh, he did things well, that one! From then on, it was all Arthur. "Where did you spend the weekend?" Dick Rodgers asked. "Catalina," I gushed, a bit too obviously, "with Arthur Hornblow." Dick looked at me as if to say, "Oh, brother, she's hooked." And I was.

That was a momentous time for me: Arthur and a new awareness of my abilities struck simultaneously. Rouben had conceived Valentine as a pent-up aristocrat hungry for life and men, so bloody bored that she'd always be sleeping—on the stairs, on the furniture, anywhere. She's napping on a little Empire sofa at one end of this huge salon when Charlie Ruggles calls, "Valentine, Valentine, could you go for a doctor?" She perks right up: "Yes, bring him in!" During the hunt sequence, she's going on as usual about her favorite topic when Jeanette's character says, "Don't you ever think about anything but men?" Valentine replies: "Yes, schoolboys." They're the corniest lines in the world when you hear them now, but that house ripped open. I mean, the preview audience just yelled. This was my first realization that I could make people laugh, that sort of insouciance or something in my voice worked. Throughout all those sober parts, you see, it hadn't dawned on me that I could be funny.

For me, the highlight of the picture was a young actress named Myrna Loy, recalled Joseph L. Mankiewicz while introducing *Love Me Tonight* at the Museum of Modern Art in 1986. *Light and lissome and lovely, Myrna's the reason you forget who played opposite Chevalier—she was a singer; she sang. She got Chevalier, but, as I remember it, Myrna got the picture.*

Rouben's revelation of my comedic talents didn't faze M-G-M. They dropped me right back into the vamp mold, loaning me to RKO for *Thirteen Women*. As a Javanese-Indian half-caste, I methodically murder all the white schoolmates who've patronized me. I recall little about that racist concoction, but it came up recently when the National Board of Review honored me with its first Career Achievement Award. Betty Furness, a charming mistress of ceremonies, who had started at RKO doubling for my hands in closeups when I was busy elsewhere, said that she'd been dropped from *Thirteen Women*. (Despite its title, there were only ten in the final print.) "You were lucky," I told her, "because I just would have killed you, too. The only one who escaped me in that picture was Irene Dunne, and I regretted it every time she got the parts I wanted."

Metro then tossed me into *The Mask of Fu Manchu* as Fah Lo See, the nefarious daughter of the title character, played by Boris Karloff. That script was really the last straw. In one scene, she has this beautiful young man tied down, then whips him while uttering gleefully suggestive sounds. Well, I'd been reading Freud, and apparently the writers hadn't. "I can't do this," I told our producer, Hunt Stromberg. "I've done a lot of terrible things in films, but this girl's a sadistic nymphomaniac."

"What's that?" he said.

"Well, you better find out, because that's what she is and I won't play her that way." I did play her, of course; there was nothing I could do about it. But Hunt Stromberg was no fool; he simply hadn't been reading Freud. He did some research, and in the end the character's worst excesses were toned down. She wasn't Rebecca of Sunnybrook Farm, but, as I remember, she just watched while others did the whipping.

As I went into another scene, Charles Brabin, the director, said, "Put this on your lap." I turned and someone was handing me a python. "What?" I groaned, eyeing this endless creature that could easily squeeze me to death. After much cajoling, I allowed them to put the snake in my lap. I touched it, expecting a cold, clammy body. Instead, it was warm and doped within an inch of its life so that it wouldn't harm me. Well, my heart went out to that poor creature. They all mumbled, "Crazy woman," on the set, but I was very attentive to my pet python after that.

That was a crazy part, yet when Roddy McDowall tricked me into seeing it recently, it astonished me how good Karloff and I were. Everyone else just tossed it off as something that didn't matter, while Boris and I brought some feeling and humor to those comic-book characters. Boris was a fine actor, a professional who never condescended to his often unworthy material. There's a wonderful scene where he says, "I want you to meet my ugly daughter," and in walks this ravishing creature wearing a jewel-encrusted Chinese ensemble by Adrian. Despite such moments, I insisted that Fah Lo See be my last exotic, and she was. In fact, that phase of my career would be completely obliterated by the next. Thirty years later, someone suggested me for the Chinese empress in *Fifty-five Days at Peking*. "Myrna Loy?" came the incredulous response. "She can't possibly play Chinese."

Ned Griffith wanted to borrow me for *The Animal Kingdom* at RKO, where David O. Selznick was head of production. Ned and I had become friends during *Rebound*. I had great admiration for him as a director, and he knew what I could do as an actress. Selznick disagreed, giving him an argument about casting me. David later said that he "leaped at the idea," since those Oriental siren roles were a joke to anyone who knew me. The truth is, however, he wanted Karen Morley for the role of the wife. "No, she isn't sexy enough," Ned protested, because in Philip Barry's play the wife is more of a mistress and vice versa. Katharine Hepburn, who was fired from the Broadway production, claims that she wanted the part, but "Myrna Loy got it because she was beautiful." Actually, David wouldn't even let me test, until Ned tricked him by talking Leslie Howard into making a test with me at night when nobody was around.

I stayed in bed all day, resting up and studying the scene. My wonderful Mexican maid, Carolla, who always pampered me, fixed scrambled eggs laced with garlic sausage before I left for the studio. The scene went well, but Leslie Howard seemed constrained, unusually standoffish. "What did Mr. Howard think of me?" I asked Ned.

"He thought you were very good," Ned answered, "but wondered if you always eat so much garlic."

Leslie was not only a fastidious Englishman, I learned later, but a vegetarian, very persnickety about food. The smell of those Mexican sausages had made him quite ill, but of course he bore it like the gentleman he was. Oh, working with Leslie was heaven . . . *heaven*. What a strong, brilliant actor, yet how easily he seemed to accomplish it, always taking time to encourage me, to ease me into a role that would be another big step away from exotica. We grew very fond of one another on that picture. I mean, it could have been a real scrambola—if I'd allowed it to be. Leslie was far more impetuous than his gentle screen image indicated. That cool, lean exterior belied a passionate nature, which manifested itself on the set. I resisted the temptation, so he stormed my house, imploring me to run away with him to the South Seas. He really wanted to chuck everything and take off. And don't think he wasn't persuasive. But he was married, and I didn't go in for that sort of thing. Besides, Arthur, who happened to be in New York on business, returned in the nick of time. But, oh, I *loved* Leslie.

Not too long ago, while visiting London, I heard a voice calling, "Myrna! Myrna!" It was Ruth Howard, Leslie's widow. "Have you seen Ronnie?" she asked as we chatted. "He's so like Leslie." That's their son, who became an actor, and does resemble his father. I remember Ruth saying that day, which was very sweet of her, "Myrna, Leslie loved you so much." And I thought, Oh, brother, little does she know. . . .

Around the time of *The Animal Kingdom*, I finally left my mother's house. Realizing that Arthur and I were serious, she began bearing down. She didn't want me to marry, she wanted to maintain her control. I had slaved, and she was having a good life, but she knew that would continue. She just didn't want to let go. She needed to be a mother, but I was twenty-seven and in love. One night, I just packed a bag and went—I sent Lou MacFarlane back for the rest of my things. Mother was so furious that she went to Europe for a year.

I rented an apartment in Beverly Hills, not far from Arthur. Juliette had taken their son back to her family home in Warrenton, Virginia, and returned briefly to the stage. She was definitely finished with Arthur, but they hadn't divorced. He claimed that Juliette wouldn't give him a divorce, although she evinced no hostility when he took me to see her in *Dodsworth*. The problem that evening was Arthur's total lack of feeling. Not only did he blithely bring his lady friend backstage to meet his estranged wife, but he thought nothing of waiting in the wings while a critical stage director rehearsed her after the performance. The fact that our being there might embarrass her escaped him, an example of his insensitivity that I observed, then discarded. When in love, one diminishes such perceptions.

The columnists could have had a field day with our relationship, but we managed to keep it out of the public eye during four years of courting or living together. Everybody did it, but nobody talked about it. Only the blatant ones were publicized, the ones that didn't hide, not the quiet ones. In fact, in all that time I recall only one crack about us—something in the *Hollywood Reporter* about Leslie Howard "carrying a torch for Arthur Hornblow's paramour."

In those days, you understand, everything had to seem perfect on and off the screen: every relationship proper, every hair in place; no wrinkles in your costumes or your private life. David Selznick, the ultimate perfectionist, always aimed for an improbable ideal. He thought my ears stuck out too far, and kept urging me to have them fixed. If I wore my hair up or swept back in a scene, he'd have the makeup man glue them close to my head. As the lights got hotter, my ears came unglued and popped loose. The director would call, "Cut! Where's the makeup guy?" Then we'd start all over again. It frustrated and exhausted me. I hated it.

Despite my ears, David arranged to keep me at RKO for *Topaze*, another chance to work with John Barrymore—this time as his leading lady. On my way to see the director, Harry D'Arrast, I ran into Jack, who walked right past me without saying a word. Oh, God, he doesn't want me, I thought, recalling our troubles on *Don Juan*; but that was six years ago—how could he possibly still hold that against me? I went to Harry, who said, "Don't pay any attention to him."

The next morning, someone knocked on my dressing-room door. It was *Mister* Barrymore himself: "Myrna, Harry tells me that I slighted you yesterday. Well, I was a bit confused. I saw *three* of you and didn't know which one to bow to."

It hadn't occurred to me that he'd been drinking, but what a graceful way to cover an oversight. I kept harking back to *Don Juan*, expecting him to blow up somewhere along the line, but we had no problems after that first day. He often made jokes about his drinking, yet remained sober on the set, very serious about the picture. I think *Topaze* meant a lot to him. No longer the rogue I'd known at Warners, he was very supportive in our scenes, generous, but preoccupied, sad. He'd gone in for exotic fish at this point and kept them around in tanks. He developed passions for different things—raising chickens at one time, I recall; always something. Fish were his new passion, and he'd added a pond to what he called his "Chinese tenement" on Tower Road. When I asked about Dolores and their two children, he talked about acquiring rare tropical fish, so I assumed things were shaky at home. On the set, though, he was a lamb, absolutely angelic. He may have been merely running out of steam, I don't know, but I feel fortunate to have participated in one of his best films.

Back at M-G-M, Irving Thalberg sent for me. You always heard of Thalberg as the ultimate producer, but I'd seen little evidence of it. I didn't know then that he brought me to Metro or held any particular interest in me. He kept me waiting interminably in his outer office. When I finally got in, he turned his back on me, looked out the window, and started talking. Well, my back went up. I'm very sensitive to bad manners. That was *Miss* Loy, you know. As I started to walk out, he swiveled his chair back toward me. "Thank you," I said rather pompously. "I was brought up to look at people when I talk to them."

"What?" he replied, startled but not displeased. Although always a little bit ill, with shoulders that hunched forward slightly, he was an attractive man, really beautiful, I thought, with a great face and deep, penetrating eyes. "Myrna," he observed, despite my outburst, "you're terribly shy. There's no reason why you should be. It's hurting you, putting a veil between you and the audience. You've got to cut through the veil and take hold of that audience. Make it yours. It's there and they like you. They adore you. You're beautiful enough for the movies, you're making good progress here"—both of which I myself had doubted—"so make it work for you."

Well, my shyness was nothing new to me, but I hadn't realized it affected my work. It's interesting that Thalberg discovered it. He didn't know me at all—oh, we met at parties and things like that, but we never had spent any time together. Yet he discerned this and, strangely enough, it was around that time I'd finally decided to leave home and make a life for myself, cutting the veil in more ways than one. After that meeting with Irving Thalberg, I felt for the first time that M-G-M had plans for me.

They were starting to build her at Metro, Minna Wallis corroborates, *and they were working her like crazy. I went to Louis B. Mayer for a raise. I'll never forget that day. Mayer and I were good friends outside the studio, but when I walked in, he said,*

"Now what do you want?" I said, "I want a raise for Myrna Loy." He said, "She's getting so much . . . so much . . . so much . . ." I said, "That's not enough." Then—I'll never forget it—he began to cry. Tears poured out of his eyes, and he kept moaning, "What are you doing to me? You're trying to ruin me." I'd heard about those little fits of his, so it didn't throw me. After enduring a bit of his pretending to cry and carry on, I got Myrna's raise.

Every woman's dream of heaven in the twenties was to be carried off to an oasis by Valentino, Ramon Novarro, or any reasonable facsimile. Well, that's just what happened to me in *The Barbarian*. Ramon, an Egyptian dragoman, succumbs to my charms, throws orchids in my window, and abducts me. Unfortunately, in 1933 fashions in screen lovers were changing. Ramon was still a big star, Metro's reigning exotic lover, but things were beginning not to work so well for him. His career was shaky, and he knew it. He'd invested his earnings wisely, so that wasn't a problem, but it's still a very sad thing, that irrevocable slide from stardom.

Like many of those so-called great lovers, Ramon was really a gentle, quiet man. We became friends on that film, but the studio exploited it. I picked up a newspaper and discovered the intimate details of our "torrid romance," which apparently was common knowledge to everyone but the participants. It was preposterous. Ramon wasn't even interested in the ladies, and I was seeing Arthur exclusively, so the publicity department had chosen a most unlikely pair. That particular thing hadn't happened to me before. It infuriated me and I raised hell. Whether or not that had anything to do with it, I don't know, but it never happened again.

Otherwise, *The Barbarian* was a wild, crazy picture, with locations in the big sand dunes around Yuma, Arizona. I rode a camel for the first time. To this day I remember her name, Rosie, because that beast was full of nasty habits, biting and spitting all over the place. Another hazard awaited me on the sound stage: a classic Hollywood bathing scene. After I was safely submerged in a sunken marble tub, they scattered rose petals on the water, stationing men to keep them circulating with long, toothless rakes. They kept pushing those rose petals closer and closer to cover me—somewhat overzealously, it seemed. I looked up and saw a ring of familiar faces, Culver City friends and neighbors who worked in the studio. Unaware that I wore flesh-toned garments, they were diligently trying to protect the virtue of a local girl. It was so sweet, but it didn't work. Some magazine photographer got in, took a picture that made me look stark naked, and syndicated it all over the world.

Once, when Ramon and I were being driven from one set to another, we noticed a commotion up ahead, people running helter-skelter, gaping at the sky. Sam Wood, our director, ran over to us, shouting, "We've just had an earthquake!" Ramon and I had been in the moving car, so we hadn't felt the initial shock, but the aftershocks were so strong that they called off the day's work. M-G-M looked like the Mack Sennett lot that day with people dashing frantically in every direction. When the lights went out in the sound booth, Robert Montgomery got lost in the baffles, those sort of winged panels, and ran around like a whirling dervish trying to escape. When the old executive building shook, Louis B. Mayer, followed by terrified associates, ran for the outside stairway leading from his second-floor office. Mayer was quite corpulent, and those usually deferential lieutenants kept rushing and shoving, trying to squeeze past him, until they all got stuck on the rickety wooden stairs.

When George Bernard Shaw visited California in 1933, he stayed at the Hearst ranch at San Simeon with William Randolph Hearst and his mistress, Marion Davies. That amused me no end, because for years Hearst's newspapers had roasted the playwright for his Socialism and liberal doctrines. I'd seen or read most of his plays, and knew something about his life and politics, so this struck me as a very strange relationship. I never went to San Simeon, although Marion had quite a crush on me. She was a sweet soul, and we used to have fun together talking and laughing at parties. But my politics and Hearst's simply didn't mix. With Shaw, apparently, it was a case of noblesse oblige.

Marion remained Shaw's official guide in Hollywood. Since she was still at M-G-M, Mayer got a chance to give one of his inevitable celebrity luncheons. We were advised on the *When Ladies Meet* set that after lunch Shaw would pay a visit. Well, Bob Montgomery got so excited he literally jumped up and down. I mean, he was an absolute wreck at the thought of meeting the great man. The prospect impressed me as well, but not to the point of giddiness. "Let's go up to makeup and get a lot of long white beards like his," Bob proposed. "We'll all put them on and surprise him." I said, "N*oooo*, we don't do that . . . we don't do that." That's how disoriented Bob was.

We were in the middle of a scene, Bob, Ann Harding, and I, when who should appear? After formal introductions, he walked right up to me and questioned the necessity of one of my lines—nothing constructive, just an attempt, I thought, to get a rise out of me. "Well, Mr. Shaw," I explained, "that's the line, and that's the way the director wants it. That's the way it goes." In other words, I offered him a slight argument. He just gave me a good looking at, sized me up, which, with his piercing blue eyes and satyr's smirk, should have been intimidating. As usual, however, *Miss* Loy wasn't having any. Having been brought up by people who respected themselves, I wasn't easily done in by any of these great figures. Of course, I regretted not having more of an exchange with Shaw, but as it turned out he really was a devil, a very naughty man, who derived humor from ragging others.

He apparently did these things deliberately, because after failing to goad me, he tried Ann Harding. Polite and deferential, Ann mentioned that she'd appeared in *Captain Brassbound's Conversion* at the Hedgerow Theatre in Pennsylvania. "Did you, now?" he boomed. "It was probably a piratical performance." He behaved very badly—berating her, threatening legal action, thoroughly demoralizing her—then just walked off the set.

Ann ran to her dressing room and burst into tears. That upsetting incident, curiously, presented me with my only opportunity to know Ann Harding at all. We'd both done *The Animal Kingdom*, but hadn't worked together. Although, as the title implies, *When Ladies Meet* gave us several scenes together, she remained a very private person, a wonderful actress completely without star temperament, but withdrawn.

Alice Brady was a different case altogether. Her father, William Brady, was a famous theatrical producer, and her own stage and silent-film careers had been formidable, but it hadn't turned her head. She was charming, funny, and wonderful. Having starred in O'Neill's *Mourning Becomes Electra*, she considered it appropriate that her pets—dogs, cats, all kinds of creatures—should be named for characters in the original Greek version. It was typical of Alice's impulsive irreverence that canine Agamemnons, feline Clytemnestras, and twittering Electras overran her house. Bob Montgomery adored her, and, both being great wits, they made very entertaining companions. We became a little coterie of three, occasionally going to her house or having something to eat after work. That kind of easy camaraderie is rare in pictures; everything goes so fast you very often don't get to know people.

The big thing about *Penthouse* was that W. S. Van Dyke directed it. That turned out to be one of the most important things that ever happened to me. "This girl's going to be a big star!" he started yelling down in the commissary. "Next year she'll be a star." Oh, some of them do that, you know, go on and on about this, that, and the other, but Van Dyke actually came up with the first part that was written specifically for me. It started out as *The Sailor and the Lady* for Clark Gable and me, and ended up as *The Prizefighter and the Lady* for me and Max Baer, a real prizefighter. Frances Marion's story was better than it sounds from the title, and Woody Van Dyke, as usual, made it even better.

Woody, the fastest director I've ever worked with, still managed to give a personal stamp to everything he did. Spontaneity was his byword on and off the set. Full of practical jokes, like having chairs wired so you'd sit down and get an awful shock, he gloated when someone mentioned Max Baer's fear of mice. Nothing would do but that he should put a mouse on Max's chair just as he sat down. Well, this marvelous hunk of man got one look at that tiny mouse, let out a scream, and took off like a bat out of hell. He nevertheless remained a stalwart figure on screen, giving a fine performance despite his lack of acting experience. And he certainly looked the part. I loved to watch the way he would lean up against the ropes, then throw himself back again, that beautiful body just glistening. The climactic fight pitted Baer against Primo Carnera, with Jack Dempsey as referee. They came from all over to watch us film that one, because Carnera was actually world heavyweight champion and Baer the outstanding challenger.

Primo Carnera was an extraordinary creature, gigantic, almost seven feet tall, with enormous hands and feet. After the entire cast had autographed one of his shoes for him, there was still ample space for the crew to sign. He seemed to be a sad man, for he really was a freak of nature, in a way, and this troubled him. The following year, he lost the heavyweight title to Max, who, ironically, had been studying Carnera's technique during their scenes in *The Prizefighter and the Lady*.

Squeezed in there someplace is *Night Flight*, notable for its all-star cast—the Barrymore brothers, Helen Hayes, Clark Gable, Bob Montgomery, and, for the first time, billed up there with the studio's best, Myrna Loy. We did that picture in bits and pieces, episodes with different characters who never met. I didn't see Jack or Helen or anybody but Bill Gargan, whom I'd adored since *The Animal Kingdom*. We had a very nice scene as he goes off on a fatal flight, which everyone seemed to do in that picture.

I didn't work with Clark Gable on *Night Flight*, but Minna Wallis introduced us around that time. The so-called Hollywood élite in those days used to give an annual Mayfair Ball—everyone who was anyone would get all dolled up in best bib 'n' tucker, go down to the Ambassador, and dance. "I'm taking Mr. and Mrs. Gable," Minna said. "I thought maybe you'd like to meet Clark." By that time he was hot, the big rage; all the women in Hollywood, including my friend Lou MacFarlane, were talking about him. I'd heard that he was always on the make at the studio, after everyone, snapping garters left and right. At the dance, though, he acted like a perfect gentleman—attentive, but not aggressive. Whenever I hear "Dancing in the Dark," I think of him, because we danced to it that night and he was vibrant and warm, a marvelous dancer. It was *divine*. . . .

Coming home, we dropped Minna off first, leaving the three of us, the Gables and me, in the back seat of the limousine. Clark's second wife, Rhea, who had been charming all evening, was much older than he and somewhat matronly. As we drove toward my mother's house, I could see that Clark was beginning to feel a bit amorous. He started edging toward me—with his wife sitting right there beside him. Of course, he was probably loaded by that time. We all were, to a certain extent.

Clark escorted me to the door. As I turned to unlock it, he bent down and gave me a "monkey bite." (It left a scar on my neck for days.) I turned around and gave him a shove, sending him backward two or three steps off the porch and into the hedge. As he stumbled back, I remember, he laughed a little, which infuriated me all the more. It was just the idea of his wife sitting out in the car. I'd had quite a few beaus, but this was different, you see, this was not right. I wanted no part of it.

I stormed into the house and what did I find? Lou MacFarlane on her hands and knees peering out the window. She was spending the night in hopes of catching a glimpse of her idol. "What could you

TUDIO PORTRAITS

ese portraits were taken at private sittings in the
d-twenties by Witzel Studio and Walter F.
ely, pioneer Hollywood photographers not
liated with any particular studio.

LEFT: Henry Waxman captured Myrna in the wig and costume that Adrian designed for Natasha Rambova's *What Price Beauty?* BELOW: During her slinky years at Warner Brothers, she posed for this publicity shot entitled "Halloween."

RIGHT: The feathered cloche was worn in *Midnight Taxi*, 1928. BELOW: The harlequinesque outfit was merely the notion of Warners' photo department.

ABOVE: In the Irving Chidnoff portrait, Myrna bridges the centuries as a sort of
Renaissance flapper. OPPOSITE ABOVE: Warners' Elmer Fryer shot Myrna in her
enchanting costume from *Bride of the Regiment*, an early "talkie" musical.
OPPOSITE BELOW: D'Gaggeri, a Wilshire Boulevard portraitist, accomplished a
more languorous mood.

Kendall Evans in 1928 (*The Crimson City*), above, and Clarence Sinclair Bull in 1932 (*The Mask of Fu Manchu*), left, immortalized Myrna's Oriental period.

M-G-M's Russell Ball and George Hurrell took these much-used publicity portraits of the "new" Myrna Loy in 1933 and 1934.

ABOVE: This 1934 stock glamour shot in Myrna's *Thin Man* gown is by Clarence Bull, perhaps the most famous of M-G-M's portraitists, who (opposite above) caught a more wily Loy in another *Thin Man* costume. OPPOSITE BELOW: The breezy profile publicized Paramount's *Wings in the Dark*, 1935.

These striking studies are the results of a private sitting with a Los Angeles photographer called Maurine.

Laszlo Willinger, one of M-G-M's ace portraitists, manipulated light and shadow
artfully in these studies taken in 1938 (opposite) and 1939 (above).

Willinger captured the perfect horsewoman (above), costumed for *Third Finger, Left Ha* 1939, while Clarence Bull caught the sleek sophisticate (left). OPPOSITE: By 1941, the persona had taken on new luster, evident in Carpenter's photograph.

Ernest A. Bachrach caught the chic Mrs. Blandings head-on in 1948.

possibly see in that ignorant person," I blustered, "that rude, ignorant person?"

"Myrna," she said calmly, "I wouldn't care if he couldn't read."

When I saw Clark at the studio soon after that, he walked right past me with his nose in the air. Next thing I knew, we were cast together for *Men in White*. Oh, wow, this is going to be something, I thought; I'm in deep trouble. When we started the film, Clark developed a pretty serious thing with Elizabeth Allan, a lovely English girl in the cast, and greeted her with coffee and cakes every morning. The crew always put out sweet breads, so Clark would load up and, just to get my goat, walk right past me to Elizabeth. He was punishing me. We managed to be convincing lovers on camera, which wasn't easy while he virtually ignored me. That Dutchman just wasn't taking no for an answer.

In less than two years at Metro, I'd made fifteen pictures. They worked us to death. You'd go from one picture to another without rehearsal, often not knowing what your part would be from scene to scene. They would hand you your afternoon lines in the commissary to learn over lunch. Those so-called moguls used us terribly. We were little more than chattels, really, but it was valuable experience. You didn't need acting school; you learned on the job, and if they decided to build you, they built you to last.

We were in the midst of the Depression. I felt fortunate to have work and afraid not to take every opportunity. As a result, I hardly existed except on the set. I was just too tired after a day's work to bother about anything but sleep, which, needless to say, pressured my already volatile relationship with Arthur Hornblow. I became fed up entirely and called Benny Thau, the studio's talent coordinator, who always helped me: "Benny, send me my week's salary. I'm going to Honolulu and spend every cent of it." I took Shirley Hughes, my friend and stand-in, and sailed on the *Monterey* for Hawaii, where Betty and Bob Black were stationed. Bob had recently been commissioned, with much fanfare, as a second lieutenant in the Medical Corps—the only enlisted man chosen from ten thousand who had applied.

Myrna used to check periodically to see how this marriage she had instigated was working out, quips Betty Black. She was already well known, although the Thin Man *pictures hadn't started, so when her boat docked she got a royal reception; they piled leis clear over her head. She stayed at the Royal Hawaiian at first, but people wouldn't leave her alone, so she moved to Schofield Barracks with us to get some rest. People tracked her there, too. Chun Hoon, one of the island's richest men, assumed because of her name and those parts she played that Myrna had Chinese blood. He had a fabulous estate with a big lanai, where he gave this elaborate party for her. Hawaiian and Chinese orchestras played and the banquet went on for hours: thirty-five courses, beginning with bird's-nest soup, right on through. After each course, Chun Hoon would raise his glass and propose a toast to the next course. The glasses were tiny, but the drinks were strong. We almost didn't make it through the dinner. He had the Chinese consul there, and all the top people from the islands and the embassies to meet Myrna. This was something rare—remember, we were in old Hawaii before annexation—a very high Chinese patriarch opening his doors to Hawaii's international community.*

Everything revolved around Myrna and it all seemed sort of like a dream to her—all very wonderful, and so forth—but her mind was still on Arthur. When Myrna loves somebody, everything else becomes a side issue. She had left because even though his marriage was definitely finished, he wasn't getting a divorce. You see, if Myrna loved a man, she wanted to marry him, she wanted to be his wife. She's never been one for affairs—she's always wanted to be the perfect wife she would later portray in the movies.

We left the post because people were pestering her. We never had any privacy. I'd answer the door and some mother would push in with her child. Would Miss Loy just let little so-and-so touch her hand? On the boat coming over she'd met the Beckleys, prominent Scottish plantation owners, who had intermarried with the Hawaiian royal family. (In fact, Mrs. Beckley's sister Princess Liliuokalani was involved with John Gilbert at the time.) Very much taken with Myrna, they invited her to use their secluded estate on the other side of the island from Honolulu. We swam and ate fresh fruits and lived purely Hawaiian style. This was the peaceful vacation that Myrna wanted, but all this time she

*still fretted about not hearing from Arthur. When Bob went back
to Schofield, there was a wire waiting: Arthur wanted Myrna to
come back and they would make arrangements to be married. She
went back to Arthur and her work.*

Shirley and I returned from our glorious holiday on the *Mariposa*. That
voyage, in February, 1934, turned out to be a very sad coming back,
because John Gilbert was on board. One of the great stars of silent
pictures, he became the greatest casualty of sound. He would appear
occasionally on an upper deck somewhere, thin and ghostly, with a
male nurse in anxious attendance. He seemed so far gone—nursing his
wounds, I imagine—after the termination of his Metro contract and his
brief marriages to Ina Claire and Virginia Bruce. He'd gone off to Hawaii in pursuit of Princess Liliuokalani, but she had spurned him. He
was trying in his way to straighten out his shattered life, but it wasn't
straightened out. It never would be. He methodically drank himself to
death over the next two years.

They put me right to work in *Manhattan Melodrama*, which pre-
cipitated the demise of John Dillinger, Public Enemy No. 1. FBI agents
shot him down outside the Biograph Theatre, in Chicago, after he'd
seen the film. Supposedly a Myrna Loy fan, he broke cover to see me.
Personally, I suspect the theme of the picture rather than my fatal charms
attracted him, but I've always felt a little guilty about it, anyway. They
filled him full of holes, poor soul.

Manhattan Melodrama was a gangster tale, but an interesting one
that would be frequently retold. Two pals grow up in the streets of New
York. One becomes Clark Gable, a gangster; the other becomes William Powell, the governor who must order his friend's execution—hokum,
but artfully done. I start off as Gable's girl and end up as the governor's
wife. I don't recall much about my scenes with Clark, curiously enough,
but he seemed all right toward me by that time—not effusive, but then
there wasn't time. Woody Van Dyke was directing and had me running
from pillar to post. And, really, that picture doesn't get going until Bill
comes in.

My first scene with Bill, a night shot on the back lot, happened
before we'd even met. Woody was apparently too busy for introductions.
My instructions were to run out of a building, through a crowd, and
into a strange car. When Woody called "Action," I opened the car

door, jumped in, and landed smack on William Powell's lap. He looked up nonchalantly: "Miss Loy, I presume?" I said, "Mr. Powell?" And that's how I met the man who would be my partner in fourteen films.

In that picture, interestingly enough, you can see a transition in the way I play my relationships with Clark and Bill. I instinctively keyed my women to the personalities of the men. Male-female relationships were much more clearly defined in those days. My job was to vivify those relationships within the framework of the script, the mores, and the abilities of the men. Clark, for instance, suffered so much from the macho thing that love scenes were difficult. He kept very reserved, afraid to be sensitive for fear it would counteract his masculine image. I always played it a little bit tough with him, giving him what-for to bring him out, because he liked girls like that—Carole Lombard had a tough quality. Of course, I didn't know all this at first. It was an instinctive thing with me.

I played differently with Bill. He was so naturally witty and outrageous that I stayed somewhat detached, always a little incredulous. From that very first scene, a curious thing passed between us, a feeling of rhythm, complete understanding, an instinct for how one could bring out the best in the other. In all our work together you can see this strange—I don't know what . . . a kind of rapport. It wasn't conscious. If you heard us talking in a room, you'd hear the same thing. He'd tease me a little and a kind of blending emerged that seemed to please people. Whatever caused it, though, it was magical, and Woody Van Dyke brought it to fruition in our next picture—perhaps the best remembered of my hundred and twenty-four features.

Woody sent a script based on Dashiell Hammett's best-selling novel *The Thin Man*, which Alexander Woollcott had called "the best detective story yet written in America." I loved it and its prospect of a witty role for the first time since *Love Me Tonight*. I'd fired an occasional quip, but my roles had been very straight up to that point. When I discussed it with Woody, however, a problem had developed. Mayer considered me wrong for the part. "Powell can play the detective—he's played Philo Vance already. Yeah, that's O.K., but I don't want Myrna in the picture." There was no precedent for casting me. Oh, they had a terrible battle! "She's all right," Woody insisted. "I've pushed her in my pool." Which he had—that was his test and apparently I'd passed. When Woody threatened to walk out, Mayer relented, but not without conditions. Woody could have me if he finished *The Thin Man* in time for me to start *Stamboul Quest* in three weeks. Perhaps he expected Woody to back down, because it took two months—six weeks, at the least—to bring in a picture like that. Woody showed 'em. He finished *The Thin Man* in sixteen days, with two days for retakes!

They called him "One-take Van Dyke." If he could get it the first time, he wouldn't even bother with a cover shot. "Actors are bound to lose their fire if they do a scene over and over," he said. "It's that fire that brings life to the screen." He wanted spontaneity, and speed ensured it. Of course, he had us going like crazy, but by that time I could come in, look at new lines, and do them. You had to in those days, because they changed scripts overnight. Often you could study the day before; often you couldn't. Woody demanded extraordinary deeds and you needed the discipline to go along with it or you couldn't work with him. He ultimately became too fast; it became an obsession. But his pacing and spontaneity made *The Thin Man.*

What other director would introduce his leading lady with a perfect three-point landing on a barroom floor—even if it was the Ritz bar? I was supposed to stroll in looking very chic, loaded down with packages, and leading Asta on a leash. "Can you fall?" Woody asked. "Do you know how to do a fall?" I said, "I've never worked for Mack Sennett, but I'm a dancer. I think I can do it." I would have done anything for Woody, because I was devoted to him. "You just trip yourself," he explained, "and then go right down."

He put a camera on the floor, a mark where he wanted me to land, and we shot it without any rehearsal. I must have been crazy. I could have killed myself, but my dance training paid off. I dashed in with Asta and all those packages, tripped myself, went down, slid across the floor, and hit the mark with my chin. It was absolutely incredible!

Filming went like a breeze, because we loved what we were doing. The only problem came when Nick Charles discloses who killed cock robin. Poor Bill complained loudly that he had to learn so many lines while I just gave him those knowing Nora Charles looks every now and then. Everybody sat down at a long dinner table, waiters served oysters on the half shell, and Bill began unraveling the plot. After a valiant try, he groaned, "I don't know what I'm talking about." But Woody didn't care as long as it kept moving. So we'd begin again and those oysters would reappear. They wouldn't bring fresh ones, and under the lights, as shooting wore on, they began to putrefy. By the time we finished that scene, nobody ever wanted to see another oyster.

Hunt Stromberg, our producer, wasn't given a heck of a lot of money for *The Thin Man*. It wasn't considered a big picture, by any means— a three-week shooting schedule usually meant a B picture. We had no idea it would turn out the way it did. None at all. We knew that we liked it, that it was fun, but its reception came as a complete surprise. It *stunned* the M-G-M brass.

We attended the first preview in fear and trembling, recalls Samuel Marx, head of M-G-M's story department at the time. *The executives went down to Huntington Park, including Hunt Stromberg, who was a nervous man anyway. I'd bought this sprightly detective story for fourteen thousand dollars, and we had no idea whether this kind of comedy would go. It had two unprecedented elements that scared the hell out of the whole studio: they were having fun with murder, and they were a married couple who acted with total sophistication. Myrna joins Bill at the bar, asking, "Gus, how many has he had?" When the bartender reports "Seven," she says, "Set 'em up," and matches her husband drink for drink. That could have been a jolt to post-Prohibition audiences still uneasy with social drinking.*

The matrimonial combination of Powell and Loy—even that was a risk, because in those days you got married at the end of the movie, not at the beginning. Marriage wasn't supposed to be fun. Myrna says, "I think it's a dirty trick to bring me all the way to New York just to make a widow of me." Bill observes, "You wouldn't be a widow long." She agrees: "You bet I wouldn't!" And he counters, "Not with all your money." These are marvelous lines, but the night of the preview nobody knew how they'd be received.

I can only tell you that it was a night of great jubilation on the Huntington Park sidewalk after that preview. The whole thing broke with tradition in several ways, yet it looked like a smash. That first preview was a thermometer that told us how much heat this team was generating. They had a chemistry that came out of Myrna Loy and William Powell, plus the characters of Nick and

Nora Charles. It was automatic that you would now continue to put them together. The reaction was so great and it never stopped.

After eighty-odd pictures—an astonishing statistic brought to mind recently by Lawrence J. Quirk's *Films of Myrna Loy*—*The Thin Man* finally *made* me. It put me right up there with the public and the studio. It inspired the press. From that time on, they called me "the perfect wife," which typed me as confiningly as those vamp roles had. But at least this wife thing, perfect or otherwise, came closer to my own personality. Nora was hardly the perfect wife in the sense of being the chaste, virginal creature that seemed to be so much admired. I wasn't like that on or off the screen. There were women like that, and men married them to be the mothers of their children, but the men usually left them sooner or later.

I prefer Gore Vidal's description of my image, "the eternal good-sex woman-wife," which removes the puritanical connotation of perfect. What man would want a perfect wife, anyway? What made the *Thin Man* series work, what made it fun, was that we didn't attempt to hide the fact that sex is part of marriage. But it was deft, done with delicacy and humor. Then, too, the Charleses had enormous tolerance for each other's imperfections. It wasn't any sticky idealistic perfection that made their marriage fun to watch—quite the contrary. Ye gods! *The Thin Man* virtually introduced modern marriage to the screen. Previously people married and lived happily ever after, but you never saw the undercurrents.

Not one day in my life passes without someone asking about Bill or Asta. Recently, the boy who delivers my afternoon paper returned my payment with a note: "Never a charge for Nora Charles." Now, that's immortality! Several wirehaired terriers played our scene-stealing pet over the years, but we weren't allowed to make friends with any of them. Their trainer feared it would break the dogs' concentration. The first one, Skippy, bit me once, so our relationship was hardly idyllic. My relationship with Bill was. We became very close friends, but, contrary to popular belief, we were never *really* married or even close to it. Oh, there were times when Bill had a crush on me and times when I had a crush on Bill, but we never made anything of it. We worked around it and stayed pals. In this world today, nobody seems to understand how you can just be terribly close and love somebody a whole lot and not sleep with him. If Bill and I had been lovers, then we would have had fights. And if we'd been married, it would have been even worse.

Even my best friends never fail to tell me that the smartest thing I ever did was to marry Myrna Loy on the screen, William Powell disclosed. *And it was the pleasantest, I might add. We were married in thirteen pictures, including* Libeled Lady *(I think we were married; it was a little confusing), and I never saw Myrna go into a temperamental tantrum, rave and rant, or walk off the set in a huff. She never lets her emotions come too near the surface, and remains calm and poised in the most difficult situations. There were days on the set when she liked to sit alone, and other days when she felt rowdydow and wanted to play pranks.*

When we did a scene together, we forgot about technique, camera angles, and microphones. We weren't acting. We were just two people in perfect harmony. Many times I've played with an actress who seemed to be separated from me by a plate-glass window; there was no contact at all. But Myrna, unlike some actresses who think only of themselves, has the happy faculty of being able to listen while the other fellow says his lines. She has the give and take of acting that brings out the best.

The Thin Man *would never have been the success it was without her. When the bed rolled beneath her in the hangover scene and she looked up at me with the ice bag on her head and said, "You pushed me," she became every man's dream of what a wife should be: beautiful and glamorous with a sense of humor, provocative and feminine without being saccharine or sharp, a perfect gal who never lost her temper, jumped at conclusions, or nagged a guy. Men-Must-Marry-Myrna Clubs were formed. Hearty Nigel Bruce broke down and wrote her his first fan letter. Jimmy Stewart said, "I shall only marry Myrna Loy," while women wept.*

I made my last stand in exotica as Fräulein Doktor, the spy who captured Mata Hari, in *Stamboul Quest.* The Fräulein was still alive when I played her. She'd become a drug addict, lost her mind, and landed in a Swiss sanatorium, so fear of libel kept the script in the air all the way through. It's an intricate spy story, kind of misty to me now, except that

I wore a wonderful black picture hat and enjoyed George Brent. He was a good actor, but rather difficult—not difficult with me, but I'd see him asserting his independence from time to time, particularly when they kept changing the script. He did a lot of good work, but never became a really big star.

They rushed me into *Evelyn Prentice*, with Bill Powell, to cash in on the success of *The Thin Man*. I'm the wife of a famous trial lawyer who thinks she's murdered someone, and so on—pure melodrama made somewhat more palatable by the direction of William K. Howard, my former champion at Fox. *The Thin Man* had been so perfect for us, such a ball to make, that going into this thing was kind of a bore. It sent Bill into occasional depressions. I'd never seen that side of him. "People don't know it, but I'm primarily Irish," he explained. "We get these dark periods."

I recall little else about that picture except Roz—Rosalind Russell—who made her film début in it. I didn't see much of her then because she had a tiny part, but you didn't pass her by very easily with that wonderfully extroverted personality of hers. And John Considine, who produced it, comes to mind because of a note he sent me on the green interoffice paper that Metro executives used. I've saved it all these years, I don't know why. Perhaps as a warning:

Dear Myrna:

Mr. and Mrs. Erich Von Stroheim are in dire want and several of their old friends on the lot have suggested that we make up a Christmas Fund to at least help them out of their immediate difficulties.

If you feel inclined to join in this much needed collection, will you please give John Farrow your check for $25.00 or more and make same payable to Reverend John O'Donnell, who has done more than anyone else to help the Von Stroheims through their very serious troubles. Father O'Donnell will give Von a list of our names, together with the check, as I am sure that Von would be much happier about the matter if he knew the names of those who thought of him at this time.

John

Metro loaned me to Columbia for Frank Capra's *Broadway Bill*. I'd become box office, you see, so my home studio could make money by lending or trading me for much more than my weekly salary. Usually they wouldn't send you if you didn't like the role. Frank had tried to borrow me for his previous picture, *It Happened One Night*. I'd refused it, and Louis B. Mayer had backed me up. Frank says that Harry Cohn, his boss at Columbia, persisted, but that Mayer remained adamant: "Harry, I *never* ask one of my little girls to play a part she don't want." Oh, I've taken flak for refusing that picture. Frank gave it to me for years. Lou MacFarlane, who begged me to do it, still says, "I told you so!" But let me say, here and now, they sent me the worst script ever, completely different from the one they shot. I've had others corroborate that. In fact, Bob Montgomery turned down the male lead for the same reason, but no one believes me. That girl was unplayable as originally written. I mean, we're in the middle of the Great Depression and she's running away because being rich *bores* her. Of course, that script arrived during one of those periods when non-stop picture-making had left me numb.

Broadway Bill was a different matter. That script grabbed me right away, and making it was a delight. I saw it recently and thought, Ye gods, could I have ever been that young? Frank Capra worked at a more leisurely pace than Van Dyke did. Sometimes he'd let us go along with our own ideas before stopping a scene. Our ideas might not have been any good, but once in a while something useful came out of it. Being a Mack Sennett graduate, Frank liked to improvise business on the set. Not that I was particularly conscious of his technique—it's very bad for an actress to be conscious of such things; it restricts her performance. I simply found him resourceful and trusted him.

I spent a lot of time listening to Frank's life story—how he got started and finally became a director, a fascinating Horatio Alger tale. He never mentioned a word about my rejecting *It Happened One Night*, not a word, which surprised me a bit. Of course, it hadn't swept the 1934 Academy Awards yet, and, anyway, he'd got Claudette Colbert and Clark Gable, which worked out very well. They were marvelous in the picture, as it turned out. Besides, Claudette had the legs for it.

Later, a couple of times on the air, Frank had great fun with me, saying, "She turned me down." So I felt he might be a bit resentful. It pleased me recently when he admitted that they completely rewrote the script after I'd seen it. I've always been a little conscious of turning it down, but not terribly, because I might have missed doing *The Thin*

Man that year if I hadn't. Ironically, that same year, the Academy was bombarded with protests because Bette Davis (for *Of Human Bondage*) and I (for *The Thin Man*) weren't nominated. They actually suspended voting rules for the first and only time because of the uproar, allowing members to ignore the printed ballots and write in any name. Of course, most of the votes had already been mailed in by then, so the winners, including Claudette, were all official nominees. Bette has deservedly won a couple of times since, but I've never even been nominated. They seldom give it to comediennes.

Were Arthur and I married then? No, we still hadn't married, we'd just been together a long time. He kept saying that he couldn't get a divorce—even after I became pregnant. Years later, his first wife told me that wasn't true, that he hadn't been trying. I don't know. Perhaps he wanted to avoid the enormous divorce settlement that he eventually had to make. Perhaps he feared marrying again. I knew he loved me and that I loved him, so I submitted to an abortion and avoided becoming pregnant again. I've had my regrets, but it was a godsend in a way. It's hard enough trying to be a wife in this business without being a mother, too. It isn't fair to the children. Some people, like Joan Bennett, handled it very well, I know, but that's my feeling about it. Any regrets, any implicit feelings of sacrifice have been allayed by surrogate children: my stepson, Terry, and his family, my godchildren, the children of friends and family to whom I've always been able to relate.

Arthur was a gifted man. His eye for detail and sense of perfection, which later became obsessive, contributed to his success as a producer. After leaving Goldwyn, in 1933, he continued to make fine films at Paramount, later M-G-M, and finally as an independent producer: *Easy Living*, *Hold Back the Dawn*, *The Major and the Minor*, *Gaslight*, *The Asphalt Jungle*, *Oklahoma!*, *Witness for the Prosecution*. He exposed me to a different aspect of the picture business, because I hadn't realized the full extent of a producer's contribution. I attended previews with him, watching him gauge audience reaction, something I seldom did with my own pictures. Actors weren't encouraged to attend previews at Metro.

We went out to Huntington Park for the preview of *Mississippi*, with Eddie Sutherland, who directed it, and W. C. Fields, who appeared in it. Fields seemed just like he did in the movies; I mean, he was this roistering character—funny, very funny, always funny. I don't recall that he paid any attention to me at dinner afterward. He tolerated me, I guess. He didn't like women, you know—his mother or some other woman must have ill-treated him as a child. It was something very strange. One of his lines in *Mississippi* included: "I'd sooner stick a knife in my mother's back." Instead, he said, "I'd sooner stick a *fork* in mother's back." That's the way he wanted it, and Eddie couldn't get him to change it. There's something so gruesome about the difference between a knife and a fork in that context.

Exposure to Arthur's world contributed to my social development as well at that crucial time. When he brought Charles Laughton out for *Ruggles of Red Gap*, we all went to dinner one evening. Charles and his wife, Elsa Lanchester, were worldly and witty, with that verbal dexterity peculiar to the British. A bit awed by them, I probably said little during dinner. The next day, at the Garden of Allah, where I lived for a while, who should come out to the pool looking like the Emperor Nero with a big towel around him but Mr. Laughton himself. "Well, hullo," he called like a long-lost friend, settling his considerable girth beside me. "Myrna"—he used my first name, which pleased me—"you know what you remind me of? Venus de Milo at the intersection of Hollywood and Vine."

Well, I loved that, because I was bewildered in those early days of stardom, getting started in a new area without much confidence in myself. That apt analogy, although I was hardly a Venus de Milo, showed Charles's powers of perception. He discerned an aspect of me usually hidden by my savoir-faire. I wasn't shy at home or with close friends; but a lot of accomplished people were coming into my life, and that could be intimidating. It wasn't a crippling kind of thing; I could deal with a Barrymore or a Shaw if provoked. But most of us in the business tend to be diffident. For instance, Hank Fonda, when we were working up on Cape Cod, said, "You know, I'm very shy." And he was a very shy man. It can be misread sometimes. People think you're a terrible snob. I wasn't at all, but besides being shy, I happened to have been well brought up, which could brand you as a snob in Hollywood.

Paramount borrowed me for *Wings in the Dark*, my only Arthur Hornblow production. Unfortunately, it wasn't one of our best. Women transatlantic fliers were a phenomenon of the period, so it could have been an important story. Instead, the studio settled for melodrama. I played an aviatrix who starts out over the Atlantic in a terrible storm.

Cary Grant, my lover, who's gone blind, flies up and rescues me somewhere in the clouds. I don't remember a lot about Cary until our later pictures together, except that he was very attractive and preoccupied with his first wife, Virginia Cherrill.

Arthur hired Amelia Earhart as technical adviser but gave her little to do. We made a publicity junket out to the airport one day with her husband, G. P. Putnam, the publisher, and Paul Mantz, the famous stunt flier. We went up and flew around. Amelia didn't fly the plane, Paul did, but she was just lovely, absolutely charming the whole time. A few years later, she wanted Mantz to accompany her on a flight around the world, but she didn't get him. She went anyway, and never returned.

Paul Mantz took me up for my first flight in an open cockpit. When he started doing wingovers, half the time the earth would be up here, half the time down there. My God! I thought I would die. Yet it was kind of wonderful because I didn't fall out and kept wondering why. It didn't deter me from wanting to learn to fly, but unfortunately there just wasn't time—or I didn't make time. You can't learn to fly in one day. It would have meant saying to Mayer, "I won't do that film!" I mean, we worked on Saturdays in those days. They used to work us on Sundays, too, before the unions ruled that those would be "golden hours." So I never learned to fly, but I played lots of women who did.

Although we worked together only that one time, Arthur was generally helpful to my career, very sympathetic and interested in me as an actress. He was not, as some people thought, a Pygmalion, but he was astute and observed details that escaped me. In one film, for instance, Adrian trimmed my dress with those big buttons that he often used. Arthur said, "Myrna, those buttons completely erased your face." That's more important than it sounds, because he understood that my strong point as an actress is underplaying, and too many clever designer details distract from it. When someone says "What a beautiful gown!" instead of "How nice you look!" there's something wrong with your gown.

Arthur also got a lot of big guns like his lawyer Bill Sacks and the agent Myron Selznick to go to work for me. I agreed to have Myron represent me, but only after Minna Wallis endorsed the idea. Myron and his partner, Leland Hayward, had backed Minna in her own agency. "They're much more important people; they're tops," she told me. "You need that kind of representation now." That was Minna—always considering *my* welfare. Of course she and Arthur were absolutely right about Myron Selznick. He was a crack agent and a fighter because, as his brother David told me, "He has a score to settle." Their father, a film pioneer, had been done in by a lot of men still in power, and Myron never let them forget it.

He took me over at a time when *The Thin Man* and my other pictures were booming at the box office, yet, I don't know why, I felt that M-G-M didn't want to do very much for me. The seven-year contract I'd signed in 1931 held me there for over three more years, although the studio could get out of it at almost any time. Those contracts burned out a lot of people, which is understandable when you consider I'd made twenty-three pictures in just over three years since signing. They always assured you that your contract would be adjusted if you achieved stardom. Well, I had and it hadn't been. When I asked for more money or better working conditions, such as the right to have an occasional holiday, they passed me from one executive to another.

By that time, my contract gave me around fifteen hundred dollars a week, half of what they paid Bill Powell, and a fraction of what other stars received—and I had to make more pictures than any of them. I wanted what Bill was getting, that's all. I was his co-star—they already considered us a team—with equal responsibilities. Fifteen hundred dollars seems like a lot of money, but it wasn't compared to what my pictures brought in. I didn't want the moon or anything; I just wanted my fair share of the gravy.

When Myron requested these promised adjustments, they refused and cast me in *Escapade* with Bill. That part was all wrong for me, and I fought it: "Don't put me in this thing. I'm not that wistful little girl selling flowers on the streets of Vienna." Bill played an artist who finds this waif—a terrible script, it seemed to me, which I don't think he took too seriously either. Then Louis B. Mayer got into the act: "Myrna, you're like one of my family. If you were my mother, my wife, or my mistress, I couldn't be more sincere. . . ." What a wonderful juxtaposition: "my mother, my wife, or my mistress." I knew damn well he just wanted to coax me into *Escapade*, but it was the first time he gave me that song and dance, and it beguiled me. I said, "All right, I'll do it."

A week or so into shooting, my darling hairdresser, Eleanor, whom I had for years, arrived in a panic: "You know what they made me do last night? I had to make a test with that new Austrian girl, Luise Rainer, and she played *your* part." I said, "Oh, did you . . . did you really?" laughing to comfort her, but thinking, Well, that's *great* for me!

I had returned to the set and resumed working, doing what I was supposed to do, when Bernie Hyman, one of Mayer's henchmen, appeared. He motioned for me to come over: "You want to take a walk?" So we took a walk and he told me they were pulling me out of *Escapade*, while Bob Leonard, the director, just stood there with the guts of a snail. Bernie took me up to Eddie Mannix, the studio manager, a professional Irishman who kept a bunch of shillelaghs outside his office. Whenever I had a beef, I used to grab one. So I picked up a shillelagh and stormed in. "Oh, God!" Eddie groaned. "Here she comes."

"Now listen, kid," he hedged, "we made a mistake."

"You certainly have—you don't know what a mistake you've made." I liked Eddie; we were friends, but this infuriated me. "I told you not to put me in the damn thing in the first place, and after I go through all the preliminaries you put some new girl into it."

"Well, we were wrong, but we'll just say you're sick and going to Palm Springs for a rest."

"No, you're not going to say anything of the kind. I'm not sick and I'm not going to Palm Springs!" And I walked out.

We conspired that evening at dinner, Arthur, Myron, and I. "You go to the studio in the morning," Myron said, "and do everything you usually do, makeup, costume, as if you're going to play the part. You may even have to walk onto the set. I don't know, but I think they'll stop you before that. The point is, don't leave that studio without a written release from the picture."

I reported the next morning and went through the motions. She was there, Rainer, all ready to start work, and here *I* was. This situation was none of her doing, of course, but she looked as if it were—furtive and frightened. Our strategy was working. I called Benny Thau's office: "Well, I'm here."

"You're what?"

"I'm in the studio ready to work." Benny had always been my champion at the studio, but this really put him on the spot. "I'm not going to leave without a release from *Escapade*, and I don't want any nonsense. I'm not sick and nobody's going to say that I'm sick."

11/87

Boy! They sent that piece of paper in nothing flat. I phoned Myron triumphantly: "I *got* it!" He was so shrewd, this man. He knew what they were up to and he knew how to handle them. They were going to make a test case of me, you see, for trying to get more money. Perhaps they needed another Powell-Loy picture right away and really thought *Escapade* was a good idea, but I think they wanted to humiliate me. Well, they weren't getting away with it. I wasn't steppin' down. I had a chip on my shoulder, believe me, and all you had to do was *look* as if you were going to knock it off!

5

THE REBEL

1935-1936

*That was a rather historic time when she took off on
a strike for more money. No one was ever expecting
that Myrna would be the one to lead off a rebellion.*
—SAMUEL MARX, 1982

verybody kept asking: "What are you going to do?" And I really
didn't know. I fiddled around for a while, just resting for the first
time in years. Then Arthur left for London on Paramount business
and I decided to follow him. I didn't even tell the studio. When I called
Myron, his partner, Leland Hayward, took the phone: "I don't want
you to fly today, Myrna; it's bad flying weather. Wait and go with me
in a day or two. You're seeing New York for the first time and you
should have a proper introduction." Leland knew a lot about flying, so
I waited. That plane, the one I originally planned to take, crashed.
There were no survivors.

The weather had improved when we boarded the New York Clip-
per, but the wings iced over Cleveland and forced us down. Since we
had adjoining suites during our stopover, I could hear Leland on the
phone most of the night. "What are you up to in there?" I asked on the
plane the next day. "Oh, just talking on the phone," he answered rather
sheepishly. Well, he gets to New York and marries Margaret Sullavan.
And what he'd been doing on the telephone was trying to straighten
things out with Katharine Hepburn, who'd been his girl for a while
there.

We landed in New Jersey, as you had to then, and Leland gave me
the tour. He was a great charmer, something of a raconteur like Arthur,

so he enhanced my first awed entry into Manhattan. We drove through the Holland Tunnel, headed east, and came out on Park Avenue. And Park Avenue was really something in those days. It still is, but in the spring of 1935, to a wide-eyed newcomer, it just looked fantastic. In fact, the whole city struck me that way—vast and vivid, alive. I fell in love with New York then and there, and the romance has lasted more than fifty years.

Leland dropped me at the old Savoy Plaza at Fifty-eighth and Fifth. When I walked into my room, it looked like a funeral parlor—you've never seen so many flowers. Things had been accumulating for days because I'd changed my arrival date. I had no secretary with me or anybody from the studio to help, as I always would later on, so all this stuff just piled up in my rooms. That got me into a lot of trouble, for among the flowers and candy, I discovered later, were notes, telephone messages, invitations, and requests for interviews. I was invited everywhere, some of the time not knowing where or with whom. It just goes to show you: the little movie star in New York for the first time!

My first night there, I went to a party at Kitty and Gilbert Miller's house. I knew them, at least; they were friends of Arthur's. George Preston Marshall, who made an avocation of squiring famous women around town, latched on to me. They called him the "Laundry Man" because, among other things, he owned laundries everywhere. We were having a lot of laughs, so I went to the Versailles with him afterward to hear Harry Richmond. This was the latest café-society hangout, with high ceilings and huge murals of the palace in question all around. Harry Richmond sang wonderfully, the Laundry Man showed off this new girl in town, and *she* was having a ball.

The next morning a note arrived from Ed Sullivan: "How dare you ignore me at the Versailles last night after I've left messages and sent flowers to welcome you?" Of course, I hadn't found them in that mess, and anyway how was I to know what he looked like? He was a columnist for the New York *Post* then, a friend of Minna's, so I called—or Leland or somebody called—and straightened things out. I gave him an interview and he forgave me. That evening I collapsed in my bed, trying to rest after a hectic day, when they called up from the desk: "Mr. Fiske is waiting for Miss Loy in the lobby." It seems that Dwight Fiske was escorting me to Buff Cobb's or someplace and I didn't even know about it. "I just got caught up in so many things," I told him. "Please, come up and have a drink while I get ready." He turned out to be a delightful man, a social butterfly, who played and sang risqué songs in supper clubs. Oh, it was fun, of course, but also a nightmare until I got my life straightened out. I finally called the hotel office: "For God's sake, send me some secretaries!" It took them days to clear away the debris.

I booked passage on the *Paris* as Mlle. Myrna Adele Williams because M-G-M was tracking me. The night before sailing, I met Elsa Maxwell at another party. She started laying out all these plans for me, sort of passing me on to her fashionable friends in London and Paris. It struck me as an interesting phenomenon, and still does, the way "society" courts young successful actresses; they *use* them, really. It's a kind of game they play, getting the celebrity of the moment for their parties. I watched this happen to me and still see it happening all the time. They don't really *want* you, but they take you up to decorate their ménage or whatever, then drop you with a crash and go on and take the next one. I can't say that Elsa ever used me particularly, because I liked her. Although something of a purveyor to the rich, she had a raucous yet vulnerable nature that rather touched me. After all, she was being used, too. And, I must say, I had a wonderful time with all those people. You just had to keep your balance.

Myrna Loy's first visit to New York was a study in expert stand-offishness, wrote columnist O. O. McIntyre after Myrna sailed for Europe. As one of the most widely advertised what-it-takes ladies, many of the town's Don Juans were prepared to run through their rigmaroles. But after each shook her hand, each realized that was that. What she expresses on the screen, that warm and languorous come-hither, completely jelled in real life close-ups. She was the most expert curler-upper the Romeos ever encountered. In fact, it was reported that several of them met her and went smack into a congestive chill. To add to the frigidity, the siren wore smoked glasses at her appearances in public. Nothing repels flirts like smoked glasses.

The *Paris* sighted England after seven days. A radiotelegram reached me as we passed Land's End: WELCOME WELCOME DARLING. DON'T MIND THE WEATHER WE CAN PRETEND ITS CHRISTMAS. I CAN HARDLY WAIT BUNTY. A. That was Arthur—his knack for doing the right thing with style and attention to detail. He was an entertaining man with a gift for making life interesting, and his voice had a quiet quality that lent great import to everything he said. (That same quality when he got angry could be terrifying in its control.) As his son Terry says, "He was a great tour guide." Terry gives him that. And he certainly was, from the moment he met the boat. It was cold early spring when we drove from Plymouth to Exeter. Trees and hedges blossomed and buttercups spread yellow all along the way. We stayed overnight in Exeter, visited its magnificent cathedral, tasted its Devonshire cream on strawberries, and this poor girl who had worked all her life was in heaven.

We drove on to Nutbourne, a village in west Sussex, to visit Guy Bolton, the playwright, and his wife. Thyme grew up the walls of their picture-postcard cottage. The roof was thatched, with beams so low I kept cracking my head—people had been smaller in Elizabethan England. Our first morning there, after a hearty English breakfast, I walked into the sitting room and who's standing there in front of the fireplace with all his paunch but Alfred Hitchcock? He lived nearby and wanted to meet me. Well, the feeling was mutual. He hadn't come to America yet, but I'd seen some of his terrific English films. It was exciting to meet him and he seemed charming, droll, but I really didn't get to know him until he moved to Hollywood. He used to come up to our house in Coldwater Canyon and discuss his films in progress. He described how everything was done very technically, how an actress had to perform her role exactly as he conceived it. I thought, Oh, dear, I can't work with this guy; I don't think I can be held like that. If he'd given me the opportunity, I certainly would have tried, but I doubt very much that we'd have got along. He thought of actors as automatons, things he could move around on a chessboard.

It seemed so peaceful along the budding lanes of Nutbourne. I could have lived there just dreaming the days away. I wanted to keep out of the spotlight, but the press tracked me down. London papers sent reporters to the cottage, so I granted interviews, saying nothing about my trouble with the studio. It poured on Sunday, but all day people on bicycles came to the cottage asking for autographs. Two boys, soaked to the skin, rode sixty miles from London. After getting my autograph, they headed straight back, swearing the trip had been worth it.

In London we stayed in Edwardian splendor at the Savoy, where our windows faced the staunch Embankment and the sweeping Thames beyond. Every English novel or history I'd read, every English part I'd played, came to life. We did some touristing, of course, the Tower of London, Parliament, Westminster Abbey and its Poets' Corner, where you feel the proximity of the great writers buried there. We went out to Golders Green to see Arthur's father, who had founded and for years edited *Theatre* magazine in New York before retiring to his homeland. He'd remarried, an Irish girl, and their son Herbert became a World War II flying ace. Arthur's mother had died during his youth. Apparently she had been a terrific woman, a Polish Jew, whose warmth balanced his father's Anglo-Saxon reserve. Her family founded the Lambert School of Music in New York City. Arthur held tremendous respect and affection for her, although he preferred to emphasize his British ancestry. "You remind me of my mother," he used to tell me at Christmastime, "because you have presents for everyone." I was always very lavish when I could afford it, and I could in those days.

They gave a reception for me at the cavernous old Empire Theatre, on Leicester Square, where I autographed literally reams of paper, using my left hand when my right gave out. The resultant publicity allowed M-G-M to audit my activities. They took me off salary to punish me, then—to save face, I suppose—announced that my appearance at the Empire had been under their auspices. They feared setting a precedent, you see, because no one had done this to them before. You always hear about Bette Davis and Olivia de Havilland bucking Warner Brothers, but that happened later. It's just that I haven't kept reminding people the way Bette and Olivia have. I wasn't on a holy crusade; I just wanted what was coming to me. Bulletins from Myron Selznick kept me apprised of negotiations: MAYER IN NEW YORK. HAVE HAD SEVERAL TALKS WITH MANNIX WHO STATES THEY WILL NOT REINSTATE YOU ON PAYROLL UNTIL YOU RETURN. MY FEELING WHEN YOU RETURN NEW YORK SCHENCK WILL PROBABLY CONTACT YOU WHICH SHOULD HELP MATTERS. SHOULD ANYTHING DEVELOP WILL ADVISE YOU. LOVE MYRON. I was having too much fun to care.

After crossing the Channel on the Rouen boat, we took the train to Paris. Our superb luncheon as we clattered through the French countryside included a wine that Arthur had been searching for. Cuisine became crucial on our travels, particularly in France, because he was a great gourmet and a connoisseur of French wines. After graduating from Dartmouth and passing the New York bar, he'd served in France during

World War I. He had been one of the honor guard on the steps of the Palais de Versailles during the Paris Peace Conference in 1919. (I remember a hysterical day in Hollywood when he tried to get into his soldier uniform.) He'd made friends like Edouard Bourdet, and later translated his play *La Prisonnière* for Broadway. The sensation caused by its lesbian theme paved Arthur's way to Hollywood. He spoke fluent French, knew France, and presented it with all the trimmings. Before entering Paris, we dined at an old hotel overlooking it—a brilliant stroke on his part. I sat down and saw the City of Light shimmering in the distance. What an entrance!

The terrace of our apartment at the Hôtel Crillon faced the Place de la Concorde and the Seine. I remember the *clop, clop, clop* of horses on cobblestone as farmers brought their produce to market at Les Halles. We'd walk out on the terrace to watch those wagons circling the obelisk, their carefully arranged loads of vegetables, fruit, and flowers forming geometric patterns in the light of dawn. When we returned a few years later, there were no more horses. Produce came in on great flat trucks. Now, of course, Les Halles doesn't even exist anymore. But I still hear those horses on the cobblestones coming in.

I fell in love with that city and returned there again and again. Arthur performed his tour-guide number beautifully. We did everything you're supposed to do in Paris, including dinner at Tour d'Argent, where the maître d' ceremoniously served us the 127,317th duck since 1890. I have the voucher to prove it. We were invited out to Lady Mendl's exquisite eighteenth-century château at Versailles—Elsa Maxwell, as good as her word, had arranged it. The others there escape me now—definitely the crème of the international set, lots of titles—but we had a marvelous time. I admired Lady Mendl, who as Elsie De Wolfe had been John Drew's leading lady in the 1890s, before becoming a trend-setting decorator. She'd married Sir Charles Mendl, a British diplomat, late in life—mainly for the title, I think; but, unlike most of that set, she worked. They eventually settled in Hollywood, where Elsie fleeced the film colony, and Sir Charles primarily dined with actresses, including me. "I just like to have a beautiful face opposite me," he explained.

Arthur wanted to see Budapest, which sounded wonderful to me. As we boarded the Orient Express in Paris, I found myself wondering, Where's George Brent? because we'd supposedly met on that train in

Stamboul Quest. Having been in so many different places in films gave me a frequent sensation of déjà vu. Though it was very late when we reached Budapest, we went out for a walk in a little park near our hotel. An old woman passed us, then turned and came back. "I know who you are," she declared. "You are Myrna Loy!" She spoke Hungarian, but the "Myrna Loy" sounded loud and clear. Here I was halfway around the world in the middle of the night and this old woman recognized me. I just couldn't get over it. That came to mind recently when I read the preamble to the United Nations Charter at the annual U.N. Ambassadors' Dinner. "You know, Miss Loy," the Tunisian Ambassador told me, "we play your films all the time in my country." And then he said, "May I ask you something? Would you mind?"—and he leaned over and kissed my cheek. It still amazes me how far the movies reach.

You can't imagine the aura of romance surrounding Budapest in the years between the old war and the war that made the Continent a battlefield again. It had as much of an attraction for travelers as London or Paris. In fact, just before we arrived, Leland Hayward and Maggie Sullavan spent their honeymoon there. We stayed at the Hotel Dunapalota, the old Ritz, which may still exist, but no doubt under very different circumstances. I remember walking into the sitting room of our apartment for the first time, and hearing gypsy music floating up from downstairs. "It's true," I said. "It's really true." That's the way you expected it to sound, and that's the way it sounded. We walked along the old Fishermen's Bastion and a young man followed playing the violin. We'd stroll beside the Danube, as people did of a summer's evening, and little orchestras played at intervals all along the embankment. When we dined at the Hungaria Café, the Ritz, or the Little Royale, violinists would serenade us at our table. Our only schedule was to have no schedule, to hear gypsy music and relax.

As we walked along the strand one morning, we looked up, and there were Robert E. Sherwood and Madeleine Hurlock waving at us from a balcony. They had both been divorced from their previous spouses—she from another playwright, Marc Connelly—and were trying to get married. They'd been to Poland and all kinds of places, but nobody would marry them. Madeleine, a former silent-screen comedienne, amusingly described their exchanges with Middle European officialdom: "These suspicious old men kept saying, 'You have to be examined to see if you are . . . if you are . . . why are you getting married? Are you pregnant?' " I don't know where they finally got married, but we hung out together in Budapest.

A brilliant playwright, of course, Bob had written, among other things, *The Road to Rome*, an anti-war comedy that I longed to do at M-G-M. He was unassuming, thin, and very, very tall. When we went to the zoo near Angol Park one day, he stopped in front of the giraffe's cage and looked up in wonder at this lofty creature. All of a sudden, that giraffe turned around and looked right back at him. It was so sweet and funny, because they recognized each other. Madeleine said, "I can't believe it," but sure enough, the old giraffe was sizing up Bob, as if to say: "What kind of creature is this? He's almost getting up to me."

Idiot's Delight, his Pulitzer Prize play, was born in Budapest. We all went to a nightclub with a dance pavilion in the middle, where itinerant players would perform. Not quite good enough for the theaters, they traveled all over Europe entertaining in these cabarets to make their living. Bob watched them and got the idea of using the Lunts—you need great actors to play bad actors convincingly—in a similar situation. When he tied in the profiteering and the military activity observed on that supposedly marriage-oriented trip, his play foretold a second world war. While Madeleine, Arthur, and I were laughing and dancing, just having fun, Bob was looking for something, and he found it.

Arthur and I went on to Vienna and Salzburg, spending too little time in those magnificent cities. We visited the Spanish Riding School in Vienna to watch the Lippizaners go through their exercises. The extraordinary grace of those stallions justified, even for a balletomane like me, using terms like "pas de deux" and "ballotade" for their movements. Salzburg's Mozart Festival wouldn't begin for another month, but we managed to hear a rather shrill operetta before leaving for Innsbruck.

The impact of the Tyrol hits when you look up the Maria Theresienstrasse, Innsbruck's main thoroughfare, past storefronts and Gothic spires to sheer Alps beyond. We hired a local chauffeur, who looked just like Hitler—the mustache, everything—and spoke painstaking correspondence-course English. He drove us over the mountains through Switzerland back into the Burgundy country of France and on to Beaune, because Arthur wanted to see the famous wine cellar at the Hôtel de la Poste. We arrived during siesta time, awakening the old *patron*, who was furious. Arthur, with his marvelous French, finally convinced the old boy to show us around. Grumpy, still half asleep, he reluctantly got the keys and took us down into that vast cask- and bottle-lined cave.

That visit taught me something about wine, but more about people, particularly the French. By the time we finished that tour, the disgruntled old man had been completely seduced by our interest. The French are very proud of their culture, their art, food, wines, their language, and tourists who don't appreciate that, who think the world's made for them, incur resentment. That old *patron* brought me roses and strawberries from his garden, while rhapsodizing about preparing a fabulous dinner for us. Years later, I would use that basic example of international relations when attempting to explain the functions of the United Nations to civic groups.

I sailed on the S.S. *Champlain* back to the fray. Bill Sacks, of Chadbourne, Stanfield & Levy, who was an old friend of Arthur's, represented me, and the battle with Metro began in earnest. It seemed low-key at first: the studio submitted scripts; Myron refused them; suspension notices followed, taking me off salary while someone else, usually Roz Russell, played the part. I never officially "received" their communiqués, however, having taken the position that they had abrogated my contract by replacing me on *Escapade*.

When Myrna was off the lot getting more money, Rosalind Russell recalled, *I was put into a movie called* Rendezvous *with Bill. I felt self-conscious. Powell and Loy had been a hit in* The Thin Man, *they were an unbeatable team, so my first day on* Rendezvous, *I tried to apologize. "I know you don't want me, you'd rather have Myrna—"*

Powell denied it. "I love Myrna, but I think this is good for you, and I'm glad we're doing it together."

I was never a top star at Metro. I was in the second echelon. That was the way they ran the lot. I once said I never got a part at Metro unless Myrna Loy turned it down, and while that was meant to be funny, there was a grain of truth in it. They had me as a threat behind Myrna, the same way they had Luise Rainer behind Garbo. Every time Myrna asked for a change in her contract, or a raise, the brass could say, "Never mind, Roz Russell will do the picture," and this system worked very successfully.

Well, I don't know how deliberate that system was. They used Roz to replace me because she was there, a comedienne, and damn good. If they tried to pit her against me, it never worked—we became good friends. Building Rainer and Russell at my expense was merely part of the studio ploy to discredit me, to prove my expendability, while I bucked the system. I held out in the Waldorf Towers, cashing checks from Arthur and Myron, Leland Hayward and Bill Sacks, who had apparently put my money into some kind of fund for tax purposes. I'm not sure. All that financial stuff I would put right out of my head. Anyway, they sent me checks, and whenever I took them to the Waldorf cashier, he'd give me a baffling look somewhere between amazement and disapproval. Suddenly it hit me: Ye gods! This guy must be thinking, She certainly is well kept, this woman, with all those distinguished names on her checks!

In the beginning, I must say, playing hooky was fun. All the things I'd always wanted to do in New York—theater, concerts, museums—all the friends or friends of friends being so welcoming, left little time for reflection. Somebody introduced me to Walter Winchell at one party. He regaled me with tales of his nocturnal prowls into the bowels of Manhattan, searching out murder and mayhem: "Have you got the nerve to do that?"

"Of course I have—sure, let's do it." I had second thoughts as we drove after midnight down sinister streets in his convertible with the top down. I didn't get shot, nothing gruesome happened, but I saw the city as few people do: Winchell's beat, not the nightclubs and high life, but the streets and the underworld that attracted him as a working reporter. After that he was marvelous, taking swipes in his column at M-G-M for ill-treating me. He'd really lay them out once in a while, which turned out to be an enormous help.

Much of our battle was being waged in the columns, with most of them taking the studio's side. That didn't surprise me, considering that the studio created monsters like Louella and Hedda and the rest. The columnists started out promoting us, doing us some good, but eventually they got power and began making deals. If somebody went out and howled on Saturday night, those vultures would be on the phone to the studio: "We hear that so-and-so"—say, Errol Flynn; you could always count on him—"we hear that Errol did such and such, but we won't print it if you give us the story about Bette Davis." They traded, and the studios gave them power by submitting to it.

Louella Parsons, the most powerful of them, had the umbrella of Hearst over her. During her years as the Hearst chain's syndicated Hollywood oracle, she became an institution, rather formidable in her way, and tough. If anything happened in your personal life you were supposed to "call Lolly"—a lot of people actually did! They all vied to give her and her husband the most elaborate Christmas gifts to curry favor. She doted on that husband of hers, a physician, whom we called "Dockie Wockie," because at the end of parties she'd go looking for him, saying, "Oh, dear, Doctor has to operate tomorrow." You'd try to find Dockie Wockie, and he'd be under a table or piano, out cold. Arthur felt obliged as a producer to stay on Lolly's good side. He was always trying to include her on our guest list, but as I've said, I wouldn't have her in my house.

"I've done something you're not going to like," Arthur announced one day. "I've sent Lolly and Dockie Wockie two olive trees for their farm from both of us."

"Oh, you mean as a peace offering?"

"Well, yes, I suppose in your case, but they won't recognize that." Later on, Louella told someone about those olive trees, meaning to be appreciative. "Arthur's tree is flourishing," she reported, "but, you know, Myrna's succumbed." Well, I found that hilarious: the only thing she ever got from me, and it died.

The Hollywood columnists generally printed what M-G-M wanted them to print, painting me as greedy and rebellious, making much of the fact that my departure had facilitated the rise of Luise Rainer and Rosalind Russell. It started getting torturous, wearing me down, because I wasn't giving in and it looked as if Metro wasn't either. Sam Marx called at this point, wanting to see me. I had always liked Sam—he was the man who found all those wonderful literary properties for us. But in my condition I took him for a spy. Fearing that he'd run back to the studio with it, I guarded everything I said and did.

I was making one of my periodic trips to New York, and I knew where she was, recounts Sam Marx. I was always looking for material for our stars and I had to anticipate that Myrna would come back. She became such a superior and desirable actress that they were putting her in a great many movies, which may be one of the reasons she finally turned and fled. Nobody makes that many movies anymore. It had shocked the studio the way she took off and wasn't even on hand to negotiate, but I don't believe anyone expected it to be very serious at first; otherwise, Mayer wouldn't have said, "All right, call her up and tell her you're looking for stories for her and see what she might have in mind." They felt it was just one of our little children who was kicking up her heels for the moment. . . . "Don't worry about it. When supper is ready, she'll come down for it." M-G-M was kind of a big family. Mayer fostered that feeling. Where other studios— Warner Brothers, for instance—were much more stringent with their people, M-G-M had a very paternal atmosphere, even in the case of recalcitrant players.

I was concerned both for her and the studio, because I knew Myrna and admired her. My job as head of the writers' department included hiring and handling an amazing group of writers, and I remember how much they held Myrna in esteem. I'm not a great admirer of actors' intelligence—half the time I feel they're a breed apart, and not far enough apart. I've never been wild about association with actors, but Myrna was far superior. She always struck me as being on a higher level of understanding and intelligence. She read and she appreciated good writing. She once said in an interview: "How can you fail when you've got such a great collection of writers?" We didn't hear that very often. Sherwood's Road to Rome, *an intellectual handling of a sexy situation in antiquity, typifies the kind of script that appealed to her. That's the reason it was always a delight to find material for her. That was the kind of thing we discussed that day in New York. I had a very pleasant afternoon, although there was a slight tension between us that I didn't quite understand, because my motives were pure, truly. I didn't look for intrigue under it.*

Sweating it out up there in the Waldorf Towers with my checks, I thought about taking acting lessons, studying with somebody, planning to do theater if I learned how. It didn't happen, though, not for more than twenty-five years. Of course, M-G-M was so powerful nobody would have touched me with a ten-foot pole. Nobody, that is, but those fearless devils Charlie MacArthur and Ben Hecht. While this conflict went on and on, I visited Charlie and his wife, Helen Hayes, out in Nyack. When Ben Hecht and his wife joined us, we spent a restful afternoon sipping cocktails and hatching a plot.

Ben and Charlie were producing their own pictures then, and about to start *Soak the Rich*. They decided to get out a big press release announcing that I'd been signed for the lead. It was a ploy, of course, just a gag, but it might have meant trouble for them. They didn't care, those devils, they were intent on making mischief. Besides, Ben wanted to get even with Mayer for some grievance or other. He said, "We're really soaking the rich with this little hoax." They were. M-G-M went wild when the papers printed the news, retaliating with some serious threats. Whereupon, Bill Sacks and I composed a little press release of our own, on the back of Waldorf-Astoria stationery, stating my position and charging them with breach of contract. All the papers picked it up.

While the studio digested that, Bill Sacks implemented his crowning strategy. "I'm going to pit Schenck against Mayer," he told me, a brilliant tactic, since those two were natural adversaries. Nick Schenck, as president of Loew's, Inc., M-G-M's parent company, held the purse strings and oversaw Mayer's authority as vice-president in charge of production at the studio. The two men resented each other, which Bill knew, and used to my advantage.

Schenck didn't like me and the feeling was mutual. He was a tough, shrewd man, who had been operating an amusement park when Marcus Loew found him. He'd risen to the top—deservedly, I suppose—but he was no gentleman; he expected all actresses to be whores, and treated them accordingly. I wouldn't stand for that attitude, so we always had an edge of antagonism between us. Schenck was first a hard-nosed businessman, however, and exhibitors were clamoring for Powell-Loy pictures. After Bill Sacks planted the seed, Schenck started blaming Mayer for my departure, pressuring him into settling with me.

While I continued my New York vigil, Mayer called Arthur in Hollywood: "Would you be good enough to come down and have some breakfast with me?" He summoned Arthur, I imagine, because he hated giving in to his old adversary Myron Selznick. "I'll tell you," Mayer said, "we've decided to bring this thing to an end. Myrna's been off the screen for almost a year, and we can't fool around anymore. We'll give her what she wants and a twenty-five-thousand-dollar bonus." Incredible! That was an awful lot of money in 1935.

When I returned, there was no animosity toward me. None at all. In fact, Arthur and I became Mayer's honored guests at the functions of the charities so dear to his heart. He liked decorating his table with his stars. Mayer was wily, but he wasn't crude, like Schenck. I liked Mayer. I didn't trust him, but I liked him. I was apparently one of the few who did. You knew he was lying through his teeth with that recurring spiel about "my mother, my wife, or my mistress," but I have to say he usually knew what was good for me. I went to him once after reading a book about a kind of slavey, a low-down girl who suffers all sorts of tragedies. The title, or why in the world I wanted to play it, escapes me now, but the studio owned it and I asked him for it. "Never! Never!" he boomed. "You'll never scrub floors. You're a lady in my book, Myrna, and you always gotta be a lady." And, of course, he was right so far as my "perfect wife" image went. No telling where my career would have gone had they not hung that title on me. Labels limit your possibilities, but that's how they think in Hollywood. If you're successful at something, God help you!

David Selznick, Mayer's son-in-law for a while, once told me, "Myrna, you don't really understand L.B." I said, "Yes, I do. I like him, but I won't be manipulated by him." Perhaps David meant that L.B. expected more *Gemütlichkeit*, which he got neither from me nor from many of his other stars, because they used to joke about him and his transparent ploys. It's true that I fought him and nearly drove him crazy at times, but in spite of our battles, I always held my own and earned his respect. I never had to play kneesies with him.

One of our clashes involved a script that Joe Mankiewicz, an M-G-M producer then, wanted me to do. While I admired Joe, a witty, intelligent man, I hated this script and refused it. I used to do that occasionally, and have to deal with Mayer's pleadings, but this time he included the entire Loew's, Inc., board of directors, who were meeting in the boardroom next to his office. He summoned me, put me at the end of this long table, and they tried to coax me into changing my mind. There they sat commanding both sides of that endless table, Nick Schenck and all the company bigwigs, and I kept shaking my head.

All of a sudden Mayer got up and rushed out, followed by a little man named Sam Katz. I don't know what Sam was, sort of innocuous, a flunky, but he came running back into the boardroom: "He's fainted! God help us, L.B. has fainted!" That broke up the meeting, so Joe and I went into Mayer's office. He was sprawled on a couch, hands folded over his chest, eyes closed, his face drained of color. I'd heard about the phony fainting spells he pulled to get his way, but I thought, My God, he really *is* having a fit. Henchmen were hovering over him, one fanning him with a handkerchief, another phoning the studio doctor. Sam called, "Myrna, go and find some ice." I knew where the bar was, because Mayer had taken me there one day to give me a bottle of Southern Comfort. That's all he ever kept there, and he was always giving it to people. So I brought them a towel and some ice.

Meanwhile, Joe Mankiewicz wasn't buying this act for a minute. Seeing Mayer lying there like a fallen bishop surrounded by fluttering acolytes, he started making cracks. As I mentioned, Joe was a very witty man. He got me laughing so hard that we retreated behind a piano at the other end of the room, assuming they couldn't hear us there. When the doctor arrived, we left.

I went right to my dressing room to avoid getting into anything with Joe. He could be very persuasive, and might have talked me into doing that picture. I was fussing around, getting ready to go home, when the telephone rang. It was Mayer, sounding like an abandoned waif: "Myrna, you wouldn't care if I died, would you?"

"Oh, no, Louis, don't say that. Of course I would care." I hadn't been in that dressing room five minutes. That son of a gun must have leapt off the couch to get to the phone. He'd been fully conscious, aware of everything, including my laughter. He wasn't calling to work on me about doing the picture; that never came up again. He merely wanted reassurance.

Mayer was a character, devious and manipulative, but how could you dislike him? Judy Garland and I used to discuss the "M-G-M syndrome," as she called it, all the people who ended up on the psychiatrist's couch or worse after the coddling ended. "You should have run away as I did," I told her, "instead of staying and taking more pills." Judy said that Mayer, contrary to the popular myth, had been good to her throughout those troubled times. "Schenck and the others wanted to throw me to the wolves," she told me, "but Mayer sent me to Boston for therapy. He tried to help me, while the others cried: 'Off with her head!' "

Mayer was a businessman, of course—he was smart and knew how to handle people—but he loved film. He had helped to establish Metro-Goldwyn-Mayer, it carried his name, and he took personal pride in its accomplishments and its employees. He was no absentee tycoon. Benny Thau and Eddie Mannix were there as buffers, but he would always be available to me. And he was known to say, "Well, I'll take a chance on that." I just don't know what's going on in Hollywood now. The only concern is to get the film out and earn millions of dollars. It seems that too many shoe companies are making films. There are times when I long for the Louis B. Mayers.

It was hell getting started, but once you were in, they coddled and cared for you. They groomed you and made you look wonderful. They saw that you played lots of different roles, and if the public responded to a particular characterization, the studio would exploit it. That was a two-edged sword, because it established an image and made stars of us, while usually limiting our range. There were writers writing for you, deftly promulgating that image. We had such writing talent at our fingertips! If you got into trouble, you could call up the Hacketts or Bob Benchley or Ben Hecht; Charlie MacArthur and Anita Loos were there sometimes, and Harry Kurnitz, George Oppenheimer, Norman Krasna . . . I could go on and on.

There were publicists working full time to promote you. Howard Strickling, director of studio publicity, was a genius. There was so much coverage, so much invented glamour. When you finished a picture, you went to Clarence Bull or George Hurrell, Laszlo Willinger or Ted Allan, those great still photographers, and you did two or three days of sittings with your co-stars. Then you would have portraits taken for hours on end. We posed for thousands of photographs, which went out with appropriate, if not necessarily accurate, copy to publications all over the world. Once you were an M-G-M star, that's the way it was. It helped to have talent, of course, but that constant saturation created this legendary kind of thing. We couldn't help becoming legends.

I feel sorry for these talented youngsters today. They do something wonderful, and before you know it they're out looking around for the next person who wants them. Unless they're terribly hot, as it were, nothing happens. There isn't that underlying continuity we had in the studios, that sense of being developed, of being guided. Mayer never even permitted publicity shots in any sort of candid, careless pose. Nowadays there's very little mystique left. These poor kids are totally exposed. They have to hit the talk shows . . . for practically nothing. They step off a plane without any sleep and the flashbulbs start popping. I came along before the candid camera. Now the worse they can make you look, the better. Glamour is dead. Not that there aren't beautiful men and women now, because there are, but I'm talking about a different sort of thing. You look at those old studio portraits and you say: "My *God!* Were there people that really looked like that?" Scrupulous attention was given to achieving an ideal of beauty. It was considered a treasured, wonderful thing. I'm not sure it was the best thing—a lot of people with talent and personality got lost in the shuffle—but it created an image, an aura, a myth that endures.

Sometimes achieving that ideal became exasperating. None of us is perfect. Everyone who has beauty must pay in one way or another. I have a little bone on the side of my nose that casts a shadow in certain lights. It drove the cameramen crazy, because they never knew when it would appear. They'd see the rushes, groan, "There's that thing again," and have to retake the scene. It looked like a tiny smudge on my nose. I mean, you could hardly see it, but that's how far the mania for perfection went. Of course, the retakes got kind of expensive, so they called me into the makeup department one day: "We think maybe we're going to have to fix your nose." I was horrified. I used to be known as "The Nose," for goodness' sake—thousands of women went to plastic surgeons to have it duplicated. I said, "Never! Nobody's touching this nose!" and got out of there fast.

I was glamorous because of magicians like George Folsey, James Wong Howe, Oliver Marsh, Ray June, and all those other great cinematographers. I just trusted those men and the other experts who made us beautiful. The rest of it I didn't give a damn about. I didn't fuss about my clothes, my lighting, or anything else, but, believe me, some of them did. Dietrich actually had mirrors rigged on her sets to check her angles, and Colbert and Crawford knew more about lighting than the experts did.

There never seemed to be much competition for roles among the M-G-M ladies. Most pictures were written or purchased with a certain actress in mind, and tailored especially for her. Sometimes properties were juggled; for instance, they bought *Love on the Run* for Robert Taylor and me, switched it briefly to Bob Montgomery and Jean Harlow, and finally assigned it to Clark Gable and Joan Crawford. But that happened because of availability before any of us even saw the script. We were all quite friendly, although there was little chance for socializing. Often there wasn't even the time or inclination to lunch in the commissary, so a busboy would serve Shirley Hughes and me in my dressing room.

The so-called star dressing rooms, built in 1935, were rewards for our accomplishments, Mayer claimed. They moved me from the old coed building—men downstairs, women upstairs—with open verandas running along the front, which we traversed in our dressing gowns to and from the bathrooms. For obvious reasons we called that building "the bordello." The new one indicated how far M-G-M. and I had come in ten years, comprising a two-story wing for women, another for men. Our wing, as I recall, had three suites upstairs and three down. I was on the upstairs front, with Garbo next door. The one behind us was always left for visiting stars. Janet Gaynor used it for a while, I remember, because that's where she met Adrian, whom she later married. Jeanette MacDonald had the first-floor front below me, and Jean Harlow was next to her, below Garbo. Joan Crawford had the rear suite on the first floor. The studio's head gardener, Tony Mendozza, planted special little gardens for each of us, with our favorite flowers: roses and gardenias for Joan; lilies for Norma Shearer, who had her own bungalow; French heather for Garbo; and for me, "all kinds," he decided, "because you like so many."

Stars would meet on the run, but my most vivid memories of nearly ten years in that dressing room include the wonderful company that worked with me: Shirley, my stand-in; Eleanor, who did my hair; Margaret, from wardrobe; the makeup people who came in; and especially Theresa Penn, my maid, who came to me as a replacement for her sister Ivory Brown. Isn't that a wonderful name? Particularly since she was black as coal. Ivory found another job when I fled to Europe, so she sent Theresa to fill in. Very young but very bright, she quickly learned to anticipate my needs, which is important in films because everything goes so fast. She's a beautiful person and still a dear friend.

We were laughers in the morning, my jolly crew and I. Some people take hours to come out of sleep, but we always arrived bright and cheerful to prepare for the day's shooting, carrying on like schoolgirls, and getting Jeanette MacDonald's Irish up. "For God's sake, Mrs. MacGillicuddy," she would phone from downstairs, "will you pull it down? Why do you have to be so cheerful in the morning?"

Garbo, according to her maid, would actually put her ear to the wall to hear all our hilarity. This intrigued her, these women having such a good time, but she never had the courage to join in. "Well," I finally decided, "if she's so curious let's ask her to come in for a cup of coffee." Theresa said she wouldn't come, but I invited her anyway; in fact, I made several friendly gestures. Garbo never responded. One day we ran into each other in the hall, and there was no way she could avoid me. I looked at her and smiled. She lowered her head, and in that low, lingering voice said, "Hallooo . . ." and hurried on by. That was my only exchange with Greta Garbo.

I never knew what to do with her after that. I became intimidated, afraid to approach her, because she always put me off. She never encouraged anybody. In her dressing room, behind her wardrobe, she had a secret door put in for quick getaways. She's a very scared lady, very shy. She wants to be alone, she really does. She moved down to Santa Monica and lived in a house with guards around it. You couldn't get anywhere near her.

After the war, when Mary and Doug Fairbanks, Jr., were my neighbors in Pacific Palisades, I used to see Garbo at their parties. They were tennis things, you'd sort of come and go, so there was no necessity to speak unless we chose to. We didn't choose to. She made no effort and I made no effort. I had nothing to say to her. By that time, I was bored with all the nonsense she'd carried on for so many years, living right next to me at the studio and never making a polite gesture. To me it's an act. Oh, her fear was genuine at first, I'm sure, but she apparently has made no effort to overcome it. After a lifetime in the public eye, it seems to me that maintaining it becomes an affectation—rude and rather childish.

You wouldn't believe it now, but I know what it means to be shy. I was scared as a mouse growing up. Although busy and doing many things, I had difficulty talking to people for years. I've worked to overcome it. There isn't anybody I won't take on now—within the bounds of propriety, shall we say. But you still can't get anywhere near Garbo. She's right here in New York, on Fifty-second Street. She goes out and walks, and people say, "Guess who I saw today?" And it's always the hat pulled down or the hand over her face, the furtiveness and apparently the fear.

Metro kept me working steadily for the next seven years after we settled our dispute. My first picture, *Whipsaw*, they rushed through and released quickly to get me back into circulation. I was a jewel thief, Spencer Tracy a detective.

> *I couldn't at first figure her out,* Tracy observed at the time. *I'd just come from the* Riffraff *set, where Jean Harlow had spent her leisure time making life merry for me and the rest of the crew. But here was a girl who finished her scene and retired into a corner to study her script. There must be something wrong with one of us. I prowled around for a day or two, then I marched myself up to her:* "What's the matter with me? Have I got leprosy or something?"
>
> Myrna *smiled.* "I've been wondering when you were going to come over and pay me a little attention." *That was all I needed. Twenty-four hours later we were on ribbing terms.*

He'd keep contrasting me to Jean, telling me what a good sport she was, what a prima donna I was, and how her Victrola had cheered them up on the set. In self-defense, I finally took the hint. That began his long torch-carrying: I was running and Spence was running after me. He would go out to a country club somewhere and call my friend Shirley Hughes to find out where I was. "What difference does it make?" Shirley told him. "She isn't going to see you." Which I never did. I liked him, but not enough. I was in love with Arthur, really in love; of all the men I've known, he was the one. As I mentioned earlier, I don't believe in having affairs when you're married or living with a man, and I was married or about to be a good deal of the time. Otherwise, goodness knows? Spence was an appealing guy.

We still managed to stay friends throughout. Working in pictures is a very transitory life in many ways, and, as I've said, you seldom have the chance of getting to know people. However, one of the benefits of the studio system was that you worked repeatedly with the same people, as I did with Spence and Bill Powell and Clark Gable. Consequently, I enjoyed great friendships with these men. It's nice being friends with men, you know—it sounds corny, but it's true. And the more I think about it, the more worthwhile it seems. If we'd had affairs, they probably would have blown up and left bad memories. As it was, we stayed friends and I keep them dear.

Following *Whipsaw*, I went right into *Wife vs. Secretary*, with Clark. Recalling our contretemps on my back porch and his dirty tricks afterward, I thought, Oh, boy, here we go again! Not at all. He was very sweet, very warm. He'd probably forgotten all about it. He brought me coffee in the morning, and we began to be friends.

Jean Harlow played the secretary of the title and I, needless to say, was the wife. I'd met Jean for the first time shortly before that. Bill Powell brought her along when we did some scenes from *The Thin Man* on Louella Parsons's radio show. We didn't want to—those scenes don't come across on radio—but the studio made you do it to keep in Louella's good graces. Talk about blackmail! "All right," I told them, "I'll do her show this time, but never again!" And I never did. Radio generated a lot of publicity in those days, and the shows were treated like Broadway first nights. They had studio audiences, so you'd get all dolled up, Metro would send limousines, and you'd go in style. Dashiell Hammett was in town, working on our planned sequel to *The Thin Man*, and somehow the studio roped him into doing this show with us. Afterward, Dash, Bill, Jean, and I went back to Arthur's apartment.

Hammett was an attractive kind of angular man, compelling and rather like the operatives of his early stories. He told me that he'd fashioned Nora after his friend Lillian Hellman, which I found interesting. I suppose in some ways she does resemble Lillian, particularly in the book, which is tougher than the film.

As we talked that evening, Dash drank heavily and began turning a little green. He went on and on about Lillian, while aiming overt passes at me, lunging and pawing, with my lover beside us. Arthur finally pulled him into the bedroom. "You look terrible," he said. "I think you'd better go home." Dash could be intransigent, but, by God, they got him downstairs and sent him home in a studio car. That was a great disappointment to me, because I really wanted to talk to the man. I never got the chance again—Metro let him go soon after that. Apparently he couldn't handle the job.

That same night, when Bill introduced me to Jean, I thought, My God, I've never seen such beautiful skin. That creamy complexion and platinum hair really knocked you out. She was being very careful and shy, since this was her first time out in public with Bill. They'd been going together for quite a while, but kept it quiet to avoid being talked about. Jean was beautiful, but far from the raucous sexpot of her films. As a matter of fact, she began to shake that image in *Wife vs. Secretary*, playing it as straight as she could with her obvious endowments. As the efficient secretary, she had no love scenes with Clark; in fact, you had the feeling that she was doing the same thing to him on screen that I was doing off. I mean, they were just friends. She'd begged for a role that didn't require spouting slang and modeling lingerie. She even convinced them to darken her hair a shade, in hopes of toning down that brash image. It worked. She's really wonderful in the picture and her popularity wasn't diminished one bit.

Actually we did kind of a reversal in that picture. Jean, supposedly the other woman, stayed very proper, while I had one foot in bed throughout. That's the sexiest wife I've ever played. In one scene, Clark stands outside my bedroom door and we banter, nothing more, but there's just no question about what they've done the night before. Clarence Brown, our director, made it all so subtle, yet, oh, so wonderfully suggestive. (In fact, the only vulgarity in that picture is in the breakfast scene, where I discover a diamond bracelet that Clark has hidden in the brook trout I'm about to eat. It didn't seem chic or funny to me— merely messy, typical of Hollywood's misguided notion of upper-class sophistication. I tried to get them to take it out, but they wouldn't. Needless to say, it's the scene everyone remembers, so what do I know?) Where sex is concerned, the double entendre, the ambiguity, it seems to me, is much more effective than being too explicit. This is something the moviemakers don't seem to understand today. In the *Thin Man* series, Bill and I were required by the code to sleep in twin beds, yet those scenes had more sophisticated "sex" than anything I see now.

Of course, the self-styled new morality is a valid reaction to all those years of often ridiculous censorship. When Goldwyn reissued *Arrowsmith* after the Production Code was established, they virtually deleted my role as the mistress. When Paramount reissued *Love Me Tonight* in 1950, they cut my chorus of "Mimi" because I wore a silk nightgown and the outline of my navel showed. Imagine! That was censorship! These days, however, young actresses tell me they can't attend auditions anymore without undressing. The boys have to do it, too. Nudity is beautiful when essential to a picture, but not when it's used for gratuitous titillation. Most of the current pornography is boring. That's it—boring! It just doesn't amuse me; I'm not a voyeur, I guess. Not that the truth they've been telling isn't wonderful, because it is; but they have sacrificed too many good elements to that. And there's nothing like a four-letter word when you need it, but you don't need it in every sentence. What a shame if it all triggers the return of censorship! I hate censorship, but I'm afraid we're heading in that direction.

Pictures came fast and furious. *Petticoat Fever* comes to mind only because of Bob Montgomery's shenanigans. We used to have such a ball working together, just a lot of crazy nonsense. As I recall it, the picture wasn't as funny, which is a shame. Bob was a deft comedian and there were so many other things we could have done together at Metro: *Private Lives*, for instance, which he did with Norma Shearer. I hadn't emerged as a comedienne yet, so Mrs. Thalberg got that one. In *Petticoat Fever*, we end up in an isolated cabin in Labrador. The snow was feathers and cornstarch, but our parkas were authentic, salvaged from Woody Van Dyke's *Eskimo*. While shooting arctic scenes on the hot sound stage, we'd get steamed up and have to stop. Bob would unzip his parka, squirt in some perfume, and groan, "God Almighty, do you know how many people have lived and died in this thing?"

The Great Ziegfeld, one of M-G-M's most expensive, spectacular productions, won the Best Picture Academy Award for 1936. And although Luise Rainer won Best Actress as Anna Held, Florenz Ziegfeld's first wife, it's Bill Powell's picture. He actually is *great* in the title role. In the famous telephone scene, which won her the award, Luise dramatically acknowledges her former husband's second marriage with repeated cries of "Flo . . . Flo . . ." Nearly fifty years later, in New York, Luise began a eulogy for Arnold Weissberger, the theatrical lawyer, with dramatic cries of "Arnold . . . Arnold . . ." Naughty Joan Fontaine, a few seats from me, leaned over and whispered, "Flo . . . Flo . . ."

I played the second wife, Billie Burke, not much of a part as written, but what there was of it was charming. I felt self-conscious about playing it, though, because Billie happened to be very much alive. Ziegfeld and Anna Held were gone, but here was Billie, bless her heart, trotting around Hollywood playing all kinds of parts. This is awful, I thought, playing a great star who's perfectly capable of doing it herself. She could have been very catty about it, saying, "Who does this upstart think she is?" Not at all. She was so pleased and so tickled by this thing that she insisted on having our pictures taken together, and kept bringing friends on the set to meet me.

You really need a party to celebrate the end of a picture. It's always a big letdown, because the work is terribly concentrated, terribly hard. God! How we survived I don't know. I must have been very strong. *The Great Ziegfeld* party, on the stage where we filmed it, was more elaborate than usual. It had been a big picture filled with stars like Frank Morgan, Fanny Brice, Ray Bolger. We had lots of champagne and everybody got looped, including Theresa, my maid. As we were leaving, she pointed to the sound stage looming across from us as big as an airplane hangar. "If that's in your way, Miss Loy," she said, "just tell me and I'll move it."

Fox borrowed me for *To Mary—with Love,* which was produced by Kenneth MacGowan, a singular man who later retired from a top position in the picture business to become chairman of UCLA's Theater Arts department. Nearly forty years after we made *To Mary—with Love,* when I was back in Hollywood doing *Ironside* or one of those television things, Kenneth came for tea. As we chatted, he recalled the scene where Warner Baxter visits the hospital to tell me that our baby is dead. That's when I utter the famous line: "They say the movies should be more like life; I think life should be more like the movies."

"You didn't become hysterical," Kenneth remarked. "All you did was turn your face away from him. You turned your face to the wall and it was devastating."

"I just felt that was what I should do," I told him; "I didn't want him to see what was going on." Oh, I could have cried all over the place in many of my films, but it just didn't feel right. The audience loses respect for the character. It seems that instinctively I've done this kind of underplaying a good deal in my work. That brand of acting had impressed me since first seeing Duse. She had an inner light, you see; you've got to have it. It's got to be inside you somewhere. You can't be thinking about how many people you're having for dinner. I've always felt that inside thing, especially in films, because so much is in the eye, so much is in the face. You cannot lie; you just can't. You can get away with much more on stage than in films—you can do a lot of tricks on stage, but I never do, I don't believe in that. In both media, I believe in honesty and discipline.

To Mary—with Love seems to be generally forgotten now, but it gave me a welcome dramatic challenge among those breezy characterizations at Metro. Also, its turbulent romantic theme sort of paralleled developments on the home front.

A year or two after Myrna visited us, Betty Black recalls, Bob and I came back from Hawaii to find nothing jelling as far as her marriage was concerned. Myrna was just getting fed up and needed to get away from Arthur's house in Bel-Air. She took me, Shirley Hughes, and her Mexican maid to Lake Arrowhead, this mountain resort above San Bernardino. She and her mother owned a cabin there, which Arthur didn't like. Oh, he liked the idea of having a place at Arrowhead, which was very fashionable then, but he informed Myrna that the rustic cabin didn't meet his rigid standards. She took her money, worked with a decorator, and completely redid the place. When she talked Arthur into going back up there, everything was of the finest you could have in a mountain home, including a canopy for the master's bed.

Anyway, we ran away to Arrowhead and had ourselves quite a time. A blizzard hit, leaving us snowbound for days. We would trudge as best we could down to the Arrowhead Inn to check for messages from Arthur. Finally he called and said he just wasn't living; life wasn't worthwhile without Myrna, and if she'd come home he'd definitely make arrangements to marry her. So we came home from the mountains.

After nearly four years of obstacles and delays, we slipped over the Mexican border at Tijuana, giving our names to immigration officials as M. Williams and A. B. Giles. Shirley Hughes and her fiancé, Ray Ramsey, a Metro cameraman, came along to be our witnesses. We drove sixty-five miles over mountains, through cactus-laced valleys, and along the winding coast road to Ensenada. Playa Ensenada, where we stayed, resembled a Moorish palace on a smooth horseshoe bay. Strolling musicians in white baggy pants, wide red sashes, and huge sombreros sang witty love songs: "With the bones of my mother-in-law / I will build a ladder up to the room of my sweetheart." Afterward, on my birthdays, Arthur would send Mexican musicians to play beneath my window.

We were married on June 27, 1936, by Justice Jaime S. Pardo, quietly, without one Hollywood columnist, reporter, or photographer tracking us.

That's what I wanted. I wanted marriage. Women all did, and whatever they say to show off, they apparently still do. I don't anymore, and if life was then the way it is now, perhaps I wouldn't have married so many times. You see, I thought I had to. Now people don't care if you're married or not, and it's wonderful. I think it's terrific. But in those days we were conditioned for marriage. Not only for propriety's sake but because even working, financially independent women were supposed to be traditional wives. Betty Black says I wanted to be "the perfect wife" of my films. Well, I'll go her one better: I wanted to be an *Oriental* wife. That wasn't Arthur's concept; it was mine, because of the atmosphere I'd been raised in.

My father was hardly a domineering man, and Mother was anything but subservient, yet society dictated that they fill certain roles. Women obviously have been as much infected by that conditioning as men have. As a result, women of my generation who do things feel a certain amount of guilt about it. I certainly did. It wasn't a conscious awareness then, but it was there just the same. Of course, being rich at the time, I didn't have to wash dishes and do ironing. I always had dependable people, good cooks, maids, but there's still a great deal that you have to do. If you've got a house, you have responsibilities besides getting up at five-thirty in the morning and sometimes not returning until seven at night by the time you've seen the rushes. You meet yourself coming around corners. Women in my business were liberated early in many ways, but the desire persisted to cater to a husband's needs, to compensate for the fact that you worked. How in the world I expected to get home from the studio in time to put out his slippers, God only knows!

6

THE QUEEN OF
THE MOVIES
1936–1942

*They called her "the perfect wife" in the movies. I
thought she was the perfect movie star.*
—HENRY FONDA, 1980

After our wedding we drove back to Palos Verdes Peninsula. We'd leased Villa Narcissa there from Frank Vanderlip, a banker with a passion for Italy. That magnificent house, a copy of Villa d'Este, overlooked the sea at Portuguese Bend. We used it on weekends and retreated there when those hot, dry Santana winds blew. Oh, I have fond memories of those Santana days when our crowd piled down from Hollywood to escape the heat.

Ernst Lubitsch headed straight for the ocean upon arrival one weekend. There had been an oil spill out at sea, and Ernst got into the residue. I'll never forget his husky, hairy body covered with this black stuff, emerging like some mythological monster from the sea.

Mitchell Leisen, who directed several of Arthur's Paramount pictures, brought Natalie Visart, a designer for Cecil B. De Mille. Bright, funny, and warm, she has remained one of my closest friends through thick and thin.

Collier Young and his first wife, Valerie, participated when they came out from New York. Collie, one of Hollywood's wittiest men, later became a screenwriter, a producer, and married Ida Lupino and Joan Fontaine. "My favorite ex-husband," Joan always called him. In those early years, though, starting out as an agent, he could hardly make ends meet. Knowing Arthur's taste for fine wine, they arrived one weekend with a bottle of rare vintage they could ill afford. We came to table, the wine was served, and the Youngs watched with great expectation as Arthur ceremoniously tasted. "An agreeable little wine," he decided, leaving our guests absolutely crushed. Collie loved telling that story, because, of course, Arthur was not only pompous but wrong.

Eddie Sutherland, another Villa Narcissa regular, had been Chaplin's assistant in the early silent days, weathered a brief marriage to Louise Brooks, and kept a talent for comedy on and off the screen. Eddie absolutely adored Loretta Young, a lovely, exuberant girl. He claimed to have spent a fortune trying to get the Vatican to annul her first marriage; but they never married.

When Myrna married Arthur Hornblow and they had this beautiful sort of Italian villa down on the coast, Eddie Sutherland took me there, Loretta Young relates. *Remembering that aloof creature of our films, I was a little scared, but she greeted me warmly, saying first thing: "I suppose you have to go to mass on Sunday?" I said, "Yes," and she arranged for somebody to take me. That whole weekend was really just marvelous for me, easy and pleasant, but elegant—beautifully appointed house, beautiful service, wonderful food. It set a standard for me. Myrna was just as good a hostess as she was an actress, and that was something to shout about.*

She's one of the substantial, one of the very important people in the motion-picture industry. Even when she started out, she had a quality about her, but by the time she got to Metro she was so well seasoned I loved that part of her career. That had real elegance, I thought. That's where she realized her full potential, because Myrna's one of the rare people with humor in our business. I mean real *humor. It permeated her roles, this kind of understanding or acceptance of relationships that leading men and ladies didn't have in those days. You played it very feminine and he was very macho and there was always conflict there. But with Myrna you always felt: Well, yeah, as mad as she got, oh, well, all right, she'd understand that, she guessed. She was always a little bit wiser, more compassionate and sophisticated. And she really has those things, too, as a person. Of course, she's a born lady, a quality that would have been enough for most*

*people. It was enough for—oh, God help me—Jeanette Mac-
Donald. You know what I mean: Myrna, particularly with William Powell, had the beginning of the modern-day sort of relationship between a man and a woman. She paved the way for all
of us.*

My mother and I were looking at Too Hot to Handle *recently, Myrna and Clark Gable, and she looked so gorgeous. My
mother said it was just too bad that they don't make more pictures like that. I said, "Well, Mama, they don't want pictures
like this apparently anymore; otherwise, they would make them."
I think the producers are the ones who are sick in the head. But,
really, how can they do it again? It's like saying, "This girl will
play the Myrna Loy part." Well, there's no possible way you can
play Myrna Loy without Myrna Loy's humor, Myrna Loy's nose,
no way! There just won't be anybody like her because she's already been the first—an original.*

I hadn't seen Loretta for years, but recently we dined at her exquisite
little house in Beverly Hills. Her mother, who's still going strong in her
nineties, decorated it from top to bottom, discreetly placing Loretta's
Oscar and Emmys on the top shelf of the front-hall coat closet. More
exposure, she decided, would be ostentatious, and Loretta wouldn't move
so much as an ashtray that Mama has placed. Loretta remembers the
details of those Villa Narcissa weekends, which surprised me, and we
laughed about the boys' little hunting expedition.

You see, the Vanderlips raised peacocks, which strutted around the
estate making a terrible racket. Have you ever heard a peacock? They
make the most god-awful sound, a shrill, plangent scream. They had a
little game, those creatures: climbing the stone stairway behind the house,
taking off, and landing on the roof. In the middle of the night, hearing
this *clumpf*, you'd wait for the roof to fall in on you. There was nothing
you could do about it. Those creatures were sacred to the Vanderlips.

Early one morning, Arthur, Eddie, and Jean Negulesco mysteriously disappeared from the house. They returned before lunch with a
peacock. I mean those devils went out and *shot* one! Loretta and I,
absolutely horrified, carried on the way women do, but to no avail.
They put their kill in the back of the car and brought it to the chef at
the Bel-Air Country Club. Nobody since Nero had eaten peacock, as

far as they knew, and by God they were going to have it. So we all went over to the Bel-Air and dined on the Vanderlips' peacock. It was delicious, I must say, but didn't taste like pheasant, as I'd hoped. It tasted like turkey.

That was the extent of our bacchanalian revels, roast peacock—and, oh, yes, an all-girl skinny-dip. We had a houseful one hot Santana weekend when the girls decided to sneak away for a midnight swim. We went in with very little on, frankly, since this was supposed to be a private hen party. Well, those rascals got wind of it, drove down in automobiles, and turned their headlights on us. We just stood there screaming, frantically trying to cover ourselves with seaweed. Mary Martin claims that she attended a mixed nude swimming party at our house. If she did, I wasn't there—perhaps Arthur carried on after I left—but we never did that kind of thing. Nobody else in our group did either, as far as I know. We had a good time, but this myth about Hollywood people being so bacchanalian is ridiculous. We worked too hard.

There were always blatant ones, of course, the ones that got into trouble; but no more than anyplace else. It's just that a famous name makes those things news. We knew there were problem drinkers, drug users, "great lovers" who liked the boys, "great ladies" who liked the girls, or sweet young things with a sharp eye on their futures. If they were quiet about it, nobody cared—that was their own business. We certainly didn't gloat about it as they do now. A lot of girls who later became stars used to slip over the border for wild weekends with the President of Mexico, getting jewelry or money for their favors. They were looking out for themselves, that's all. Most of them were girls who'd had rough times on the way up. Now they've gone way above all that.

We built our Hollywood house in Hidden Valley, at the top of Coldwater Canyon. Well, almost at the top. We knew that Boris Karloff lived somewhere above us, because his bowling green wasn't properly engineered and the balls kept tumbling down the mountain. Moss Hart considered building on the hill between us and Karloff, until, he claimed facetiously, stray bowling balls deterred him. The sport was very big among the English and Sam Goldwyn at that time.

Despite bowling balls and the proximity of Beverly Hills, Coldwater Canyon consisted of wild, bush-covered hills and valleys. The only sign of civilization when we started building was the narrow white macadamized road climbing our hill. Our architect designed a sprawling clap-board house combining Colonial grace with the contemporary freedom we wanted. Below the house on another level, we built tennis courts and a pool and pool house, with dressing rooms and bar. Below that on the valley floor, we had a wonderful lime orchard, where Jim, our gar-dener, one day caught a dogged fan digging up a tree for a souvenir. And everywhere we planted gardens. Oh, the flowers were magnificent! When I think what I put into that place, it makes me sick. Arthur and I were making combined yearly salaries of around three hundred thou-sand dollars and we lived up to it, believe me. I'm terrible about money. Awful! I always had people to handle my finances. Then all I did was make money and they'd put it in the bank and Arthur and I would spend it. But we had fun. It was worth it.

One spring I drove up to Myrna's house, recalls Betty Black, *and it was the most gorgeous sight I ever saw in my life. The gardener had just thrown wildflower seeds around, every kind and color, a whole hill of them that led to her house. It was a very well-run estate, the way Arthur wanted it run, like the stately homes of England. Everything had to be very English: his friends; his clothes were from London; he even started watching everything Myrna put on, so that her clothes were sort of English, too. Myrna never really cared about those things, but Arthur was twelve years older, set in his ways. He wanted to live like a millionaire, as did Gene Markey later on.*

The first time my mother saw Myrna's house, she said, "Gosh, she must have to work awful hard to support all these people." Sometimes they'd have as many as seven gardeners at a time. They had a butler, live-in maids, a laundress who doubled as Arthur's valet, a German chauffeur named Helmut, a wonderful Russian cook, Sergei. Everybody in Hollywood talked about the food they served—everybody, that is, who was lucky enough to be invited.

Myrna's whole life and friends revolved around Arthur, and he was very much of a snob to all her old friends except Bob and me. He liked us, probably because Bob was an officer. That was the Britisher in Arthur. He would have Della—and Auntie—over every once in a while, because it was Myrna's mother and Myrna was still a little under her influence; you don't break away just like that. Myrna bought a car for her, hired a chauffeur and a maid, and Arthur always sent things down to her house. But all the time that Myrna was married to Arthur it wasn't a family kind of thing. It was always writers and composers from New York or Who's Who in Hollywood and the British colony—the Laughtons, the Nigel Bruces, Louis Bromfield, Alfred Hitchcock, the Goldwyns, the Selznicks. Those people were always there and there was tennis and elegant buffets prepared by Sergei and his wife.

One afternoon, Bob played doubles with David Niven, who wasn't all that well known then. But Myrna saw his future. "He's a darn good actor," she predicted; "he'll go places." After the match, I was having a delightful time talking to him, when Gene Markey arrived with his wife, Hedy Lamarr, and Bob was crazy about Hedy Lamarr. I was charmed and always have been with Gene, who later on I would know pretty well when Myrna married him. He was doing some writing then besides his picture work, and I had read his books, and told him how much I liked them. I always felt sort of . . . not in awe of these people because they were celebrities—they always were very nice to me—but because of the knowledge, the conversation. Myrna didn't have time for the ones who were partying every night. You had to have your wits about you at Myrna's house.

It was a rich landscape of creative people out there. Everybody was working; everybody was doing something. People didn't just sit around unless they had time off, which wasn't often. There was so much wit, so much energy. The kind of sophisticated comedy I did in films came from those people and that sort of environment. They observed and recreated with an edge the so-called leisure class, the élite of that era. The Noel Coward type of rich characters with butlers and maids—that formal way of life did exist then. It doesn't now, not to that extent, so it's not being written about. Life is somewhat grimmer these days. It's extremely difficult to be witty. I knew people who talked that way: Noel himself, who always visited my set when he came to Hollywood; Herman Mankiewicz; Moss Hart; George Kaufman; Dorothy Parker; and Arthur was no slouch, either. In fact, it used to get pretty rough. I'd be exhausted after a conversation. I'd sit there and wonder: When will I think of something witty to say?

Harry Kurnitz was one of the great wits, along with Dorothy Parker, but his humor was never cruel, as hers could be, unless he turned it on himself. We were immediate friends from the first time Collier and Valerie Young brought him to my house—long before he wrote *I Love You Again* or *Shadow of the Thin Man* for Bill and me. We all went to a crazy, *crazy* party one night, and apparently we all had enough to drink and Harry had more than enough. He arrived at our house for a prearranged tennis game the next day looking absolutely desperate. "I want a record of the way I feel today," he groaned. "I'm going to put it in a time capsule to show the world in many years hence what modern man was like."

Our house became quite a gathering place, and the tennis matches continued even while I worked. Our courts were cut right out of the mountain, leaving dirt and brush above that gardeners kept cutting back. While Arthur and my brother David played doubles one day, somebody screamed. A rattlesnake was crawling down the wall of the court. I went for Jim, the gardener, who was always killing those creatures, and we ran back to find David holding the snake down with his tennis racquet. They're lethal, one bite and you're gone, but David just held the bloody thing down until Jim killed it. I considered that very heroic of my little brother.

David wasn't there very often, I'm afraid; Arthur was rather snooty toward my family. He had no reason to be just because he happened to be born on the West Side of New York and finally made it to the East Side—it's as simple as that! I'd have Mother and Aunt Lou to dinner and it wasn't exactly pleasant for them. But my mother was always on his side—she was that way with all my husbands. I went down to her house after a fight with Arthur one night. "You can't stay here," she said. "Go home to your husband." She wouldn't put up with me. I had trouble quite a bit with him after that, but I never went to Mother.

The rattlesnakes had some competition after Arthur bought a ferocious black police dog that scared me to death. "Why in the world are you bringing that kind of dog into this house?" I asked, but Arthur would have him. Sidney Howard, out from New York to write the *Gone With the Wind* script, was chatting contentedly with me on the porch one afternoon, when all of a sudden Arthur came running for his life toward the driveway with this dog in hot pursuit. Sidney and I were terrified, paralyzed, not knowing what to do. Finally I called Jim, as usual, and we went after them down the drive: Arthur, with the snarling black dog at his heels; Jim, the gardener, with Sidney Howard and me frantically bringing up the rear, looking for all the world like a Mack Sennett chase. When we reached the bottom, Arthur hadn't been mauled, but that police dog wasn't around for long.

Arthur had a gift for attracting interesting, amusing people. I'd met Charlie Chaplin at one of the De Milles' parties, but it was after he and Arthur got together somewhere that he'd come to see us. He was a very self-involved man, not terribly interested in anything that didn't have to do with him or his work, so a lot of people avoided him: "My God! Is *he* coming to pester you? Watch out, you won't get any sleep." It's true. He would go on and on into the night, but I found him fascinating. He held forth, loving to be the center of attention, telling wonderful stories about things that happened on his sets. He would explain how his routines developed, cannily aware of the process, acting out every bit of business as if he were blocking a scene. You saw this inventive mind at work and realized how those brilliant films evolved.

One night he'd been holding forth in our library for hours when I excused myself, hating to leave, but assuming he would understand: "I have to work tomorrow and you know what it means to get up at five-thirty." And God knows what time it was then. Charlie was still surrounded by rapt listeners, but I will never forget how puzzled he seemed, and a little bit offended. He couldn't imagine anything taking precedence over his performance.

Reginald Gardiner was another spellbinder, a raconteur with a difference. With his versatile voice and dexterous hands, he could become a stone wall or whatever he chose to be. His wallpaper was amazing— you could actually *see* rolls of repeated patterns. When we traveled from New York to Hollywood together once, he lightened that usually tedious train trip. At Albuquerque we got out and walked up to the engine just to stretch our legs. They had steam engines then, which went *shshshsh*, making all those wonderful sounds. "This engine is *livid*," Reggie said, "absolutely livid," personifying it before doing a perfect imitation.

The first time I met Hedy Lamarr, she was with Reggie. She always said he was the man she should have married. She had sprained her ankle and Reggie was sort of hauling her around, but you didn't miss that beautiful face of hers. Oh, it was fabulous, just fabulous! People assume, apparently because of her beauty, that Hedy is a blank. Not at all. She was always charming when I knew her, with a nice sense of humor. When she married Gene Markey, they became part of the group that used to come to my house.

Arthur made several musicals at Paramount, which put him in touch with the composers who came out from New York. Our house became a gathering place for them. I had a fine piano, a medium grand Steinway handmade from pearwood. My mother was always very fussy about pianos—nothing but a Steinway would she ever touch. One night Richard Rodgers, Jerome Kern, George and Ira Gershwin fought for that instrument, practically knocking each other down getting to the piano. One would get up and another would jump in. They played and played. Augustine Lara, the Mexican composer, was there. He sat in absolute ecstasy at this display of musical wealth. The talent—good Lord! But we really had a musical theater then.

Dick Rodgers played a beautiful piano, which is not always true of composers. We had become friends making *Love Me Tonight* and stayed friends through the years. I would always see him and Dorothy when they came out to California. Besides that marvelous *Love Me Tonight* score, he wrote a song for *Manhattan Melodrama*, which, after several changes of lyrics by Larry Hart, became "Blue Moon," a very New York song. It has a quality about it that is the city at night. He played those and other songs at my house—always his own songs, of course, vying with his peers for that pearwood piano.

Jerry Kern came into my life while composing that lovely score for *High, Wide and Handsome*, one of Arthur's Paramount musicals. He was dear and diminutive, with an impish sense of fun. I adored him. Sometimes I'd come home from the studio in the evening and find him sitting on our front porch. He would drive up from his house in Beverly Hills and just wait for us. Once, planning to surprise me, he climbed into an enormous ceramic jar on the porch and got stuck. We had one hell of a time extricating him. Arthur and I, with some of the servants, had to overturn that heavy thing and pull, coax, and squeeze, nearly breaking his little bones. This was Jerry, full of whimsical pranks to relieve what seemed a constant flow of creativity. He worked late at night, which was hard on his wife, a lovely woman, patient; they all had to be, married to those mad men. As he composed by an open window one night, a bird's insistent call annoyed him. "Close that window!" he shouted to his wife. "It's driving me crazy." But the birdcall came back to haunt him, and, dozens of melodies later, it became the first seven notes of "I've Told Every Little Star." Beautiful melodies poured out of him.

George Gershwin ended up at the piano that memorable evening in Hidden Valley. George never wanted to go to sleep, you know. He just kept playing and gradually people began to leave. Eventually, only the two of us were left in my living room. He was still at the piano at four in the morning. I really never could figure George out. Of course, I didn't see as much of him as I did of Dick and Jerry, but I spent time with him and listened to his music. There was an intensity about him, but he didn't talk very much, he just played. His passion was his music. During that long session at my house, I don't remember what he said, only what he played. It was the most extraordinary thing, because one week later he was dead from a brain tumor. I don't think he knew about it that night, but the untimely loss revealed the irony of the last song he'd played: "They Can't Take That Away from Me."

The most cherished of all the people from those years is John T. Hornblow, Arthur's son Terry. No more than six when his father first introduced us, he bowed so low that he almost fell over. I adored him from that moment. When he returned to his mother, in Warrenton, Virginia, he wrote: "Dear Minnie," which was Arthur's nickname for me, "I am sorry I went away from you." From the very beginning it was a big love affair.

When he spent summers with us, usually accompanied by a nurse or his French governess, we'd have baby animals around and all that kind of thing. He joined boys' clubs and broke his arm, and we went through all one does with children. His father, who hadn't spent much time with him, tried to compensate by enforcing a regimen of activities without really participating. I tried to do what Arthur didn't do, like taking him fishing for speckled bass on those excursion boats from Malibu pier. Terry and I were friends. We did things together. When we gave parties for him with David and Irene Selznick's sons, or Steve Broidy and Buff Cobb's son, all those Hollywood kids, Arthur did the planning and I did the playing. We'd have gunny-sack races and every imaginable children's activity. Those kids went home looking as if they'd been through a war. So did I.

Of course, I was working most of the time. In order to see more of Terry, I'd take him to the studio in the morning. He loved listening to Hawaiian music on the car radio and conversing with Helmut over the little microphone from the back seat. At the studio he'd watch me work occasionally or take a tour; then we'd have lunch in the commissary and Helmut would drive him home.

People who gauge such things consider the last part of that decade my "golden years." They were certainly working years. From *The Thin Man*, in 1934, to *Another Thin Man*, in 1939, I made twenty pictures. They varied in quality but all bore the stamp of experts and artists combining to create mass entertainment. Movies then were what television is now to the public—and they can never be again. The amazing thing, really, is that so much of quality came out of what were essentially entertainment factories.

Libeled Lady was one of the best of the so-called screwball comedies, with a great cast, and Jack Conway directing us at breakneck speed. I didn't work too much with Jean Harlow and Spencer Tracy on that one; Bill Powell and I usually played separately from them. But Spence carried on during the shooting, because it was the first time we'd worked together since my marriage. He moped around pretending to pout, playing the wronged suitor. He set up a "hate Hornblow table" in the commissary, announcing that only men I had spurned could sit there. So all these men joined him who were supposed to have crushes on me, which they didn't have at all. It was just a gag, but Spence made his point.

We went into the California mountains for exteriors—Bill and I and Walter Connolly, that darling man who played my father. That's where they shot the fantastic fishing sequence when Bill does everything wrong and ends up with the prize fish. I see it now and scream. It's a hysterical piece of work, but then Bill was a very gifted man, able to do great comedy and tragedy, everything.

Arthur came up there with us, the only time he ever accompanied me on location. He liked Bill, fortunately, and they became good friends. We stayed there almost a week, living in little cabins with a chuck wagon to feed us and the crew. Those chuck wagons, a vestige of the old West, developed into a service the studios used on locations. The food was great, probably the kind my father had cooked over a campfire at roundup time. It was beautiful up in the mountains—glorious sunsets, deep, quiet nights, a welcome relief from claustrophobic sound stages.

"A sequel," Irvin S. Cobb warned me, "is like a second helping of casaba." We were lucky with *After the Thin Man*. Picking up where the original left off, Dashiell Hammett wrote an original story, which the Hacketts again adapted for the screen. Hunt Stromberg produced, Van Dyke directed, and Bill and I returned as Nick and Nora, with Asta in tow. Jimmy Stewart, in one of his first film roles, played the deranged culprit, and darn well, too. He was very excited and enthusiastic about it all, rushing around with his camera taking pictures of everybody on the set, declaring, "I'm going to marry Myrna Loy!"

We shot exteriors in San Francisco, so I went up on the train with Bill and Jean Harlow. She wasn't in the picture, but he had somehow managed to get her away from her mother. The grip she had on that girl was unbelievable. Bill and Jean were unofficially engaged, and he'd given her an enormous star-sapphire ring, which she proudly displayed on the train. It really was *too* big, I thought, and Bill kept making jokes about it, but Jean was thrilled. This meant so much to her. I realized during that trip how deeply she loved Bill, a total childlike love, full of the exuberance and wonder that characterized her. She wanted marriage, but he was afraid to marry her. And, of course, that was the great guilt he bore after her death. He loved her, but he'd been married twice—to a woman in New York years before; more recently to Carole Lombard—and both marriages had gone bust.

At the St. Francis in San Francisco, they had reserved the Flyshaker Suite for Bill and me. The management assumed we were married. Already they considered us a couple after only five pictures together! Well, of course, it was hysterical. Here was Jean, but we couldn't be obvious about the situation with the press on our heels. To complicate matters further, conventioneers had taken every other room except a little hall bedroom downstairs somewhere. I didn't know what to do, but Jean was marvelous. "There's nothing for you to do," she said. "We'll just have to put Bill downstairs." I never saw his room, so I don't know how bad it was, but Bill complained bitterly, let me tell you, angling to get upstairs.

That mix-up brought me one of my most cherished friendships. You would have thought Jean and I were in boarding school we had so much fun. We'd stay up half the night talking and sipping gin, sometimes laughing, sometimes discussing more serious things. She talked about Paul Bern, the Metro executive who killed himself during their marriage. That was still very much on her mind after four years. She told me how terrible that had been, because she loved him. She became involved with him because he treated her like a lady, not a sex symbol; he never put her down, but showed kindness and consideration. She told me all about this. She didn't tell me in so many words that he couldn't consummate the marriage. Now, how do you say things like that? I assumed that was his problem, though, intensified no doubt by her sexy image, because I sensed some guilt in her reaction—there's bound to be in a situation like that. But mostly there was love, great affection and admiration, an implicit acceptance of his deficiency. He couldn't bear the burden of disappointing her, however, and she blamed that sexy image to some extent.

One never confused the parts people played with their actual personalities, as so many of these would-be biographers seem to do. Jean was always very cheerful, full of fun, but she also happened to be a sensitive woman with a great deal of self-respect. All that other stuff—that was all put on. She wasn't like that at all. She just happened to be a good actress who created a lively characterization that exuded sex appeal. Being a sexpot is no fun, I can tell you that. My tenure in that department was brief—and I always had one foot up, anyway—so I didn't have quite as much trouble as some of them did. My God! When you think what this country does to those women—look at Marilyn Monroe! I guess it's a sin to be sexy, but a little vicarious drooling from the public, that's all right. This covert lasciviousness must stem from our puritanical past. I don't know; but thank God I wasn't a sexpot. All the sexpots are dead or about to be.

Remember that awful book that was written about Jean? That's typical of the school of biography that seeks to fit the reality to the image. It was claimed she ran around San Francisco getting drunk and sleeping with cabdrivers. She was with me or Bill, for God's sake, and when we worked she hung around the set. Oh, it makes me wild when I think about the rubbish that's printed! Most of it's trash, believe me, but the worst part of it is that people believe what they read. The written word has some kind of sanctity. I can't even discuss the book that Joan Crawford's daughter wrote; it makes me ill to think of it. Joan and I were friends for fifty years and the person I knew wasn't like that. Why don't people consider the source? I worked with Christina and saw how that mind operates. The book Margaret Sullavan's daughter wrote is just as bad. Maggie gave up the best years of her career to raise those children, and that's what she gets. And these so-called secret lives infuriate me. That stuff used to be confined to the *Police Gazette*. Now there seems almost a diabolical desire to destroy—the rule of sensationalism at any cost. Imagine calling Errol Flynn a Nazi spy. My God! He was never sober long enough. How can they print such things? Recently some bird in Toronto swore that he recruited me as a United States spy during World War II. How idiotic! I spent the war years in New York and Washington working for the Red Cross. What do they want of us? They're really having a field day tearing apart all these people they adored for so long.

We worked terribly hard on that San Francisco location. We shot all over town, with about sixty principals and crew and hundreds of local extras; but Woody Van Dyke always liked a festive company, so there were lots of parties. I noticed that Jean tired easily and in the morning her usually snow-white skin sometimes seemed slate-gray. I sensed that she was a sick girl. Knowing how hard it was to get Jean away from her mother, a devout Christian Scientist, I got in touch with Saxton Pope, a friend of mine at the University of California Medical Center in San Francisco. I always went to him for my checkups—I never had them in Los Angeles. If you were a movie star and entered a hospital there, the columnists would say you were having a baby or an abortion. They go right after you. That's why I'm still very quiet about my illnesses. They're ghouls. If I go in for a checkup now, they're dusting off the obituaries.

I invited Saxton and his wife, Jeanne, to a cocktail party at the St. Francis. "Take a good look at this girl," I told him. "Besides your interest in her, which you unquestionably will have, see what you can find out about her health." So he said, "I'm a doctor," and flirted with her, taking her pulse, fiddling around, and she didn't catch on. He couldn't make any kind of diagnosis at a party, but he told me later, "When I took hold of that girl's wrist, it was almost as though the veins were hardening." As I remember, he surmised that she'd had some kind of blood disorder as a child, which had something to do with that white, white skin of hers. He wanted to give her a thorough examination, so I made her promise me then that she'd come back there for a proper checkup. I even arranged for an appointment at the medical center, but she never made up her mind to do it. She became friendly with the Popes and talked them out of it. Jean could be very persuasive.

Let's get one thing straight about my next picture. Whatever critics and commentators may say against *Parnell*, I like it. I think Clark Gable is wonderful in the title role and I like my Katie O'Shea. The best love scene he ever played is in that picture. It's the first meeting between Parnell and Katie, when he talks about having seen her in a white dress at the opera. It's a beautiful scene. You can feel the beginning of this love that would rock the British Empire.

Clark gave a subdued, sustained performance as Parnell, which apparently was the problem. He had been so typed as those red-blooded Blackie Nortons that people didn't want to be reminded he was an actor. They went after the macho stuff. And I was breezy Nora Charles, which prohibited me from donning Adrian's nineteenth-century finery and creating a more sober characterization. Disgruntled fans wrote to the studio by the thousand—they did that in those days. Some of the critics complained that we played against type. We were actors, for God's sake. We couldn't be Blackie Norton and Nora Charles all the time. It's interesting that Joan Crawford was originally assigned Katie O'Shea, while I was scheduled for *The Last of Mrs. Cheyney*, with Bill Powell and Bob Montgomery. They switched us at the last minute because Joan's previous attempt at nineteenth-century characterization, *The Gorgeous Hussy*, elicited the same kind of public resistance. Clark, Joan, and I—so many of us—were the victims of our carefully nurtured images.

Matters weren't helped in *Parnell* by putting us up against a lot of heavy-weather Englishmen, those veddy British character actors with their painfully precise West End accents. My sort of mid-Atlantic accent stood up pretty well—even against Edna May Oliver, who wasn't English but might as well have been. She was a terrific lady, very amusing, a staunch Yankee spinster living in a little house out in Westwood. But Clark was the last person in the world to attempt an English accent, and the contrast worked against him. It wasn't intentional. Those Britishers, Edmund Gwenn, Donald Crisp, Alan Marshall among them, were generous actors, marvelous men. In fact, we shared a dramatic incident while shooting before a replica of the House of Commons. Work was halted, a radio produced, and the British contingent gathered round to hear the abdication speech of Edward VIII. Absolutely *stunned* by his decision, they all objected vehemently, considering it a terrible mistake, as the grim, gray Parliament set loomed behind us, intensifying that touching moment in history.

I really can't understand the great outcry that persists against *Parnell*. That script, written by John Van Druten and S. N. Behrman, no less, does not totally disregard history. It dealt with such issues as Home Rule in more depth than did most of the so-called historical dramas. Metro strove for accuracy. When young Randolph Churchill, feeling cocky, visited the set, he insisted that Gladstone would have been addressed as "Mr. Prime Minister" in the House of Commons. John Stahl, our director, stopped the scene while the research department cabled the clerk of the House to verify the fact that "Mr. Gladstone" was indeed proper in 1887. *Parnell* was far from the critical fiasco that hindsight has made of it. Many reviewers admired it at the time and, contrary to the popular myth, it made a healthy profit. It certainly didn't hurt our popularity. During its release, Clark and I were voted King and Queen of the Movies, in the most comprehensive national poll ever held.

I can give you the specifics of that thing because Aunt Lou tucked a 1937 New York *Daily News* into an old scrapbook. That yellowed relic explains that fifty-three newspapers in the key cities of the United States and Canada polled over twenty million people for the results. Ed Sullivan even came out to Hollywood with these tin-and-purple-velvet crowns for a formal coronation. Clark always after that called me "Queenie," which sounded like someone in a Western saloon. The whole thing was a scream. Bill Powell, who came in fourth in the men's division, sent me a florist's box as long as a couch filled with sour grapes. The card read, "With Love from William IV." We never took that stuff seriously, any more than we did the box-office polls that kept placing us in the top ten during those years. Funny, but those measures and titles didn't mean as much to us as you might imagine. Clark and I felt like a couple of kids trying to make out: we went to M-G-M together. We were serious about our work, studying and observing, learning our craft, but we were having a ball. As Clark said later, "We never expected to be legends."

If we had thought about it, we might have realized that this legend business was an inevitable result of all the exposure. Interviews, as I've said, were like Presidential press conferences then, because there were so many newspapers. You always had to have somebody from the studio to help you through them. Larry Barbier, one of Howard Strickling's assistants, was my protector. If I went to New York or anywhere on studio business, Larry accompanied me, reinforced by people from the local Metro office once we arrived. There would always be a phalanx of people around to protect me. We were so coddled by the studio. This was the "M-G-M syndrome" that Judy Garland and I used to talk about, a strange kind of conditioning that wasn't good for us. I considered it great sport to shake them, to escape the constant surveillance. Others, like Judy, became too dependent on it. On the other hand, you had the public to deal with, which I rudely discovered on a trip to New York with Arthur.

Like all native New Yorkers, Arthur loved to shop there, and in that day, before cut-rate chain stores and suburban malls, New York shops were really something. We went down to Macy's one morning to buy place mats and things for the house. I'm a pretty fast shopper; I don't fool around, so a salesgirl took me behind her showcase to show me what they had. I'm examining this stuff, when all of a sudden I look up and there's a sea of faces crowding in on me. Two big Macy cops appear, grab my arms, and start pulling me: "Word's out that you're in the store; we've got to get you out of here. They're coming up the elevators and the stairways." They were scared; they really had a mob on their hands. Just then some woman yells, "I luf you! I luf you!" and cracks me on the back of my neck. I actually saw stars. She almost killed me with her luf. I'm staggering, calling for Arthur, who's wandered off to another department, with these two cops dragging me downstairs, all the while bawling me out: "Don't you know better than to do a thing like this? Don't you ever come in here again." They got me to a side entrance and literally *threw* me out of Macy's. Imagine! I stood there absolutely nonplussed until Arthur found me. "They just threw me out," I gasped. "I mean, they actually told me never to come back." The irony started us laughing as we headed toward Fifth Avenue for a shot of brandy.

But to get back to my relationship with Clark Gable, when I think of it now, considering the way it started, it was curious. We became devoted to each other. We weren't lovers—he was in love with Carole

Lombard by that time. In fact, after I repelled his initial attack, we eventually became more like siblings. Nobody believes that, and you can understand why when you consider Lou MacFarlane's line after I pushed him off the porch: "I wouldn't care if he couldn't read." That's how Clark affected women. But our relationship was unique. Oh, he sometimes gave me the macho routine when people were watching, but he changed when we were alone.

We always used to celebrate together at the end of a picture. Clark insisted on it. Maybe we'd include the director, maybe not. It was just a kind of ritual that the two of us had. We would share a bottle of champagne while he read poetry to me, usually the sonnets of Shakespeare. He loved poetry, and read beautifully, with great sensitivity, but he wouldn't dare let anybody else know it. He was afraid people would think him weak or effeminate and not the tough guy who liked to fish and hunt. I was the only one he trusted. He never wanted me to tell about this, and here I am giving him away; but I never mentioned it while he was alive.

He had to keep up the masculine image for Carole. Though she joked and teased about it, somehow he kept having to prove it to her. Carole was beautiful and feminine, but she could swear like a stevedore, really take off, and he would just sit back and howl. He loved it, yet it challenged him. That may be why older women generally attracted him. His first two wives were much older. Of course, they helped him: one was a drama coach, the other a rich Texan. But Clark wouldn't marry for those things; he was too independent. I think he just felt less pressured by them. He more or less continued that through his life. After Carole died, he used to see Dolly O'Brien, who was a lot older. He had some kind of mother fixation, and although I was younger, that's probably what I represented to him.

We have an awful macho thing in this country and he was cursed by it. People kept reminding him that this was what he had to do. He happened to be an actor, a damned good one, and nobody knew it— least of all Clark. Oh, he wanted to be an actor, but he always deprecated his ability, pretending that it didn't matter. He was really a shy man with a terrible inferiority in him somewhere. Something was missing that kept him from doing the things he could have done. In *Test Pilot*, he had a moment when he talked about the girl in the blue dress—the sky. That scene terrified him, scared him to death. He got

IGHT: The uncomfortable creature anging on for dear life (far left) is Myrna Williams, who made her Im debut as part of this "human handelier" in *Pretty Ladies*, 1925. ELOW: The nominal star of I-G-M's *Pretty Ladies* was ZaSu itts (center), but the first and econd "snowdrops" in the front row, ucille Le Sueur and Myrna Villiams, would later reign at the ewly established studio as Joan rawford and Myrna Loy.

LEFT: Monte Blue was a top star at Warner Brothers when he made *Bitt Apples* with this buoyant newcomer 1926. BELOW: Myrna's first talking sequences were shared with Conrad Nagel in Warners' *State Street Sadie* 1928. BOTTOM: That same year she cavorted silently with Victor McLag and Robert Armstrong in Howard Hawks' *A Girl in Every Port* at Fox. OPPOSITE ABOVE: Warners' art department must have worked overti to create this evocative Burmese background for its resident native gir and Lowell Sherman, her prey, in *Evidence*, 1929. OPPOSITE BELOW Azuri, the native dancing girl, Myrn tried to seduce a large portion of the Foreign Legion in *The Desert Song*, Hollywood's first "all talking, all singing, all dancing" operetta.

ABOVE: Alexander Korda directed Myrna as an oversexed gypsy in *The Squall*, 1929.
OPPOSITE: Myrna depicted characters of decidedly mixed origins in John Ford's
The Black Watch, with Victor McLaglen (above), and Victor Fleming's *Renegades*,
with Warner Baxter (below), both in 1929.

In the early thirties, *Devil to Pay* with Ronald Colman (above) and *The Animal Kingdom* with Leslie Howard (left) led Myrna out of the Orient and into the more suitable drawing room.

rna matches profiles with
bert Roland in *The Woman
Room 13*, 1930.

She works her wiles, as Morgan
le Fay, on Will Rogers in
A Connecticut Yankee, 1931.

rna comforts her pilot
band, William Gargan, in
ht Flight, 1933, her
official billing as a star
M-G-M.

ABOVE: When Jeanette MacDonald stole Myrna's costume in *Love Me Tonight*, Myrna retaliated with contrasting black and stole the scene. MacDonald "got Chevalier," says Joseph L. Mankiewicz, "but Myrna got the picture." LEFT: In *Thirteen Women* she returned to exotica with a vengeance, playing a Javanese-Indian half-caste who murders ten schoolmates. Only Irene Dunne, pictured with her, escaped her wrath. OPPOSITE ABOVE: John Barrymore was intrigued by the sophisticated Loy in *Topaze*, 1933. (The doorman is silent screen idol and pioneer director King Baggott, reduced to playing bit parts.) OPPOSITE BELOW: Myrna was moved by the imprisoned Gable in 1934's *Manhattan Melodrama*.

ABOVE: In *The Barbarian*, Ramon Novarro carried Myrna off into the desert. This time *he* was the native! LEFT: The movies' most popular trio: Nick and Nora Charles (as played by Powell and Loy) and their irascible pet, Asta, in *After the Thin Man*, 1936. OPPOSITE: After a brief return to exotica as Fräulein Doktor in *Stamboul Quest* with George Brent and Lionel Atwill (top), it was clear sailing… or flying, as she did with Cary Grant in *Wings in the Dark* (middle)…or fishing, as she did with Bill Powell and Walter Connolly in *Libeled Lady* (bottom).

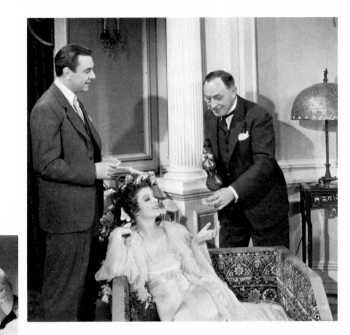

LEFT: Loy and Spencer Tracy
matched their brand of understat[ed]
intensity frame for frame as they
watched Clark Gable take a peril[ous]
flight in *Test Pilot*, 1938. BELOW
That same year, Gable and Loy w[ere]
reunited by popular demand in *T[oo]*
Hot to Handle: she as an aviatrix [he]
rescues after he causes the crash [of]
his newsreel truck. OPPOSITE: R[obert]
Taylor does not look very menac[ing]
wielding his pillow in *Lucky Nig[ht]*
(above), but Myrna packs a wallo[p]
with a canvas in *Double Wedding*
(below)—artist Bill Powell's portr[ait]
obviously displeased her.

In 1939, Myrna won the coveted role of the dissolute Lady Esketh in *The Rains Came*, with George Brent as a former lover (above) and Tyrone Power as the innocent Indian doctor whose love redeems her on her deathbed (below). OPPOSITE ABOVE: The Charleses chose to ride in the baggage car in *The Thin Man Goes Home* rather than be separated from their pesky wirehaired terrier, Asta. Made in 1944, this was the fourth of the six popular *Thin Man* films. OPPOSITE BELOW: *The Best Years of Our Lives*, produced by Samuel Goldwyn in 1946, defined the postwar generation and became one of the most honored films of all time. Fredric March co-starred, with Harold Russell and Hoagy Carmichael, visible at the piano in the background, lending solid support.

LEFT: 1960—The alcoholic mother of Paul Newman in *From the Terrace*. BELOW: 1979—Th long-suffering but smitten secretary of ruthless tycoon Alan King in *Just Tell Me What You Wan* BOTTOM: 1950—The working mother of twelve opposite Clifton Webb in *Cheaper by the Dozen*.

so upset when we shot it I had to keep reassuring, comforting him. Not that he couldn't do the scene—he did it beautifully—but he was afraid it would make him appear too soft. He had this macho thing strapped on him and he couldn't get out of it.

Clark never again challenged his public after *Parnell*; even Rhett Butler was an extension of the kind of character everybody expected from him. He finally believed that was all he could do, and maintaining that macho image plagued him to the end. It finally killed him, roping and being dragged around by all those horses in *The Misfits* when he was way past the age for doing such things. You know the only thing that bothered us about Clark playing *Parnell?* The fact that nobody would believe he could die of a heart attack in the role. Ironically, that's just what happened in real life.

During my early years in the studios, movie people were too busy getting a foothold to concern themselves with social conscience. I once asked, "Why does every Negro in a film have to play a servant? How about just a black person walking up the steps of a courthouse carrying a briefcase?" Well! The storm *that* caused! That was in the early 1930s. But later in the decade Hollywood began to acknowledge the rest of the world, mainly through the political efforts of transplanted New Yorkers. The Motion Picture Artists Committee, with Dash Hammett as chairman, brought Ernest Hemingway out to raise money for the Spanish Loyalists. Hemingway spoke and showed the stirring anti-Fascist documentary he wrote and narrated, *The Spanish Earth*, which financed eighteen ambulances and numerous medical supplies. Many actors put their names on ambulances, among them Bob Montgomery, who was afraid he'd never live it down when he became an Eisenhower Republican. I don't know what happened. He'd always been so faithful to F.D.R. I used to tease Bob about his defection: "You look more like a Republican every day."

Hemingway was pretty much the king, enjoying himself thoroughly as everybody bowed and scraped and gave him money. He came soliciting on the set while Bill Powell and I were shooting *Double Wedding*; but he was more interested in booze than contributions. Bill got a bottle and Hemingway stayed around all afternoon. We had a picture to make, but he and Bill had a wonderful time getting roaring drunk. Hemingway was traveling with Martha Gellhorn, whom he later married. She impressed me as a woman of substance then and later when I saw more of her in Italy. The great man, however, usually in his cups, boisterous and self-important, struck me as rather a washout.

Admittedly, I wasn't at my best during *Double Wedding*. It had more slapstick than most of my comedies and seemed hell to make. We spent three weeks shooting in a trailer with two sides knocked off and dozens of people jammed in and around it. I hated that picture, although I may never have seen it. Perhaps it became the scapegoat for concurrent despair; during the filming, Jean Harlow died, leaving Bill and me absolutely devastated. Oh, it was horrible, an awful blow; I loved Jean, deeply. I felt a sickening mixture of grief, guilt, and frustration because I hadn't been able to do what might have saved her: get her away from her mother for an examination. I hold that woman responsible for Jean's death. With proper treatment, the cerebral edema that killed her would never have developed in a twenty-six-year-old girl.

Bill and I tried to carry on with this slapstick comedy, but he collapsed and the picture kept being delayed. He blamed himself for Jean's death: he had loved her but hadn't married her and taken her away from her mother. He'd call me for comfort when he got low. One day he phoned, moaning, "This is a good throat-cutting day." I put on my hat and ran, but he was over it by the time I arrived. "It was an Irish funk," he explained. "It's just the Irish in me."

Man-Proof was lighter going. We had a wonderful cast and I had an unusual part featuring a terrific drunk scene—everyone said it was, anyway. Walter Pidgeon, who played the man between Roz Russell and me, was always a delight. Pidge and I managed to work together once or twice a decade over a forty-year span. And that was the only time I worked with Franchot Tone, an attractive man, whom I never got to know very well, unfortunately. He and Joan Crawford were married at the time and things weren't going well for them. I remember him sleeping a lot on the set. He was always asleep.

Roz was her exuberant self—lively and full of fun. We became friends during that picture, despite all the studio nonsense about pitting her against me. She lived down a hill from me and gave very entertaining parties, during which she invariably joked about getting my rejects. "Those scripts," she'd say, "they all have your name scratched out on the cover. You wait until dark, shove 'em out of your house, and they roll down the hill and hit my front door. That's the way they're cast. I'd like to send you around the world to get rid of you." When Arthur and I were in Scandinavia, I sent her a card: "Well, you've succeeded. I'm halfway around the world." I'm sure there were several roles I played that Roz would have liked. They seldom used her very well at Metro; they missed things sometimes. It was difficult to tell what people were going to accomplish. Although my rejects occasionally brought her better roles, she didn't really get her big opportunities there. She *certainly* did all right afterward!

Test Pilot, one of M-G-M's blockbusters, is a personal favorite of mine. It really stands as an example of what big-studio filmmaking could be: the writing, the directing, the photography, the technical expertise, the casting of that impeccable stock company. Imagine playing opposite Clark Gable, Spencer Tracy, and Lionel Barrymore in one picture! What actress wouldn't look good? I adored Lionel, but unfortunately we just had a couple of brief scenes together and a wonderful telephone conversation that we each filmed separately. His injured leg bothered him, so his scenes were written for a seated position. He seemed cheerful nevertheless, and understandably so, since we all pampered him outrageously—particularly Clark and Spence, who both held Lionel in great esteem.

With Clark, as I've said, I played a tough, independent woman. He always tried to put me on the spot when people were watching. There was a constant one-upmanship, despite our gentle poetry sessions, and I was usually a bit feisty with him. Metro's writers sensed this and wrote our pictures accordingly. That was fine with me—it gave my parts a little more variety. In *Test Pilot*, we have that marvelous scene on the porch where I breezily seduce him without so much as brushing hands.

Spencer Tracy and I always played well together. We had the same technique. At the time, I didn't know it, of course; one didn't ponder such things then. We didn't intellectualize. But later on, analyzing what we did, I came to realize that it was true of Spence and me. He was a perfectionist, aware of everything he did with a part. Those seemingly relaxed, easygoing performances were carefully thought out, structured creations. He was always so afraid he'd go too far; he knew you had to measure your distance in films. That's one of the reasons he was so good.

When he made retakes, he wouldn't let me leave. "No, no, you wait," he'd say. "You've got to tell me how I'm doing." He'd do the scene and rush back to me: "Did I ham it up? Did I do too much?"

Sometimes I'd say "Yes," although it wasn't true, just because he seemed to want that challenge. Or perhaps I was responding to his vulnerability, for he had a lot of that in him and it was hard to resist. So he'd do the scene over again. Of course, it would be just the same, marvelous, but I'd say, "That one's O.K., that's all right." And he would believe me. He never caught on. I could do no wrong as far as Spence was concerned.

Spence and Clark weren't great pals off the set, but they liked each other and worked well together. They had a lively exchange, which actually very seldom went on with many people during filming. We all had nicknames on the set: Clark, as I've said, called me "Queenie"; he was "the King," Spence "the Iron Duke," and Victor Fleming, our director, "the Monk" for some reason I've long forgotten. Of course, Clark sort of envied Spence's acting reputation, while Spence coveted Clark's standing with the public and the studio, so their raillery had an edge to it. After our would-be coronation, Spence would hail Clark as "Your Majesty"; Clark would call Spence a Wisconsin ham, and Spence would counter with "What about Parnell?" It was just macho against macho, but it got a little out of hand when we went on location to March Field, in Riverside.

After a morning of shooting exteriors around the airfield, we were having sort of a *gemütlich* lunch with some of the officers. They wanted to fly Clark, Spence, and Victor over to Catalina in one of the big Air Corps bombers we were using in the picture. I overheard Spence say, "Thank you very much, I don't want to go." I noticed that the fliers seemed to understand what he was about, but Gable and Fleming started in on him, ragging him for not going. You know how men are. They made all sorts of demeaning cracks, while Spence just sat there. It infuriated me, but not having heard the buildup I kept my mouth shut.

The minute the others left, Spence jumped up from the table, grabbed me, and out we went. "What's the matter?" I asked. "What's going on here?" He wouldn't answer. He just swept me across the field, rigidly gripping my arms, until we reached the car that drove us to and from Riverside. On the way back, he finally blurted it out: "Well, Goddamn it, you know what would happen if I went with them. When they get off that plane, the first thing they'll do is head for a bar. You know I can't do that." Then it dawned on me. He was afraid of going on a bender. He'd had a drinking problem for years; one drink could set him off. It was a real problem and he knew it, but he had the discipline to abstain during shooting. Between pictures, sometimes, he would just disappear for a spell, but not while he worked. Gable and Fleming didn't understand this; I mean, they refused to understand and had simply kept ragging him. Rather than risk a relapse, Spence had sat there in front of all those men and taken it. "You know I can't do that," he repeated in the car to Riverside, trembling with anger. I tried to comfort him: "Yes, darling, I know you can't do that, I know. Calm down, now. Quiet down." He was so mad I resolved then and there not to let him out of my sight.

We were staying at that funny old Riverside Inn, with its caverns and cataracts and musty charm. "Look, why don't we have an early dinner," I suggested, hoping to keep him out of harm's way. "Let's eat before the others get back." I alerted Shirley Hughes. They'd become friends when he used to call her all the time, trying to find me. He had stopped doing that by this time . . . well, to a certain extent; anyway, I wasn't having too much trouble with him. We just settled down to being good friends, but he did hang on to me and trust me. He knew I'd understand him.

We were finishing a very glum dinner when the prodigals returned. "Look at 'em!" Spence growled. "Didn't I tell you?" They had indeed gone to a bar and got clobbered. "All right," I said, "so what are you going to do now?" He answered ominously, "Well, I don't know." As we passed their table, Gable and Fleming were being relentlessly buoyant. I stopped to blast them, but Spence, after a very curt nod, bolted. When I ran after him, he had vanished. I called Shirley: "For God's sake, we've got to find him. We've got to get hold of him before anything happens." We combed every bar and watering hole in and around Riverside, but never found him.

He didn't show up for work the next morning. Everybody went crazy, assuming he'd gone on a bender. They couldn't replace him, you see, he was already so identified with the picture. We were stuck there on location unable to shoot without him while calls buzzed between March Field and M-G-M. "My God," Victor moaned to Benny Thau, "we've got a situation on our hands!" I thought, Yeah, you sure have, and you damn well deserve to have one, too.

A few minutes before noon, Spence strolled nonchalantly onto the set, bid everyone a jaunty good morning, and went to work. When

Gable and Fleming started threateningly toward him, I headed them off, took them aside, and gave 'em hell: "Haven't you clowns done enough? How dare you do a thing like that? You know he has to be careful. Where are your brains?" I really laid them out while Spence worked smugly on. To this day I don't know where he had been, but he'd let them suffer and taken his revenge.

Spence and I never worked together again, but we stayed friends. Occasionally the studio presumed upon that, thinking I could handle him when he gave them trouble. We both happened to be in New York when Benny Thau called from Hollywood: "Myrna, we're waiting to start Tracy's picture and he's there on a bender, holed up at the River House with his male nurse. See what you can do?" I called; Spence asked, "Where are you?" and I told him. I shouldn't have. He was at the door of my St. Regis suite in no time. Days of drinking had left him belligerent. He made his usual play for me, bringing his fist down with such emphatic frustration at one point that he smashed a glass-topped coffee table. Then he turned defensive. "You don't have to worry about me anymore," he said like a sulky child. "I've found the woman I want." As he outlined the virtues of Katharine Hepburn, I was relieved, but also a bit disappointed. As selfish as it sounds, I liked having a man like Spence in the background wanting me. It's rather nice when nothing's required in return.

Spence happened to be a decent but complex man, an independent spirit full of Irish-Catholic guilt. I had never thought of him as such a good Catholic, but apparently he was, because he would never divorce his wife. Years after he first told me about Katharine Hepburn, I saw him at the Beverly Hills Hotel, where he lived by himself. His home life was a mystery to me—if he had a home. Usually he didn't have one. I asked him: "Why don't you marry the girl?" And he said, "Well, because of Johnny." I knew his son Johnny. He was deaf, but always visited my sets because, according to Spence, my enunciation was so clear he could understand me.

"What do you mean 'because of Johnny'?" I snapped. "That's no excuse. Johnny's been married and divorced himself." But, of course, things were different then. We were still living in that chauvinistic world. And I don't think Kate, as he called her, wanted to marry anybody.

They put Clark and me right into another picture to capitalize on the success of *Test Pilot*. I played an aviatrix who, as the title implies, was *Too Hot to Handle*, but it wasn't much of a part, rather routine. It really was mostly Gable. He's wonderful, very comical, as the newsreel reporter who fakes stories. The whole thing was fun, though, and a bit hazardous. Clark supposedly saved my life on that picture. The script called for him to rescue me from a burning plane wreck after causing it. They turned on controlled fire from a valve behind the cameras, and Clark ran over to pull me out. He yells, "Come on, those gas tanks will blow any minute!" I counter, "What did you expect 'em to do, you clumsy jackass?" Supposedly, the controlled fire went wrong at this point, but Clark kept coming and yanked me out as the plane burst into flames. Ten seconds later, according to news reports, I might have burned to death. That incident received enormous coverage, but it could have been pure publicity. You do a lot of crazy things in pictures, but it all happens so fast and you're usually well protected. I don't recall feeling extreme heat or anything; I can't honestly say if Clark really saved me or not. Such was the power of Howard Strickling and the M-G-M publicity department.

World events dwarfed the rigors of picture-making in 1938. In fact, I felt sure that war was inevitable after England and France sacrificed Czechoslovakia to appease Hitler in Munich. It didn't take a genius to perceive this as another of Germany's steps to war; yet people preferred to believe Neville Chamberlain's naïve assurance that handing over the Sudetenland would ensure "peace in our time." Wasn't he aware that they'd given Hitler the military keystone of Central Europe? I'd read *Mein Kampf*—not too many others had, apparently. I kept saying, "Hitler's book outlines everything he's going to do, and, believe me, he's going to do it." Most people paid no attention. Arthur did, of course; he was astute politically. Generally speaking, however, apart from a kind of conversational concern, like discussing the weather, few cared to face this very real possibility of total war.

We used to lease a house in Malibu from Madeleine Carroll, one of our Hidden Valley visitors, a bright, accomplished woman, a great beauty, and a great gourmet. I still have wonderful recipes she gave me. We were down there with a houseful of guests the last week of September when they sold out Czechoslovakia. As I sat riveted to the radio trying to digest the aftermath of Munich, Jan Masaryk, Czech Minister at London, came on the air. It must have been four in the morning London time when he finally delivered his speech after a day of fruitless dealings with the British Cabinet. The quality of the man and the fate of the world were evident in that voice spanning the wires from London to Malibu. His country obviously meant everything to this man whose father had virtually democratized it and become its first President—a noble experiment destroyed by Munich. "This is the beginning of the end," he predicted; "the start of a terrible war." The pain and logic of his words motivated me to send a cable offering support and encouragement to this man I had never met.

Edward R. Murrow, who was then doing his powerful broadcasts from London, told me years later he had spent that fateful morning with Masaryk. They had returned to the Czech Embassy after his speech to make a soufflé or something, since Jan loved good food and preparing it always relaxed him. My wire was the first delivered that morning, according to Ed, before those of kings and presidents, heads of state.

A reply from London—addressed "Myrna Loy, Hollywood"—reached me two days later. It simply said: BLESS YOU. JAN MASARYK.

Picture-making persisted, a tiresome necessity in a chaotic world. A lame bit of whimsy called *Lucky Night* was co-written by Vincent Lawrence, who, strangely enough, did so well with *Test Pilot*. The studio thought it would be a good idea to team me with Robert Taylor, Metro's reigning heartthrob. Our first day on the set I played records, which we did sometimes to fill those endless waits between shots. In fact, Joan Crawford employed someone just to operate her phonograph. I was listening to some wonderful Cuban music when Robert Taylor approached: "Do you have to play that sexy stuff all the time? It's the dirtiest music I ever heard." That was my first day with him. I thought, Oh, brother!

He was a bit stuffy, but we got along all right—during the picture, that is; later on I didn't get along with him. He became one of the tattletales, one of the guys who named innocent names to the House Un-American Activities Committee in 1947. Come to think of it, he acted somewhat deviously on *Lucky Night*. He was engaged to Barbara Stanwyck, whom I always liked, but for some reason he tried to cook up a little triangle; he wanted her to think I was after him. Barbara's maid mentioned this to Theresa, who assured her that nothing could have been farther from the truth. I'm not sure Barbara believed her, because on the last day of shooting she came by in a limousine and whisked him off to be married.

Marlene Dietrich, Kay Francis, Tallulah Bankhead, Ina Claire, among others, campaigned for Lady Esketh in *The Rains Came*. For months Roz Russell kept telling me I'd be a fool to change my type for the part, freely admitting that she wanted it herself. I was surprised when Darryl Zanuck asked to borrow me for that role. He had never particularly respected my abilities, and I'd never really thought much of him—at least in the early days at Warners. I had no inkling then of his capacity for making powerful pictures like *Gentleman's Agreement*, *Pinky*, or *No Way Out*, and he certainly never foresaw my development. Of course, his background was writing, and story values were always the most important thing to him. Oh, he knew it was a good idea to have Betty Grable under contract, but he wasn't as concerned with finding vehicles to fit a particular star's personality as they were at M-G-M. He and his wife, Virginia, became friends of mine over the years—I would spend Sundays at their Malibu beach house—but he continued to irritate me professionally. The social life was usually very separate from everything else in Hollywood.

I'll never know why Darryl took things out on me. Perhaps he wanted to justify the fact that he'd fired me from Warners and I'd become a big success. Don't forget that. He wasn't lettin' me off the hook, I guess, because a quarter of the way through *The Rains Came*, he called me up to his office and started in on me. Questioning my interpretation, but never being specific, he offered no constructive alternatives. That's a terrible thing to do to an actress. "Oh, my God, what do you mean?" I groaned. "Let's get Clarence in here. He knows me." Darryl had also brought Clarence Brown over from Metro to direct the picture. "No," Darryl snapped. "I don't want Clarence in here." As his pointless harangue wore on, I started to leave. "Well," I asked from the door, "what do you want me to do?" He said: "Show up for work." That was it. He never made any sense, really. He may have been afraid Lady Esketh would turn out to be the vamp he'd written for me in *Across the Pacific* in 1926.

When I discussed it with Clarence, he said, "Forget it. Don't let him upset you." Louis Bromfield, who wrote the novel, used to spend those Santana weekends with us at the beach. I asked if he liked my interpretation of his character. "As far as I can tell, everything looks beautiful," he told me. "In fact, I think you're giving the best performance of your career." So I stuck to my guns.

Despite Darryl's machinations, it was a happy film. Nigel Bruce, who played my husband, was a darling man we called "Bunny." He and his wife were denizens of the English colony, which we dipped into quite a bit. Arthur, being half English, after all, enjoyed that crowd. So did I.

Maria Ouspenskaya played the Maharani. Oh, Maria was so dear, a tiny little thing, just a bag of bones but just beautiful. And such an accomplished woman! She had been with the Moscow Art Theatre in Russia, then played on Broadway and ran an acting school before coming to Hollywood. The first time I saw her, she was lost in the maze of lamps and cables outside the set. You can't believe what a jumble it is—hazards everywhere. And here this tiny creature stood, all done up in her costume for a test. "Oh, my gootness," she enthused, "iz such fun to be barefoot." Her exquisite little feet had only skimpy strings of pearls around them. "You have to watch out for nails and things," I warned, swooping her up and carrying her onto the set.

Clarence Brown and I worked together several times. He had a deft hand, and I had a lot of confidence in him. Darryl did his best to break that up, but it didn't work—we just went right on. "You know, people don't die with their eyes closed," Clarence suggested during my death scene. "Why don't you try dying with your eyes open. You've just got to hold your breath." I held my breath, staring at some fixed object until I began to see stars and everything started to blur and run together. I was turning a little blue when he finally called "Cut!" When you trust a director, you'll do anything for him.

I had another near-miss on that picture. They created an amazingly authentic Indian street on the old 20th Century-Fox back lot—which no longer exists; you have all these hotels and office buildings there now. Tyrone Power and I rode horseback down that street to a temple where the rains of the title started. I thought nothing of doing my own riding, having been raised on a horse, but when they let go with the rain my horse reared up, turned around, and headed back up the street. Further disoriented by all the stalls and hawkers and racket, he shot out of there hell-bent for the main part of the studio. As we raced past little roads between deserted sets, I still felt some control, but when we hit the cobblestone courtyard in front of the commissary, let me tell you, I've never been so scared in my life. If he'd dumped me there, it would have been all over. I lay very low, hanging on to the bridle and his mane. He darted toward the commissary, reached the steps, and, by God, stopped—just like that, as terrified as I was.

All these wranglers and so forth came running; you know, they were going to *save* me. In a pig's eye! Why I wasn't thrown I'll never know. Oh, was there a scandal afterward! The people who supplied those animals were usually trustworthy, but they'd run out of experienced horses and, without telling anybody, sent one that had never worked in films. Heads rolled over that blunder.

I went right on with my next scene, a romantic interlude with Tyrone Power in the temple. Poor Ty seemed more upset about my impromptu ride than I did. He was out of his mind because a wrangler had taken his horse to come after me, leaving him helpless to join the rescue attempt. Ty Power was one of the nicest human beings I've ever known, a really divine man, perceptive and thoughtful. That happened to be a bad time for me. There were problems at home, the beginnings of real trouble with Arthur. I felt my world falling to pieces around me. I never discussed it with Ty—I didn't know him that well then—but he sensed it and made it his business to cheer me up. When I came on the set one morning, he approached with a long-stemmed bird of paradise in a Coke bottle, bowing and making a grand gesture of presenting it to me. That typified the little things he would do. I'm sorry to report that we weren't lovers, but close to it. I loved him, but he was married to that damn Frenchwoman.

He had a very strong sense of other people, heightened by a kind of mysticism, a spiritual quality. You saw it in his deep, warm eyes. It seemed perfect casting when he played that sort of person in *The Razor's Edge*. That was Ty. He used to invent games for us to play on the set, just to keep my mind off other things. "If you weren't who you are," he asked, "what would you like to be?"

"I haven't the slightest idea," I replied. "Do you know what you'd like to be if you weren't Ty?"

He made a graceful sweeping gesture with his hands: "I would like to be the wind, so I could be light and free and be anywhere I want at any time. I could go all around the world and look in people's windows and share their joys and sorrows." When he died, that's all I could think of. I said to myself, "Well, all right, he's the wind."

I had three weeks between pictures that summer of 1939, so Arthur and I sailed for Europe. I hoped travel would ease the tensions between us, which to a certain extent it did. Arthur, as always, was at his best as a tour guide, even with forebodings of war. We found fear in Paris. The statues around the Place de la Concorde were draped in purple, dramatically protesting, as only the French can, Germany's usurpation of foreign territory. Yet when we flew to Sweden, the war I considered inevitable seemed curiously remote as an army of fans closed in. The M-G-M representative, fortified by roses and a fawning entourage, hustled me into the lounge, where dozens of reporters and photographers waited for a promised press conference. It seemed ludicrous with Hitler on the warpath, but there was no avoiding it if I wanted to get out of that airport in one piece. We had arrived during the Midsummer celebration. It rained on Midsummer Night, so everybody gathered in a great hall to drink frothy mumma and waltz to "Black Rudolph." It was a festive introduction to my grandfather's homeland.

We went over to Norway by train, hiring a car at Oslo to take us to the fjords—strips of sea cutting jagged cliffs, with cottages and little cherry trees perched on top. We drove way, way up into the mountains, shivering from the height and the chill air, until we reached an inn with fires blazing in huge open hearths and brandy served in warmed snifters. I remember going outside and finding brave little blossoms popping through the snow. We came down and took a boat across the fjords to Bergen. Oh, Lord, that's close to heaven. You could just hear Grieg's music in the hills. You expected to find trolls under every little bridge.

A hydroplane flew us to Amsterdam, where reality struck. An agitated Paramount representative met us: "You didn't go into Germany, did you?"

"No," Arthur told him, "we flew over it on our way to Sweden. Why?"

The representative turned to me: "Don't you know you're in Mr. Hitler's little black book? You're right at the top of his blacklist—he's banned your pictures." It seems that my wire to Masaryk had appeared in the London *Times*, and that, along with my support of an economic boycott of Nazi Germany and my outspoken defense of German Jews, had reached the Führer. Well, as far as I was concerned, my pictures damn well should be banned. Why should I be entertaining the Third Reich? The bigwigs of Loew's, Inc., M-G-M's parent company, saw it differently. I received a letter later on from Arthur Loew, the founder's son, who ran foreign distribution. The company's international greeter approached me on the set. "I've been carrying this letter around for a long time," he told me. "I just haven't had the nerve to give it to you. I still don't, but I must and you can tell me what to do with it."

The letter started out very nicely before making the point that I should beware of mixing my "politics" with my "career." I handed it back to that man, suggesting, "You know what you can do with this." He replied, "Yes, that's what I thought you'd say." Oh, Lord, this still makes me so mad I could spit. Here I was fighting for the Jews and they're telling me to lay off because there's still money to be made in Germany. Loew and many of the company's executives were Jewish, but they condoned this horror. I know it's incredible, but it happened.

We flew from Amsterdam to London. There was fear in London. They were piling sandbags in front of Claridge's, that's how close it was. But you wouldn't have known it when the *Normandie* reached New York in July. We had a large contingent of movie people on board, so several film reporters met the boat. I avoided them, but the others submitted to interviews about the movie business abroad. Whether from optimism or ignorance, the threat of war was never mentioned. Arthur reported that French pictures were gaining popularity in Scandinavia and threatening Hollywood's B product, but other matters were preoccupying my husband. Minna Wallis, who met the boat, always recalled a bit wryly the infinite care with which he supervised the unloading of the vintage wines we'd brought from Beaune.

Hal Wallis, Warners' executive producer, told reporters that they planned to produce twenty-six quota pictures a year in their British studio at Teddington. Herbert Wilcox, the British producer, would collect his star and future wife Anna Neagle in New York before immediately returning to Scotland to make *Bonnie Prince Charlie* for RKO. Elsa Lanchester, en route to join Charles Laughton in Hollywood, said they'd return to England early in October to appear in *The Admirable Crichton* for Paramount. Well, it all proved to be merely academic; six weeks later, American filmmaking in Europe virtually ceased. Germany invaded Poland on September 1, 1939, and Great Britain and France declared war two days later.

I returned to business as usual for the time being. The third *Thin Man* started shooting the day after we got back. I got there bright and early to greet Bill Powell, who was returning to work after a two-year bout with cancer. They'd cut it out and he survived it—and *how!* I called him a few years ago for his ninetieth birthday. He still seemed a bit frail when we started *Another Thin Man*, but he wasn't giving up a thing. They'd added Nick Charles, Jr., to the script, leaving Bill incredulous. "Why do we want this kid?" he groaned. "First thing you know, he'll be in kindergarten, then prep school, then college. How old will that make us?" Bill, only in his forties, was very conscious of aging. When I saw him in the hospital after his operation, it amazed me to find him with gray, almost white hair. I never knew he'd been dyeing it all those years. He really didn't like being seen that way, even by his screen wife. "There's a factory down here that gives off silver dust," he explained. "It blows through the window into my hair."

Another Thin Man was the last of the series to have an original story by Dashiell Hammett scripted by Frances Goodrich and Albert Hackett, that prolific husband-and-wife writing team. Do you know I never saw them at Metro? It's terrible, really, but unless they sent for the writers to get us out of a hole, we seldom saw them on the set. Apparently there weren't any problems, because I didn't meet the Hacketts until I moved to New York in the fifties. We became friends, I'm happy to say, and Albert facetiously explained one day why they didn't write the last three *Thin Man* pictures: "Finally I just threw up on my typewriter. I couldn't do it again; I couldn't write another one." Perhaps we all should have concurred; those last three never really touched the previous ones.

After finishing *Another Thin Man*, I visited Montana with Mother. Arthur made a point of coming to the train to see us off. There had been rumors of discord, not entirely unfounded, and he intended to dispel any hint of estrangement. I certainly wasn't leaving him then; I simply wanted to go home for the first time since we'd left after my father died. It turned out to be too much of a state visit for my liking. The studio planned to get some publicity out of it, so Larry Barbier, my protector, and a photographer came along. There were endless local interviews. The mayor and the Marlow Theater, the scene of my dancing début in 1917, gave formal receptions.

I managed to make time for friends and family and a visit to the ranch. Grandmother's orchard, Grandfather's split-log buildings were still intact, but everything seemed smaller, the distances greater. "Don't forget," Uncle Elmer explained, "your legs are longer now than they were then. Now you look down on the things you used to look up at."

Uncle Elmer, a wild young man and a delightful older one, always had an appropriate comment. Twenty years later, when they pulled *This Is Your Life* on me and brought him to Hollywood, he stole the show with his wonderful tales of old Montana days.

People seemed pretty much as I remembered them. Of course, at first they scrutinize every move you make, expecting to find horrible changes wrought by fame. It's wonderful when they tell you they can't find any and start trusting you again. When discussing past events, they never asked if I remembered this or that. They took it for granted that I would, and I usually did. Someone would mention that the wild roses I had loved were coming into bloom; someone else would bake my favorite cake. Nobody made a point of these things; they were accepted facts that time couldn't change.

I kept thinking of the Scandinavian people I'd seen living similar lives, now under Hitler's boot in one way or another. All those peaceful people living so contentedly—where were they now? Ours is such a good way of life, I thought; we should all be happy as kings, and we should be ready to fight like hell to keep it. I was a warmonger in those days.

I returned to Metro expecting to play the Roman senator's wife who beguiles Hannibal in *The Road to Rome*, a role I'd longed for. Joe Mankiewicz had scheduled it for production with Clark Gable as Hannibal. Bob Sherwood had adapted his play into one of the wittiest scripts I've ever read. I'll always love the scene where Hannibal shows her a great bunch of keys, saying in effect: "They are the keys to the cities I've conquered. What good are they now?" He wasn't depicted as a great war hero, but as an honest-to-God man who feels he's wasted his life. That was the trouble. It decried war and half the world was fighting. "If we should get involved in the war," Joe reasoned, "public morale will be largely in the hands of the entertainment industry." A script outlining the idiocy of war obviously lost its humor in 1940. We suspended production. I've always regretted that.

Instead, they gave me *I Love You Again*, with Bill Powell. While no *Road to Rome*, it turned out to be one of our best marital comedies, a clever script with a great piece of directing by Woody Van Dyke. Bill had some hilarious moments, including a Boy Scout hike filled with pratfalls and business that still makes me scream with laughter. He was back in top form after a bad, bad period following Jean's death and his bout with cancer. Diana Lewis, a petite Metro player, had entered the picture. He brought her to my house so I could have a look at her—not that it would have made any difference; he was mad about her. I gave a dinner party and asked mutual friends like Ronald Colman and Reggie Gardiner. "Mousie," as Bill called her, was adorable, pretty and charming, but twenty-six years younger than he. We were all properly skeptical, predicting that a marriage would never last. Well, it lasted for over forty years, until his death, and she was a wonderful wife to him.

Third Finger, Left Hand was a departure for me. In most of my pictures I complemented the male character, who usually carried the story. This often meant that my roles were subordinate, but that's the way I wanted it. The Bette Davis type of classic woman's role wasn't for me, nor was the Roz Russell female-executive routine, which is what I did in *Third Finger, Left Hand*. Melvyn Douglas helped me through that one. I adored him, as did Theresa, my maid—she liked Bill Powell, but Mel was her passion. He had a kind of warm attentiveness that people responded to. He was a great person, a tireless fighter for liberal causes. In fact, during that picture cries of "Communist" came from certain factions of the American Legion after Mel had been appointed a lieutenant colonel in the California National Guard. Don't think all the hysteria started with Joe McCarthy.

In 1940, we had Representative Martin Dies and his committee accusing people like Jimmy Cagney, Fredric March, and Humphrey Bogart of being Communists. These were all good, liberal-minded citizens who weighed the issues and fought for what they believed in. Because Mel and his wife, Helen Gahagan, contributed to the Spanish Loyalists and gave holiday feasts for the children of poor migrant workers, they were branded radicals by conservative elements. It's always good publicity, you understand, for these crusaders to attack Hollywood. I knew Mel and Helen very well in the old days, and supported her later when she opposed Nixon for Congress. We all fought the good fight together.

With the characteristic generosity of show people, everybody joined forces to battle an even greater evil. Long before Pearl Harbor, Hollywood rallied one thousand strong at the Coconut Grove to raise $15,000 for Franco-British War Relief. Merle Oberon, Claudette Colbert, Annabella, Maureen O'Sullivan, and I were among the cigarette girls, while Charles Laughton, Herbert Marshall, Laurence Olivier, Ronnie Colman, Ian Hunter, Charles Boyer, and Bill Powell formed an unlikely chorus line to belt "The Man on the Flying Trapeze." I sold peanuts with Cary Grant, Roz Russell, and Charles Boyer at a Buy-a-Bomber Benefit. Carole and Clark, Sam Goldwyn, Ty Power, and I broadcast for Greek War Relief, among countless broadcasts for countless worthy causes. Bill and I turned over our earnings from a Lux Radio Theater broadcast—$10,000—to the Red Cross. Hollywood's English colony banded together and sent a fully equipped ambulance to the British Red Cross every week. Bob Montgomery not only donated an ambulance but went over to England to drive it. The war was still "over there" but coming closer.

On June 14, 1940, the Germans entered Paris. Arthur and I were again at the Malibu beach house when the news came over the radio. Paris—it seemed impossible. . . . Soon after that disquieting development, Jerome Kern turned up with Kitty and Gilbert Miller. Jerry spied the piano that had stood there winter after winter in the fog, and sat down to play a song he and Oscar Hammerstein had just written. Gathered around that old wreck of an upright, recalling those bistro pianos you hear in Montmartre and on the Left Bank, we all began to cry as Jerry played "The Last Time I Saw Paris."

I left Arthur in November. It's the hardest thing I have ever had to do. I loved him—of all the men in my life he was the one—but I couldn't live with him. I left him five times and kept going back, which, believe me, is hardly my usual style. Having once made a decision, I not only stick to it but dismiss the alternatives from my mind. Self-recrimination is unproductive.

I walked away that first time never expecting to return, leaving the house and everything in it. We had quite an accumulation. Our wedding presents alone could have supplied several dealers; Hollywood people give elaborate gifts. "There's so much silver," Betty Black said, "the sideboards groan." Those things were very important to Arthur, and he considered them his gifts not ours. It didn't matter to me. I simply left it all for him and took a little furnished bungalow in the Hollywood hills.

It shattered me, walking out on a marriage that I thought would last forever. God knows we hadn't been impetuous; we'd courted and lived together four years beforehand. I was in a state of turmoil—no question about it—and the press didn't help. As quiet as you try to be about these things, they find out. Louella Parsons was doing a personal appearance in New York when news of our separation broke. To the delight of her audience, she actually stopped the show and dictated a bulletin for her column then and there. Imagine having your personal problems bandied about that way? The vicissitudes of my life with Arthur are still hard for me to discuss, because I have a stepson and his family who are precious to me. And, after all, he's Arthur's son.

I think most people who knew Arthur would say he just put you down. He put everybody down—friends, servants, colleagues. He became a very difficult man, fastidious to the point of mania. Everything had to be perfect. Well, that's generally true of most artists. It's true of me as far as work goes, but it isn't true in my private life. It became an obsession with him. One day, I saw him sticking little pieces of tape under the figurines on the mantel so the maid would place them exactly where he wanted them. After a while you get to the point where nothing's ever right; everything you do is put down. I guess I was a hard one to get down, but he finally succeeded.

Many of our friends were aware of this, but they didn't have to live with it. Collie Young never took him seriously; he just laughed at him. I always wished I had that gift. Billy Wilder could make a joke of Arthur's pretensions. When someone asked why I'd finally left, Billy said, "Well, she just got tired of watching him test the Burgundy for room temperature."

Intending to start divorce proceedings, I engaged an attorney, then took no further steps. Arthur wasn't letting go that easily. He courted me again while interrogating my friends about what I was doing and with whom. He plagued Natalie Visart after she returned from my cabin at Arrowhead. Poor Nat had an office next to his at Paramount, so whenever she came or went he'd come charging out to question her. She'd tell me about it later and we'd howl.

Four months after leaving him, I went back. He had sold our Hidden Valley house and moved to Cherokee Lane in Beverly Hills. Whatever his motives were for that transaction, I didn't care; it seemed as if we might make a fresh start there. Arthur made an effort in his way, doing the tour-guide bit again, taking me back to Mexico, where we always had wonderful times. In Mexico City, we stayed with friends on a hill near Diego Rivera's house, where barefooted maids brought water in earthen jugs. We drove along the dusty road to Taxco, where I slept in a hammock overlooking the sea. Clouds of wild flamingos still crossed the Acapulco sky; now it's built up with rich people, rich hotels.

Bill and I made two more films in rapid succession. *Love Crazy*, cashing in on the success of *I Love You Again*, had Bill pretending to be crazy so I wouldn't divorce him. He was hilarious, as usual, but my part wasn't much, really, just this stodgy woman who puts up with him. I don't recall much about *Shadow of the Thin Man* except that Bill's prediction about Nick Charles, Jr., came true. He was already off to military school. That turned out to be the last one of the series that Woody Van Dyke directed. He died in 1943, quite suddenly, leaving a great void as a friend and as a director. He seems to be neglected now, which puzzles me; he was one of Hollywood's best, most versatile directors. Perhaps that very versatility is the reason they haven't started honoring him yet. Critics and commentators, whoever makes those judgments, seem to go for genre directors—it's easier. But they'll get around to Woody one of these days.

Things were still pretty rough at home, so I went to New York to catch my breath, shall we say. Natalie Visart came along, in need of rest after nine months on De Mille's *Reap the Wild Wind*. She was the only designer in those days who dressed not only women but men and animals as well. I didn't have my studio protectors with me, which gave Nat a taste of traveling with a movie star. We were both fascinated by Fifth Avenue, with its shops arrayed for Christmas, but we'd stop to look in a window, Nat would turn to say something, and there would be a big head between us, gawking at me. We couldn't really walk anywhere without being mobbed, until we discovered that the streets were relatively clear at dinnertime. So every evening at seven we'd take our walk and do our window-shopping.

I decided to visit a plastic surgeon. David Selznick used to rag me about my ears, since women were wearing their hair swept up in Empire variations then. "Oh, Myrna," he'd say, "you'd look wonderful with your hair up, but you've got to fix those ears." I made an appointment as Marjorie Williams, thinking the doctor wouldn't recognize me. It seems incredible, I know, but I had very little ego at that time. After I explained the problem, he said, "Let's take some pictures and see what can be done." He photographed me from every conceivable angle: left side, right side, front and back, even getting up on a chair to shoot down at me. I thought he was being unusually thorough. "Well," he disclosed finally, "I've got your nose, Miss Loy." That son of a gun knew me all along, and intended to make a fortune on it. "I get so many requests for a 'Myrna Loy nose' these pictures will be invaluable to me," he explained. "So I really shouldn't charge you to fix your ears." I laughed and told him I'd think it over, but never went back. More urgent matters intervened.

The next afternoon, Sunday, I was spending with my stepson, Terry, when his mother called. "My God!" she declared. "We've been attacked!" That's how I heard about Pearl Harbor. Bill Sacks, my friend and lawyer, had planned to take us out that evening. We didn't much feel like a night on the town after the day's events, but we went anyway. New Yorkers were going mad in the clubs and in the streets. Somewhere along the line, we ran into the Robert Youngs and stayed up all night. Everybody was in such an emotional state, horrified, resembling macabre New Year's Eve revelers. We planned to see the Youngs again the following evening, but I became overwrought, worried about Arthur and my family on the vulnerable West Coast. "I can't possibly come," I told Bob. "I have to go back."

When we landed in Burbank, you couldn't see the airport. Thanks to Hollywood ingenuity, they'd completely camouflaged it in the short time since Pearl Harbor. The studios had donated their experts and equipment to turn the airport into a nondescript mass of greens and yellows. Arthur met me there, brimming with news. He'd become an air-raid warden and the house was cluttered with tin hats, sand buckets, the paraphernalia of his new calling. Right above us on the hill perched an anti-aircraft artillery, manned by boys from Brooklyn. They kept complaining, "We're freezing to death in California," so I sent a stove to keep them warm. It seemed incredible. Our world had changed in forty-eight hours.

Everything went into gear very fast. Everybody was doing something—*everybody*. Hollywood abounded with spirit, titles, and organizations. Clark Gable asked me to serve in the Screen Actors Division of the Hollywood Victory Committee, coordinating talent for hospital tours, bond rallies, and camp shows. Clark chaired our division of fifteen, and at the first meeting, December 22, 1941, Carole was first to stand and pledge proud support to her husband. No one could have imagined that three weeks later, returning from a bond-selling rally, Carole would die in a plane crash. Bill Powell, her first husband, Spence, and I were Clark's only fellow Metro actors invited to the small private funeral. Clark, beyond consolation, would talk only to Fieldsie, Carole's great friend and manager, Madalynne Fields. He wouldn't talk to anyone else, no matter who it was.

Losing Carole, in a sense Hollywood's first casualty of the war, devastated all of us and strengthened our will to participate. I got into uniform for the Hollywood Chapter of Bundles for Bluejackets, helping to run the Naval Auxiliary Canteen at Long Beach, sharing the night shift with Kay Francis. Kay was part of a group of friends from Arthur's first marriage that sort of stuck with him after I came in. Edmund Lowe and George Fitzmaurice were others. They were a sophisticated bunch, Kay most of all. She was a little ahead of her time, using four-letter words that shocked me terribly; but I liked her. We shared a reality beyond titles and organizations at Long Beach, handing out coffee and doughnuts and whatever reassurance we could to draftees bound for Hawaii. We saw untrained kids inducted, all so young and bewildered, an endless stream totally unprepared for war. It broke our hearts.

"We're on yellow alert," our military adviser warned one night. "Get ready to close up shop and be out of here by eleven." Which we did pronto. Since a Japanese submarine had recently shelled an oil field near Santa Barbara, everyone overreacted at the slightest provocation. Kay and I, bordering on hysteria, were trying to drive home when we passed what is now Los Angeles International Airport. Then it served as a private landing field for Howard Hughes and other fliers. This night— I will never forget it—there were dozens of planes lined up ominously in the dark with their propellers just turning, waiting for something to happen.

I barely reached home before all hell broke loose. It sounded like the end of the world. When I peeked from behind the tightly drawn curtains, the boys from Brooklyn were firing. Artillery fire, flares, and spotlights crisscrossed the sky. Arthur, who'd been asleep, came running downstairs in a panic. When I got through to my family, Mother was in hysterics. "Take it easy," I said. "We're all right." Which turned out to be true. We had experienced the famous false air raid of 1942 that no one has ever really explained.

During those months after Pearl Harbor, I devoted myself to war work and the ever-diminishing possibility of preserving my marriage.

There was nothing ready for me at the studio—nothing but froth, at any rate—and I wasn't in the mood for froth. That happens sometimes. You work like a dog for months at a time and then there won't be anything for a while. It took a long time to prepare a picture for production.

I still went out to the studio to shoot promotional reels for War Bond drives or Bundles for Britain, both of which I was very much involved in. Lionel Barrymore and I were working late one night on a pitch for some worthy cause when he said, "Jack's out in the car; I'm sure he'd like to see you. Why don't you go out and say hello?" *God!* I went out and he didn't know me from a hole in the ground. It was awful. The legend I had first seen striding down the corridor at Warners sat gray and crumpled in the back seat of a limousine, obviously long gone by that time. What do they say about alcohol being an insult to the brain? Two months later he was dead.

I was pretty much of a wreck myself then. It became obvious to me that Arthur could never change, whether he wanted to or not. He feared that if everything and everyone around him wasn't perfect it would reflect on him, make him seem less than perfect. I don't know if there's a psychiatric term for that phobia, but there should be. Arthur eventually realized that to a degree. "He's finally seeing an analyst," Collier Young told me after I'd left, "but he won't lie down; he's walking around."

Perhaps I should have kicked him in the teeth a couple of times, instead of trying to be the perfect wife he wanted. It's curious that I never married men like my father. My husbands tended to be rather overbearing, manipulative, more like Mother, and I always yielded to them. Arthur's demands were unattainable. His son, Terry, was expected to win everything, always to be the best. Arthur once pitted him against Bernie, the son of our laundress, in a race. When Bernie won, Arthur raised hell with Terry, absolutely tormented him. He became a tyrant, foisting his distorted sense of perfection on us. You shouldn't do that to people. It just isn't that important. It certainly isn't important enough to destroy someone. It almost destroyed me, because I went through it myself and then saw it happening to my stepson.

It's a difficult thing when you realize you don't like one of your parents, discloses Arthur's son Terry, now Dr. John T. Hornblow of Farmington, Connecticut, and Watch Hill, Rhode Island. *That's not easy to talk about. I tried very hard to establish a relationship with him, but every attempt was met with a rebuff. He just really didn't want to have a child, and yet, curiously, he compensated by being punctilious, paying the bills, writing the necessary letters, doing everything a parent should do except the one vital thing: relating to the child and allowing the child to relate to him. He never touched me physically except an occasional shaking of hands when I arrived or left. When we met, it was as though by appointment. Everything was programmed. During the time that Myrna was married to him, she succeeded in softening some of those lines. She would take me to the studio sometimes and do all sorts of spontaneous things with me, cutting to some extent his coldness with her warmth.*

He could sit behind his desk and slash and cut with his tongue better than anyone I've ever known—and without raising his voice. Someone should play him; he was very good. He could instill in a vulnerable individual, be it a child, a woman, or an employee—he could instill terror. I'm not overstating that. On one occasion, the terror was so completely disabling that I wet my pants.

The things that made him angry with me—or with Myrna, for that matter—were unpredictable. Once he'd ordered Swiss chard for a luncheon at Hidden Valley, but none was served. "Where's the Swiss chard?" he demanded. Myrna told him there was none at the market. "I know there is some," he insisted, berating her in front of the guests. He stopped the luncheon right there, sent everyone back to the living room for more drinks, and went out after Swiss chard. When it had been procured and properly prepared, luncheon resumed. Nobody could have been very hungry.

Another time, after I'd accumulated enough black marks in the book he kept to record my daily transgressions, he decreed that no one in the house should speak to me for a week. One day, Myrna passed me in the hall, started to say something, but caught herself in time. I actually recall a look of fear coming into her eyes. She turned up that exquisite nose and continued on her way. It probably was as hard for her, that punishment, as it was for me. But I think she felt the terror, too.

Just before I left Arthur for the last time, John Hertz, Jr., came to a dinner party at our house. He was a New York advertising executive, the son of one of America's richest men, bright, appealing, and extremely attentive. During dinner, he took my hands in his. "You're the beloved of millions," he told me, "but your hands are cold and sweaty." Arthur had driven me to this point, no question about it. I was a wreck, nervous and obviously vulnerable. John started working on that immediately. It didn't occur to me that I might be leaping from the frying pan into the fire.

7

THE EXPATRIATE

1942-1947

Though the fact may disappoint members of other fan clubs, the President's favorite actress was Myrna Loy. He plied Hollywood visitors with questions about her, wanted very much to meet her, and to his great regret, when she at last came to the White House for a March of Dimes celebration, he was out of the country at an overseas conference. "Well," he asked when he returned, "what was she like?"

—GRACE TULLY, F.D.R., My Boss, 1949

ow a year is nothing, it seems, but time in those days didn't go so fast. You seemed to get in quite a lot of living between one year and the next. In March of 1942, after finally telling Arthur that I wasn't coming back, I headed East on a Navy Relief fund-raising tour. He dutifully saw me aboard the Super Chief expecting me to relent, but this time I meant it. My nerves, my general health depended on it.

John Garfield, Janet Gaynor, Loretta Young, and I rallied in New York to promote a big Navy Relief show that Walter Winchell had arranged. Walter herded us to the Stork Club, where Sherman Billingsley participated in publicity for the Madison Square Garden extravaganza. My first live appearance before such a huge audience succeeded, thanks to a bright routine written by Georgie Jessel; but the show's highlight was Ty Power's recitation of lines by Stephen Vincent Benét challenging the appeasers and calling for unity between America, Britain, China, and the Soviet Union. Patriotism ran high and that event alone raised hundreds of thousands for the cause.

While tabloids exploited my latest separation from Arthur, I ran into his first wife, Juliette, near St. Patrick's one afternoon. "What have you done to my son?" she asked. "He's been in his room crying for three days. He thinks he's lost you." I rushed home and called him: "This thing doesn't make any difference between us. It doesn't mean that we won't be friends." It didn't, thanks to Juliette's unfailing generosity over the years. "You amaze me," I told her when we became closer toward the end of her life, "sharing your son all this time. Why did you do it?"

"When you were married to Arthur," she explained, "I wanted Terry to have a friend at court, but he became so fond of you that I didn't want him to lose you just because of a divorce." Juliette's willingness to share him has enriched my life immeasurably.

During my three weeks of fund-raising in New York, John Hertz, Jr., started a barrage of flowers, phone calls, and invitations—the full assault. He was crafty. Aware that my situation with Arthur had left me pretty much of a wreck, he continued to play on it as he had when we met in Hollywood. I didn't know it then, but he'd had ample exposure to psychiatrists and analysts. Susceptible but hardly ready to commit myself, I returned to Hollywood expecting to start a new *Thin Man* picture. I took a small apartment, again leaving the house and its furnishings to Arthur, intending to start preliminary divorce proceedings. When the picture was delayed, however, I decided to get a quick divorce in Reno.

It's a miserable business—all that cut-and-dried legality to end a relationship that had been so deep and all-important. During the time required to establish residence there, I cried a lot, reflected, withstood any second thoughts, and found myself depending more and more on the continuing long-distance barrage from John. After receiving my final decree, I brushed back a recalcitrant tear, pushed past persistent reporters, and made the two-ten plane for New York.

Six days later, in his sister's house on East Sixty-second Street, I impulsively married John Hertz, Jr.

After years of being put down by Arthur, I had been disarmed by John's relentless understanding and whirlwind pursuit. A bit younger than I, he was bright, appreciative, and insistent, a bachelor-about-town who squired débutantes and celebrities to the haunts of fashionable New Yorkers. I remember him telling about a date with Paulette Goddard, when he presumptuously inquired about her early life. "Wasn't your first husband a gambler?" he asked. "Didn't he play the boats, with you as sort of a shill?"

"Oh, no," she told him, "he was just a kind of Robin Hood, taking money from the rich and giving it to me." Which I loved—it's so typical of Polly's forthright, unaffected humor.

So John was a member in good standing of what they called café society in those days. It's the "jet set" now, but still includes all those rich people whose shenanigans fill the columns. John's father, one of the richest, was another embodiment of the Horatio Alger story. Brought to America from Austria at the age of four, he left home at twelve, drove delivery wagons, worked as a copyboy on the Chicago *Daily News*, became a sports reporter, a fight promoter, and a motorcar salesman, utilizing his trade-ins as taxis. After establishing the Yellow Cab and Fifth Avenue Coach Companies, he merged with General Motors, acquiring the first of his many millions while still a young man. Canny ventures and investments continued to build his fortune and his prestige; even his stables turned a profit with such proud names as Reigh Count, winner of the Kentucky Derby and the Coronation Cup. They named a filly after me later on, but she never won anything.

John, who dwelt, understandably, in his father's shadow, didn't have to. As executive vice-president of Buchanan & Co., he had achieved success and respect in the advertising world. But in his mind his father's accomplishments always dwarfed his own. He admired and resented him. Mr. Hertz loved and challenged his only son. Constantly at odds, they were not even speaking at the time of our wedding. His father didn't understand that John's resentment and often violent reactions had a psychological base. Neither did I at first, when they extended to my own career. His aversion to my working delighted me; I was tired of work by that time.

Filmmaking was important to me, but I wanted to live, too. I didn't gear my life to whether I was making a movie or not—the war had made other things far more essential. My M-G-M contract had four years to run, but nothing the studio offered seemed tempting. Nick Schenck, furious at me for not working, said, "She's just fiddling around in New York." For God's sake, I was married. They all had to accept the fact. My box-office standing was still way up there, but I never realized that was so important. I didn't take it seriously enough, I guess. I can't even remember if they still kept me on salary—that's how little it meant to me at that point in my life. After struggling for twenty years to get to the top and stay there, I wanted to taste life, to see things and do things. My relationships were more important than my career. At that time, it was absurd for a woman to expect a marriage and a career to flourish simultaneously. Men were not conditioned to cope with this—

certainly not John. I decorated our apartment, a spacious duplex with enormous windows overlooking East Fifty-seventh Street, and assumed everything would be just dandy.

At first it was, enriched by the infinite possibilities of New York and the quality of my new husband's associations. That was when I met Jan Masaryk. Recalling my supportive cable after Czechoslovakia had been sacrificed to the Nazis at Munich, he approached a mutual friend of his and of John's sister Helen. "Take me over there," he demanded. "I want to see Myrna Loy." So they came over to our apartment and we had a wonderful evening—the beginning of one of my most cherished friendships.

Whenever Jan came to this country after that, he would call me or I would call him and we would spend at least a few hours together. He was usually involved in covert diplomatic negotiations to aid his occupied country, but he would arrive, warm and charming and generous, laden with flowers, a book or something for me, and presents he was taking on to somebody's children. When we settled down to tea and good talk, he was very gay, very cheerful on the surface, a witty conversationalist who made rich humor of his early marriage to a Crane plumbing heiress, played rolling Slovak folk songs on the piano, and cooked like a cordon bleu chef. He was cooking one night during the London blitz when a bomb jolted his building. "Uncivilized swine, the Germans!" he fumed. "They have ruined my soufflé." That was the way he hid pain—with a casual bon mot and his big smile, insisting that what he really loved was wine, women, and song. Underneath it all, however, was the serious, dedicated man who had set up an underground news service in Czechoslovakia before the Nazi invasion, then broadcast via the BBC to his beleaguered compatriots, giving them hope and assuring them of Allied support.

My main interest in those days was politics, so we would usually discuss world events during our visits. While amusing and delighting me, he always inspired me, too, with his enlightened and creative views. He talked about his father, a coachman's son who became Czechoslovakia's first President, and about his Brooklyn-born mother, whom I was scheduled to portray in a film that, regrettably, never reached the screen. He talked about his overriding dream to return his country after the war to the democracy his father had established. Jan was always a great dreamer, but he became a realist, as well. With the advent of Russia as our wartime ally, and the wincing memory of Munich, he considered the possibility of a democratic future for his country precarious. He nevertheless resisted cynicism by aiming for a greater goal; long before the war ended, he began working for world peace through the creation of a United Nations. "During the first effort, after the First World War, there was a tremendous outburst of idealism," he maintained, "and I was one of those whose heads were rather in the clouds and whose feet were not too definitely on the ground. This time it is essential to keep our feet on the ground, but also occasionally to look above the horizon and into the clouds." That, in short, was Jan Masaryk's philosophy of life.

Another extraordinary person came into my ken when John met with Mrs. Roosevelt to generate more aid for Greek War Relief. He brought me along for my first visit to the White House, a prospect that left me in a flurry of nervous excitement and euphoria. Not because of Mrs. Roosevelt, I'm afraid—not that first time, anyway—but because I absolutely idolized Franklin Delano Roosevelt—who, by the way, happened to be a fan of mine. He made no bones about it: I was his favorite movie star. My pictures were always shown at the White House. He even had one on board when he secretly met Winston Churchill at sea for their Atlantic Charter Conference, and supposedly the old boys sat around watching my picture after dinner. We carried on a correspondence all during the war. I'd send him telegrams whenever I approved of something he did, which was often, while he kept trying to get me down there for bond rallies or other fund-raising events, which previous commitments had precluded.

Unfortunately, the President was away during my first visit, but Mrs. Roosevelt was charming and helpful, pledging her support to Greece as she did to so many worthy causes throughout her life. Merely an observer that day, I never imagined that we would be drawn together by numerous other projects in years to come. She was so hospitable, excitedly introducing me all around and making me feel welcome. She left us in the Blue Room at one point, I remember, and returned with Frances Perkins, the Secretary of Labor. "Would you mind meeting Mrs. Perkins?" she asked, somewhat nervously, as Mrs. Perkins hovered in the background. "It would be an honor," I said. So we met and chatted, and she was charming.

"Wasn't it nice of Mrs. Roosevelt?" I said to John as we left the

White House. "I mean, taking Mrs. Perkins away from important things so that I could meet her."

"You're so naïve," he said. "Didn't you realize *she* wanted to meet *you?*"

Soon after this, when the Roosevelts were entertaining Queen Wilhelmina of the Netherlands at Hyde Park, they asked me to come out and repeat a sketch I'd done in John Golden's Army Emergency Relief show. Well, I was elated, thinking, At last I'm going to meet the President! Unfortunately, there was some trouble in paradise at my house. John came home very loaded one night and we got into a terrible fight. I don't know whether he hit me himself or hit me with something, but in any case I woke up the next morning with a terrible mouse under my eye. Reluctant to do so, but unprepared to face the Roosevelts with a black eye, I canceled my visit and forfeited the chance to meet the President. I didn't realize what a problem that caused until we dined at the Colony with Jimmy Roosevelt a week later.

This was about the time Jimmy married that nurse. She'd just been to Washington and started making cracks about his family, which I didn't like. But Jimmy was very, very attractive. He really had all the wonderful Roosevelt charm. "Well, what's my mother been up to now?" he asked during dinner. "The papers say you were supposed to do a sketch at Hyde Park, but Mother took your place playing a movie star who visits an Army camp and gets kissed by a soldier. They're all criticizing her for it, saying, 'Who does she think she is, Myrna Loy?' "

Later on, when I knew Mrs. Roosevelt better, I told her the reason for my cancelation. "Oh, what a terrible thing," she commiserated, and countered with a confession of her own. "Myrna," she added rather shyly, "I had to do what I did. I had to replace you because none of the young women were there—no young Roosevelts. The only other person who could have done the sketch was Queen Wilhelmina." Well, the two of us began to giggle at the thought of the formidable and decidedly overweight Queen of the Netherlands cavorting with the Army. We had the greatest time over that, which shows a side of Mrs. R. that people seldom saw. They always considered her so stiff, but she was not. My Lord, that woman had enormous humanity and humor, and, despite her vast knowledge, a wonderful kind of innocence, too. There were some things that her education had not covered. For instance, the recent nonsense about her being a lesbian. I'd like to have the woman who wrote that by the neck. For God's sake, Mrs. Roosevelt wouldn't even have known what the word means.

The black eye that kept me from going to Hyde Park was not an isolated event. It became increasingly obvious that I had married a rather neurotic person, shall we say. I had always been unnerved by the way his eyes changed, rapidly reflecting his moods, but his violent temper came as a shock. He had even been barred from "21" because of it; they wouldn't let him through the door despite his connections. He became extremely possessive. When we went to the Stork Club one night with Bill Powell, John accused me of having an affair with him. He was wildly jealous of Bill, of everyone. To a certain extent, he resented my career as he resented his father's success. He couldn't take the business of my being famous, which is one problem I never had with Arthur. John resented my participation in anything that didn't include him. I was willing to curtail my picture career in hopes of preserving our marriage, such as it was, but I would not eliminate what seemed to be vital war work.

Like so many others, I continued to participate in the entertainment industry's tireless contribution to the war effort. At Madison Square Garden, for instance, one of the greatest all-time shows raised $10 million in bonds, and $200,000 for Army Relief. Charles Laughton, Dorothy Lamour, Pat O'Brien, Paulette Goddard, Al Jolson, and fifty others performed; Mayor La Guardia conducted a joint concert of the Police and Fire Departments' bands; and I did a mock striptease before the audience of twenty-two thousand to stimulate bond sales. My hat brought $30,000, a pair of elbowless crimson gloves $25,000. As a climax to the huge rally, the Assistant Secretary of the Treasury announced that the motion-picture industry—stars, producers, exhibitors—had achieved its $775-million bond-selling quota for the Treasury's September drive.

There were countless such events, but as the war continued I wanted to make a more personal contribution. That opportunity came when the Red Cross asked me to set up entertainment programs for Eastern military hospitals and rest centers. It felt so wonderful to walk down the street all by myself without studio bodyguards and go into my office at the Red Cross. As Assistant to the Director of Military and Naval Welfare of the American Red Cross in the North Atlantic Area—try that on your tintype—I became liaison officer between show business and the various agencies that sent units to hospitals. We handled transportation, hospitality, guide service, and scheduling for visiting entertainers, as well as making visits ourselves. We had as many as ten companies entertaining servicemen in forty-two East Coast centers.

My first hospital visit was to Halloran, on Staten Island, where they were bringing back burn victims from Egypt all wrapped up in bandages with only bewildered eyes showing—if they were lucky. Oh, my God, it was awful! But I managed to get through it, with the brass who escorted me watching very carefully for signs of weakness. I learned about courage from those incredible young men; their positive attitude made you try harder. You had to be completely natural with them, and sometimes I didn't quite know how. When they joked about their injuries, you wanted to cry, but they wouldn't accept pity, nor would they allow you to pretend to ignore their injuries.

There was a gang at Bethesda Naval Hospital I would visit on holidays, when hardly anyone came near them. Lying there covered with plaster, while plastic ears set or patches healed where skin had been taken from their stomachs to fix their faces, they would shout: "Hey, Myrna, how about slippin' us some skin?" They were all so cheerful. The blind boys would hear my name, put their hands over my face, get hold of my nose, and say "Yup, that's her." I would have fun with them for a little while and then go to the ladies' room and cry.

After a while, I could take almost anything, even the psychiatric wards. Apparently I had something that made them trust me, which is what you must have with mental patients. They're just enveloped with fear. It would infuriate me when after a stretch on the wards I'd go to some fancy restaurant and hear a lot of well-dressed people bitching about the butter shortage or gasoline rationing.

Performers were wonderful about entertaining, and the patients were terrific audiences. They loved comedians like Jack Benny and Bob Hope, or singers like James Melton, who frequently entertained. I remember asking Frank Sinatra to go, and Frank, who was 4-F, saying yes. Has he got guts, I thought; a 4-F to go out there and go through all that. But he was willing to do it and they loved him. You could always count on Frank. All during the war, he did broadcasts and rallies for President Roosevelt. Frank used to be a good Democrat, a fighting liberal.

The biggest hit of all was Betty Grable, who agreed to visit Halloran during a brief stop in New York. When I picked her up at the hotel, she flopped limply into the car. "Have I got a hangover!" she groaned.

"Harry James and I were out on the town last night." A game gal, direct and unaffected, she tried to make polite conversation on the way to Halloran while obviously suffering. Finally, I stopped at a little road-house and made her take some beer to appease the gremlins.

Then we get up there, and she's a sensation. Can you imagine? This was the pinup girl of the Navy, the Army, and the Marine Corps. They were so thrilled, so excited—some of them shy, some of them forward—and she was absolutely terrific, which wasn't easy in her condition, par-ticularly since she hadn't been prepared for all that horror. Overcome at one point in the burn ward, she sat down on the edge of an empty bed, looking up at me like a little girl ashamed of being naughty. "That's all right," I said. "You can sit and rest." In the last ward, to cap the climax, we ran into a sexy, life-size model of Betty. The men had built it out of cardboard, with the emphasis, of course, on her famous legs. She was a little upset by it, a bit taken aback. Betty was sick and tired of her legs. All the so-called sexpots become aggravated by the preoc-cupation with their legs or whatever it is that's concentrated on. "Oh, no, don't be upset," I told her. "They love you. They're just happy to see you." So she stayed quite a while and bore the adulation, giving kisses and autographs, putting her lip-prints on plaster casts as the men moved joyfully around her, some on crutches, some legless in wheel-chairs, some excitedly clapping their good hands against their legs, in lieu of a hand that was gone. Once you had seen those men and talked with them, watched their faces light up and heard them call you by your first name, once you realized the amazing impact of your pres-ence—to them you were something of home, however little it might have been—you couldn't walk away.

I couldn't walk away from John, either, although I should have. His doctors had warned him that drink aggravated his precarious mental state, but he ignored them. He would go into rages during which my life was almost threatened. Once he hurled a Rodin sculpture at me— even at his worst, John always had great taste. During those spells, I would have to leave so he couldn't find me. No one, not even his sister Helen, who loved him and understood about him, went near him at these times. You just didn't know where you stood.

Helen was supportive and helpful to me during that period. No mat-ter how bad my marriages were, something good always came out of them. From Arthur, I have his son, Terry. From John, I have my enduring friendship with Helen, although we couldn't ostensibly see each other while he was alive. She's marvelous. In spite of the fact that she's always had lots of money, she's not in any way a snob; she doesn't have those kinds of friends, and she's not ruled by riches. One day, she turned up for lunch at the St. Regis carrying an old shopping bag. "What's in there?" I asked. "Oh," she said, "pearls, diamonds, emeralds—all my jewels. I'm taking them to be appraised." Recently she called me after I'd had some serious surgery. "Need any money?" she asked. "I'm so rich it's disgusting. I'm even making money on my horses."

During my troubles with John, Helen talked to a psychiatrist about it. "You'd better get her down here," the psychiatrist told her. So Helen took me in to talk about her brother. Well, that was the second good thing that came out of my marriage to John Hertz, Jr. I met Ruth Mack Brunswick, then considered the foremost analyst in America, who had worked with Freud for twenty-five years in Vienna. She was a wonderful woman, wonderful, one of the great psychiatrists. She even analyzed Karl Menninger. They all had to be analyzed before practicing.

She refused to see John, determining that he would not benefit from analysis but needed intensive psychiatric care. "My dear girl," she told me, "your husband is insane." But she took me on, twice a week for ten months, because she discerned a great anger in me, anger that I had repressed about Louis B. Mayer and M-G-M, about the responsibilities my father had burdened me with, and particularly about Arthur. It was very hard for me to get over Arthur and those years of being put down. I was on the verge of cracking up, because just too much had happened too fast.

I left John during that period, aware that he was beyond my help. Having deteriorated to a dangerous level, he became increasingly violent after I left, perpetrating some hair-raising incidents. My brother David, whom I had brought to New York to work for John's agency, was sort of stranded there with his wife, Lynn, after my hasty retreat. John took them on a reckless ride one night, went into a wild-eyed tirade about my departure, and scared the bejesus out of them. David and Lynn weren't sure if they would get home alive. They quickly followed me back to California. Later, when John's nurse didn't answer his bell promptly, he tried to shoot her, actually putting a shotgun blast through the bedroom door. Oh, yes, I escaped with my life—barely.

After three years, related William Powell, *the* Thin Man, *his perfect wife, and their pooch with personality took up where they left off, on Stage 9 at M-G-M. The reason for the lengthy layoff was that Myrna up and got herself married and moved to New York. The* Thin Man *pictures had always been big money-makers, and naturally the M-G-M boys were eager to keep them going. They announced new Noras, like Irene Dunne, from time to time— merely as a ploy, I suspect, to lure Myrna back—but every time such sacrilege appeared in the columns, there was an uproar. The studio was deluged with fan letters. The fans wanted Myrna, and they didn't want anyone else. I wanted Myrna, too. Besides the favorable reception our pictures always received, I must say it was certainly a pleasure to work with her. She's—well—compatible.*

When Myrna wired Mr. Mayer that she was ready to start business again at the old stand, I learned that she was arriving on the Chief, so I borrowed Asta for the day and rushed out to Pasadena to meet her. As she got off the train, I quickly told her that Asta and I had just arrived from Palm Springs and that I thought it was a hell of a nice gesture on her part to come three thousand miles to meet me. Myrna looked weary and a bit thin, I thought. "When the studio sees you," I said, "they'll change the title of our picture from The Thin Man Goes Home *to* The Thin Woman Comes Home." *Well, it was hot in Pasadena, and no one was listening except Asta.*

The first day of the picture, everybody wanted to hug and kiss Myrna. I've never seen a girl so popular with so many people. Everybody from wardrobe was over on the set, everybody from makeup, everybody from property, everybody from miles around, it looked like. There were big signs across the stage flamboyantly announcing, WELCOME HOME, MYRNA, *or* DON'T LEAVE US AGAIN, MYRNA, *and somebody pelted her with papier-mâché roses left over from* Maytime.

The second day, we got down to the business of bringing Nick and Nora to life again.

We missed Woody Van Dyke's certain inspiration on the fifth *Thin Man* picture. There were expressions of disappointment for a while, but we got over that. Richard Thorpe was a good director and it turned out to be a funny movie. Some of the sequences are hilarious, as I recall, although I haven't seen it for ages. The only thing I can remember is that wonderful sequence in the yard. Bill's lying in a hammock, and I come out and try to open this garden chair, which goes awry. "Oh, I'll help you," he offers, never moving a muscle. "Don't bother," I tell him; "you might get all sweaty and die." Dwight Taylor, who wrote the script with Harry Kurnitz, claims that I ad-libbed that line. I thought he wrote it. Anyway, it's a funny line.

When I first met Dwight at the studio, his looks really struck me. Oh, boy, was he a good-looking man. He was Laurette Taylor's son and had inherited a lot of her humor and style, as well, so I invited him to one of my parties. Having shed Hertz in Mexico, I was a bachelor girl again, occasionally dating men like Helmut Dantine and doing quite a bit of entertaining. M-G-M had rented a beautiful house for me facing the Bel-Air golf course. Life on the edge of a golf course was quite a show, with strange men skulking about my garden in search of lost golf balls. Clark Gable and Bob Montgomery, home on leave, were two of my more familiar trespassers; I told Clark I was going to set up a lemonade stand and make a fortune. Bing Crosby used to stroll in off the golf course to join my weekend gatherings. Arthur Schwartz or Hoagy Carmichael would be at the piano playing their songs, and Bing would sing along.

The night Dwight Taylor came to that house, he met my old friend Natalie Visart. She was very down after an unfortunate love affair, sort of dragging around, so I had insisted that she come. The first person she saw happened to be Dwight, and that was the beginning of that. "Myrna had her eye on him," Katie De Mille told her later, "but you certainly pushed right in." That wasn't strictly true. Of course I admired him and thought he was gorgeous to look at, but Gene Markey had entered the picture by then. He came to my house while on leave from the Navy. "I went looking for you after your divorce from Arthur," he claimed, "but you married John Hertz before I found you." So that was already brewing.

"You can have Dwight," I told Natalie, "but if you marry him, you've got to give me your blouse." I was mad about this blouse she'd made from a slendang, a Javanese sarong, while preparing costumes for *The Story of Dr. Wassell.* Its sort of chartreuse, yellow-green colors were perfect for me. The first time they came to dinner after their marriage, she walked in and handed it to me. We almost died laughing while Dwight and Gene stood there, utterly perplexed.

I returned to New York after finishing *The Thin Man Goes Home*, moved into the Waldorf Towers, and resumed my Red Cross work. It seemed essential as the war wound down to make sure that the entertainment and hospital tours, the morale-lifting would continue when the bands stopped playing. People were in a fervor of patriotism then, but later, when they were back to normal, the men on the so-called Purple Heart circuit would not be.

Visits to Bethesda and Walter Reed took me frequently to Washington, where another meeting with the President was proposed. Henry Morgenthau, Jr., Secretary of the Treasury, approached me during a reception at the Carlton, where I always stayed. "You're causing us a lot of trouble," he said. "The Old Man keeps asking us, 'What are you doing? Why do you keep her away from me?' So let's see if we can't get you over there this time. I'll tell you what you do. Tomorrow morning, put your hat on the dresser and I'll call for you." Well, he telephoned the next morning to say that the President had gone to Toronto for a meeting with Mackenzie King. That's how tight security was—even the Secretary of the Treasury didn't know he was going.

Soon after that, someone called from the White House and invited me to participate in the President's sixty-third birthday celebration. Each year, the President invited a contingent of movie people to the birthday balls given to raise money for the Infantile Paralysis Fund, becoming one of the first Presidents to involve us in White House activities. They hated to give me an invitation at the last minute, they said, but the President had particularly wanted me to fill in for Gary Cooper, a staunch Republican, who didn't want to come. Can you believe such a thing? He'd been invited and refused! George Murphy, another Republican, was part of that delegation, and I was very pleased with the way he handled himself. But Gary—I just don't believe he said that; some secretary probably said it for him, which happens sometimes. Anyway, it gave me the opportunity to be there.

Needless to say, I was thrilled at the prospect of finally meeting my hero. In fact, Dr. Brunswick was somewhat concerned. "Now don't be disappointed," she cautioned during one of our sessions. "Nobody could possibly live up to your ideal of him." I called John Harburger at John

Frederic's: "I'm going down to the White House to meet the President and I want something that will really knock him out." He made me the most wonderful hat out of white organdy to wear with a great black dress, and just before I left the Carlton for the White House he sent a big bunch of violets to complete the ensemble.

So over I went to the White House. Knowing my way around a little bit, I looked down toward the East Room, but he wasn't there. There was no sign of him or his chair. I walked down to the receptionist and there stood Mrs. Roosevelt. She looked at this glamour girl all done up and said, "Oh, my dear, my husband is going to be so distressed!" And I thought, Well, you're something! I fell in love with her then and there. What a terrific thing for her to say. Wartime security prevented her from telling me when or where he had gone, but later it came out that he had been on his way to meet Churchill and Stalin at Yalta.

Of course I was terribly disappointed to miss him again, but Mrs. Roosevelt was wonderful. She did a very sweet thing that first day, taking some of the Hollywood contingent—Joe E. Brown, Gene Kelly, Jane Wyman, Danny Kaye, Alan Ladd, Veronica Lake, Victor Borge—on a tour of the White House. She took us into the President's private study above the Oval Office, where he kept his memorabilia, all the little gifts that people sent him. Aware of my interest, she made a point of opening his desk drawers to show me personal mementos. She knew all about my telegrams and the President's invitations, our long-distance infatuation, and she was always so sweet about it.

The birthday celebration lasted three days and nights. We sped in Red Cross motor corps buses from event to event—official luncheons and dinners, radio broadcasts, shows at service hospitals, midnight shows at local theaters—raising several hundred thousand dollars to fight the disease from which the President himself had suffered. I followed Mrs. Roosevelt around, and I want to tell you, she was something to follow around. That lady could cover more ground, and trying to keep up with her was no joke. Wearing a wonderful white fox-trimmed ermine coat, and keeping me at her side for moral support, she swept to birthday balls at six Washington hotels, the Lincoln Colonnade, and the Stage Door Canteen. The instant we stepped through the door of the Canteen, the G.I.s spotted her and gave a rousing ovation, cheering and clapping and stamping their feet. They thought she was just terrific. So did I. Here was a shy, private woman whose vital participation changed for all time the concept of the First Lady as simply a glorified house-wife. "I am my husband's legs," she explained.

At midnight, merrymaking paused while she read the President's birthday message over a nationwide radio hookup: ". . . We will never tolerate a force that destroys the life, the happiness, the free future of our children any more than we will tolerate the continuance on earth of the brutality and barbarities of the Nazis or the Japanese warlords. We combat this evil enemy of disease at home just as unremittingly as we fight our evil enemies abroad."

That was January 31, 1945. Our First and Third Armies, a hundred thousand men, were smashing the Siegfried Line. The Russian Army was seventy-three miles from Berlin. The President, the Russian Premier, and the British Prime Minister were approaching Yalta to discuss the anticipated German surrender and the continuing war in the Pacific. We couldn't have known that whirlwind birthday celebration would be his last, that Franklin Delano Roosevelt would die that April—one month before the war in Europe ended. As I was leaving the Carlton one day, some bigwig jumped out of his car and shouted, "Germany has surrendered!" Washington went into a frenzy of celebration, diminished somewhat by the loss of the man who had guided us through the darkest days.

I continued to commute between New York and Washington, but the capital seemed desolate somehow without the man who had been hope and strength and conscience to the American people for twelve years. No man had a harder act to follow than did Harry S. Truman, and there was not a little skepticism as he assumed the Presidency at that crucial time. I had met him briefly at the White House during his Vice-Presidency without really forming an idea of him. The next time we met was at a charity show at one of the Washington theaters just after he became President. I was sitting in one box, and he was in another, and the boxes below us were filled with G.I.s who wanted our autographs. Little pieces of paper signed "Harry S. Truman" were passed to me and I would sign underneath, or they would come to me first and then he would sign.

Outside, after the show, we laughed about it and chatted awhile. "I'm leaving for Independence in the morning," he said. "I'm going out to Tom Prendergast's funeral." That impressed me, because I knew Prendergast, who had put money into the coffers and helped Truman get where he was, had a lot of scandal attached to him before he died. The papers were playing it up, but that didn't faze Harry Truman. He had been a friend and the new President was going back to his funeral and the rest be damned. Well, I thought, this fellow has guts; I like this. He's all right. And that was my first inkling of the forthright, gutsy spirit that would characterize his Presidency.

Washington became a little brighter then, helped immeasurably by the advent of Commodore Gene Markey, assistant intelligence officer on Admiral William F. ("Bull") Halsey's Third Fleet staff. Gene, a brilliant raconteur, a man of unfailing wit and humor, could charm the birds off the trees, although birds were never his particular quarry— women were, the richer and more beautiful the better, and I never knew one who could resist him. I certainly couldn't. His first wife, Joan Bennett, a friend of mine, finds physical similarities between herself and Hedy Lamarr, his second wife, and me. She thinks he chose for type, which is probably true, but he had the ability to glorify any type. He could make a scrubwoman think she was a queen and a queen think she was the queen of queens. After long days of hospital visits and Red Cross business, I would drag myself to the Carlton and change for nights on the town with him. He was indefatigably social, so we went every-where and met everyone, often making a foursome with our old friends Collier and Valerie Young, since Collie was a lieutenant commander also stationed in Washington.

The capital was the hub of the world during those final months of World War II, a heady combination of immediacy and frivolity, diplomacy and intrigue, tight security and political blunders. As we entered one of Marjorie Merriweather Post's dinner parties with a group including Senator Tom Connally, a big, blustering Texan, he spouted insultingly about the French. He walked along absolutely reviling them, oblivious to the fact that behind him, listening to every word, was the French Ambassador. Those things were always happening in Washington.

That was my first visit to the fabulous Foxhall Road home of the Post cereal heiress, who was then Mrs. Joseph E. Davies. Our hostess struck me as lovely and charming, but her rich surroundings upstaged her. The house was hung with Gobelin tapestries and filled with rare Russian art treasures purchased during her husband's ambassadorship in the Soviet Union. We dined off solid gold plates with solid gold cutlery.

She was really the rich person's rich person. They were absolutely fascinated by her. She had the courage to do what no one else dared to do. "Does she really have little moats around the trees in her garden for the convenience of her dogs?" Babe Paley wondered aloud, years later, like a fan curious about a favorite movie star. "Is it true she has a rusticated escalator of simulated birch at her Adirondack lodge?"

When Japan surrendered, I was back in Hollywood feeling a new sense of self-understanding and well-being after ten months of analysis. "You're finished," Dr. Brunswick had decided, and threw me out. That was one of the most beneficial experiences of my life. She really straightened me out. There wasn't that much difference in my looks or demeanor, but Tyrone Power immediately sensed a change when he saw me at the Zanucks' house one Sunday. "What's happened?" he exclaimed. "You look absolutely wonderful!" It was our first meeting since I'd come back from New York and he'd been discharged from the Marine Corps, so there hadn't been time to share my experiences. He just knew, with his instinctive sense of other people, that I was in one whole piece.

After thirteen years with M-G-M, I was resolved to get out of our contract a year before it expired. Of course, my great days took place there to a large extent—they certainly did well by me—but I had the feeling Joan Crawford had when she finally left after eighteen years: that I would just be drowned, that they wouldn't go out of their way to find material, and so forth. I wanted to get out before they finished me off. They used to do that in the studios—they'd either get very careless or do it deliberately. Somebody new comes along, they get all excited, and all their interest goes there. Even if you're still bringing in shekels at the box office, they have a tendency to ignore you. They were pushing another redhead, Greer Garson, and deservedly so, but they also were bringing in stars who did my sort of thing—Claudette Colbert, Katharine Hepburn, Irene Dunne—and giving them roles that should have been offered to me. Admittedly my wartime hiatus had probably diminished my market value and created some animosity at the top. Nick Schenck, for instance, kept telling them at the studio that I didn't want to work.

Metro's other female stars of the thirties—Garbo, Norma Shearer, Eleanor Powell, Jeanette MacDonald, and Joan—had already gone. The studio just didn't know what to do with us, Joan especially. We all knew that they were easing her onto the skids, and I was always cheering her for going out to Warners, making *Mildred Pierce*, and beginning a whole new career. You see, they had set ideas about her; they still thought of her as a jazzy girl. They had set ideas about all of us, forgetting that we had aged a bit and might be able to extend our range. We were stuck with our images. Sometimes they lacked imagination. When I went with M-G-M after starting out as a slant-eyed exotic, they didn't know what to do with me for a long while. I didn't fit into the usual glamour-factory pattern. *The Thin Man* didn't fit into the pattern, either; finding it was an accident—for me a lucky one. But ten years of that kind of luck was enough. The essentially comic treatment of marriage and murder belonged to a more cynical, satiated prewar era. The noble, self-sacrificing Minivers and Curies supplanted the flippant, sophisticated Charleses. The whole world's sense of values had changed, and I wanted to go along with it.

Metro wanted to keep me available for an occasional *Thin Man* or marital farce with Bill. Otherwise, I didn't exist. They had bought Conrad Richter's story *Sea of Grass* for Spencer Tracy and me. Its Western setting and pioneer flavor, similar to my own background, promised the kind of role I'd always wanted to play. They kept postponing it, however, and when they finally announced a starting date without informing me, I called Benny Thau and raised hell: "What happened? Who's playing it?" When he said "Spence is doing it with Hepburn," I realized what had happened. "Oh, well," I said, "that figures." I was mad as hell at Spence, at everyone.

They were willing to pay me my thirty-five hundred dollars or so a week, but they weren't giving me anything interesting to do, nor would they allow anyone else to use me. Howard Lindsay and Russell Crouse wanted to star me on Broadway in *State of the Union*. M-G-M wouldn't let me do it. Noel Coward tried to borrow me for Elvira in his film of *Blithe Spirit*, a role I was born to play. It was my part. Remember the scene where she materializes, sees her rival's garden, and says, "It looks like an old salad"? Oh, it's a wonderful part. M-G-M wouldn't let me go. "Do you want me to wait around until I'm dead?" I asked Mayer.

It took a lot of courage, I suppose, to leave the Metro womb, but I wanted to make my own choices. Mayer at first refused when Leland Hayward asked for my release. Myron Selznick, only in his mid-forties, had recently died, a tragic personal and professional loss. Leland, his partner, represented me until he sold out to MCA and Lou Wasserman took me on. Can you believe it, Lou Wasserman who became head of MCA and Universal Pictures and God knows what? Anyway, I was in good hands but decided to approach Mayer myself. I don't think he cried, but he came close. All the people who worked for him were like his children, you see, his possessions, but his former "wife, mother, mistress" routine had taken on new refinements since he had divorced his first wife and married a much younger woman. He was raising thoroughbreds at that time and, for some reason or other, brought one of his champions into the conversation. "You're very ungrateful after all I've done for you," he railed. "I couldn't care more about you if you were my own horse." He never could get over the fact that I wanted to go. He couldn't understand it, but after I agreed to return for any future *Thin Man* picture, he finally consented to abrogate my contract. It was a terrible blow to him, because I was the last of the ladies from M-G-M's heyday to depart.

Arthur Hornblow, who had taken up residence as a Metro producer, sent word for me to come by when he heard I was in Mayer's office. During a sort of general exchange, he said, "What do you mean by walking out on all these men who love you so much?" That somewhat ironic observation, coupled with Mayer's heartfelt assurance that I meant as much to him as a horse, provided my only valedictory after thirteen years at Metro-Goldwyn-Mayer.

There was no formal leave-taking or anything of the kind. This was a factory, for God's sake—there was never any kind of sentimentality about the studio. You had that feeling for your hairdresser, your makeup woman, some of the actors, and the wonderful crews, people with whom you had close working relationships. You did not have that kind of devotion to the bosses or the company, you really didn't. It was all a way of making a great deal of money for everyone. When I say it was a factory, it *was* a factory. You walked onto the set and people were still hammering and putting things together. There was actually no glamour, just damned hard work. You got up when the only other creatures stirring were the wild foxes that came down from the hills to rifle garbage cans. Even my servants were sleeping, because they were needed at night. I became an agricultural authority during those rides to the studio; the only thing on the radio was the farm report. You reported for makeup by seven, sat under the dryer and dealt with wardrobe, then went to the set at nine. You got up there on the set and you had to create, to sustain a performance within the strictures of cables and lighting and camera setups until noon. After an hour for lunch, when maybe you got out of your costume, or maybe you didn't because it took too long to put on again, you went back and worked straight through until six.

I don't want to disparage it all; being a part of Hollywood's Golden Age had its wonderful aspects, too. There was the satisfaction of being productive, professional, and totally involved, and being well paid for it besides. There was the pleasure of working with so many talented people and associating with so many beautiful ones. That was the norm in those days—you had to be a beautiful woman; you had to be a handsome man. But so far as its being inherently glamorous, it was not. The ones who got caught up in that myth didn't survive it. People who live what they call normal lives don't believe this, because they've been taken in by all the glamour stuff. But that's the truth of it. The thing that fascinates me, considering what goes into making a film, is that it turns out all shiny and bright. The glamour, of course, is in the way it comes out on the screen.

I had returned from the wars, as it were, and bought a house in Pacific Palisades that had belonged to Avery Rennick, a noted California craftsman. He had made all kinds of furniture for me over the years, beginning with some hand-carved Italian pieces when I still lived with my mother. We went through several periods together. The house was a red Connecticut saltbox, a ridiculous kind of house to have in Southern California, but charming nonetheless. He built everything, including the furnishings, meticulously to scale, copying the paneled walls and fireplace of the sitting room from one in the American Wing of the Metropolitan Museum. I loved that little house. Perched on three lots on Rivas Canyon, it had a lime orchard, a beautiful lawn, and an English garden like Grandmother Johnson's in Helena. The Will Rogers ranch covered much of the land above us, so the country was still pretty wild. There are probably nine thousand houses there now.

Oh, that was a really lovely place—beautiful flowers and my wonderful cat and my big, boisterous poodle. I always had dogs, but unfortunately my schedule seldom allowed me much time with them. The poodle became attached to my secretary, Leone Rossen, who came to me after the war and is still with me as secretary, business manager, and friend. She's a wonderfully loyal, capable person who does all the things that I can't do with mathematics. She loves figures, while I look at them and blanch. She's really my alter ego in that sense.

As I've mentioned, Mary and Douglas Fairbanks, Jr., had a house above mine. Doug's an old friend, a nice man and a talented actor who has managed to overcome the burden of his father's fame. I've seen him do some awfully good work—his Rupert of Hentzau was magnificent—but they never got behind him and built him up to his full potential. He and Mary were denizens of the British colony whom Arthur and I had fraternized with. Many of my old friends gathered there, which lent comforting continuity to my Hollywood return, particularly after Gene Markey came home on terminal leave from the Navy. Very ill at the time, he moved in and I nursed him.

Gene decided we should get married when Admiral Halsey, the hero of the Pacific, came to town to lead the Tournament of Roses parade. This would be convenient, you see, because Gene wanted his former boss as best man. He was always very casual about that kind of thing, which infuriated me. I was busy making *So Goes My Love* at Universal, my first picture since leaving M-G-M, and he was arranging our wedding around Bull Halsey's schedule. Gene's charm and humor usually won me over to his point of view—shades of Arthur Hornblow, despite ten months of analysis! Gene gleefully arranged a full-dress naval affair, sparing me the details while I finished my picture, a pleasant period comedy with a pleasant leading man—Don Ameche.

"You've got to have something to wear," Natalie Taylor said as the wedding day approached. She designed a little horizon-blue suit and hat for me. Just before I left for the church, we decided that we didn't like the hat, so Nat turned it upside down and it worked. I drove to the Terminal Island Naval Operating Base with my mother and the Collier Youngs—Lieutenant Commander Young, that is, and Valerie, who was my matron of honor. While speeding south from Los Angeles, our car was blocked by a Pacific Electric–crossing wreck at Long Beach, making us twenty minutes late for the ceremony. Who should be standing outside the tiny white chapel when we finally arrived but Captain John Ford, U.S.N.R. He looked at me and growled, "For Christ's sake, you would be late for your own wedding!" Remember my old friend Jack Ford? Well, unaware of the little crush that he had nurtured for years, Gene put him in the position of giving the bride away. I stifled my laughter as he glumly escorted me down the aisle past a sea of fidgeting naval uniforms—brass from San Diego and high-ranking friends like Robert Montgomery, Douglas Fairbanks, Jr., and John McLain. Gene waited nervously at the altar while Bull Halsey, grinning broadly, comforted him: "You see, I told you she'd be here."

Reporters and photographers closed in as we left the chapel, while platoons of sailors hoisting seabags passed on their way to the base separation center. We drove in the admiral's car with its five-star license plate to a boisterous luncheon at Mike Romanoff's, hosted by Gene's Navy friends. You would have thought Bull Halsey was the bride the way everyone catered to him. My groom was so busy delivering the admiral to his subsequent appointments that he let Collier take me home. We all gathered that evening for a big party at Mocambo. It was really wild, a typical Markey extravaganza, but hardly a wedding celebration.

Soon after my third marriage, I began what is probably my finest film. Sam Goldwyn and his wife, Frances, after reading a *Time* article on the return of injured servicemen, visualized a picture. He commissioned MacKinlay Kantor to write an original story of veterans adjusting to postwar life, from which Robert E. Sherwood adapted the screenplay that became *The Best Years of Our Lives*. Sam and his director, William Wyler, wanted me for Milly but feared that I would refuse the relatively small role. With the intention of persuading me, the Goldwyns arranged a dinner party that included Bob Sherwood, apparently to lend credibility, although he was suffering from conjunctivitis and barely able to see or participate. Undaunted, Sam launched his offensive, enumerating the advantages of accepting a small role that not only required me to play Teresa Wright's mother but wouldn't even have a designed wardrobe, because he wanted me to shop with Irene Sharaff for clothes that a banker's wife would wear. He needn't have bothered; those things didn't trouble me at all. The story had won me in synopsis form—even before he had Bob expand my part into a beautifully realized character.

It was typical of Sam, an old friend of mine, that after getting me to agree, he used a variation of the same pitch with my agent—small part, mother role, no costumes—to get my price down. I had agreed to do the part for $100,000, which was less than my usual free-lance fee, but Sam tried to renege on that. Leland or Lew said, "No hundred thousand, no Myrna," so he finally relented.

My only reservations about doing that picture concerned working

with William Wyler, because of stories from Bette Davis and other actors about his endless retakes and bullying. "I hear Wyler's a sadist," I
told Sam.

"That isn't true," he replied, with a genuine Goldwynism; "he's just
a very mean fellow."

"Look, Sam," I continued boldly, showing off, "I don't want any
trouble from him. You just tell him when he starts pickin' on me, I'm
takin' off."

I had my first exchange with Wyler while making wardrobe tests.
He checked my bathrobe for a bedroom scene, then pointed to my hair,
which had just been done: "How are you going to wear your hair in the
scene?" I bent down and shook my head so that the careful hairdo all
fell down. "That's better," he said, "mess it all up. You've just gotten
up and haven't had time to comb your hair." I smiled, nodded, and
started to leave. "Are you afraid of me?" he asked abruptly. "No," I
lied, "I'm not afraid of you." And I was scared to death, having heard
all those stories and knowing how great he was. "You don't have to be
afraid of me," he said gently.

Apparently, Sam had spoken to him, which seems so ridiculous in
the light of what followed. That first exchange characterized our relationship. We got along like silk; no two people ever got along as well as
we did. "I can't believe the radar you two have going," Fredric March
marveled. "You don't even need to talk. You just sort of grunt." We
had extraordinary communication, a kind of telepathy. Willy would start
to speak and I'd say, "Oh, yes, I know what you mean." Despite rumors
to the contrary, if he trusted actors, he gave them a chance to be creative. We could do whatever instinctively we felt like doing. Although
that is perhaps my most serious film, as moving and meaningful today
as it was then, Freddy and I did it with great humor; otherwise, it could
have been trying. Willy even gave us credit in several interviews for
improvising. I've never heard of another director doing that.

The only quarrel I ever have with critics is when they try to pin a
specific virtue or fault on one individual, William Wyler ob-
served. When, for instance, you work with people like Freddy
March or Myrna Loy, a director might improve their work, but
he certainly can't make a performance, because they are too
knowing. After Myrna gets Freddy to bed in his drunk scene, I

thought she should have an exit line, but there was none in the script and Robert Sherwood wasn't there. "We don't have any words for this," I told her.

"You don't need words," Myrna said, and made the exit just sort of hitting her head with her hand in a gesture of amused exasperation. It worked perfectly. How many actresses would cut their own line to improve a scene? But she always considered the good of the picture and the impact of her fellow actors. Take the hangover sequence. In rehearsal, Fred was mixing a bromo in two glasses and suddenly lifted the empty one to his mouth by mistake. He stopped the scene to do it over again, but it was Myrna who suggested that we keep the business in, and it brightened up a sequence that had more talk than action to start with.

It was great to get Myrna for that part. On paper it didn't look like much for her, but she had the unusual intelligence to choose a picture instead of a part. And because she played it the role became much bigger than it seemed in the script. Our peers of the Academy neglected to nominate her for an award, but she won Best Actress at the Brussels World Film Festival. CONGRATULATIONS, *I wired.* NOW YOU ARE THE BEST ACTRESS IN THE WORLD. *And I meant it.*

As for Willy's legendary penchant for retakes, I experienced it only once. After the famous homecoming at the beginning of the script, Freddy's character becomes restless and wants to go out and raise some hell. Poor Teresa and I go along to Hoagy Carmichael's bar, where he finds his equally restless pals, Harold Russell and Dana Andrews, who gives a fine performance in what is really the film's central role. As we entered, I was to say, "Old buddies, old buddies," which seemed out of place. "I don't like that line," I told Willy, but he insisted on keeping it. We did it over and over again, every possible way—upside down, backward, everything—without ever satisfying him. The repetition rather embarrassed me, because when somebody gets into a spot like that it becomes the joke on the set. Everybody went around saying, "Old buddies, old buddies."

At the end of the picture Willy phoned me: "I owe you an apology, Myrna. You remember 'old buddies'? Well, you were right and I was wrong. That did not belong there. It held up the scene and I've cut it."

"This is the nicest thing that's ever happened to me," I told him. "No director has ever called me up to apologize for anything." Willy's methods never got to my ego because I felt that he respected actors. I'm sure there were some he considered bums, but generally speaking he had a great respect for them.

I'd seen Willy be very hard on other people in the two previous pictures we did together, Teresa Wright relates. *He could wear people down with the amount of takes he'd make. But there was less of that on* The Best Years of Our Lives. *It was more spontaneous because he really liked his cast. He seemed to be sitting back and enjoying himself. He just got a terrific kick out of watching Myrna and Freddy together. So did I. To me their scenes still stand as the epitome of married love on the screen. You can take all the erotic pictures of the world and they won't compare with that bedroom scene the morning after. She brings that breakfast tray in and he looks at her and sets it aside. It's a marvelous moment because you've seen them the evening before dancing and coming together with the beautiful subtle things that both of them did. What's being felt and played underneath is exciting.*

Since they shared the same easy rapport off the set, it was hard to separate them from their roles. When he asks her to dance in the bar scene, they began to kid and ad-lib, contributing texture that wasn't written in the script. Willy liked it, so that's what you see in the film. Myrna is just exactly the kind of actress Willy loved. He never liked things that seemed too theatrical, overstated. She exudes powerful yet quiet femininity. It's so inner. The subtlety of what goes on within her amazes me. You feel her sensual quality, her deep womanliness, while underneath there is always this little laugh lurking. She would look at Fred, and the distance caused by months and months of separation just vanished. It was a lovely thing to watch in rehearsal and in the actual scenes. You seldom realize during shooting when a scene is very, very special, but I was always aware of it in their scenes.

Although there's only about twelve years between us, I played Myrna's daughter. (Ironically, when we did a television movie twenty years later, every time there was a shot of us together she looked like my daughter!) Some of her contemporaries complained that she was setting a bad precedent by playing the mother of a grown daughter, but she never, never said a thing about "I'm really too young to be doing this." She's very professional, very easy, and has that wonderful sense of humor. It's not big and bawdy and loud; it's very, very quiet. She can say something with that little lilt to her voice that isn't funny if you try to repeat it, but her timing and underlying wit make it funny. She has a way of quietly observing and coming out with things that don't make you laugh out loud but just make you enjoy the moment.

I'm so fond of Myrna. I admire her and consider her a friend, yet it's hard to really know her. She's so self-contained that she could have been in turmoil, had any number of problems on that picture, and I wouldn't have known it. On the other hand, you always felt that you could have gone to her with your problems. She's understanding yet reserved. Most of us probably wonder what else happens in her life when she's away from the set. It always came as a surprise when you realized that she was now married to a different person, because each time you really felt, as with The Thin Man *or with Freddy, that this was the perfect mating of two people.*

Thirty years after we made *The Best Years of Our Lives*, the American Film Institute gave William Wyler its Life Achievement Award. All these jokers who had worked with him were out there—Charlton Heston, Eddie Albert, even Greer Garson and Walter Pidgeon—making their jokes at his expense. Streisand didn't do it. With all the problems they apparently had on *Funny Girl*, she was very gracious. The others said some nice things, too, because I'm sure they all admired him, but there was entirely too much kidding about his retakes and perfectionism. People think they're supposed to get laughs, you see, because they're on television.

I kept getting madder and madder as I looked down the table at Willy and saw his discomfort. Harold Russell, sitting next to me, didn't like it either. Finally, at the end, it came time for me to speak. "I'm going to defend you," I began, explaining that the reason for his repeated takes was that he "suspects some wonderful new thing is going to happen—and it usually does."

He called me the next morning to thank me. "Well," I ventured, "you weren't very happy last night, were you?" And he said, "No, I wasn't very happy," which was a damn shame.

Willy's detractors should consider his gentle handling of an amateur like Harold Russell on *The Best Years of Our Lives*. After seeing an Army documentary about Harold, whose hands had been blown off in boot camp, Willy tested him and decided to cast him as one of the returning veterans. "It's a tricky thing," he told me. "It would be awful if he doesn't work out." But Harold turned out to be an extraordinary man and a born actor. Outgoing and lighthearted, he had adjusted to the loss of his hands and to the hooks that replaced them. Willy coached him with infinite patience and Harold worked very hard, earning and deserving every honor bestowed upon him.

The first time we met, Harold made a point of reaching out with those hooks and taking hold of my hand. You didn't put him at his ease; he put you at your ease. It was unbelievable—before long, you didn't even notice them anymore. Yet somehow that very acceptance of his was an indictment, inspiring a deep, gnawing resolve to see that this would never, never, never happen again. The tragedy, of course, is that it keeps happening—in Korea, in Vietnam, in the Middle East and Central America. I've spent most of my life opposing war. Harold is more practical. He has devoted his life to rehabilitating war's casualties.

The Best Years of Our Lives garnered honors throughout the world for addressing just such issues, touching a responsive chord in anyone who had experienced the war in any way. But it had by no means been a sure thing. The subject of returning veterans, of rehabilitation and adjustment, was controversial and touchy at the time. Who would make a picture like that but someone with guts? And Sam Goldwyn had guts. Everybody warned him against it, but he had faith in it and the results proved him right—not only in regard to the quality but also in solid Hollywood terms at the box office. This was an astute man, an extraordinary man, the same man whose verbal blunders made "Goldwynism" a Hollywood synonym for malapropism. And he really did say those things.

One evening, as I sat in the Goldwyns' projection room awaiting the inevitable after-dinner film, Sam burst in calling, "Hail Selesia!" Assuming he was proffering some sort of salute, I returned a tentative nod. "You know," he continued, "that little king. I wonder what ever happened to him?"

"Oh, Haile Selassie," I said. "I don't know. Things are very quiet in Ethiopia these days." He didn't care whether he had it right or not— he knew politics interested me and he just wanted to make conversation. Sam came to this country as a boy and sold gloves before joining up with Zukor, De Mille, and Lasky, the boys who virtually invented Hollywood. Very early on, however, Sam broke all ties and became a truly independent filmmaker, setting his own standards, never wavering. And the extraordinary thing was that this man had such taste, an innate taste that told him when something was good or bad. There was no question about it, he just knew. When Bob Sherwood invented a sequence of G.I.s rioting over the housing shortage for *The Best Years of Our Lives*, Sam objected. "Bob, listen," he cautioned the great playwright, "you said to yourself: 'Now I'm in Hollywood, writing a Hollywood picture. I'll have riots. That's Hollywood.' But I don't want you to think of this as a Hollywood picture. I want something simple and believable."

He found his match in Frances Howard, the former actress he married, a great beauty and a great lady, who inspired him throughout their fifty-year marriage. Theirs was a great love affair that never faltered, even after Sam became virtually comatose toward the end. Although she had nurses round the clock and all the proper equipment for him, Frances neglected herself. She was twenty years younger than Sam but beginning to go downhill, and it worried me. I urged her to institutionalize him. "Oh, no," she declared ingenuously. "I could never do that. My boy is going to stay right here."

She had always soothed and protected him, participating astutely in business and creating a stimulating environment at home. They always had the most interesting friends, and the distinguished visitors to Hollywood inevitably came to them. Our friendship dated back to the early thirties, when Arthur worked for Sam. Frances adored Arthur, but she didn't take sides after our divorce, as so many people do. Long after my move to New York—until 1974, when Sam died—I spent Christmas or Thanksgiving or other celebration days with them if I happened to be in Hollywood.

The last time I ever saw Sam was at one of their Thanksgiving gatherings. Having been away for quite a while, I was startled to walk into the living room and find a frail old man hunched over in an armchair that seemed far too big for him. With trembling hands he held a hearing aid to one ear, an earphone to the other, trying to hear the radio. Unsure that he could respond, I approached him, threw out my arms, and cried, "Sam!" He didn't say "Hello, Myrna, how are you? Kiss your foot?" or anything. He just looked up with undiminished eyes and said, "Guess what, Myrna? *Wuthering Heights* got the highest ratings out of Cleveland last week." Over ninety and unable to work anymore, he would not give up. He was following his old films around on television.

What we are missing now, with conglomerates owning the studios, is that love of film. The conglomerates have other businesses, so if this doesn't work, then something else will. During the actors' strike, for instance, they said, "Oh, let them strike. That's all right. We've got plenty of other interests; we're selling jeans"—or this or that. I don't know what is going on in Hollywood now. Someone told me that people out there have dollar bills for eyes. They might have been difficult, the Goldwyns and the Mayers, but I wish we had some of them back, some of those monsters. They were businessmen, of course, and we were slave labor, making very little money compared to what they made. When I think of the millions they made on me, and I had to fight for a five-hundred-dollar raise!

They are still making money on us. In 1960, this whole gang of producers got together and talked the Screen Actors Guild into accepting an unsuitable residuals agreement. The actors were scared in 1960. The studio system was collapsing, and they feared the demise of the movies. So they made a deal that was fine for the young, who had the bulk of their careers ahead of them; but those of us who'd had tremendous careers before 1960 were wiped out. At first, 1948 was to be the cutoff year, which would have been somewhat better for me, but then they traded off for a pension plan that actors can draw on. It doesn't amount to much—nothing like what residuals would bring. For God's sake, the *Thin Man* pictures alone are always playing in revival houses and on television! Mickey Rooney wants to fight it now. He called recently, but I told him it was a bad time. The actors were striking and nobody was interested in the grievances of living legends. It's terribly unfair, but I don't think anything can ever be done about it. I think it's too late.

So those monsters or their successors are still profiting from our names and talents. But, in spite of all that, there was always a feeling of creativity, a sense with Goldwyn, with Mayer, with Zanuck, with Warner, with all of them, of making that picture! They had started the film business and this is what they loved; this was their life. I can't tell you what a difference that makes.

Dore Schary, head of production at RKO, convinced me to do *The Bachelor and the Bobby-Soxer*. The two roles were really Cary Grant's and Shirley Temple's, but the script amused me, the pay was good, and playing a judge for the first time seemed like fun. Also, I would be working with Cary. Since we did that turgid aviation melodrama for Arthur twelve years before, he had emerged as a very fine comedian. So I got my clothes and went to work.

The "fun" picture got off to a miserable start. Cary was uncomfortable with the young director, Irving Reis, whose previous output consisted mostly of B pictures. In those days Cary was very persnickety about such things, wary of newcomers lacking proper credentials. (He got much easier later on.) The fact that I liked and worked well with our director threatened my insecure co-star even more. When I asked Irving to redo my first scene twice, Cary got his back up and left the set to phone Dore. "What's going on here?" he said. "You've got a director down here who doesn't know what he's doing and Myrna's getting away with murder!" Dore came down to the set and Irving walked out.

"Cary's very suspicious of you," Dore told me. "He thinks you're trying to put one over on him." Having worked with me before, Cary should have known better. I have always behaved very well professionally; but he thought I had an in with Irving that was getting me special privileges. Sometimes on your first day's work you don't make a lot of sense; it's just nerves. He had the jitters, that's all, probably about other matters. He had just met that little girl he finally married—Betsy Drake— and it was a big, flaming affair at the time. Eventually, Cary and Irving came to terms, but Dore stayed close by until the picture was finished.

As we began to know each other better, Cary learned to trust me. But I still had Shirley Temple to contend with. Playing her older sister wasn't easy, because I had to treat her rather severely on screen. You had to be careful in pictures about being too hard on dogs, children, and Shirley Temple; otherwise, you could really alienate audiences. Perhaps I was too convincing in the role, for the little devil began to needle me. Among her tricks was blocking the movie-camera lens with the still photographer's used flashbulbs during my close-ups, which ruined the shots. It wasn't vicious—she considered her little pranks funny—but we had to be on guard every minute to prevent her from holding up production. "What about this child?" I asked Gene, who had produced several of her childhood pictures at Fox. "Did she behave that way with you?"

"No," he said, "but she was much younger then." She was eighteen on our picture and already married to John Agar—not very happily married, I suspected. "Just send her some flowers," Gene suggested. It hardly seemed adequate, but I did it. After that it was night and day, everything was fine. Having had my hands full with Cary for the first part of that picture, I probably hadn't paid enough attention to her—she was just looking for affection and attention. Shirley and I became very close, very friendly. Whenever we meet, she still calls me "Sis." Our politics differ—she is a confirmed Republican—but I really applauded her accomplishments in the United Nations. Her appointment caused general skepticism. "What have we got here, Myrna?" Ralph Bunche asked. "What have we done now?" They doubted her capability, but she concentrated, worked very hard, and wound up Ambassador to Ghana.

Those postwar years that seem so rosy now in the glow of hindsight were really quite miserable politically. We were building up to the McCarthy era then. You could feel this cold wind blowing into Hollywood from the East, chopping the city into factions. There was a clash between the liberals and the conservatives. All you had to do was know someone of questionable political persuasion and you were labeled "Commie." There were perhaps six or seven hard-core Communists in Hollywood then, and they were not dangerous people. What could they do? The notion that they could make subversive movies within the strictures of the studio system and the Production Code—it's insane! But the right wing organized, saw Hollywood as a perfect place to promote a "Red scare," and looked about for scapegoats. I was one of the first they went for in 1946. If you were a staunch Democrat, politically involved, and a friend of Eleanor Roosevelt, if you advocated peace and the United Nations, you were ripe for the pickin'.

I woke up one morning to find myself listed in the *Hollywood Reporter* as "part of the Communist fifth column in America . . . serving a possible treasonable purpose," along with Edward G. Robinson, Orson Welles, Burgess Meredith, James Cagney, Lionel Stander, and J. Edward Bromberg, most of us just good liberals. One or two may have got involved with the Communist Party briefly—just as I might have if my intellectual curiosity had run in that direction—but none was a committed Communist. And even if there were any, isn't political freedom an American right? That is what always horrifies me about these righteous purges: the implicit denial of our constitutional rights. We forget sometimes that the essence of democracy is to question. In those days, people thought—some still do—that liberal meant Communist. To me a liberal is one who moves slightly left when the Fascists get too strong and slightly right when the Communists get too pushy. A real liberal has to be flexible that way. Frankly, nobody could be more anti-Communism in its present form than I am. I believe in liberality of thought and have no time for any kind of totalitarianism—be it right or left.

When the crash came, I was, fortunately, still working at RKO, on *The Bachelor and the Bobby-Soxer*, of all things. Dore Schary, the production chief, was waiting when I arrived that morning. "The studio's yours, kid," he said. "I'm locking the gates and you can have the publicity department, anything you need." Dore was marvelous about it, supportive and stalwart, which lightened those dark days. A bright, concerned man, he became one of my most cherished Hollywood friends and political allies.

Another staunch ally, my lawyer Martin Gang, would later represent gratis many people in similar trouble who couldn't afford him. "You want to sue?" he asked. "Probably," I answered, "but first let's try for a retraction." Martin served the *Hollywood Reporter* with written notice that the statements were libelous, demanding a retraction of the article, which they had picked up from the *American Photo-Engraver*, a trade-union publication. Written by Matthew Woll, a vice-president of the A.F.L., that article was instigated by Hollywood right-wingers who feared any kind of intellectualism—much like Agnew with his references to "effete snobs."

Instead of a retraction, the *Reporter* republished the libelous statements.

Two days later, October 4, 1946, I filed a one-million-dollar suit against the Hollywood Reporter Corporation and its publisher, Billy Wilkerson, for twelve counts of libel. Greg Bautzer, representing Wilkerson, called me in to give a deposition. My husband, under duress, accompanied me. Gene was so nervous, so jittery about it, that he provided my only laughs during those anxious days. I always called him a Bourbon, but he never quite decided what he was politically. He generally played it safe, although he did stand up to Adolphe Menjou, who was running around Hollywood crying communist. "Now, listen, Adolphe," Gene admonished, "you stop this slander. Myrna's no Communist."

"Well," replied Hollywood's foremost reactionary, "she'll do until one comes along."

Bautzer grilled me about supposed Communist publications. "No, I'm sorry, I don't know anything about that," I kept saying as he continued probing, getting nowhere. He had obviously investigated me beforehand, because I later learned that he called Wilkerson and said in effect, "There's nothing here, Billy. You've got the wrong girl—she doesn't know anything."

Edith Wilkerson, Billy's wife, called me from the *Reporter* later that day. "When are you coming down to take over?" she asked.

"Oh," I said, "any day now." We treated it with great humor, but she was worried. Of course, I didn't want the damn thing; I wouldn't have touched it with a ten-foot pole.

They printed a front-page retraction stating that a thorough investigation had disclosed "that a grievous injustice had unwittingly been done Miss Loy and the others. Miss Loy, for example, has at all times been a loyal citizen of the United States." Woll, under my threat of legal action, also backtracked, claiming that his "personal inquiry" proved that I hadn't supported any activity "harmful or inconsistent with the American way of life." His "inquiry" was answered by a most unlikely source—Edward Arnold, president of the Screen Actors Guild and a conservative Republican. Putting aside our political differences, Eddie met with Woll. "So far as Myrna Loy's concerned," he stated, "you're barking up the wrong tree."

There's a bright saying in Hollywood: "If you're not careful, they'll put you up against a cellophane wall and shoot you from both sides." That's what happened to me: hate mail arrived from archconservative kooks, along with subversive propaganda from every radical organization. While the retractions painted me as a patriotic torchbearer second only to the Statue of Liberty, one Communist publication pictured me as a heroine of the left, holding a big bunch of red roses while reading the preamble to the United Nations Charter at Carnegie Hall. That event, the American Slav Congress, had inspired Woll's attack, although we had then been allies of Yugoslavia and Russia. In order to curtail the publicity, the hate mail, and the propaganda, I decided to settle for retractions and withdraw my suit. The Wilkersons, relieved beyond measure, hired clipping services to send me the retractions reprinted in hundreds of American newspapers. The right-wingers never hit me again after that—not in public, anyway.

While *The Best Years of Our Lives* reaped awards and honors and box-office receipts, M-G-M beckoned for *Song of the Thin Man.* "Well, how about you?" said Benny Thau. "Look what you've been up to. You've really stunned them around here with your success." He was delighted for me but furious that Metro hadn't made such a picture and given me such a part. Dear Benny was a great friend of mine all through my Metro years, helping in the early days to get me tested for various parts, later getting me into Mayer whenever I wanted him, always comforting me and advising me when I had problems. That was part of Benny's job—liaison between management and contract stars—but he was genuinely kind and appealing. In fact, he was Greer Garson's great love before she married that actor who played her son in *Mrs. Miniver.* Long after I left the studio, Benny would take me to lunch or dinner at Hillcrest, the Jewish country club, which delighted me. Jews could never get into the Los Angeles Country Club because of all those snooty people, all those racists, so they built a better one practically across the street.

Song of the Thin Man was a lackluster finish to a great series. I hated it. The characters had lost their sparkle for Bill and me, and the people who knew what it was all about were no longer involved. Woody Van Dyke was dead. Dashiell Hammett and Hunt Stromberg had gone elsewhere. The Hacketts were writing other things. Surprisingly, though, that last *Thin Man* was pretty well received, particularly in England, where, according to the *Hollywood Reporter,* "Most of the cricks gave a cordial welcome back to old-timers Bill Powell and Myrna Loy. . . ." I know that only because Bill sent me the article with "old-timers" circled in pencil and this note scrawled at the top of the page: "Dear old girl! I know you wouldn't want to miss this. Love, Willy (old boy)."

After we finished that final *Thin Man* picture, George S. Kaufman, who was directing Bill in *The Senator Was Indiscreet,* called me: "Do you think it's possible for you to do a bit at the end of the picture as Bill's wife? We can't hire you. We couldn't afford your salary. It's just a gag." "Great!" I said. "Of course I'll do it."

When the senator has troubles, he gets on the phone and calls "Momma," his wife, whom you never see. At the end of the picture he has to leave the country and winds up on a tropical island. They cut to him saying "Momma" or something, then cut to me in a sarong with a gray wig and the whole bit. It was a yell and it made George happy on the only picture he ever directed. They gave me a brand-new Cadillac for my day's work, which was fine—I was driving my old Ford station wagon around at that time. And, of course, the joke worked wonderfully well with audiences, who by that time simply took the Powell-Loy relationship for granted.

While I went from picture to picture, Gene returned to 20th Century-Fox for *Moss Rose*, producing and working on the script. The writing part of it pleased me; that's where his real talents lay. In fact, I kept after him to write a book about the war, but he never did. He squandered his wit, his verbal brilliance, his creative energy on society, a tendency that, I must say, afforded me considerable amusement during our years together. He was popular and entertaining, and, although ten years my senior, rather disarmingly boyish in many ways. It was always such a delight to take him to his London tailor for fittings. It was also expensive, but Gene just happened to be the kind of man you did those things for.

He loved parties and people. So we participated in the postwar festivities that imitated but never quite duplicated the social whirl of the thirties. We danced when the Zanucks transformed their Santa Monica beach house into a flower-bedecked campaign tent in honor of General Mark Clark. We gathered at Mocambo, two hundred and fifty strong in our finery, to honor Walter Winchell and his work for the Damon Runyon Cancer Fund. Picture people worked and played as they always had, but their world was no longer isolated. Strikes and ideological infighting, anti-trust laws that severed studios from their theaters, runaway production, and the specter of television would irrevocably alter the social climate, the very nature of Hollywood.

I still preferred more intimate gatherings at the Fairbankses' next door or at Cole Porter's in Brentwood. Cole gave wonderful little dinners, always graced by his taste and charm. Although in constant agony from a freak riding accident that had crushed his legs, he would sit at the piano and play his songs, suggestively enunciating his witty lyrics in a thin, chirping voice. He didn't get out much then, so he was always anxious for gossip, which generally doesn't interest me. Gossip diverted him from pain and the boredom of virtual confinement, but his informants included several Hollywood scavengers who dined out on their often erroneous tales.

"I hear Joan Crawford's bearing down on her children," Cole observed during one of my visits.

"In what way?" I asked.

"Well, she's making them bow and curtsy."

"There's nothing wrong with that," I told him. "Terry Hornblow bowed so low when I first met him he almost fell on his face, but that's what they did in the schools he attended. They were being taught how to behave." It rather surprised me that Cole, of all people, questioned that sort of social training, because he was a great gentleman, courtly and gracious, despite his constant pain. After my visits he would send beautiful yellow roses to my house just to thank me for coming to see him.

Of course I knew about the problems Joan was having with her two intransigent older children. They were unruly and obstinate and she was trying to make a lady and a gentleman of them. But she was being criticized for it. To anyone who knew Joan, those melodramatic excesses described by Christina are incredible, yet the seemingly harmless gossip that piqued Cole's interest was repeated and exaggerated over the years until, as usual in Hollywood, it gained commercial credibility.

You could always count on the Fairbankses to have interesting houseguests and gatherings. That's where I'd see, but not engage, Miss Garbo. Doug, as English as an American could be, had a penchant for all things British. Our great friend Fulke, the Duke of Warwick, often stayed there, as did Clemence Dane, the novelist, a delightful lady whom we later visited in her lovely mews house in Covent Garden. Somerset Maugham may have been a better writer, but he certainly lacked her charm. He was always cranky toward me because I'm not a cardplayer— when he wasn't writing, that's all he ever wanted to do. "Why don't you play cards?" he'd snap. "What's wrong with you?"

Evelyn Waugh also had a reputation for being difficult, but I found him charming. When his novel *Brideshead Revisited* became a best-seller, M-G-M wanted to purchase the film rights. Having had previously unfruitful negotiations with them, Evelyn said, "I won't consider it unless I can direct it." The studio offered him an all-expense-paid trip to America just to discuss it. When he got to California, they gave him the big hurrah treatment and optioned the book. Then they stuck him in a writers' row cubicle to adapt it and forgot all about him. What was worse for Evelyn, who was very conscious of such things, Hollywood neglected him socially; with the exception of some English expatriates, we were the only new friends he had in the business. I tried to compensate by planning activities for him and his wife, Laura, a lovely person. When I called one day to ask them to lunch with me at the commissary, she said, "I'd love to, but I'm not sure where Evelyn is. He leaves here in the morning and he's gone all day. He doesn't go to the studio anymore, so I thought he might be at your house. I don't know what he's doing." Around that time, the effort to develop an adaptation of *Brideshead Revisited* ran into censorship problems. Evelyn, refusing to emasculate his novel to appease the Production Code, left Hollywood in a huff.

We quickly found out what he had been doing all those days Laura couldn't find him. He had been visiting Forest Lawn to get material for *The Loved One*. That brilliant book couldn't have been more on target. While flying East in a terrible storm, I once scrawled on a little piece of paper: "Don't put me in Forest Lawn." I had attended funerals there, and the artificiality repelled me—all those stuffed canaries in that little chapel making bird sounds. It's a beautiful, scrupulously manicured park, no question about it, but to me it represents a peculiarly Southern California tendency to avoid the inevitability of death. Instead of coming to grips with it, which is the best thing to do—although not the easiest—they seem to move away from it.

My mother died in 1966, and my brother had her cremated at Valhalla, a North Hollywood mortuary; then I returned the ashes to Montana for burial. There was something so different about the two ceremonies. I went into that old cemetery beneath Mount Helena, full of worn crosses and moss-covered stones, and it was real. There wasn't this hiding, this getting away from the idea of death. Not that one should indulge oneself in a situation like that, God knows, but face it. The difference between that and the Forest Lawn implication that it hasn't happened is what Evelyn so brilliantly captured in *The Loved One*. He

avenged those Hollywood slights with a comic masterpiece. But his ultimate victory against Metro's shortsightedness and Production Code re-
strictions came after his death, with a superb television production of
Brideshead Revisited.

The ranch mother in *The Red Pony*, based on John Steinbeck's
beautiful novella, was as close as I've come to playing a woman like my
pioneer grandmothers. Although it was an independent production released by Republic, a so-called "poverty-row" studio, the creative lineup
was irresistible: Lewis Milestone, whose previous work I admired enormously, directed; Aaron Copland composed an original score; and John
Steinbeck adapted the screenplay himself. Also, it was my first picture
in perfected Technicolor. The color sequences in my early talking musicals had been filmed in the experimental two-color process.

It wasn't a great part for me, despite the interesting aspect of the
woman being stronger than her husband, because the story is really
about the little boy and the horse. Milly, as Milestone was called, wanted
the mother depicted from the boy's point of view, so I played her with
an austere, quiet strength. Several critics, missing the point, wondered
what had happened to Nora Charles. I loved working with Milly again,
for the first time since our early days at Warner Brothers. With *All
Quiet on the Western Front* and several other wonderful pictures, he
became one of Hollywood's finest directors, working in a strong, straight-
forward manner without any particular gimmicks. Of course, I wasn't
thinking in terms of technique in those days. In retrospect, we try to
make more of those things than there was. With the exception of some
of the eccentrics like Von Sternberg, with whom I worked briefly early
on, good directors just made the picture, keeping their technique as
unobtrusive as possible.

I was surrounded by marvelous fellows. Little Peter Miles actually
carried the picture as the son, and Shepperd Strudwick did so well as
the husband. Louis Calhern, full of stories and fun, was wonderful as
my father, an old pioneer who spins oft-told tales of "westering." The
character particularly interested me because my grandparents had done
the same thing. Robert Mitchum, who played the ranch hand, was
a devil, one of those men who got a great kick out of teasing me. He
just about tortured me with his pranks during shooting—particularly
when he had an audience. He seized one opportunity when Hedda
Hopper came out to the ranch where we were shooting to interview me.

We asked Myrna if she considered singing one of the best ways to exercise a dog. She said hers enjoyed going for a tramp more than anything.

PUBLICITY SHOTS

Although her cheerful demeanor belied the fact, Myrna considered posing for endless publicity pictures a tiresome necessity. ABOVE: Warners sent their new starlet to Malibu to sing a bizarre duet with their top box-office star, Rin Tin Tin, in 1925. LEFT: The following year, she was back on the deserted beach, where the Malibu colony now stands, posing between location shots for *Across the Pacific* with Monte Blue. (The palm trees and Myrna's dark hair and flesh tones for her first exotic role were studio created.) BELOW: A decade later, she returned to civilization, strolling down the main street of the 20th Century-Fox backlot with Ian Hunter, Warner Baxter, and their director, John Cromwell, while filming *To Mary—with Love*.

M-G-M included its directors in formal a[nd]
informal publicity shots. LEFT: Charles [Brabin]
stood his ground with Boris Karloff and M[yrna Loy]
as the nefarious Fu Manchu and daughte[r on]
the futuristic set of *The Mask of Fu Manc[hu].*
BELOW: Clarence Brown was understand[ably]
more relaxed with Harlow, Loy, and Gab[le in]
Wife vs. Secretary.

Richard Thorpe oversees Powell, Florence Rice, and Loy on the claustrophobic trailer set for *Double Wedding*.

Conway clowns with le and Loy between takes *oo Hot to Handle*.

Victor Fleming directs Gable and Loy in a scene for *Test Pilot*, as Lionel Barrymore, with his head turned, looks on.

LEFT: In 1937, Gable and Loy were officially crowned King and Queen of the Movies after the New York *Daily News* and fifty-two other newspapers in the United States and Canada polled over twenty million readers. (Doug Whitney Collection) BELOW: Sid Grauman was not amused when Powell and Loy wore oversized clown's shoes to the footprinting ceremony in the famous forecourt of his Chinese Theatre.

ABOVE: Ed Cronenweth photographed Myrna in flying garb for *Too Hot to Handle*. RIGHT: She was stranded with Gable and Tracy between scenes of *Test Pilot*, strolling at March Field.

Nothing garnered publicity like romance, which our
heroine supplied in abundance, compliments of
Clarence Bull, with Powell (right) and Gable (below).

More romance, captured by Bull, with Robert
Taylor (left) and Robert Montgomery (below).

Powell and Loy, considered the supreme screen team of the thirties, made fourteen films together in thirteen years, including *I Love You Again,* 1940 (above), *Love Crazy,* 1941 (opposite above), and *The Thin Man Goes Home,* 1944, with Asta (opposite below).

ABOVE: The stellar cast of *The Great Ziegfeld* posed for Clarence Brown in full costume: Powell in the title role, Luise Rainer as Anna Held, Myrna as Billie Burke, and Virginia Bruce as a Follies showgirl. OPPOSITE: Two million-dollar quartets: Loy, Franchot Tone, Rosalind Russell, and Walter Pidgeon shot by Eric Carpenter for *Man-Proof*, 1938 (above); Powell, Loy, Harlow, and Tracy shot by Ted Allen for *Libeled Lady*, 1936 (below).

Movie sets always drew famous visitors. ABOVE: Amelia
Earhart coached Myrna for her role as an aviatrix in *Wings in
the Dark*. RIGHT: Billie Burke frequented the set when Myrna
played her in *The Great Ziegfeld*. BELOW: Ernest Hemingway
stopped by the *Double Wedding* set and stayed to get drunk with
Bill Powell.

ABOVE: Quite an august crew gathered on the *Thin Man* set in 1934: Maureen O'Sullivan, William Powell, Dashiell Hammett, its author, W. S. Van Dyke, its director, and Ronald Colman, who just happened to drop in. (Douglas Whitney Collection) BELOW: J. Edgar Hoover's visit to the *Man-Proof* set brought old friends Loy and Crawford together for a group shot: Richard Thorpe, Clyde Tolson (Hoover's assistant/companion), Myrna, Joan, Hoover, and Franchot Tone (Joan's husband at the time).

ABOVE: Shirley Temple is caught betwee
Cary Grant and Myrna Loy in this shot fc
The Bachelor and the Bobby-Soxer in 194
(Douglas Whitney Collection) LEFT: My
and Montgomery Clift were much less
strained off camera than this 1959 shot fr
Lonelyhearts would imply. (Douglas Wh
Collection)

ABOVE: In 1960, Myrna played Doris Day's aunt in *Midnight Lace* and actually enjoyed the experience. BELOW: *Airport 1975* mingled Hollywood legends with relative newcomers: Gloria Swanson, Jerry Stiller, Susan Clark, Sid Caesar, Myrna (in curlers), Martha Scott, and producer, Bill Frye.

ABOVE: Old pros Loy and Pat O'Brien responded to fledgling director Burt Reynolds on *The End* in 1978. BELOW: Sidney Lumet directed Myrna in her last feature to date, *Just Tell Me What You Want*, in 1980. (Douglas Whitney Collection)

As she angled for a story, Mitchum sat there on the porch watching. "You know," he suddenly interjected, "at one point Myrna comes out into the corral and does a dance of the seven veils," which he demonstrated in vivid detail, managing to fluster even a tough old bird like Hedda.

Oh, yes, Bob clowned around, but when it came to actually working he was all business. He is one of those artists that make it look easy, a fine actor and an intriguing man with so many sides to him. He has that smooth, masculine surface, seemingly without a care in the world, yet you saw an underlying sensitivity and intelligence. It was typical of his contradictory nature that this macho man who loved bedeviling me should ask me to sign a photograph for him at the end of the picture.

Myrna had a feminine, upright way of dealing with my outrages, Mitchum discloses, visibly delighted by the memory. *She used it—probably to teach me a lesson—one unbearably hot day on location. The crew took their shirts off, but Myrna sat there cool and crisp in her high-buttoned dress. I wanted to remove my own shirt but felt uncomfortable about it in front of this prim creature. "Aren't you hot?" I asked, trying to unbend her a bit. "Not particularly," she replied. So I got to the point: "Why don't you undo a button?" She lifted that wonderful nose like this, very haughty, and said, "Would you have me be unattractive?" Needless to say, I kept my shirt on. I don't want to imply that this woman was in any way an iceberg. She just knew what makes a heroine, and what keeps a queen a queen.*

I don't remember John Steinbeck being on the set, but we met afterward in New York. I was lunching at this restaurant with big armchairs at the Drake where everybody went in those days; friends like Dick Rodgers would always be there and we'd meet up and have wonderful times. One day, John Steinbeck was sitting at the next table. We were introduced, but he seemed preoccupied and said little beyond the amenities. Needless to say, I was disappointed and thought it rather rude when he left the restaurant without so much as a nod in my direction. No sooner was he out the door than a waiter delivered a note: "Miss Loy, I am glad you were in *The Red Pony*. You were the Ruth Tiflin I visualized. John Steinbeck." All he had to do was get up and walk two steps to my table, but he couldn't do that. He was too shy, afraid of approaching me in any but his own proven way.

I went back to RKO for *Mr. Blandings Builds His Dream House*, with Dore Schary again producing and Cary Grant in the title role. Oh, that was a joy, sheer heaven from beginning to end. Our director, Hank Potter, who had done theater, worked in sequence, which was nice. We started at the beginning, with that bedroom scene where Cary and I are asleep with the masks over our faces as Melvyn Douglas gives that witty narration about modern cave dwellers. It's a wonderful opening because it captures workaday New York. The alarm rings; he turns it off, she turns it on again without opening her eyes. He finally gets up and goes out to get the coffee. "Don't lie down again," Hank told me; "sit up, but keep your eyes closed." So Cary, the dutiful husband, brings me a cup of coffee, putting it under my nose so the aroma will wake me up. When he did this, it suddenly dawned on me how to play that role to complement his individual style. I had my easy way with Bill playing the sort of vis-à-vis. With Clark, as I've said, I was often tough because he liked that kind of woman and I instinctively reacted to it. But Cary was terribly funny when he was frustrated, when he was upset. That's one of the things that made his comedy so hilarious, so I immediately decided to play the "little woman" who leans on him and drives him crazy. With the help of a clever script it worked.

Have you ever been married? asked Cary Grant, who had. *If you haven't been married, then you can't understand what it meant to have Myrna play your wife. Even when she fed me lines off camera, I'd look over and she'd be pulling down her hem or straightening a stocking in a subconscious wifely gesture, instinctively doing the things that married women do. Acting is like playing ball. You toss the ball and some people don't toss it back; some people don't even catch it. When you get somebody who catches it and tosses it back, that's really what acting is all about. Myrna kept that spontaneity in her acting, a supreme naturalness that had the effect of distilled dynamite. She really became the perfect wife. Melvyn Douglas and I used to talk about it on Blandings. All the leading men agreed—Myrna was the wife everybody wanted. The only problem we had was her photographic memory. She seemed to look at a page and know her lines*

and mine. It was harder for me. "Careful," I told her, "you'll
make me look bad on the set."

That picture was as smooth as glass. It just worked—the characters, the whole thing. It was a picture that I thoroughly enjoyed. Since Cary was sure of me and my methods by then, we worked well together; our acting styles meshed and we had fun in the process. He was very sweet to me, a charming companion full of information and humor and hilarious stories about his early days in America as a Coney Island stilt-walker. I marveled at the contrast of that young hopeful clattering on stilts along the boardwalk and the symbol of elegance he had become. Cary's impeccable timing and delivery, his seemingly effortless performances resulted from hard work, concentration, and a driving demand for perfection. And wonderful Mel, bless his heart, managed to excel in an extremely difficult situation, because the script had him playing off us without really being a part of us. What a paradox that such delightful working conditions should provide a backdrop for another installment of what self-styled pundits called "the Red Star Follies"!

Representative J. Parnell Thomas, chairman of the House Un-American Activities Committee, began his attack on the film industry early in 1947. At first, tired of being exploited by publicity-seeking congressmen, the Hollywood establishment protested the unfounded accusations of Communist infiltration. Representative Thomas persisted, however, and rapidly the studio bosses, manipulated by their Wall Street investors, began to capitulate. It was a conspiracy, I think, put together by these money men to protect their investments and implemented by Hollywood's right-wingers to promote their warped brand of Americanism. As a matter of fact, I know it was, because later on there was a kangaroo court, made up of John Wayne, Ward Bond, and other right-wingers, that decided who would work and who wouldn't. I'm not sure if Jack Ford was a part of that. I hope not; but then, so many people surprised me in those days. Presuming to make Hollywood and the world safe for democracy, they assailed the very precepts of democratic freedom when they appeared as "friendly witnesses" before the Thomas committee. I expected it from Adolphe Menjou, the standard-bearer of the right, or Jack Warner and Louis Mayer, who thought they were protecting their studios, or conservatives like Robert Taylor and George Murphy. The shock came from people like Robert Montgomery, whom

I'd considered intelligent and open-minded, or Gary Cooper, who shared my vigorous Montana background and whose father was a fair-minded jurist.

Despite my open criticism of their smear tactics, the inquisitors didn't come near me this time, because I had fought and defeated their predecessors. They aimed at people less likely to have the power and the means to fight back, which is one of the reasons we established the Committee for the First Amendment. Can you believe such a thing? Having to form a defense for the First Amendment?

John Huston and Willy Wyler came on the *Blandings* set and asked me to help establish a committee to protest these attempts to curb political freedom and set arbitrary standards of Americanism. I joined and gave a thousand dollars to further the cause. Mel Douglas also joined, but Cary didn't want to get involved. I don't know what his politics were, if he had any; he wasn't unsupportive, but he didn't say, "I want to belong to this thing." You couldn't blame him. You couldn't blame anybody, in a way, for not getting involved. As Dore Schary told us after returning from Washington and his bout with the Thomas committee: "A man could get killed out there."

Many professed liberals ran and hid when I tried to recruit them, but ultimately the Committee for the First Amendment consisted of several hundred Hollywood liberals and thousands throughout the country. We gave radio broadcasts, issued pamphlets, and generally tried to present an opposing view. But the investigation reached epidemic proportions when a producer, a director, and eight writers refused to answer the Thomas committee's questions, invoking the First—not the Fifth—Amendment. After these "Hollywood Ten" were cited for contempt of Congress, film-industry bigwigs, many of whom had instigated the purge, met at the Waldorf-Astoria in New York and voted to fire them. Dore Schary, as RKO's head of production, was forced to go along with the so-called Waldorf Statement or go out of business. Frustrated and appalled, he told reporters: "Producers who were afraid to stick their necks out before are still afraid. Those who have always shown courage will continue to make the pictures they want. The Goldwyns and the Zanucks and our own studio will not be frightened off." Back at the studio, he told Mel and me, "I'll hire any Communist that's around!" But the Hollywood Ten—men like Ring Lardner, Jr., Dalton Trumbo, Albert

Maltz, and Alvah Bessie, who had written some of the most stirring patriotic pictures of World War II—became "un-American" and unemployable.

On the *Blandings* set, we had a taste of the underlying prejudice that accompanied this self-righteous crusade. During a House debate on the contempt citations, Representative John Rankin, a Mississippi Democrat, made covert racist remarks to Representative Helen Gahagan Douglas about her husband's real name—Hesselberg. Mel countered with an eloquent response: "I am proud to inform you that my father's people, of Russian-Jewish ancestry, fought against the kind of persecution which the Nazis developed to a point of revolting perfection and which you seem to advocate in America; my mother's people, of Scotch-English ancestry, whose name I adopted professionally, fought in the struggle for the independence of this country. . . ." He forcefully challenged Rankin and his cohorts to bring him up before the committee, which, of course, they never had the guts to do.

They stayed away from Mel after that, but the purges continued into the fifties, spreading to New York and shattering countless other lives and careers, before climaxing with the McCarthy circus. They eventually discredited our Committee for the First Amendment, listing it as a Communist-front organization. So membership in what was plainly a public-spirited attempt to ensure civil liberties became a factor in determining employability during those dark days.

I don't think my career was affected, although there is no way of knowing. I was certainly luckier than some of the others. I hadn't left my car out in front of the wrong house or worn red to church. And at that time I happened to be rich and powerful—as powerful as you are in Hollywood when you are making money and bringing shekels into the box office, which is pretty powerful. During that decade of purges, major box-office stars were never considered fair game. The grand inquisitors, in the league with the money men, needed scapegoats, but not at the risk of box-office returns. They persecuted actresses like Marsha Hunt, Jean Muir, and Anne Revere, actors like Lionel Stander and J. Edward Bromberg, whose careers suffered from the slurs.

Seeing this happening around me, I decided to get in touch with Ronald Reagan, a professed liberal finishing a five-year term as president of the Screen Actors Guild. It seemed to me that the Guild should damn well do something for its beleaguered members, although I already suspected Reagan of veering toward the conservative camp. For the sake of our endangered colleagues, I tried to find him anyway, sending out all kinds of messages and signals but getting no response. Even then he had an eye on his political future. He'd taken off for the mountains. He didn't want any of that on his shoes.

8

THE ACTIVIST
1947–1950

Not all of Hollywood's stars shine brightest only in the world of tinsel and papier-mâché. There are some who have emerged into wider and still more influential spheres. Of these, perhaps the most conspicuous is Miss Myrna Loy. As an eloquent and energetic champion of the United Nations, she is exerting an influence which will be felt far beyond the cinema box office.
—United Nations World, 1949

After completing *Blandings*, I headed for New York, ostensibly to promote *The Bachelor and the Bobby-Soxer* before its Radio City Music Hall première. My interviews drove RKO's publicity people crazy. Instead of touting the picture, I used the exposure to blast the continuing smear-and-run campaign of the Thomas committee. As my fury at that injustice intensified, my outbursts became more frequent, less guarded. A few courageous entertainment columnists, notably Earl Wilson, actually printed my controversial remarks. I appreciated that. Not many of them were taking stands in those days.

Another cause diverted me during that trip: the fledgling United Nations. The U.N. reporter for *The New York Times* guided my first visit to Lake Success, where the U.N. was located before the Rockefellers donated the East River property. I still recall the impact of the proud circle of international flags flying outside those temporary headquarters. A vague concept of world peace had engaged me since my childhood support of Wilson's League of Nations. Firsthand exposure to the wages of war in burn centers and psychiatric wards intensified it. The founding of the United Nations in 1945 gave it direction, a sense of commitment that my picture career had never inspired.

Open sessions of the third General Assembly drew me to Lake Success. I also wanted to find my friend Jan Masaryk, who was walking a political tightrope as the democratic representative of an increasingly Communist-dominated Czechoslovakia. Having endured his country's prewar sacrifice to Germany, Jan now faced Western equivocation as Russia blatantly strengthened its postwar foothold. I assumed that he could use some moral support after giving the General Assembly the bad news. "Europe has gone definitely to the left," he warned, while at the same time endorsing Soviet Foreign Minister Vishinsky's proposals for armament reductions and an atomic weapons ban.

Such forthrightness alienated the wary Western Powers in 1947, and publicity-minded commentators like the Alsops denounced him for attempting to build a bridge between his country and the Soviet Union. Is it so bad to build a bridge? He knew that the Czechs had to co-exist with the Russians or, as he put it, "they will eat us up." But he never discarded his goal of returning to the democracy instituted by his father. Jan wanted the best for his country, for everybody. He always tried to build things. He was that kind of man, a man of peace—the first president of the World Federation of United Nations Associations, whom Trygve Lie called "the voice of the United Nations."

I left several messages for Jan at the Carlyle before he finally called back. "I can't come to see you this time," he said. "It's impossible." He sounded strange, very disturbed.

"In that case," I offered, "I'll come over and see you." That simple courtesy seemed to please him inordinately.

"My goodness," he replied, "that would be so wonderful of you." On the way out, I had the Plaza florist send a big vase of roses over to him.

The man who greeted me was far from the jovial Masaryk of old. The people around him had been his aides and servants for years, but he seemed furtive, guarded. He had recently received a package containing a bomb. Its failure to detonate did not diminish its shattering implications. Although it was generally considered a Communist plot, he suspected that radical Czechs opposed to his conciliatory stand might have sent it. A bitter irony for the man who had kept the dream of democracy alive throughout the war! Political allies were also deserting him, he told me, leaving him to attempt rapprochement alone. After the United States turned down Czechoslovakia's request for much-needed wheat, Jan went to Washington, where he obtained neither wheat nor satisfactory explanations from former friends. The sorrow of this man was very apparent to me as we sat and talked that day.

His spirits lifted when my elaborate gift of roses arrived. Delighted and a bit embarrassed, he indicated the toque-shaped container. "What do you expect me to do with that vase," he teased, "put it on my head?" He relaxed and began once more to beguile me with rich humor and reminiscences. A story about the San Francisco Conference to draft the U.N. Charter revealed his true estimate of what he ironically labeled "Russian democracy."

"One day during a break in our meetings, Molotov invited me to lunch," Jan related with infinite relish. "We got into his long limousine and drove for almost an hour while he lectured me about the inequities of democracy and the virtues of Communism, particularly its concern for the common man. On and on he droned about his rapport with 'the people,' until I wearily insisted on lunch and he ordered his driver to pull up at a little suburban restaurant. The proprietress, delighted by such distinguished company, warmly welcomed the Russian representative with a friendly slap on the back. Molotov stiffened, angrily pushing away the startled woman. 'Go shake hands with her,' I whispered. 'She means well.' But the man of the people did not understand."

I was returning to California that afternoon. Gene had telephoned, frantic about a leaking roof and other minor domestic problems that he was typically unable to cope with. Jan begged me to stay in New York for a few days, but my impulse was to get him out. "Come back to California with me," I urged. "That's what you need—rest and sun. We'll go to the desert."

"No, I can't." He sighed. "I couldn't do that now. Things are very bad in my country." He understood the risk of returning to Czechoslovakia then, yet he would not forsake his people. As I was leaving, he held me back a moment. "I don't want much," he said, "only to be able to walk down by the river in Prague and watch the children play."

Five months later, Jan Masaryk jumped to his death from the window of his Prague apartment—so claimed his country's Communist-controlled press. I doubted it. He was depressed, but not suicidal; that was not Jan's way. "Jumping from a window is what a servant girl would do," he had observed when a colleague tried it after the ultimate Communist coup. Even then he had kept fighting. Shortly before his death, he assured a convention of Czech war veterans that the usurpers would be defeated in the next general elections. As bleak as things became, he would never have lost faith, he would have continued, in his own words, "to look above the horizon and into the clouds."

As two hundred thousand Czechs filed reverently past his casket in Prague, I visited the Czech consul in Los Angeles. I had to go somewhere with my grief. The consul's politics baffled me; he represented the Communist government, yet seemed to worship Masaryk. He even gave me what must have been classified information and documents, including transcripts of Jan's last radio broadcasts. To the very end, he had continued selling democracy, reminding his people that they still had friends in America.

In his final broadcast, to my everlasting gratitude, he included "Myrna Loy, whose words of encouragement in the darkest hour of my life and the history of my nation helped to give me courage during the seven long years that followed." What his example and the privilege of his friendship have given to me is as incalculable as his bequest to the world. Even in death, Jan spoke for democracy as an instinct born in man. The European Recovery Program (called the Marshall Plan) came before the Senate, backed by his message of faith. "There are arguments of facts, there are arguments of figures, but the final argument is that of pure and sacrificial emotion," *The New York Times* editorialized. "This is the argument that Jan Masaryk represented. What we hope to do with dollars he did, in his final splendid moment, with his heart's blood."

It is really immaterial whether Jan killed himself or someone else killed him. Either way, he was murdered, just as the liberties of his country were. As witnesses have escaped from Czechoslovakia, however, the true story has emerged. A few hours prior to his compulsory appearance as a minister before the new regime's puppet Parliament, he had tried to escape, intending to continue the fight for freedom on neutral ground. Five Central Committee officials, alerted by Jan's Party-planted secretary, followed him to the Prague airport. When he saw his pursuers and started running for the plane, they shot at him. The fatal bullet entered behind his left ear. They carried the body home and dropped it headfirst to the pavement below. I could only think of our last meeting. "What do you want me to do with that vase," Jan had playfully asked, "put it on my head?"

The Communists were quick to use their victim for propaganda. They spread the suicide story and laid his bruised, broken body in state before his grieving countrymen, concealing the incriminating bullet hole with a bunch of snowdrops. Jan would have liked that touch—a bunch of Czechoslovakian wildflowers to hide totalitarian infamy. He always believed beauty overcame ugliness, kindness overcame cruelty, common men could overcome tyrants, because democracy is not something historical; it lives in men's hearts. To preserve it, a Masaryk dies for his country, or actors fight for persecuted colleagues, or citizens challenge the smug élitism coming out of the Reagan White House. The right of men to speak their minds and think their thoughts is the essence of freedom. Whatever passion I possess has been dedicated to fighting for it. After Jan's death, the fight took an international direction.

As program director of the American Association for the United Nations, relates Estelle Linzer, *I was arranging a dinner at the Waldorf-Astoria to honor Trygve Lie, the first U.N. Secretary-General. Like all dinners it required a dais, and every dais needs famous people. When Douglas Fairbanks, Jr., a board member, asked if the dais was closed, I assumed he had someone famous in mind. "There's always room for a friend of yours," I told him.*

"Good," he replied. "I have a friend who's very interested. I'll get her on the phone." He dialed the number and said, "Hello, Minnie? [Minnie? I thought; this I've got to see! But for Doug we'll do anything.] I'm with a remarkable gentleman who wants to speak to you." He handed the phone to Clark Eichelberger, our executive director, the man who had nurtured the AAUN from the old League of Nations Association. Doug and Clark went back and forth with Minnie a while, until Doug finally said, "Put on your best dress and just come."

"If you give me this Minnie's full name," I offered unenthusiastically, "we'll be happy to have a place card, receive her, and—"

"Oh," Doug interjected, "it's Myrna Loy!"

Myrna appeared at the Waldorf ballroom looking absolutely radiant. When they introduced her, there were gasps just because the lady was there; but she wouldn't rely on her image. She graced that dais between Nelson Rockefeller and Under Secretary of State

Benjamin Cohen, from the old New Deal days, and met them on their own terms. The two men were so startled by this phenomenon: a glamorous movie star who knew what she was talking about. Myrna was already well grounded in politics.

That evening came off smashingly and she was a great part of its success; she added something unexpected. That distinguished gathering was expecting the usual speeches from U.N. people and politicians, and look what it got!

When I returned to California, Elsie Jensen Brock, the AAUN's West Coast director, invited me to tea at the Ambassador. I committed myself that afternoon to work for the association. The object of the AAUN was to serve as a link between the public and the United Nations, which is dependent for its success on the understanding and support of the people. It can only survive with public opinion behind it. The people make foreign policy in a democracy, and they make it out of their ignorance or out of their understanding. Only out of people's understanding can the world be organized for peace.

This basic message was not easy to deliver in that postwar era, despite the example of men like Ralph Bunche, Acting Mediator for the U.N. in the 1949 peace mission to Palestine. The Arab-Israeli armistice he negotiated made peace a workable concept for the public, while underscoring this man's extraordinary achievements in the shadow of Jim Crow. Raised in poverty by a grandmother born to slavery, Ralph became the first black American to hold a desk job in the State Department, before going on to greater accomplishments. I was fortunate to have him as an avid supporter during those early years with the U.N. and as an inspiration always.

Nevertheless, Americans tended to back away from the U.N. as the "cold war" began. The concept of world peace seemed as threatening, somehow, as the horror of total war. We are a cocksure nation, rankled by claims—which are not true—that others might be stronger than we are. Working for peace rather than arming for war is branded as subversive by conservative governments.

In Washington today, for God's sake, we still have an anachronistic administration promoting the age-old fallacy of aggression for ultimate peace. It serves their interests to debunk, as Reagan has, the efforts of the U.N. and its subsidiary agencies, castigating them as idealistic luxuries. The World Health Organization (WHO), while providing emergency aid in epidemic control, has wiped out several of the world's diseases. The Food and Agriculture Organization (FAO) includes among its priorities aid and instruction to farmers in underdeveloped countries. The United Nations International Children's Emergency Fund (UNICEF) feeds, clothes, and houses displaced and underprivileged children throughout the world. The United Nations Educational, Scientific, and Cultural Organization (UNESCO), in which I became involved, to me means education for all by all. The universal right to education and the duty to educate brings freedom from ignorance, and freedom from ignorance brings freedom from fear.

Mr. Reagan and his bunch, and others before them, have self-righteously deprived us of such "luxuries" in favor of so-called defense spending, implying that democracy can be maintained and spread by force. Naturally, problems arise when new nations come into their own, some of them under certain influences we as Americans would wish they weren't under. But we must tolerate that. Many Third World countries are influenced by the Soviet Union—they would not like to be told that, but it's a fact—and at a recent UNESCO conference they attempted to restrict the press. This is anathema to an American. We demand a free press—although I could throttle them sometimes—and we work for it wherever we go. But you don't achieve it by ignoring those who think otherwise. You must work with the Soviet Union. You must work with all these people. We have finally brought Red China into the U.N. What was accomplished by ostracizing them for so long?

So the U.N. is not merely a rhetorical forum that conflicting nations run to when it's usually too late; it is an organization dedicated to nurturing co-existence as a viable alternative to armed confrontation. Idealistic? Certainly! But what more essential aspiration could men and nations have? I was expected to address such concepts in order to bring West Coast civic groups into the AAUN.

I had never made a speech in my life. Elsie Jensen Brock drafted the first one and patiently coached me. My stage fright was scarcely eased, however, by her warning that the first political group, from Long Beach, would be hard to get, even hostile. They considered the goal of co-existence pointless as we veered toward war with the Soviet Union in that spring of 1948. Stressing that it was more important than ever, I aimed a bit warily to present the case with facts and logic. You can imagine my relief when they began to listen and understand.

My presentation improved with my confidence as I covered other West Coast cities. I discovered that Americans, particularly the middle-class suburban women who comprised the majority of my audiences, are highly constructive in their discussions and resolutions regarding world affairs. This country is fantastic. There are so many concerned people, so many clubs and political organizations everywhere. That's what keeps democracy going.

In May of 1948, I went to San Francisco as a delegate to UNESCO's Pacific Regional Conference, which aimed to promote local-level support groups. I was stimulated on several levels: getting my first taste of a full-scale government conference; addressing San Francisco youth associations; touting the cause on radio shows. One of my most productive relationships evolved when George V. Allen arrived late from a diplomatic mission to Iran. As Assistant Secretary of State for Public Affairs, he was in direct charge of UNESCO and scheduled to address the conference the day he arrived. I was assigned to brief him on everything that had happened beforehand. This impressed Luther Evans, the Librarian of Congress, and Dr. Clarence Dykstra, Provost of UCLA, who, along with George, advocated the participation of the movie industry in the cause of world peace.

Having already narrated a film short for the U.N.'s Crusade for Children, I knew that documentaries met with a certain audience resistance. During meetings with these influential men, I expressed my belief that one little incident to battle international prejudice dropped into an entertaining film is worth all the documentaries ever made. It gets to the people. With that in mind, the State Department and the National Commission for UNESCO appointed me chairman of a preparatory committee to establish a grass-roots Hollywood support group, which became the Hollywood Film Committee.

We were just a handful of concerned people at first: Joseph Roos; Kenneth MacGowan; Celeste Holm; Sheridan Gibney; Alice Evans Field, a director of the Motion Picture Association; and Margaret Herrick, executive secretary of the Academy of Motion Picture Arts and Sciences. We had our headquarters at the Academy, thanks to Margaret, and began to apprise the Hollywood establishment of its potential for nurturing international cooperation and understanding.

> *Within a year of that first Waldorf dinner, Estelle Linzer observes, Myrna was elected to the AAUN's board of directors—not on a whim, but for her tireless efforts to strengthen our Pacific Coast organization. She became one of our most effective speakers, because she never depended on being Myrna Loy. Although her presence, her celebrity, would bring people in, Myrna realized they would lose interest and never come back if she merely sat there looking pretty. She wanted to understand every aspect of what she was advocating. She also wanted to prove herself as a person of some depth and knowledge. She achieved this because she reads and studies and learns. She's as good a student as she is an actress.*
>
> *Although her acting career was in full swing, she remained a loyal board member and a hard worker on the Pacific Coast. In New York she never turned down our invitations to work. In fact, we had to be careful about that. Clark Eichelberger, who became her dear, close friend, had to protect her from herself. That was friendship! We learned early on never to waste Myrna on anything unimportant. You know—you didn't ask her to open a supermarket, because she would do it.*

With *Blandings* in profitable release, *The Red Pony* in the can, and a non-exclusive three-picture deal with RKO, I could afford to give the U.N. my undivided attention. Gene had other plans. He terminated his writer-producer contract with 20th Century-Fox to organize Charter Films, Inc., our own film and television production company. We purchased four story properties, including two of Gene's early novels, and hired Larry Barbier, my former M-G-M protector, to handle publicity. It seemed like a good idea at the time, but before our independent venture got under way, Gene and Gregory Ratoff, a fellow Fox refugee, involved me in another project. Contingent on my participation, they arranged to write and direct, respectively, a picture for Alexander Korda. "I tink eet would be wonderful part for Myrna," Gregory told Gene. "Why don't we all go to Europe and make eet?"

So, leaving several more promising offers, I sailed away to make *The Case of Lady Brooke*. That was really a trip! My secretary, Leone Rossen, who came along to deal with my U.N. correspondence, tended to be protective of me and wary of Gene. She remained the one woman he couldn't charm. She was incredulous when he turned up at the boat with several steamer trunks—more than I had brought—to accommodate the wardrobe I'd bought for him. I got even in Rome, when the Fontana sisters fitted my costumes. They were heavenly, the most elegant clothes I've ever worn in a picture. That was Alex Korda, always the best at any cost.

We shot locations on Capri. Alex arranged for us to stay in the Villa Crespi, overlooking the Faraglioni, those majestic rocks that pierce the island's coast. We also used the villa as a set. That, too, was Alex—always get the most for your money. Automobiles were forbidden on that side of the island, but beautiful old paths ran down the hillside to the town and the sea. Long before dawn made shimmering blue of the Bay of Naples, I would wend my way down to the hotel where they made us up, greeting the only Caprisi who were about that early—fishermen heading out to sea.

Gregory Ratoff, despite his broken English and explosive temper, managed to get the best from a fine cast, including Richard Greene, Roger Livesey, whom I adored, and Peggy Cummins. Sometimes dismissed as Zanuck's court jester at Fox, Gregory was more than that. He was a very funny man, keeping us in hysterics with imitations of his fellow Russian Boris Chaliapin. But he was also a creative, stage-trained director who made some good pictures. It wasn't his fault that ours didn't turn out to be one of them. It didn't start out that way, either. It was a shambles, particularly after Gene, a terrible hypochondriac, collapsed under his mosquito netting in the Villa Crespi, moaning and being pampered and getting behind on the script.

When we moved to London for exteriors, Sir Alexander Korda himself, no less, greeted us at the airport with open arms and a battery of cameramen. He whisked us off to his elegant penthouse apartment at Claridge's, suggesting that we take a suite there—at those prices! I don't remember whether Alex paid or we did; I never bothered about such things then. But Leone did, so I have a feeling *he* paid.

Alex had directed me in *The Squall* when he came to Hollywood at the end of the silent era with that protean contingent of Germans and

Hungarians. He never let me live down my barefoot cavorting as Nubi, the oversexed "geepsy."

"Oh, well," I told him, "that was a long time ago, and I was only a child actress."

"Yes," Alex countered ironically, "and I was a child director."

He had become rich and famous—the King had knighted him—and several people warned me that it had gone to his head. I never saw that at all. He was wonderful to us, an attractive, charming host, who introduced us to the international élite comprising his social world. My great interest was in meeting Winston Churchill, which Alex promised to arrange. It never quite happened. So, although we came close, I never met Roosevelt or Churchill, the two men I most admired.

Thanks to Alex's associations and Gene's social energy, I met practically everyone else. We used to hang around with some pretty hot stuff. Gene, sociable and enormously charming, made all kinds of friends—principally in the upper strata, but not exclusively, thank God. He was an amiable Irishman, whose great talent happened to be accumulating people. He discovered, for instance, that Marina, the Duchess of Kent, liked dancing at Ciro's, where she had gone with her late husband. How he found out such things, I don't know, but he invited her to accompany us, and she accepted. I liked Marina immediately, and she liked me, so we started taking her around with us. This was the woman held second only to the Queen in the esteem and affection of the English people, the Greek and Danish princess who had married the youngest son of George V. Yet she was always so easy with me, always so charming, as warm and amusing as she was beautiful.

Marina had become a symbol of noble widowhood for war-ravaged Britons after her husband was killed on active duty in 1942. She served as a more intimate model for her niece Princess Margaret, who emulated her aunt and frequently exasperated her. We were at Ciro's one night when Margaret arrived with her entourage. She was still young then, not yet twenty, and Marina was upset. "That girl is always staying out late," she told me, fretting about her niece's proclivity for nightlife and café-society companions. Aunt Marina was on her case, and Margaret knew it. There were strained glances between tables, but she never approached us. We met soon after that, though, and she was sweet— petite and much prettier than her pictures, with skin as smooth and white as English porcelain.

Unlike many so-called noble ladies, Marina deserved the designation. She took the duties and responsibilities of her rank seriously, while despising their stultifying formality. As a regular-duty nurse during the war, she used the pseudonym Sister Kay to avoid special treatment, winning everyone with her commitment and energy. I remember her returning annoyed from an official visit to a candy factory. "One would have expected it to be less formal than wartime visits to steelworks," she observed; "but no, the same entourage and the same script went with me. I was required, as Noel would say, to stick to the script, forbidden any spontaneous exchanges. I stood there like a mannequin, watching them dip endless chocolates. I never want to see another sweet!"

Movie stars were not the only ones with tedious public responsibilities, I discovered, although royalty had its advantages. Marina loved going to the movies, but I dreaded being recognized and mobbed by English fans, who are even more avid than the American variety. One night it happened. Someone spotted me, and triggered a chain reaction in the crowded lobby. They grouped and started for me, bearing down until they recognized the Duchess of Kent beside me. This was royalty, you see, no two ways about it. They backed away, bowing and scraping, never requesting so much as an autograph.

Marina was an intelligent woman devoted to the arts. Her friends included Noel Coward, Ninette de Valois, and Sir Malcolm Sargent. Her tastes were sophisticated. She introduced me to Kafka's work during a visit to Coppins, her country house in Buckinghamshire. That was my kind of house—cozy old pickled-pine paneling brightened by pale green-and-blue chintzes. Pictures of her late husband graced every room, and two pianos stood side by side in the music salon, where she and the Duke had amused themselves playing duets. She and their three children still played hers; his was never touched.

The country charm of Coppins gave way to medieval grandeur at Warwick Castle. Fulke, the Duke of Warwick, had been a friend since he visited Hollywood in the thirties, so handsome they tried to make a movie star of him, but he didn't need Hollywood. After some brief appearances as Michael Brooke, he retreated to England and his ancestral home. Who wouldn't have? I remember waking my first morning and looking out over those ancient crenellated walls and towers dusted with snow. I crossed the hall, where Gene was ensconced in Cardinal

Wolsey's bed, to see the River Avon winding toward Stratford with serene swans cutting its surface, snow frosting its edges.

It seemed highly romantic to be living as if knighthood were still in flower within massive chambers holding history and priceless treasures. One room contained the most beautiful Canalettos I've ever seen; another, the Great Hall, displayed armor and weapons and a ferocious iron executioner's mask from the days of the powerful barons. Not that Fulke allowed us to indulge our initial awe. Relaxed and gracious—it was his home, after all—he made us feel as if we had always lived in a castle. In fact, he and Gene made a playground of it, abetted by several ancestral ghosts.

"Have you seen the lady on the stairs?" Fulke would whisper ominously. "She materializes at the oddest times."

"Oh, yes," I lied, "I've seen her several times. We're old friends."

One night, I entered my bedroom to find the executioner reading in the fourposter. Those devils had propped that huge mask on my pillow with an open book in front of it and a light behind it to make the gruesome eye slits glow. I yelped and pretended to swoon until the perpetrators had their fill and removed my ferocious bedmate.

Fulke had given the castle to the state by that time, so, excepting his private quarters, they opened it to the public on certain days. He simply couldn't afford the upkeep; he was even having trouble trying to keep his own section intact for his son. "Well, we have to go out and shoot for the pot," he would joke when they went after pheasant or grouse.

Tradition, nevertheless, required that Christmas Day be celebrated in the Great Hall with an enormous tree and a baronial banquet. The dozens of guests included Lord and Lady Selsdon and their little daughter, who left her doll and baby buggy underneath the tree. When she wanted them the next morning, her mother and I, still in dressing gowns, went after them. We opened the door just as some tourists were entering at the opposite end of that truly Great Hall. As we made a run for the tree, our pale gowns flowing behind us, a woman let out a bloodcurdling scream. We grabbed the buggy and vanished through the doorway, leaving a cowering crop of tourists believing fervently in Warwick Castle's ghosts.

Our petty pace continued in town, even after I developed appendicitis. They nursed me along while I finished the picture and participated in the Royal Film Performance, a charity gala at the Empire. Laurence Olivier and Vivien Leigh led the British stars, and the U.S. studios sent over a contingent of their best. The women wore fabulous gowns— mine was a new Dior of rose-colored net and lace—which we were expected to show off while descending a steep, treacherous stairway into the lobby. As we started down, Elizabeth Taylor, delicate and lovely with her white, white skin and violet eyes, turned to Robert Taylor and groaned, "I'm gonna throw up!"

I had sat on those stairs during rehearsals with the cream of English actors at my feet, the acting knights urging me to perform the show's big skit with them. But Hollywood studio representatives said, "No, one of our regular contingent has to do it!" The fact that I was living in England made me ineligible to represent my country, for some reason. They finally worked me into a bit with Sid Field, one of England's most popular comedians, a much-beloved man. When he kissed me during our turn, the entire audience went wild. You could hear them scream-ing—it was a great moment for them. After the show, we lined up alphabetically for presentation to the royal family. King George, gravely ill, could not attend, but Queen Elizabeth (now the Queen Mother) appeared with her daughters, Elizabeth and Margaret. A little tremor ran through me as the Queen took my hand; you could tell she hadn't slept for nights. That round, pretty face was drawn, those bright eyes bloodshot. But she was swathed in glittering silver and covered with jewels, all done up in a diamond tiara and bracelets, emerald necklace and earrings. She clearly believed that if you're a queen, you look like a queen.

"You are a great friend of England," she said, her sweet smile tran-scending fatigue and finery. "Mrs. Churchill told me about the hospital beds you sent over during the war." I was amazed as she recounted my wartime services to England—amazed not by what she said, but because she had done her homework. With the King perilously ill, she had taken time to learn about all the show people she would meet that evening. She was not born a queen, she became one reluctantly when her brother-in-law abdicated and her husband succeeded him, but she was everything a queen should be.

Gene, meanwhile, was indulging his penchant for nobility in a rather disconcerting manner. When I came home from Shepperton Studios in the evenings, there would be a flurry in Claridge's lobby, employees rushing for telephones when they saw me, obviously alerting my philandering husband. One evening his well-tipped sentries weren't quick enough. I caught him with lipstick on his face, so to speak. The whole business resembled a tawdry bedroom farce as he promised to reform and swore that I was the *one*—which was probably true.

That was the curious thing about this man; as deeply involved as he was with me—and he was very deeply involved—he could not resist other women. If a woman went after him, she could have him. It helped if she had money or a title, of course—nothing less for Gene than a duchess or a countess. The inherent humiliation was bearable, I suppose, because I wasn't really in love with him, not the way I had been with Arthur. I liked Gene, loved being with him, so I put up with this situation for a long time. Preserving our relationship seemed worthwhile at that stage.

Although doctors considered my appendectomy "very successful," they kept me in the London Clinic for two weeks, then recommended a year of rest. "Are you serious?" I balked. "*Me* rest for a year?" They were serious, so Gene suggested returning to Italy to recuperate in the sun. Our departure was delayed by the first anniversary of Jan Masaryk's death and the daring escape of Josef Josten from Soviet-held Czechoslovakia.

Proclaiming himself one of Jan Masaryk's collaborators, Josef got in touch with me after reaching London. He documented the true story of Jan's death, adding that my late friend's radio broadcasts had left me something of a symbol of freedom to the Czechs—an honor for which I was grateful but hardly worthy. "I consider myself in exile in London until democracy is returned to my country," Josef told me, to which end he established the Information Service of Free Czechoslovakia. I supported his efforts, as well as those of the United Nations Association of Great Britain to establish the Masaryk Memorial Fund.

With Winston Churchill as chairman, a battery of distinguished Englishmen devoted themselves to honoring Jan—out of admiration, but also, I suspect, out of guilt for having sold him out at Munich. Miscalculation followed by altruism is a peculiarly British paradox to which America of late has fallen heir. Nevertheless, I wholeheartedly backed their effort to erect a statue and a Masaryk center for international studies in Geneva.

My doctors believed me safely in Italy when I attended Jan's memorial service at St. Martin-in-the-Fields. Still rather drawn and weak, and moved by the powerful service, I blasted invading representatives of Fleet Street: "I'm here to honor Masaryk, not to be photographed!" It didn't faze them. They circled like hungry mosquitoes as I commiserated on the church steps with Viscount Cecil, a recipient of the Nobel Peace Prize and the honorary life president of the U.N.A. As we spoke, a bedraggled old street woman watched from the sidewalk. Finally, she mustered the courage to approach us.

"Who was that for?" she asked.

"Jan Masaryk," I told her, "the former Czech Foreign Minister." Elaboration was unnecessary.

"Really"—the old woman sighed, surpassing the day's eloquent eulogies—"to think that such a man is dead!"

After a valedictory dinner party at Ciro's with the crème of Gene's social conquests—the Duchess of Kent, Mark Bonham-Carter, Captain David Bruce among them—we headed for Santa Margherita on the Italian Riviera. That little fishing village, burnished blue and gold, had yet to be spoiled by its postwar resort status. From our rooms at the Hotel Miramare, where the Mediterranean glinted through open windows, we could stroll unmolested through town. I was recognized but never pestered beyond graceful bows with charming greetings of "Madama."

We made passing acquaintance with the bustling fishermen and with the Franciscans, who walked the town barefoot in sackcloth robes. Polite but usually remote, they unobtrusively tended the sick, delivered babies, then returned to spare cubicles in the nearby monastery. One of them, an ascetic but congenial man of God, always paused to pass the time of day. I was out alone one morning when he stopped me and hesitantly, rather shyly, requested an autographed picture. I returned to the hotel, bursting: "What am I going to do? That brother we like wants my photograph. What will he do with it? Put it under his cot?"

"Oh, give it to him," Gene coaxed. "Let him have his fun." But I never did. I was afraid the poor soul might break his vows.

Gene had not chosen Santa Margherita merely for its fishermen and Franciscans. Artists and writers, many of them his friends, inhabited the surrounding hills. We visited Alan Moorehead at Portofino, a gleaming stack of whitewashed building blocks. Alan's *Nile* books are among my favorites, and unlike many other authors he embodied the grace and perception of his work. We spent an exhilarating day with him and his friend, a charming young man whose untimely death soon afterward devastated Alan.

We took tea with Max Beerbohm at Rapallo. His villa was modest but wonderful because its walls were lined with his witty caricatures of the great and famous. They were as much as I got of the celebrated Beerbohm wit. Far from the sharp-tongued sophisticate I expected, he seemed rather sweet, gentle, spending most of our visit in nostalgic reminiscence with Gene. They had known each other in younger days—Max had even done a caricature of Gene somewhere along the line. So I spent a pleasant afternoon seeing his pictures and chatting with his wife, a charming woman much younger than he.

It was quite another story with Bernard Berenson, the legendary collector and art historian, who inhabited a Florentine hilltop near Sir Harold Acton and several of our other English friends. I expected our visit to I Tatti, Berenson's Renaissance villa, to approximate a museum tour. But I never got to see many paintings. As if his treasures were part of him, to be taken for granted as he settled into his eighties, he dismissed them in favor of human exchange. A frail, austere old man, with penetrating eyes and a wide Tatar nose, he surrounded himself with doting secretaries—aging beauties who formerly had been more than secretaries to him. Not that he was giving up a thing!

He positioned me between himself and Gene on the deep sofa in his sitting room before a blazing fire. The shawl over his knees, I assumed, was also for warmth. It turned out to be a cover for a flank attack. That rascal began stealthily inching toward me. I would move over a little bit and he would keep coming, trying to make contact with a knee or an elbow. It could only have been academic with my husband beside us, but Berenson obviously didn't think so. It was so funny, so dear. ("He's an old man; he's cold," Gene speculated later. "He just wanted to get warm.")

"I want you to come into the garden and hear my nightingales," Berenson told me. "This is their time of the day." He held my hand and guided me down a deep, cypress-lined walk. Scented air and stillness provided a backdrop for the story of his love affair with Italy. "We English cherish our damp little island, but we long for warm places," he confessed. "I first saw Italy as a young man and loved it with a young man's fervor. I knew that it was where I would stay. I have never regretted it."

We waited at the bottom of the garden for nightingales that never came. It was too early. The sun hadn't gone down. But he insisted that they would sing. We listened in the stillness until Gene, afraid that we might miss our evening's diversion, hustled me reluctantly away. The last I saw of Bernard Berenson, he was still waiting in the garden for his nightingales.

During our six months in Italy, fascinating places and people blended. While absorbing the wonders of Rome, we saw a lot of Martha Gellhorn, who lived there. She had impressed me when she and her former husband Ernest Hemingway visited Hollywood in the thirties, so I wasn't surprised by her warmth and intelligence. Besides her daring stint as a *Collier's* war correspondent, she wrote damn good fiction, which remained inevitably overshadowed by the Hemingway affiliation.

The decadent magic of Venice was not upstaged by its film festival. Although designated as the Venice International Film Festival, it still seemed essentially a showcase for the burgeoning postwar Italian film industry. Names that later became household words in America were not generally known then. Fortunately, my months in Italy had familiarized me with them. As one of the first American participants, I endured full assaults from the paparazzi and the international press while trying to communicate with Vittorio De Sica and Anna Magnani, whose English was only slightly better than my Italian. In any language, Magnani's unkempt sensuality made an impact. She was an original and she knew it, giving the press and the public measured doses of the earthy appeal that would catapult her to world fame.

We returned briefly to England, where Korda assigned Gene to write a film in Bavaria for Bobby Henrey, that little boy who made such a hit in *The Fallen Idol* with Ralph Richardson. After a stop at Bad Gastein, where Gene outfitted himself like a central-casting Bürgermeister, we crossed into the majestic reaches of Bavaria. At end of summer, the land was rich and closer to the sky, really heavenly. Gene worked and, for a change, I just explored hills and fields—until the State Department summoned me to Paris.

I had visited Paris earlier that summer to study the International

Theater Institute, whose plan to use theater as an educational tool co-
incided with my aims for film. Assistant Secretary of State George V.
Allen, whom I had briefed at the San Francisco Conference, invited
me back as a consultant on mass communications to UNESCO's General
Conference. So I returned to my beloved Paris, although there was little
time to enjoy it, with non-stop meetings, receptions, and broadcasts for
UNESCO Radio. We worked like dogs, which our congressional adviser,
my fellow Montanan Mike Mansfield, fortunately observed.

Congress usually sent a representative as a diplomatic gesture, but
also because some of its members were always a little bit suspicious of
the U.N. and wanted information. I remember sitting with the congressman from Montana and explaining what UNESCO was all about.
He returned to Washington with enthusiastic reports of our work, publicly acknowledging my efforts in areas where women, let alone actresses, were not taken seriously.

That was a much-appreciated affirmation, since I had encountered
a certain hostility at first, though not generally from the foreign dele-
gations, who freely mixed artists with scientists and statesmen. The
British delegation, in fact, gave a dinner for Lord Russell and me.
The distinguished diplomatist and the lowly movie star were their guests
of honor. It was a fabulous evening, although Lord Russell was very
naughty, teasing us with "Oh, you're just a bunch of do-gooders—
saints, nuns. . . ." Actually, he embraced U.N. ideals and made a
rousing speech to that effect the next day.

No, it was a certain faction of the U.S. delegation that resented me.
We had some marvelous representatives—university presidents, scientists, politicians—but there existed an obvious division between the down-
to-earth people who understood my reasons for being there and the intellectual snobs who looked down their noses at the movie star invading
their ranks. This ivory-tower mentality, particularly from the universities, which evaluates in terms of caste and shuts out the mere artist,
infuriates me. I certainly do not think we are second-class citizens. I
was taught from childhood that it was my divine right to be involved.
But I also believe that a performer should do his homework before getting involved. "Considered as artists," Albert Camus said, "we perhaps
have no need to interfere in the affairs of the world. But considered as
men—Yes! The miner who is exploited or shot down, the slaves in the

camps, those in the colonies, the legions of persecuted throughout the world—they need all those who can speak to communicate their silence. . . ."

At first, I followed my Grandmother Johnson's old admonition: "Listen and learn!" It was probably just as well. In my enthusiasm, I might have tried to monopolize every discussion. Then George Allen changed all that during a delegates' reception. "Look," he began, "you're going to have to address the U.S. delegation tomorrow morning." I stared at him incredulously. "You've got to say something—people are so curious about your being here." It was then nearly midnight. I stayed up most of the night, pacing, studying, agonizing over a speech that would tell the ivory-tower boys what artists could bring to this political forum.

I entered that meeting scared to death but prepared and dressed to the nines. Women should never be intimidated into dressing down to strengthen their professional image. Display your femininity proudly. A woman needn't don horn-rimmed glasses and orthopedic oxfords to prove she has brains. My speech emphasized the difficulty in selling peace, and the rare few throughout history who had managed it—the saints by their lives, Gandhi in his march to the sea. "This was a man of peace," I said of Gandhi, "yet he had a great sense of public relations." I stressed the need for public relations, as crass as it seemed, because that was my job, really, *selling* the idea of UNESCO. I explained that the artist by virtue of his work was best equipped to interpret the man of peace. "Peace is a *dramatic* idea," I concluded. "It is *positive*, and does not mean merely not going to war. The cause of peace is the world's greatest drama."

Well, the place came down; they just kept applauding. One of the scientists—a pioneer in cancer research—came up, took my hand, and said, "You belong." That meant a lot to me. Despite my unruffled exterior, I was afraid, unsure of my abilities.

Although my independent-producing career seemed lost with Gene in the Bavarian Alps, I still had the non-exclusive contract at RKO, where they wanted another Grant-Loy picture. With that in mind, I had talked with Terence Rattigan in London about purchasing *O Mistress Mine*, his play that the Lunts had played to perfection in England and America. "There has been, as you probably realise," Terence wrote to me, "considerable confusion over the question of rights and a few days ago these were definitely and finally sold to R.K.O. I've heard nothing of their plans but I gather they want to go into production very soon and I presume will be using my script. Would you like me to write to them saying you would be interested, or would it be better if you got into touch with them yourself? I should be so happy if you played the part which, after all, was written for you."

I assumed the part was mine. But Howard Hughes had just taken over RKO. Now, there was a curious man. The first time we met, in the early thirties in Howard Hawks's garden, a buffet was laid out on several long tables. Hughes tailed me from one to another, like a bloodhound on the scent. That day I just kept moving. I never really *knew* him—few people did—but I knew he kept women stashed all over town and I didn't care to be involved with him. Although he could be charming when he wanted something or someone, he always struck me as kind of a sad man, which, coupled with his deafness, contributed to his later reclusiveness. Even in those years you felt something strange about him, something that would eventually blow up.

Hughes grabbed *O Mistress Mine* for the largest sum paid for a play in 1949. Then he put it on the shelf. Despite continued interest from Cary and me, he never filmed Rattigan's play—one of the inexplicable decisions that lost RKO nearly $40 million during Hughes's six-year reign.

Concurrently, *The Case of Lady Brooke*, which Korda released as *That Dangerous Age*, was doing well in Europe. Korda's recent deal with David Selznick, however, prevented Fox from distributing it in this country, as originally planned. Corporate infighting kept it off American screens for another year, until Eddie Small finally released it—"sneaked it out" would be more accurate—through United Artists as *If This Be Sin*. That ridiculous title did not lure many Americans into theaters to see what would be my last major romantic role. But we got them in their homes. It became one of those pictures that hit television in the early days. I had a little set in Washington—you could hardly see anything—and they played that picture to death.

I was about to rejoin Gene in Bavaria after the Paris conference when Darryl Zanuck offered me the role of Lillian Gilbreth in *Cheaper by the Dozen*. What an irony! Zanuck, who typed me as the sloe-eyed exotic at Warners, casting me as the wholesome mother of twelve. I didn't see much of my old friend and nemesis then—around that time he left his wife, Virginia, and their children and went to France. He gambled heavily and got mixed up with a succession of French girls, trying unsuccessfully to make stars of them. Darryl, undersized, with prominent buckteeth, always seemed to be overcompensating to prove his potency. I felt sorry for him, because his compulsion toward young women who were probably exploiting him led to a sad restlessness. Virginia hung in there, though, and finally he came back to her in Palm Springs to die.

Several of my colleagues considered that playing the mother of twelve was career suicide for a forty-five-year-old actress. "For heaven's sake, you're letting us all down," some of them complained. "If you start playing mother roles, we'll all have to do it." To a certain extent, I suppose, they were right. I perceive that period now as the first stage of the transition female stars must face in middle age. At that time, however, I was unconcerned with such things in relation to my own career. It never occurred to me to fight to hold on the way Joan and Bette did. I am an actress always, but I am also a woman. As a woman, I needed increasingly to participate in more essential areas. Making pictures was a financial necessity for me, yet by that time, if the truth be told, my priorities were elsewhere. United Nations work brought me a kind of fulfillment I hadn't found during twenty-five years of picture-making.

As far as *Cheaper by the Dozen* was concerned, I liked the book and admired Mrs. Gilbreth, who combined motherhood and management engineering on a grand scale. It seemed like a good role for me. So, fitting speaking engagements and meetings of my Hollywood Film Committee around the shooting schedule, I went back to work. Fortunately it was a fun picture with all those adorable kids, and Jeanne Crain, sweet, lovely Jeanne, an incredible girl. She looked like the fifteen-year-old she was playing, yet she was a top box-office star and on the way to having quite a slew of kids herself.

After having the best dramatic role of my career in Pinky, *admits Jeanne Crain, I was absolutely crushed when they cast me as a teenage ingénue in* Cheaper by the Dozen. *"There are lots of things you don't understand," Zanuck said. "There will come a day, my dear, when no one will ask you to play a fifteen-year-old." Well, I accepted the role and the whole thing turned out to be a very joyful association.*

The thought of working with Myrna Loy intimidated me at

first, because I held her in such awe. I had adored her in all those wonderful pictures with Bill Powell and in the original of The Rains Came with Tyrone Power—I have a tape of it today and play it over and over. And perhaps because of that she seemed inscrutable to me. Although her features and coloring are not in person Oriental in the faintest degree, I can see why they typed her in those roles when she was terribly young. She projects a kind of serenity, a quiet, very calm, controlled type of movement, and yet you think, Oh, so many fascinating, mysterious things are going on behind that. It wasn't easy working on an intimate family picture with someone you worship. Myrna must have sensed that, because she set about putting me at ease right away.

It was an incredible lesson for me when the totality of Myrna as a woman and actress began to emerge. I think of her as woman incarnate, truly multifaceted and very, very deep. As in a pool, a deep, deep pool, you only see the surface, but all the drops from different sources flow into it, immediately becoming part of the whole. This depth is manifested in her acting. The slightest thing she does has a force, while others could chew the scenery and it wouldn't mean a thing. When Myrna does a scene, she appears to be so low-key and doing practically nothing discernible, yet when you sit in the rushes the next day, she zings out of the screen. It's the most amazing translation. Does she have an instinct the rest of us don't have? I don't know. It's as though she has something, an elusive quality, that only the camera can see. It must be a gift, a God-given quality that somehow is captured. She was absolutely made for motion pictures.

Clifton Webb, who played her husband, was just the opposite kind of person and actor. He was very temperamental, bombastic, and dictatorial, and that was his style. It always amazes me that certain actors can get away with murder if it's absolutely true to them. Myrna was the perfect foil for Clifton, letting him fly all over the place, while she remained serene and submissive and really in charge of the whole thing. Their surprising chemistry made the picture believable and successful.

I played Myrna's daughter three times—again in Belles on Their Toes, the sequel to Cheaper by the Dozen, and later in a live television production of Meet Me in St. Louis. It amuses me *because Myrna, who never had children, was so perfect as a mother, while I, the mother of seven, was never considered the motherly type. I begged to play the mother in* Please Don't Eat the Daisies. *I nearly jumped off a precipice over it, knocking on doors and everything. "Oh, no," they said. "You couldn't play that." But Myrna sailed gracefully from perfect wife to perfect mother and everybody just took it for granted.*

I never had a problem with my dozen kids. From Jeanne on down to the babe in arms, they were professional and disciplined. My only troubles on that picture came from two old friends: Walter Lang and Clifton Webb. I liked Walter, who had married Fieldsie, Carole Lombard's great friend, but he was the kind of director that drove me crazy. After going through my scenes ahead of me, acting out every detail without giving me a chance to try it, he would call, "O.K., let's shoot!"

"Look, I can't work this way," I finally protested. "How about letting *me* do it?" I have to do it myself. I have to see how it *feels*, how my body responds. It's essential. Walter and I straightened that out and we never had another problem.

Clifton's transgressions were more subtle. As a stage-trained actor of the old school, he considered scene-stealing his duty. Apparently it was kosher to do this on stage in his day. It isn't in films. You are absolutely nose to nose and cannot move or you've turned your partner around with the back of his head or some awkward angle to the camera. We were trained to consider the camera supreme, and if you turned this way or that the scene was most likely ruined. No professional film actor ever does that—ever—so I wasn't looking for it.

During one of my scenes with Clifton, our cameraman Leon Shamroy suddenly hurled his hat to the floor. "Goddamn it, Myrna!" he shouted. "When are you going to learn? Look at your marks." He was absolutely right. I had moved way back to keep up with Clifton. "I've marked you both three times, but he keeps moving back on you and you don't know it!" Leon stormed off the set in utter disgust. This is the man who probably got more Oscars than any other cinematographer, one of the great innovators. It was a bad moment, but I went out and convinced him to come back.

When I returned to Clifton, he was standing stock-still where I'd left him. We finished our scene without a hitch. There was no apology, no reference to Leon's outburst, but I sensed a touch of sheepishness cracking Clifton's otherwise imperturbable veneer. We had no more stage tricks, and our friendship stayed intact. I went to his house for bashes, where his mother, Maybelle, who looked like Clifton in drag, held court. Maybelle was the quintessential stage mother, her son's promoter, adviser, and inseparable companion since his youthful Broadway years. They used to say Clifton and Maybelle were Hollywood's happiest couple. Everybody went to their house. He was very social and very dear in his way—it just had to be *his* way.

Clifton came in to watch us shoot the touching ending, where I, as his widow, assure our brood that they will not be separated. The scene took a lot out of me, and I was resting in my dressing room when Clifton started hammering on the door. "My dear Myrna," he intoned, "what are you trying to do? Take the picture away from me?"

I hadn't heard much from Gene since my return, except indirectly from an Army friend of his who had seen him in Vienna. "Gene asked me to drop you a line cautioning you not to make any uncomplimentary remarks about the Russians when you write to him," Colonel John Corridon transmitted via the Army Postal Service. "The mail coming by the Austrian post is strictly censored here and if you spoke your mind about our dear allies, it might result in some annoyance to the company." That was Gene, always covering his flanks.

Meanwhile, I kept getting curious calls from Louella Parsons. "I've had another letter from Gene," she prodded. "What's going on with you two, anyway?" I wasn't sure if she had really heard from him—I certainly hadn't—but that's the way she was, calling just to start something. As I've said, she gave me the willies. Gene, however, was one of the people who liked to keep her informed. You were supposed to if you wanted favorable publicity. I never did. In fact, it delighted me when that group out there, the Hollywood press or whatever, named me their least cooperative actress one year. Granted, my exposure as a movie star opened doors that Myrna Loy of the U.N. couldn't open by herself, but I got plenty of coverage without catering to the sob sisters. My private life was none of their damn business.

Louella's prodding continued, while my husband remained in England, chasing some Irish countess. It really was a riot, when you think of it—all these ladies had to be at least countesses. It was painful, too. So finally I said, "O.K., buddy, I've had enough of this. Nothing's gonna change." Apparently, Joan Bennett and Hedy Lamarr had faced the same problem when they were married to him. It was pathetic, really. Even when I called to say I'd had it, he kept insisting that he loved me, that I was the *one*. He probably still believed it, but since the rumormongers had already got hold of it, he agreed to a separation.

After herding twelve kids around on the set all day, I often changed and went directly to address such diverse groups as the Los Angeles Advertising Women or the Motion Picture Industry Council. I was meeting with various studio heads or arranging meetings for visiting State Department officials in our continuing campaign to involve Hollywood in the workings of UNESCO. I spent a whirlwind Christmas week in Washington as the guest of Alice Curran, special assistant to my mentor, George Allen. I reported on the progress of my Hollywood Film Committee to Librarian of Congress Luther Evans, George, and his assistant Howland Sargeant, whose ideas impressed me as we developed, the procedure for studying the effects of American films abroad while upgrading their message. I attended working luncheons, receptions, dinners in my honor, and countless State Department functions, including a farewell for George Allen, who was leaving his post as Assistant Secretary of State to become Ambassador to Yugoslavia. Professional and personal relationships began to emerge that would become increasingly important in subsequent years. I was no longer the new girl in town. I was a worker, a participant, and treated as such.

I returned to Hollywood fired up for action, and many screenwriters and producer-directors succumbed. Frank Capra got excited about United Nations Children's Fund material I sent him and used it in *Here Comes the Groom*. George Seaton incorporated UNESCO ideas into *Anything Can Happen*. Ida Lupino and Collier Young, who had married and set up a production company, offered help. Roberto Rossellini wanted to make a film in Europe for us—many people did. The problem was getting money. UNESCO did not have funding to make its own films.

My progress was hampered when certain anti-U.N. and anti-Communist factions united in yet another attack on Hollywood. This relatively small-scale smear job was spearheaded by Gerald L. K. Smith in his rabid monthly *The Cross and the Flag*, and by Myron Fagan, a curious crusader whose off-the-wall output included *Red Treason in Hollywood*. These fanatics made quite some headway in Republican women's groups and the more conservative film organizations—particularly the Motion Picture Industry Council, an amalgamation of nine vital guilds and associations. Its executive secretary, Art Arthur, worked wholeheartedly with me to establish a fact film program. "We did a great job for war," he reasoned. "We should be able to do an even greater job for peace." But the council's co-chairmen, Ronald Reagan and Roy Brewer, ultimately thwarted our attempts.

At this time in California, remember, we had Richard Nixon exploiting the "Red scare" in his fight against Helen Gahagan Douglas for the Senate. Nixon employed cheap, Red-baiting tactics to win, giving an early indication of the opportunism that would eventually, but not soon enough, discredit him. Eleanor Roosevelt, who had Nixon pegged from the start, enlisted my aid in the fight against him. As a vocal campaigner for Helen, I had the honor of being put on Nixon's blacklist—the one in the bottom drawer that included Katharine Graham, owner of the Washington *Post*. Helen's supporters began pushing me for the congressional seat she had vacated to run for the Senate. I nipped that in the bud. "I've been away from California so long I don't feel eligible to represent the people there," I told reporters. "I don't know enough to be in Congress. I'm learning to be a diplomat, but I'm no politician."

Fagan and Smith questioned more basic qualifications. "A dispatch from Paris now reveals that Myrna Loy has been in Paris to advise the American delegation to UNESCO," noted an editorial in *The Cross and the Flag*. "Anyone stupid enough or cunning enough to join the Red organizations of Hollywood has no expert wisdom to offer." Such libel may have impressed Hollywood's more rabid conservatives. It didn't fool my mother.

"Why, Myrna's always been interested in public affairs," she informed inquisitive reporters, "and she has wisdom to spare! Her father ran for the Montana legislature when he was twenty-one—he cast his first ballot for himself, and he was elected, too. Her aunt was county treasurer for years. Myrna was raised to be involved."

Nor was my credibility in Washington affected. On April 19, 1950, Secretary of State Dean Acheson appointed me to a three-year term on the National Commission for UNESCO.

The National Commission consists of one hundred members handpicked from the realms of education, science, religion, and culture. There were damn few from that last, a rather abstract category. In fact,

Archibald MacLeish and I were the only so-called artists appointed to the Commission. The United States tends to trust plutocrats, politicians, and career diplomats rather than intellectuals and artists. We generally shun them, are scared to death of them. While serving on the U.S. delegation to the Fifth General UNESCO Conference in Florence, I was reminded that other countries harbor no such prejudice. François Mauriac headed the French delegation. Julian Huxley and Alan Moorehead represented England. Jaime Torres Bodet, UNESCO's Director-General, had introduced the concept of "each one teach one" in Mexico. So many countries sent philosophers, poets, and teachers who lent a necessary note of idealism and vision to often bureaucratic proceedings. We forget that our greatest politicians were visionaries. Thomas Jefferson, for instance, whose inspiring creed I repeated in my speeches: "I have sworn upon the altar of God eternal hostility against every form of tyranny over the mind of man."

India sent its greatest philosopher, Sarvepalli Radhakrishnan, who gallantly claimed to be a fan of mine. I certainly became one of his, impressed by his blend of spiritual and political awareness, and frequently consulted him. The next time I saw him, he was Vice-President of India. The last time I saw him he was President. His participation on so many levels awed me, but I discovered that educated Indians tend to be that way. I never worked with Nehru, unfortunately, although we met at the mayor's house when he visited New York with his daughter Indira. He was very charming, a handsome and compelling man, who flirted with me throughout the reception. Well, let's just say he spent a lot of time looking at me, and I was not unreceptive. I could understand how Edwina Mountbatten might have been attracted to him. They were the basis, supposedly, for the characters of Lady Esketh and the Indian doctor in *The Rains Came*.

The Italians really put on a show for us in Florence. The opening ceremonies began with pomp and circumstance at the Palazzo Vecchio, the Town Hall facing the Piazza della Signoria, where Savonarola was burned. They laid a long red carpet to the palazzo for us, flanked by a resplendent honor guard wearing scarlet-and-gold state uniforms. For our regular meetings we used the Palazzo Pitti, where Botticelli angels cavorting on the ceiling diverted me during conferences. "How will anybody get any work done here?" I asked Alan Moorehead. "It's too seductive." But we did. We got a hell of a lot of work done.

State Department documents, to put it mildly, are difficult to comprehend. After poring over them, taking copious notes, I would question Howland Sargeant, who headed our delegation, or run to the British Library. I then went into those meetings and discussed, reasoned, argued into the night or as long as my voice held out, until a vote was taken. Sam Goldwyn, who happened to be in Europe, was amazed by my participation when I invited him to audit a meeting. He sat beside me wearing earphones for English translations of the various speeches, listening with the wonderment of a child. I remember his pride at being there and his willingness to help. Of course, Sam had already produced films that espoused U.N. principles. At that time he was making tough little pictures like *Roseanna McCoy* and *Edge of Doom*, which in their way fostered our goal of co-existence.

"I don't think we'll get to you tonight," Howland whispered during a particularly exhausting session. "Why don't you go back and get some sleep?" My room at the Excelsior was tiny, but its balcony jutted out over the Arno, allowing a panoramic sweep of Florence. I was just falling asleep when someone knocked at the door: "Miss Loy, you're on!" I dressed quickly and rushed back to the Palazzo Pitti. Still groggy, I stepped out of the car and stumbled on the cobbles, sending my carefully arranged notes flying around the courtyard.

I managed to get through my speech, which Alan Moorehead claimed impressed at least one fellow delegate. "There you were, tired, losing your voice," Alan recounted, "while nearby slumped an old fellow from one of the Arab countries who had slept through most of the speeches. The minute he heard your voice, he sat bolt upright, his turban comically askew, and hung on to your every word." My presence generally puzzled the Arabs. The Lebanese delegation sent me flowers daily, without quite understanding what this Western woman was doing there.

I spent my few free evenings at Alan's house, which had belonged to the poet Poliziano, a protégé of Lorenzo the Magnificent. One night— I have never seen such a night—the moon shone like the sun. We were sitting in the walled garden, its flowers and olive trees and old stones silvered by moonlight, when the nightingales that had eluded me at I Tatti began to sing. You've never heard anything so beautiful. The closest thing in this country is the mockingbird, but there's no comparison, really. Read Keats, read the other poets, only they can verbalize that crystalline call.

We worked six days a week, usually making good-will appearances for the State Department on the seventh. When we reached Piazza del Campo, in Siena, the city's historic annual horse race was over. They ran another one for our group, which included Maria Montessori, who had addressed the conference. The fact that I'd seen the colorful race before, with Gene, didn't diminish its excitement, particularly with Montessori along. That innovative educator, well into her seventies, depended on her son and, occasionally, a wheelchair to get around, but she bristled with energy and curiosity. She would not be left behind when the mayor led us up some steep City Hall stairs to a terrace over-looking the piazza. I will never forget Montessori's excitement as she leaned over the railing, cheering the riders on.

At one point she turned to me, her sweet Italian features animated by fierce, probing eyes. "Do you know how much power you have?" she probed. "You have *tremendous* power!" She had just returned from India, so at first I thought she meant mystic power. No, she meant the power of film, and she implied in no uncertain terms that I should use it.

As if to prove her point, while my fellow delegates toured, the State Department kept me in Florence for a propaganda mission. The local Communist government was showing an American documentary about the Tennessee Valley Authority, with the narration dubbed to serve their ideology. My appearance was meant to counteract the anti-American atmosphere, but Party officials never acknowledged me. I felt like a sacrificial lamb among all these women wearing black dresses and crosses, who I later learned had been ordered to ignore me. As I headed sheep-ishly for the door after the film, some brave soul shouted, "Myrna Loy, we love you!" Then there was hell to pay—autographs, embraces, fur-ther protestations of love—as officials tried vainly to stem the "power" of film.

Howland Sargeant, the head of our delegation, also stayed in Flor-ence that day. He was allowed to take me to tea in Fiesole at the Mon-astery of St. Francis—after the brothers had lent me a homespun shawl to cover my bare head and neck. Within that fitting monument to the gentle patron of birds and flowers, where Franciscans tended enchanting gardens, I began to know Howland. He was thirty-eight then, attractive in a masculine, staunch New England way, possessing the integrity once implied by the designation "Yankee." A Phi Beta Kappa at Dartmouth, a Rhodes Scholar at Oxford, he joined the State Department and served F.D.R. as chairman of the Technical Industrial Intelligence Committee for the Joint Chiefs of Staff. Truman elevated him to Deputy Assistant Secretary of State. Drawn by his intelligence and expertise, I found myself depending on him not only in the general course of business but in rare free moments as well. Along shadowed stone passages into sudden piazzas, across the jumbled Ponte Vecchio, we discussed pertinent issues, to be sure, but the Flower of Italy's seductive aura did not elude us.

When the conference ended, some of us repaired to various European cities before going home. Our group made a good-will visit to Munich, which was sad at that time after the war, devastated. Then we went to Paris, a city Howland knew and loved. He introduced me to charming, out-of-the-way bistros all over town. La Bourride, on the Rue Paul Cézanne, resembled a ship's interior and had birds flying around the dining room. Chez Marcel, on the Rue de la Folie-Méricourt, was run by an exuberant little Basque man, who greeted us like long-lost relatives. Paris worked its magic and, my God, this thing with Howland developed into a romance!

9

THE
WASHINGTON
WIFE
1950-1960

Miss Loy's work for UNESCO *has made news wherever she has gone and has made friends for her wherever the news has gone.* —Washington Post, 1950

Ten days after we returned from Paris, in June of 1950, the North Koreans crossed the 38th parallel into South Korea. The United Nations Security Council acted quickly, certifying the act of aggression and authorizing resistance—a classic example of collective security. Had the old League of Nations been as decisive when Japan entered Manchuria or Germany attacked Poland, it would have altered the course of history.

In response to President Truman's forceful stand on Korea, sixteen United Nations countries sent fighting forces and forty others sent hospital units or material aid, ultimately averting a chain of aggressions that might have triggered a third world war. The price: three bloody years of combat in Korea, which never inspired the home-front spirit of World War II. Even in Washington it was business as usual. The Korean "skirmish" remained, to paraphrase Oscar Wilde, the war that dared not speak its name, a harbinger, perhaps, of our national rejection of Vietnam. The bands had indeed stopped playing, yet the needs of our wounded remained the same.

I resumed my hospital rounds, delivering armfuls of fresh pink and white lilacs flown over by the Dutch for our military hospitals. Occasionally I met nurses who remembered me from my Red Cross days. "You still have your knack with the boys?" one of them asked. "I have one now, a Negro, who won't respond to anything or anybody. See what you can do." I found the young man strapped to a kind of cradle bed, staring vacantly at the ceiling—at nothing, really. I stood there wondering what one could possibly do to reach him. Finally, I placed some lilacs on his pillow where he could smell them. Slowly, very slowly, he turned his head toward the flowers, then looked up at me and smiled. The memory of that beautiful black face beside those white lilacs will stay with me forever.

Gene Markey's international version of open marriage persisted during our eight-month separation. A born courtier—witty companion, skilled lover, dynamic partner—he simply found it impossible to concentrate on one woman. We had a lot of fun, a wonderful time, until his promiscuity became more than I could bear. I couldn't take any more of those goings-on. One should take a certain amount, I suppose, in order to preserve a marriage. I took more than a certain amount and ultimately the marriage wasn't worth it. I once more made the twenty-seven-hour flying trip to Cuernavaca, filing my petition in the same dingy provincial courthouse where I had divorced John Hertz. Leone, resisting "I told you so," joined me on that depressing pilgrimage. She helped to ease the inevitable sense of loss that follows even an amicable divorce. "I'm very upset about it," I told pushy reporters at Los Angeles airport. "It's too painful even to talk about." And although I harbored no second thoughts about divorcing Gene Markey, it was.

Gene subsequently married a very rich woman, the owner of Calumet Farm, and lived out his life in his accustomed grand style, raising thoroughbreds. One of them ran second in the Kentucky Derby. I didn't have money on it. Gene wasn't a horseman when I married him; he was a sailor. He died in 1980, still maintaining, according to his stepdaughter, that I was the *one*.

My priorities were in Washington. I bought a charming little frame house in Georgetown, and the U.N. Information Office gave me a space in their temporary headquarters near the State Department. At first, gaping neighbors and autograph hunters hounded me on my brisk morning walk to Wisconsin Avenue to hail a cab for the office. Soon, however, I gratefully became just another resident of Georgetown, which is really a pleasant, friendly, naturally sophisticated place to live.

On another level, instant recognition spared me the ordeal of the capital's rigid pecking order. People—even those at the top—would listen to me because they felt that they already knew me. After all, communication is the essence of UNESCO, and I found that a bridge had already been created for me. Celebrity got me to the podium, shall we say, but once there I was on my own. Myrna Loy the actress might be invited to speak at organizational teas, luncheons, and dinners, but Myrna Loy the UNESCO spokesperson had to stress the heightened importance of international understanding in light of Korea. "More than ever now free people need to be reminded that liberty and freedom are their most cherished possessions," I told the American Newspaper Women's Club when they fêted Philippine Senator Geronima Pecson and me. I became a frequent last-minute speaking replacement for busy government officials. Anna Rosenberg, for instance, Assistant Secretary of Defense, asked me to fill in at a World Brotherhood meeting at the Shoreham. "It was really splendid of you," she wrote with becoming modesty, "and I know that the audience got a good 'break' by the substitution."

Howland Sargeant became a steady, stimulating beau for nearly a year after my divorce. He had been divorced several years before we met, so we both eschewed rushing into marriage. We avoided the more publicized political parties in favor of small dinners with friends or picturesque restaurants on the outskirts of town. I wanted to spare him the commotion that still accompanied my more public appearances. All that exaggerated attention activates an insecurity in a man, a jealousy probably planted in their formative years. I was conscious of it always, conscious that my fame exacerbated it. You couldn't avoid it. We were together in some remote part of Florida when an idiot photographer burst in, disrupted our lunch, and infuriated Howland. "You'd better think it over," I warned him. "I'm a famous woman and this is what you'll have to put up with. There's nothing I can do about it."

When we finally decided to marry, it happened very quickly. The press had made such a point of our relationship that we considered it prudent to attend the forthcoming UNESCO conference in Paris as Mr. and Mrs. Sargeant—idle gossip could have harmed Howland's credibility in the State Department. Holding off tickets and passports until after the ceremony, we hurriedly set the date for June 1, 1951, five days before our scheduled departure. Although that day dawned oppressively hot, I got all decked out in a new silk suit with fresh flowers and headed for the Presbyterian rectory. Howland wanted to be married by a minister, so we chose my Scottish grandmother's denomination. That turned out to be a big mistake. The Southern Presbyterians had recently ruled that a year must elapse between marriages; since my divorce had been final for only ten months, the minister refused to marry us.

There we stood at the altar, so to speak, with our attendants, my old friends Betty and Bob Black, damp and frustrated and no place to go. Suddenly Bob, who had realized his early potential to become Pentagon Chief of the Medical Corps, remembered that the chaplain at Fort Myer owed him a favor. He telephoned only to find the chapel booked solid. Bob persisted. "All right, Colonel Black," the chaplain relented. "I'll try to squeeze them in." Wedged hurriedly between two military weddings, wilted bouquet, creased suit, and all, I became Howland Sergeant's somewhat depleted bride in time for the Paris trip.

U.N. Secretary-General Trygve Lie, a massive, exuberant, peace-loving Norwegian, visited Paris during the conference. Jacob Malik, the U.N. Security Council's Soviet representative, had proposed a Korean armistice, and Lie sought international support to implement it. While political analysts weighed Malik's motives, Trygve confided, "Propaganda or not, we must take advantage of his move and start peace negotiations." That possibility, ultimately unrealized, permeated the Paris conference and strengthened my argument for the uses of film. *The Best Years of Our Lives*, for example, was having a tremendous impact in the European countries that had been at war a few years before. They identified with the characters, realizing that people are the same the world over, and that war, even for the conquerors, is hell.

"That's one thing our films can do," I told an international gathering of newsmen; "erase national stereotypes that pop into your head when someone mentions another nationality. Usually it hasn't anything to do with the character of the people, and usually it's unkind. For years, it's been a joke that all Englishmen carry umbrellas, but when you make it clear that they do so because it rains so much in England, it doesn't seem so absurd." Not a terribly profound observation, to be sure, but in context it made a valid point. Well, not in Congress, it didn't.

When we returned to Washington, I discovered what it meant to be a State Department wife and ripe for the pickin'. During a House debate on UNESCO's budget, a Republican congressman led the attack: "Miss Myrna Loy, the Hollywood *actress* [uttered with great scorn], a member of the organization, was concerned with explaining to the world certain national customs—such as why Englishmen carry umbrellas." That prefaced allegations that Howland and I had married when we did only to ensure a free wedding trip. "I admire Mr. Sargeant's choice of Paris as a place to honeymoon," he said sarcastically. "My only regret is that the average American taxpayer is not able to arrange a honeymoon there at the government's expense." Fortunately, Representative Prince Preston of Georgia, our adviser in Paris, stood and refuted the charges, explaining that my UNESCO job was unsalaried and I had even waived expense money. But I would continue to be a good visible target for U.N. opponents.

Apropos of salaries and expenses, I returned to Hollywood for a picture after a two-year hiatus. Since George Sanders was renting my Pacific Palisades house, 20th Century-Fox supplied a Beverly Hills apartment for the duration, which was fine with me. I had no intention of staying away from Howland any longer than necessary. In fact, I would have preferred not to work so soon after my marriage, but the picture, *Belles on Their Toes*, was a sequel to *Cheaper by the Dozen*. It seemed only fair that I continue playing Lillian Gilbreth, whose character comes into its own in the sequel, allowing me to strike some long-overdue blows for working women. I finally met Mrs. Gilbreth at a Washington luncheon afterward. Our hostess, Oveta Culp Hobby, wishing to surprise her, didn't say I would be there. It worked. Mrs. Gilbreth was so flabbergasted, so stunned to see this woman who had played her in two films, she peered at me out of the corners of her eyes and barely said a word.

If you got along well the first time, observes Jeanne Crain, *a sequel's like a family reunion. Clifton Webb, being the way he was, kind of set the tenor on* Cheaper by the Dozen, *but Myrna became the dominant one in the sequel. So we were all much closer and the set was more festive. Hoagy Carmichael was in the picture and played the piano at every opportunity between scenes, while we all reminisced about this or that and sang along. Since Myrna's character really came into flower, and mine grew up, we had more of a mother-daughter relationship in the script and on the set, too. She was playing a living woman with a worldwide reputation, and, of course, Myrna was that kind of woman her-*

*self. One day, a Japanese delegation from the San Francisco Peace
Conference arrived on the set to present a scroll honoring her
achievements as an actress and a* UNESCO *representative.*

*I remember Myrna between scenes dictating to her secretary,
carrying on* UNESCO *business. It was really with her in heart and
mind all the time. We used to talk about the United Nations
view of the world and what must be done to eliminate disunity.
Intelligent and tremendously caring, she brought so much into
my ken that I had never really thought about before, a world of
consciousness about social issues and individual participation.
During our private conversations, for the first time, I saw that
underneath her composed exterior was a very, very passionate
woman concerned for life and the world.*

Before I left Hollywood, Jerry Wald and Norman Krasna proposed reuniting Bill Powell and me in *Three to Make Ready,* based on Katherine
Turlington's delightful best-seller. It was the most tempting of several
film prospects, but I rejected it. After all, a new husband and another
life waited in Washington.

Washington is a political town, obviously, but it's just as much a
social town with rigid codes of behavior. Believe me, you've got to look
out on both counts; you've got to watch your step. I remember thinking
at first, Oh, they're really going to get this movie star. And anti-U.N.
politicos and gossip-oriented reporters did when it served their purposes.
One columnist in particular—her name, fortunately, escapes me—always angled for something negative about me to spice her column. When
I gave a series of parties after my marriage, she had a field day specu-
lating about who this actress thought she was, coming from Hollywood
and flouting protocol and blah, blah, blah.

Since Howland had accepted so many invitations as a bachelor over
the years, some of which we'd accepted together, the time had come to
reciprocate. Our professional and personal associations were involved—
hundreds of people—so I decided to give three days of parties: first, the
UNESCO relations staff; then, his State Department colleagues; and, finally, the politicians. When someone questioned the protocol of having
the politicians last, I said we were building to a climax.

We had taken a spacious apartment at Friendship, Evalyn Walsh
McLean's former mansion, which was perfect for entertaining. I served

the best of everything—beluga caviar, the works. This all occurred in the heat of summer, when Washington's climate is unbearable; but you were considered a sissy if you had fans or, God forbid, air-conditioning. Now they all have air-conditioning, but at that time they actually disdained anyone cowardly enough to employ cooling devices. That's the kind of provincial thinking you were up against. Self-styled arbiters had been hammering away at me: "We don't do this in Washington. . . . We don't do that in Washington." I finally said to hell with it and did it all anyway, including placing a great big electric fan in my living room. When old Alben Barkley, the Vice-President, arrived, he made a beeline for that fan. "Ahhh," he sighed, "this is wonderful; you're a smart girl," and held court right in front of it throughout the party. Fans became de rigueur in Washington after that, a petty victory that, I must admit, brought me inordinate satisfaction.

I never aspired to be one of those political partygivers. I wasn't rich enough or so inclined. They were an interesting breed, though, those Washington hostesses, working hard to galvanize the essentially provincial, workaday town. Perle Mesta was a Midwestern lady who never pretended to be anything else. She loved bringing people together, taking as much pleasure from her frequent, lavish entertaining as her guests did. It would have been easy to consider me just another bauble to spice the action, but she wasn't like that. Perle was as lavish with genuine warmth and welcome as she was with food and spirits. She never put on airs of any kind, even after Harry Truman made her Ambassador to Luxembourg. She was definitely the President's kind of gal. Mine, too, using her money to such congenial ends, as did Lillie Vogel, another great hostess and character-about-town. There's something heartening about people with that kind of generosity.

Marjorie Merriweather Post was no less generous, but her garden parties and charity fêtes tended to be more structured and elegant. When first entering her Foxhall Road realm during the war, I had been overpowered by her great wealth and its obvious material rewards. On subsequent visits, however, her beauty and charm took precedence. Despite her unquestionably grandiose life-style—moats for her dogs; rusticated escalators—she remained a genuinely nice person committed to charitable causes. Yes, she had extraordinary wealth, but she used it well. And her daughter Dina Merrill, whom I first met when she was a young girl in her mother's house, possesses all those qualities, besides a talent that would have made her a front-rank star if she had concentrated on her acting career.

These were relative newcomers compared with the old-guard hostesses who had survived the vicissitudes of our capital. Foremost among them was Alice Roosevelt Longworth, Teddy Roosevelt's daughter. They never needed to build a monument for her father in Washington—they had Alice. She used her lineage like a pedestal. Spoiled and pettish, always expecting to be pampered because of age and rank, she would constantly put forth half-baked political ideas without knowing what she was talking about. I avoided her like the plague. But I adored another old-guard Republican lady, Mrs. Robert Lowe Baker, whose quaint "at homes" and Old World teas offered such a marked contrast to Perle Mesta's breezy bashes.

Washington was a haven for extraordinary women, and I'm proud to say that many of them became my friends. India Edwards, whose husband ran the State Department's overseas photography and film section, was a very political person. Everybody down there is in one way or another, but India was exceptional—a beautiful, dynamic woman, who happened to be executive director of the Democratic National Committee, a great friend of Truman's, and a real power behind the scenes in Washington. They almost nominated her for Vice-President at one of the Stevenson conventions.

Maureen Mansfield was another formidable woman. I knew and admired Mike as a brilliant politician with great powers of persuasion, a man who became Senate Majority Leader and Ambassador to Japan without losing the look and feel of a rugged Westerner. But Maureen was the one who had schooled this rough Montanan in their early years together. In fact, someone wrote a script about them and wanted me to play Maureen. Like most of the projects I really cared about, it never happened.

Another extraordinary woman occupied the White House, and despite the intimidating aura of the executive mansion, Bess Truman invested it with a sort of down-home hospitality. The President absolutely adored his wife, so she never felt pressured to be anything but herself. I've never known a less ostentatious person than Bess Truman. And don't think that Alice Longworth and her crowd didn't try turning that into a liability. Bess couldn't have cared less. She never made a fuss about things being this way or that; she just did what she was supposed to do, and did it with far more distinction than some of the fashion plates who have succeeded her.

Since the White House sets Washington's social and political pace, simplicity became the keynote of the Truman years. The President's direct no-nonsense approach permeated his administration. We know Harry Truman had guts, but they went deeper than invective. His pervading sense of inner security, on a lesser level, strengthened my position. He never considered the proximity of a movie star harmful to his credibility, as do so many candidates who use us, then drop us. When issues were pertinent to UNESCO, he kept me at his side during Blair House conferences or Rose Garden functions, frequently soliciting my opinions and advice.

When the President elevated Howland to Assistant Secretary of State for Public Affairs, he placed him in the top echelon of the State Department under Secretary of State Dean Acheson. At the end of the swearing-in ceremony, Dean turned to me and smiled. "It strikes me," he said for all to hear, "that we're getting two assistant secretaries for the price of one." Even as I smiled in response to the compliment, I cringed at the thought of diminishing my husband's achievement. Not that Dean had intended anything but a graceful acknowledgment of my commitment to Howland's work.

Dean Acheson was an attractive, really stunning man, who exuded fierce dignity and forthright integrity. For me he held enormous appeal, but then I've always found brains sexy. I opposed some of his stands during his tenure and later as a bipartisan Presidential adviser—his support for bombing North Vietnam and Cuba, for example—but I admired and respected him. His demand for excellence in government made him rather contemptuous of the lesser minds in Congress. He would rail with devastating wit against the "sly worldliness" and "sanctimonious self-righteousness" that inflated government windbags and beclouded, as he put it, "the dangers and opportunities of our time with an unctuous film." How much we need men of Acheson's fiber now to shake up that smug, generally subservient bunch in Washington.

Howland and Dean met comfortably on intellectual and social levels, and since I liked Alice Acheson, we all became friends. Lacking the limitations and pretensions of so many government wives, Alice was a good painter, a gracious hostess, a warm, generous person. After receptions at her house, she would always send over beautiful arrangements of her party flowers for me to enjoy. I would attend those official teas and State Department functions, but mostly we had quiet sorts of family evenings together. That wasn't so easy to accomplish in the capital, because you seldom leave the pressures behind. I learned what it meant to go through the hell of two or three major crises a day. One had to be prepared to face them and solve them with expertise gained only from having been there. That's why I sympathized with Jimmy Carter, who was catapulted into the White House without benefit of a Washington indoctrination.

One early April evening in 1951, Acheson summoned Howland to an emergency meeting at his house. This was rather unusual. They often had evening meetings but held them at an official apartment kept for that purpose. "It will be a long night," Dean cautioned me. "Why don't you come along and keep Alice company?" So off we went to P Street with my curiosity piqued. While Alice and I sat in the living room discussing Canada and some beautiful paintings she had done there, the men were on the sun porch locked in hushed conversation. I was dying to know what was going on, but not a word of explanation came, not a peep out of anybody, only that infernal buzzing while I tried to concentrate on polite chatter.

On the way home my husband said nothing, and I had learned that a State Department wife never asks questions. A rather noncommittal person anyway, Howland became stoically closemouthed about official business. He was perfect for his role—he should have been a spy. That ability to separate home and office was symptomatic of deeper attitudes about women mixing in the world of ideas and government, a subtle prejudice that would help to erode our marriage. I went to bed frustrated the night of the Acheson meeting, respecting Howland's position, but a little bit angry nevertheless.

The morning headlines answered my unasked questions: TRUMAN FIRES MACARTHUR. The general had become obstreperous, aiming to enlarge the war by invading China, and the President had taken the unprecedented step of removing him from command. That had been implemented at the Achesons' while I discussed Canadian landscapes.

When the Hiss-Chambers case broke, Acheson foresaw the Red-baiting hysteria of McCarthyism that would follow. While himself enduring unfounded insinuations of Communist sympathies, he stood by his much-maligned colleague. "I will never turn my back on Alger Hiss," he declared. "He is a friend." Throughout the inevitable McCarthy era, Acheson fielded bitter accusations hurled at himself and his staff with a potent blend of intelligence, dignity, and contempt. He remained a reasonable voice in the wilderness as good men were unreasonably discredited and disgraced. I watched in dismay and frustration, unable to participate in the fray because of my husband's position in the State Department. Government wives cannot vote, electioneer, or fight for even remotely controversial causes. I'd been doing battle all my life, it seemed, for myself or others involved in those witch-hunts, and there, in the thick of the McCarthy horror, my hands were tied. I had to sit back and watch, giving quiet succor, as progressive, farsighted friends like Bill Benton were knocked out of Congress after McCarthy attacked. It's very difficult being a true liberal in this country. These days you're not even allowed to be a good Democrat!

Fortunately, I was allowed to continue my U.N. work. Dean, who had appointed me to the UNESCO Commission in the first place, remained supportive of my various endeavors. And various they were, whether praising the women of Japan, during International Women's Week, for "helping to bring your country back into the family of nations," or imparting the essence of UNESCO to young people during the Philadelphia *Bulletin*'s forum "What's Next for Youth?" I served as a member at large for UNESCO's Third National Conference, at Hunter College, and assembled motion-picture representatives for the Venice Conference of Artists—without including myself. Howland's work would have kept him from accompanying me to Italy, and he was not, shall we say, enchanted by my involvement as it was.

Before our marriage, there were discussions of politics and the U.N. and UNESCO, an exchange of ideas, a mutual commitment to our respective goals. I needed that kind of intellectual stimulus. He fulfilled me intellectually, sexually, emotionally, and every other way, although we were people from altogether different worlds and he could be slightly patronizing to those with less education. After the wedding, he began reverting to the way he had lived as a bachelor: a day at the State Department, a game of tennis or squash, and home to read the newspaper or watch the news before dinner. I had a maid to serve him and ordered only the finest food, which he ate with gusto and appreciation. Then, if we weren't going out, he went to sleep.

He wanted a "little woman," and for a long time I tried to bury myself in his world. We stood in caps and gowns as Mr. and Mrs. Howland Sargeant to receive citations from Fairleigh Dickinson College for distinguished service to UNESCO. But vociferous photographers marred the dignified ceremony. I stood dutifully by as he became Assistant Secretary, and headlines blared: MYRNA LOY'S HUBBY TAKES STATE DEPT. OATH. I donned a folksy sundress and attended his twentieth Dartmouth reunion, aiming to be just another alumni wife. "It is no reflection," decided the class secretary, "that Assistant Secretary of State Howie Sargeant and Congressman Tom Curtis were outshone by Howie's wife, Myrna Loy. . . ." So you start cringing and slumping a bit, holding back, thinking you can protect another ego by diminishing your own.

During a big Washington political dinner in 1952, Harry Truman stood up and said, "I'm not going to run again." He announced it as simply as that, and we who knew him didn't doubt it. I wish you could have heard the groans from that august assemblage of Democrats. It was a jolt, because after finishing F.D.R.'s fourth term, he had served only one of his own. But Harry had had it and there was no changing his mind.

The shock was dispelled by the man who ultimately became the Democratic candidate in 1952. When I first met Adlai Stevenson, at some posh affair, he struck me as charming and very attractive—not physically unlike Arthur Hornblow, in fact. Subsequently, at more intimate gatherings of mutual friends, the quality of this singular man emerged. Unlike any other politician I'd known, and Adlai was certainly a politician, he was witty and incisive without constantly measuring his words for political effect. Paradoxically, his conversational spontaneity faltered only when he strained to avoid the clichés he abhorred. Where others were glib, Adlai was eloquent; where others were clever, he was wise. The more I learned of him and his policies, the more frustrating my position as a State Department wife became. I was forbidden to do any electioneering—that's a rule. I couldn't get out and fight for this man publicly, but he always knew he could depend on me.

On election night I could only fret. Elsie Jensen Brock, my AAUN colleague from California, called when she reached Washington after working her tail feathers off on a cross-country sweep for Adlai. I implored her to come over, so we could comfort each other, but she was half dead and went to bed. So had my husband, after Eisenhower's

victory seemed inevitable. It infuriated me when Howland quietly shuf-
fled off, until I realized how deeply it affected him. The opposition was
in, and that meant the end of his tenure. I sat up alone watching the
returns on our blurry little television set and crying.

Before the changing of the guard, we attended another UNESCO
Conference in Paris, Howland's last as chairman of the U.S. delegation.
"How could you have done this?" accused colleagues from many coun-
tries, as if we were personally responsible. "How could you have lost
Stevenson?" How, indeed!

When the new boys took over in Washington, I called my friend
Margaret Mahoney at UNESCO—now she's president of the Common-
wealth Fund—to rail at the repressive policies of the Eisenhower administration. I ranted on and on while Maggie tried to silence me with
such noncommittal comments as "Myrna, you mustn't talk that way."
Later, she called me from home: "For God's sake, Myrna, don't do that!
Please don't put me in that position!" The new administration were not
only putting their policies on the desk, they were putting little wires
under them. Phones were tapped and people in the State Department
were scared to death. For the good of my friends, I finally had to shut
my mouth.

Some of my concern stemmed from increasing conservative attacks
on UNESCO, which accused the cultural organization of advocating world
government, atheism, and Communism, among other imagined infa-
mies. We dealt with this issue during the Fourth National Conference,
at the University of Minneapolis, where I was a delegate, and found an
unexpected ally in President Eisenhower, who praised our "dedicated
task of deepening international understanding."

My greatest concern, however, centered on my husband, who had
to get a job. That's what happens in bipartisan politics: wham, you're
out and that's it! It was a frustrating time for him. We went up to New
York so often for interviews that we took a little pied-à-terre on Fifty-
first and First, a neighborhood where several of our friends lived. From
a wide range of job offers, including one to head a carpet-manufacturing
company, we were tempted when Antioch College, a front-runner in
truly liberal education, offered him its presidency. Being a college president's wife would have required a great deal of time, but I could have
worked it out, and the prospect of dealing with young people in that
capacity appealed to me. Howland was about to accept that post when

the government made an offer: president of the American Committee for Liberation. He took it because it meant running Radio Liberation, a tremendous network that broadcast American news and views to Communist satellite countries.

A motley bunch of White Russians staffed Radio Liberation: nobles, peasants, Trotskyites—everything except Communists. One elegant old Polish count always wore white kid gloves in the office to avoid soiling his aristocratic hands. All refugees from countries trapped behind the Iron Curtain, these strange bedfellows joined forces in hopes of shaking, or at least easing, the Soviet yoke.

Since Radio Liberation was based in New York, we took a larger apartment overlooking the East River on the edge of Beekman Place, despite a rental agent who was wary of having an actress in the building. The basis of that kind of insecurity is akin to racism, and it still goes on. It happened to Gloria Vanderbilt when she tried to get into River House. Although I later became co-chairman of the Advisory Council of the National Committee Against Discrimination in Housing, I'm ashamed to say that I submitted to such absurdities then, actually obtaining references from friends like Dean Acheson and Dean Rusk. This relieved the agent no end, convincing her of our suitability. But I couldn't resist a parting shot after everything was signed. "Oh, there's one thing I neglected to tell you," I said. "My husband's black." That woman actually shriveled up before my eyes. Imagine the repercussions in 1952 if it had been true!

We didn't forsake Washington. We purchased and restored a small house on N Street, where I became a familiar sight in slacks, directing workmen or digging in my garden full of roses. There was time for domesticity, because I subjugated acting and even UNESCO commitments to it, still aiming to be the "little woman" Howland wanted. Months of job hunting had intensified his masculine insecurities about a working wife.

I never officially retired, although my reluctance to work and my U.N. participation caused many to assume I had. Marian Anderson, while we were lunching at the U.N. during that time, told me people thought that about her since her appointment to the United States Mission: "They forget that singing is still my livelihood." There is a bright woman, who knew just what she was doing. To think what she had achieved since the D.A.R. refused her permission to sing in Constitution Hall and Mrs. Roosevelt arranged for the Lincoln Memorial instead! That splendid moment struck an irrevocable blow against racism.

I turned down an awful lot of stuff in those days. To please Howland, yes, but really most of the offers were easy to dismiss. I won't make a picture, even a prestige picture, just for the sake of doing it; I'll do only a good honest role. If you get panicky and do everything that comes along, pretty soon nothing comes. You have to pick and choose. And even though I've done small things along the way, it's a general rule that something in them somewhere was worth doing. It wasn't only a question of parts to suit one's age; Hollywood had stopped making the kinds of comedies I wanted to do. In the thirties and forties, film comedy was, at its best, social criticism, a reflection of the times. Hiroshima, the cold war, and McCarthy put a stop to all that. People became afraid to laugh at themselves, and a dreadful lack of humor entered American life, at least in the scripts I was getting. Subtle wit and humor gave way to buffoonery, which was perfect for television. Like reflections in the distorting mirrors of a fun house, it's too far removed from reality to frighten people, so they carry on laughing.

After I'd had a three-year hiatus from picture-making, Norman Krasna, who'd written *Wife vs. Secretary* twenty years before, offered the witty role of a senator's wife in *The Ambassador's Daughter*. What a relief from the scripts I'd been getting! Norman's light touch was very much in evidence; he wrote, produced, and directed the picture. Although I liked the part, it meant filming in Paris for three months while Howland's work kept him in New York. Also, it presented the next stage of an actress's transition: the move from star to supporting player. I would be billed right up there with Olivia de Havilland in the title role, but it was her character that mattered; mine was incidental.

Despite the subterfuges of men who operate them, cameras really don't lie. In the end, an actress has only two ways to go: quit at the top, like Garbo, or shift into character parts, as I did. Actors go on playing romantic leads with a new crop of starlets; actresses are relegated to doting mothers, fluttering aunties, or monsters. While Cary and Clark romanced Grace Kelly and Sophia Loren, Claudette and I were mothering Troy Donahue and Paul Newman, and Bette and Joan were terrorizing each other. It never bothered me as an actress, but those career stereotypes foisted on women have greater ramifications. Women of a certain age are condemned for taking young lovers or even for maintaining a healthy sex urge, while men are openly admired for it. Whether such prejudice emanates from Biblical taboos or what, I don't know; but they persist.

The ego problems inherent in making the transition to supporting roles are exacerbated by the prejudice against older women in the film business here. You are considered a has-been. In England, great stars like Gladys Cooper, Sybil Thorndike, and Peggy Ashcroft all played character parts without losing face or prestige. They did supporting roles in films during the day while starring at night in the theater. They don't seem to understand that in Hollywood, where box office is the overriding concern. Consequently, many actresses of my generation keep waiting for star parts that are just not being written. "My name goes above the title," Bette Davis insists. "I'm a star!" She is, and a great one. But is it worth playing all those demented old ladies to maintain that status? I've turned down plenty of them. For me they would be a waste of time.

So it was either hang on and wait for star parts—and die of ennui or starvation—or play character roles and keep busy. I'm glad I made the transition when I did. It didn't hurt me at all. Technically, I guess you could still call me a "star," but I'm a "guest star" or an "also star-ing," and happy to do small roles if they're good. You can't play smart glamour girls forever.

With Howland's blessing and his promise to join me in Paris for New Year's, I accepted Norman's offer. In fact, before I left, Howland thoughtfully compiled meticulous lists of dozens of friends and restaurants we had enjoyed on previous visits. I took the red-eye flight, which I never do anymore. You arrive exhausted and join the day in full swing without catching your breath. They whisked me off to a fabulous lunch, before sending me for fittings with Christian Dior. He was charming, offering me the choice of the new collection he happened to be showing that day. I'm good at knowing what's right for me—I should be, having had to face enough mistakes; seeing yourself on the screen is a great teacher. But Dior left little margin for error. His perfectionism pervaded his establishment, down to the fitters and the girls in the workrooms, ensuring stunning, flawlessly made costumes. After my fittings, the cast assembled for a script reading at the Krasnas' sumptuous Bois de Boulogne apartment, which Goering had appropriated during the Occupation. That long, eventful day ended with a night at the opera.

The French studios don't keep the ungodly hours we do here. You report to the hairdresser at eight-fifteen, makeup at ten-fifteen, and get rolling around noon. Since they all do theater and film simultaneously, they won't get up at five in the morning after an evening performance to be on the set by eight. We usually worked later in the evening, which was fine for me. I could ride along the Seine to the Joinville-le-Pont studios in the late-morning light of the Impressionists and return in Pre-Raphaelite dusk.

My driver was scheduled to collect me from the Raphaël, near the Arc de Triomphe, at eight each working day. But that proud Parisian, noticing my interest, would arrive a half hour early to conduct what he called *"petites promenades."* These daily detours took us through the Bois de Vincennes, past the zoo, or into the old, sort of Napoleonic section, which, in its rather run-down state, somehow captured history. "Oh, I would love to live here," I told my congenial guide. "This is where my apartment would be." Enchanted and refreshed, we would head for the little suburb of Joinville-le-Pont, past riders training trotting ponies, and enter the vast studio that Paramount had built in the twenties.

My approach had not been entirely enthusiastic the first day. One reason for my accepting the role of the senator's wife had been that Melvyn Douglas, a dear friend, would play the senator. At the last minute, however, previous commitments forced Mel to withdraw. Who replaced him? The man who ran around Hollywood calling me a Communist, my reactionary nemesis Adolphe Menjou. Quite frankly, the prospect of working with him horrified me, but a cable waiting in my dressing room that first day eased the tension: ANYTIME YOU TURN AROUND TO LOOK YOU'LL SEE ME IN YOUR CORNER. LUCK AND LOVE. JOHN FORSYTHE.

John, Olivia de Havilland's leading man, was a good liberal Democrat who knew the situation between Menjou and me. He became a staunch ally, as tough on our side as Menjou was on his. There were two of them: dear Tommy Noonan, who is gone now, joined our camp. Olivia I could never figure out. She stayed out of it, and wisely, too, I guess. She had her own problems, after discovering during filming that she was pregnant. We got along well, within reason. Occasionally she would get upset and carry on—caused, to give her the benefit of the doubt, by the pressure of simultaneously carrying a child and a picture. She endured great discomfort throughout an unusually cold Parisian winter. Our dressing rooms were frigid. We put electric pads on our laps to keep from shivering while they applied our makeup. During location shots in an unheated church, we sat with hot-water bottles under our elegant Diors. Olivia was understandably preoccupied, but she behaved graciously toward me, which I appreciated on that transitional picture.

At first, Adolphe Menjou was true to form. "Oh, Myrna," he goaded, "I dined with Westbrook Pegler before coming over," knowing damn well how I despised the right-wing columnist who called Roosevelt "that cripple in the White House." I'd grit my teeth and say "Jolly for you," while John and Tommy retaliated with jokes about his politics. Adolphe really got bugged when the French crew read Communist newspapers or distinguished guests at chic parties turned out to be left-wingers. "Don't you know," I teased, "all the best Parisians are?" His incredulity was almost endearing.

Soon afterward, in the makeup department, Adolphe began plying John and me with unexpected reminiscences. "My wife and I were staying at Marion Davies's beach house when the big gold scare hit California," he related one day, apropos of nothing. "We rushed home to rescue the gold bars we kept in our cellar. We had to carry them out in suitcases, and, you know," he disclosed in all innocence, "I never realized what a burden gold could be." John and I laughed out loud at his utter ingenuousness, which served only to further endear us to him. It seems he had developed big crushes on us—we became the two people he liked and wanted to be with; he wouldn't leave us alone. We finally gave in and went around with him a bit and, wouldn't you know, my old adversary turned out to be a warm, affectionate man. After the picture, his wife, Verree Teasdale, wrote to thank me for "taking care of Adolphe."

Before I left for Paris, Arthur's son, Terry, had confided that he wanted to study medicine. When Arthur happened to come through Paris with his third wife, "Bubbles" Schinasi, I lunched with him, hoping to stimulate paternal support for Terry.

"That's just another pipe dream," he scoffed. "He was going to be a psychiatrist and he was going to be this or that . . ."

"Now, listen to me," I urged. "He's going to be a doctor. I've had lots of evidence of it," and I listed examples of Terry's childhood attraction to medicine. I wanted Arthur to get with it for once, but he never did. He never gave his son moral support or any other kind for his studies. Terry survived without it, ultimately becoming a fine neurologist. He married a wonderful girl, and when their first child was born, his mother called to tell me. "Myrna," Juliette announced with typical generosity, "you're a grandmother!"

Howland, who knew and loved Paris, arrived for New Year's Eve and made it the best I've ever had. New Year's, not Christmas, is the big celebratory holiday in France, and the Parisians play it to the hilt. Our festive group went from club to club, drinking vintage champagne, tossing huge balloon-like things around, and generally raising hell. I discussed international relations that evening with an expert in relations of quite another kind, when we ran into Polly Adler somewhere along the way. The infamous madam who wrote A House Is Not a Home struck me as a lonely woman with a touching yen for respectability— whatever that is. "Miss Loy," she scrawled in a childish hand on the back of a dinner check, "the highlight of my visit to Paris is meeting you. Your thoughts and efforts are not in vain. God bless you, sweet lady."

On our way home, Howland inspected Radio Liberation facilities in Spain and Portugal, two countries that had accepted the network. France, for instance, would have no part of it; the French considered it merely a propaganda machine, while we thought we were telling them it wasn't like that at all. My first stop in Madrid, even before the hotel, was the Prado. I had to see those pictures. The galleries were a little dark—it was late in the day—but the light rather suited the richness of Goya and Velázquez: opulent portraits with King Charles spaniels and powerful war scenes that somehow brought Picasso's work to mind. Goya also decorated a little Madrid church with frescoes of his mistress, the Duchess of Alba, and selected contemporaries gazing from a balcony while putti hover about goosing each other. The artist was having his little joke.

We stayed at the Madrid Ritz, which was unusual—they prohibited actors. Can you imagine the old "rogues and vagabonds" theory persisting to that day? But I was "government." I think Cary Grant is the only other actor to have got in. Ironically, the American Ambassador, John Lodge, and his wife, Francesca, both stagestruck, had acted in Hollywood in the thirties. Charming and solicitous, they compensated for the hotel's archaic policy by entertaining us at the embassy and guiding us around that ancient city of somber nights and narrow ways.

Lisbon, with all the different-colored houses on little hills, reminded me of California as it used to be. We caught up with Francis Lederer and his wife, who had been so pleasant on *The Ambassador's Daughter*. We visited some magical old castles perched on sheer crags and shared the night of Epiphany with the employees of a Lisbon restaurant. They threw out all the other customers and asked us to stay while they played haunting fado music and marched around carrying wired arcs of flowers over their heads.

We stayed in Escorial, the resort near Lisbon where deposed kings go to die. The night before we left, the hotel manager brought an enormous guest book for us to sign. Flipping through it, I was startled by an inscription from Leslie Howard. He had stayed in that same room, where Nazi spies had overheard him discussing his flight the next morning, the fateful flight that was shot down. It has always been assumed that the Germans were after Churchill and got the wrong plane. There has been speculation, however, that the British broke a German code and knew of the attack, but didn't stop the fight because the Germans would have discovered that their code had been broken. Oh, my God, I hope that isn't true. Leslie's inscription was so cheerful; he had enjoyed his stay and looked forward to returning. That was a sad moment for me. I loved Leslie.

Dreary film scripts and a desire to stay in the East drove me to television. I did quite a bit of it in the fifties—hour or half-hour comedy and dramatic shows, like *General Electric Theater*, that could be done quickly in New York. Ronald Reagan, who hosted the G.E. show and toured as a kind of apologist for the company, visited the set occasionally. We just made small talk about the pictures—he knew enough about my politics to avoid more substantive matters. He was pleasant, though, very congenial—you have to give him that—wielding the same brand of theatrical charm with which he now faces the nation. Yes, he was on the road for G.E. then, stumping for them, making speeches, and kind of got to like it, I guess. Amazing . . . amazing . . .

One series pilot, *Indict and Convict*, in which I played a judge, had some grit. The networks considered it too "relevant and controversial for consumers" and took the homespun *Donna Reed Show* instead. The humor of another, *It Gives Me Great Pleasure*, based on Emily Kimbrough's experiences on the lecture circuit, appealed to me, as did working with Robert Preston and Zachary Scott. It proved too sophisticated for sponsors. These weren't live television; they were filmed shows done with all the care of theatrical features.

My first live show, an all-star adaptation of *Meet Me in St. Louis*, came in the late fifties. It also turned out to be my last, since they pretty much curtailed live production after that. Our producer, David Susskind, actively pro–live television then, went about grumbling, "Motion pictures . . . bah . . . . fooey, fooey . . ." We rehearsed for weeks way downtown on Second Avenue in the old Jewish district, where they still had wonderful kosher restaurants. Ed Wynn and I would go across the street to lunch on delectable delicatessen. That adorable man played my father and we became great friends. Although he had been a big Broadway comedy star, he was very insecure as a straight actor. He never felt too sure about what he was doing. I always had to get him going, telling him, "You're wonderful! You're terrific!"—which he was in spades.

Despite the energy and expertise of a stellar cast—Jeanne Crain, Jane Powell, and little Patty Duke played my daughters, Walter Pidgeon my husband—we all needed encouragement on that show. After the grind and drudgery of rehearsing and blocking, you faced the technological jumble in the studio and thought your performance was gone forever. Obviously, live television required technical synchronization to the split second, but the sets, representing a house of three stories, sprawled over one huge stage. I'd be in the kitchen baking a pie; then they'd push buttons and switch over to another room a hundred feet away. You dashed through mazes of cables, wires, ropes, and lights from one set to another, with production assistants pointing and whispering, "Look out . . . Look out for that . . ." (One young assistant, who laid tape on the stage for us to follow, was Joseph Papp, now the prime mover of New York's Public Theater.) You grabbed costumes and kept running while pulling them on. You ran up the backs of portable stairs, caught your breath, and walked down the fronts into the scene as though you had just strolled in from the garden. And you were panting.

In the middle of one scene, a Christmas tree started to fall on Jeanne. Her back was turned to it and the camera was on me, making it impossible to warn her. Disaster, I thought; this is it! Then, in the nick of time, a stagehand caught it from behind. Meanwhile, the show proceeds. You say your lines, registering only what the script requires. Oh, it was incredible! When it was all over, David Susskind looked at me and asked proudly, "Well, how do you like television now?"

"I *won*," I told him, catching my breath. "That's all I can say."

But it was exciting and wonderful. Two hours went in the flicker of an eyelash, and you came out of it with a high that should be bottled and sold. The absolute exhilaration is greater even than an opening night on stage. You have all the momentum of a stage performance, but there is still the camera, the definition, the close-ups. It combines everything. What a shame that so little television today realizes its tremendous potential.

We shot most of those shows just across the East River from our apartment or in other New York studios, which allowed me to return to Howland every evening. One very special prospect, however, lured me back to Hollywood. Universal offered Bill Powell and me a television film, which I accepted enthusiastically, since we hadn't worked together for ten years. When I reached Hollywood, Bill sent me dozens of red roses—I'd never seen so many roses—and invited me to dinner. This is bad, I thought; something's wrong here.

Mousie, a great sportswoman, was playing tennis down in San Diego the night I went to their house. She was always so sweet about leaving us with our rambling reminiscences. Bill and I talked about the past, the present, what we'd been doing or planned to do. We never discussed politics—I avoided it. His crowd tended to be conservative Republicans, and I just supposed we wouldn't agree on such matters.

During dinner, Bill suddenly looked straight into my eyes. "Minnie," he blurted out, "I'm retiring." It stunned me. "I'm hitting sixty-five," he explained defensively, "and I'm tired."

"Oh, it's that bad, is it?" I scoffed, indicating the pillow and comforter on the back of his chair. Of course, he was thirteen years older than I and had a long start on me professionally. I remember admiring his consummate villainy in pictures like *The Bright Shawl* and *Romola* when I was starting out at Grauman's.

"*Mister Roberts* did me in," he continued; "that long location in Hawaii, Jack Ford getting sick, Mervyn LeRoy coming in. Minnie, I wouldn't even groom my mustache again, much less learn a movie role."

So that was the end of that. Bill's retirement was a blow personally

: Producer Arthur Hornblow,
's first husband, dutifully saw his wife
n she embarked for Montana with
ther, her Aunt Lou, and her brother,
BELOW: During that return in
er first since she had left in 1918,
posed in front of one of the split-log
ldings her grandfather had built on
row Creek Valley ranch.

Myrna and Arthur Hornblow helped to d
their magnificent Hidden Valley house i
undeveloped pocket of the Hollywood hi

The Hornblows participated vigorously in the social life of the film capital, attending premieres (above left) and fêtes such as Alfred Newman's Mozart Party (the host sits between them, above right). BELOW: They attend the studio preview of *Libeled Lady* with its director, Jack Conway, and her co-stars Jean Harlow and Bill Powell, who were engaged to be married. The shared laughter of Myrna and Jean characterizes their exuberant friendship.

Birthday parties were a fringe benefit and a publi[c] pivot at M-G-M. LEFT: Loy and Gable demons[tra]tively celebrated Victor Fleming's day on the *Te[st] Pilot* set. BELOW: Myrna's thirty-fifth mileston[e] attracted studio head Louis B. Mayer, who surpr[ised] his star during the filming of *Third Finger, Left Hand* with a visit from her husband. Also prese[nt] (second left to right) were studio manager Eddie Mannix, her director, Robert Z. Leonard, and h[er] co-star, Melvyn Douglas. BOTTOM: Mayer also made a special visit to the set of *Another Thin M[an]* to share Myrna's thirty-fourth birthday cake.

T: Myrna joined Judy Garland and Frank
gan on the *Wizard of Oz* set to celebrate
er of Victor Fleming's birthdays. BELOW:
crew, and bigwigs surprised Robert Taylor
e *Remember?* set, including his co-star,
r Garson, and, to her left, Eddie Mannix,
nd Powell, Benny Thau, and, holding the
MBER sign, Woody Van Dyke.

ABOVE: Myrna's second husband, rent-a-car heir John Hertz, Jr., was an advertising executive. (Douglas Whitney Collection) BELOW: Her third marriage, to writer/producer Gene Markey, was a military affair, with Admiral William "Bull" Halsey (right) as best man. (Douglas Whitney Collection)

en the Markeys arrived
London to make *The
se of Lady Brooke* for
xander Korda, the
ducer greeted them with
mile and a battery of
eramen.

When Myrna married Assistant
Secretary of State Howland Sargeant
in Washington, D.C., her old
friends Bob and Betty Black stood
up for them.

Sargeants honeymooned in
, where Howland was presi-
of UNESCO's Sixth General
erence and Myrna was a
ate. U.N. Secretary General
ve Lie joined them in the
ing hall of UNESCO House.
glas Whitney Collection)

At the outset of World War II, the studios were quick to support the war effort and to use it as a publicity pivot (as witnessed by the photo and caption on the opposite page from a forties fan magazine). Myrna agreed to a formal sitting with M-G-M's Eric Carpenter in her Bundles for Bluejackets uniform, but most of her time was spent running the naval Auxiliary Canteen at Long Beach, sharing the night shift with Kay Francis.

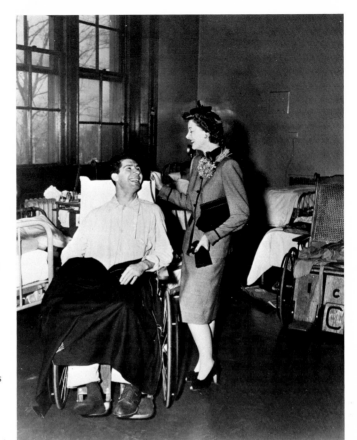

a made only one film during the
preferring to work full-time for
ed Cross instead. As Assistant to
director of Military and Naval
re, she arranged entertainment
ty-two East Coast medical
ies and frequently visited them
f. She is seen (right) with
an S. Katz at the Bronx Veterans
ital during a tour of Eastern
ary and veterans hospitals.

Chas. Rhodes

Hollywood stars aren't missing a single trick when it comes to helping out with
the war effort. At the recent Buy a Bomber Benefit Show at the Music Box Theater
they were on the job selling programs and peanuts. Among the peanut venders
who raised money were Cary Grant, Roz Russell, Myrna Loy and Charles Boyer

During two of her trips to England, Myrna had fortuitous meetings. ABOVE: In 1935, Alfred Hitchcock ambled over to Guy Bolton's cottage, where she was staying, to see this star from far-off Hollywood. BELOW: In 1949, she was presented to Queen Elizabeth at the Royal Film Performance as Margaret Lockwood looked on. Visible in the background, greeting the princesses Elizabeth and Margaret, are Laurence Olivier, Vivien Leigh, Alan Ladd, and Glynis Johns.

irty-seven years between photographs
ledy Lamarr, right, on the *Lucky Night*
1939 and with Jacqueline Kennedy
s, below, at a tribute to Josephine Baker
Met in 1976) have not dimmed the Loy
ce. These three profiles, according to a
plastic surgeons, were the most sought
y patients—Myrna's in the thirties,
in the forties, Jackie's in the sixties.

Politics and public service have permeated My
life. LEFT: She congratulates Adlai Stevenson,
whom she admired and adored, after he annou
his presidential candidacy in 1952. Senators
Sparkman and Murray are in the background.
BELOW: She performs United Nations busines
two former Speakers of the House, Republican
Joseph Martin (left) and Democrat Sam Raybu
(right).

…elegate chats with U.N.
…tary-General U Thant at a
…tion (right) and huddles with
…ant Secretary of State Francis
…ox and her admired colleague
…or Roosevelt at an AAUN
…ng (below).

‸3, Friedman-Abeles photographed Myrna
 costumed for her Broadway debut in a revival
 Women and (below) at rehearsal with her co-
 ‑im Hunter, Rhonda Fleming, and, behind
 Lainie Kazan, Dorothy Loudon, and Alexis
 . OPPOSITE ABOVE: The star responded to
 ‑ion at Town Hall when publicist John
 ‑er (right) presented her in his "Legendary
 " series. OPPOSITE BELOW: In the 1960s,
 ‑ made her stage debut in *Marriage-Go-Round*
 ‑laude Dauphin on the New England summer

The glittering honoree, captured by David McGough's camera, greeted well-wishers when the Academy paid tribute to her at Carnegie Hall in 1985.

and professionally, but I never confronted him with it. He knew how I felt; there was no need to belabor it. He found what he wanted in life: a very happy marriage, living among friends he loved. Mel Douglas did the Universal TV film with me, and no matter what offers came for us over the years, Bill stuck to his guns, contentedly ensconced with Mousie in a refrigerated house in Palm Springs.

My erstwhile screen partner bowed out that spring of 1956, but my former candidate returned. Adlai Stevenson was again seeking the Democratic nomination, and this time, with Howland out of the State Department, I could fight the good fight. A courageous man—too courageous, as it turned out—Adlai had refused to be as political as he should have been to win in 1952. He would not compromise. He remained firmly behind the goals he held for America, believing that the people would respond to truth and reason rather than jargon and hollow campaign promises. "Let's talk sense to the American people," he said. He could not be cynical about the electorate, which in retrospect, I fear, is the biggest mistake a politician can make. But then, Adlai was as much statesman as politician, a creative man of far-reaching ideas and, more to the point, ideals.

On April 23rd in Washington, I attended a reception for Adlai and the annual $100-a-plate Woodrow Wilson fund-raiser that followed. Given by eleven ranking Democratic senators, including my fellow Montanan Jim Murray, that reception launched another Stevenson-Eisenhower contest. Campaigning full time, I agreed to address a Stevenson rally the following week in Washington's predominantly black district. I telephoned Eleanor Roosevelt, who was sharing the rostrum, to coordinate our speeches.

"Myrna," she answered cheerfully, "what can I do for you?" We had that kind of willing exchange; we were always calling each other for help with causes or candidates we espoused. "She did everything," Adlai once said of Eleanor Roosevelt, "because it was worth doing; she did nothing because it would enhance her own role." As a matter of fact, I didn't do nearly as much for her as she did for me. She trusted me, I guess.

"They've asked me to talk about Adlai," I told her, "and I wanted to be sure we don't cover the same ground."

"Well, he's in trouble after the California attack," she explained, "so I must refute it." Some damn-fool union leader had accused him of being a Communist. "I must talk about his politics." She paused a moment. "Why don't you talk about the man?"

"Oh, really?" I barely managed to reply.

"Yes," she said. "I think that would be right. You talk about the man himself."

The *man!* What an order! I sweated that one out, wondering how to approach it, particularly since I had such a crush on him. To me he was the sun, moon, and stars, and, although I never presumed upon it as so many women did, I think he had a sneaking admiration, or liking, for me. Warm and charming, with eyes that seemed to see only you, he loved flirting with a certain select group of women—Betty Bacall, for one, adored him—but then he would smile and back away. He was a great tease. He didn't make a big thing about his commitments to any woman—because there had been many bad personal experiences in his life. That wife of his, who was mad as a hatter, treated him abominably. I felt for him very deeply. I also felt a bit put upon by him. But that had no bearing on my participation in his campaign. I supported him because I believed in his integrity, advocated his policies, and considered him the right man for the job.

That's essentially what I told the Washington rally, after putting on my thinking cap and writing a speech incorporating the "three H's": his humor, humanity, and humility. It worked. The audience responded and Mrs. Roosevelt approved.

"That was marvelous," she said.

"You don't know what I went through," I replied. "I hardly slept last night trying to figure out what to say." The *man!*

We flew back to New York together late that afternoon. She took out a manuscript to read. "This is about my husband," she explained. She always referred to him as "my husband" or "Franklin," never as "the President," speaking of him with genuine fondness, expressing her gratitude for the schooling he gave her in politics. I witnessed again her ingenuous, almost childlike humor when she cheerfully recounted lunching at Bernard Baruch's with Winston Churchill. "After lunch, as we adjourned to the sitting room for a chat," she related, "all three of us paused to turn up our hearing aids so we could hear one another. I laughed. They didn't. They didn't find it funny." She laughed heartily again as she told it.

Halfway to New York, she fell fast asleep. So, that's how she does it, I thought. Nobody could figure out how she accomplished as much as she did. That day, for instance, she had left New York on a morning train, stopped off for a meeting in Baltimore, continued on to the Washington rally, and was flying back to attend a dinner with her son Jimmy. She awoke refreshed when we landed at LaGuardia. We disembarked and off she went. I've got a pretty good stride, but keeping up with her was never easy.

There was a long line at the cab stand. She was late for her dinner, but there she stood, not a peep out of her. I walked over to the starter. "See who's standing over there," I whispered. "Oh, *yeah!*" he said. "Get a cab for her," I told him, "but don't say anything." She never wanted special attention, she wouldn't accept it; she would have waited until the last dog was hanged before she'd do a thing like that. But the starter finessed it, got her the cab, and I sent her on her way. As I waited, something she had said years before came back to me: "I am my husband's legs."

Her strength lay, I think, in knowing who she was—"a basic instinct for being herself," Adlai called it—while maintaining great modesty about it. Her charm, the charm of humility in high places, was irresistible. When I asked her for a photograph, she looked amazed. "*You* want a picture of *me?*" she said, apparently thinking back to her girlhood, when her mother's beauty eclipsed her own plain features. It was so touching and revealing, because people always made fun of her looks; yet she had a wonderful, appealing face with an expression of deep kindliness, which her unselfish life made increasingly beautiful. So, ironically, did a 1946 automobile accident. She was delighted when two broken front teeth needed replacing: "Now I have two lovely porcelain ones that look far better than the rather protruding large teeth which most of the Roosevelts have."

She learned, as many of us do, to overcome shyness and face the world head-on. Most charm, it seems to me, stems from confidence. You may have great kindness and understanding, but if you're shy and unsure your charm won't project. When Eisenhower replaced her on the U.N. Mission, to which Truman had appointed her, Mrs. R. wasn't cowed. She walked right into the AAUN office and offered her services: "I would like to work for you. Is there anything I can do to help?" She wanted to continue her work and knew she could do so there. Clark Eichelberger gave her an office and she remained involved until her death.

Mrs. R. adored Adlai Stevenson, seeing in him much of the "practical" idealism, humanity, and persuasiveness of her husband. She campaigned tirelessly to get him elected—many of us did. In Los Angeles, I helped Dore Schary organize a rally at big old Gilmore Stadium. We assembled a stalwart group, with a nucleus of the same old diehard liberals. Hank Fonda, dear Hank, showed up, and Robert Ryan and Mercedes McCambridge—you could always count on them—and Betty Bacall, who really had guts. Bogey was dying, but she bore up throughout that whole thing. At one point, she opened her bag and took out a little bottle of vodka. "Would you like one?" she asked. "No, thanks," I said, "but you go ahead." Betty's not a drinker; this was against the cold and the sorrow within her.

We never saw some of the others who promised to be there—Frank Sinatra, among them. I had always been able to depend on Frank, but he didn't show up. He later hopped on the Kennedy bandwagon, however, and I forgave him. When my friend and, at that time, agent Mimi Weber dragged me to Las Vegas to see the "Rat Pack" perform, Frank joined us in the lounge at the Sands after the show. "You know, Myrna," he said, crouching down in front of me. "I've always been in love with you." I patted him on the head and said, "Well, Frank, you've been a bad boy, but then again you've come a long way and I'm very proud of you." He kissed me, and it was very sweet. That was around 1960. Since then, of course, he's moved farther and farther to the right and what's he got for it all? A Chrysler? A Medal of Freedom? I've never been able to figure out how he suddenly went the other way. But that's his business.

The Stevenson rally was broadcast to several cities over closed-circuit television, and some of us had agreed to speak. As we entered Gilmore Stadium that evening, Dore handed me my topic on a little piece of paper. From his sheepish expression, I assumed the worst. I was right. Scrawled on the paper were two words: "Hydrogen Bomb"! "You gave me an easy one," I whispered with my best Nora Charles inflections. Adlai opposed using the bomb, of course, opposed even building it. That was a very unpopular stance in those days·and hurting his chances— that's how crazy this country could be! But I handled it that night, discussing the humanity of his stance and his integrity in the face of political expediency. He was too brave, not political enough. He ultimately succeeded in banning the bomb, but he lost again to Eisenhower in 1956.

"There are things more precious than political victory," Adlai observed in defeat; "there is the right to political contest. In much of the world partisan controversy is forbidden and dissent suppressed. God bless partisanship, for this is democracy's lifeblood!"

Who could have won against Eisenhower, the hero of World War II? It was political suicide and so disheartening, because Adlai would have made a brilliant President. The tragedy is that thinking men, so-called intellectuals, seem to threaten the electorate. We have in this country an anti-intellectual strain that scares the bejesus out of me. Don't we want a bright man? Don't we want a creative man? Must we always have these hacks?

In September, 1957, one hundred world figures signed a petition urging the U.N. to implement its resolutions condemning Soviet aggression in Hungary. Most of the free world had been inspired by Hungary's fight for freedom and outraged by the repressive measures taken to stifle it. With Norman Thomas, Senator Javits, Bishop Pike, and Victor Reuther, I presented the petition to U.N. Secretary Dag Hammarskjöld and Prince Wan of Thailand, president of the General Assembly. The Communist Party newspaper in Hungary responded with an article headed THE U.N. AND THE SMILE OF AN ACTRESS, claiming that I had used my "finest smile" and emphasized my "female charms" to influence the president of the assembly. "According to some reports," concluded Nepszabadsag, "Miss Loy's sex appeal had a deep effect on the prince."

After much bandying about, that tempest in a teapot subsided. But singling me out, a typical Communist ploy, served a twofold purpose: they got at Howland, whose Radio Liberation broadcast to Soviet satellites; they played down the issue of Hungary by emphasizing the actress and ignoring the other members of that extraordinary, across-the-board deputation. With repetition, such tactics ultimately discredited our attempts to effect the withdrawal of Soviet troops from Hungary.

After consulting on film for the Sixth National UNESCO Conference, in San Francisco, I returned to another bout with Communism, this one from a quite different perspective. In the mid-fifties, the House Un-American Activities Committee moved its entertainment-industry purges to New York, aiming to purge radio, television, and the theater. Concurrently, a number of radio and television personalities, including John Henry Faulk, Charles Collingwood, Faye Emerson, Orson Bean, and Garry Moore, ran for election to the local board of AFTRA (the American Federation of Television and Radio Artists). As the "Middle of the Road" slate, they opposed Communism, while condemning political black-listing and such witch-hunting McCarthy-era organizations as AWARE, Inc.

AWARE, Inc., was a private organization started by Vincent Hartnett, a man who had a supermarket in Syracuse; but the organization's influence was insidious. Oh, honey, if you've never been in one of those blitzes you don't know what goes on in this world. After the Middle of the Road slate won by the largest vote in the New York local's history, Hartnett started a smear campaign against John Henry Faulk, a sort of Will Rogers–Garrison Keillor type. When John Henry's popular CBS radio show began losing sponsors, he sued Hartnett for conspiracy and libel. Hartnett's lawyer, Roy Cohn, retaliated with obstructive tactics, which jeopardized John Henry's career and reputation.

As legal costs mounted and CBS got nervous, John Henry telephoned me. We had met while fund-raising for an asthma foundation in Denver, where he regaled me with down-home stories that packed a political punch. "Myrna," he said, "I'm in big trouble. It's getting very bad, no matter what Ed Murrow and some of the fellas at CBS are trying to do for me." I didn't know too many media bigwigs, but friends of mine did. After trying that avenue to no avail, a group of us decided to give a New York fund-raiser to defray Faulk's legal expenses and to publicize this outrage. As usual, I called Mrs. Roosevelt, hoping that she would lend her support.

"What can I do for you, Myrna?" she asked in her usual willing way. I explained the situation, and, not wishing to go into anything without the facts, she asked me to send over some material on the case. She then discussed it at lunch with Ed Murrow, a very wise, very good man in a profession where it's difficult to be either. "We both feel that something should be done to bring the case to the attention of the public," she wrote to me. "I will certainly try to get to the meeting, for I am concerned that such a thing can happen here."

She got there, and despite the prospect of a speaking engagement in Albany that night, she was terrific. When she apologized for having to leave early, it was the first time I had ever heard her sound the least bit tired.

"You do so much," I said.

"Just the way you do, my dear," she countered, with that warm smile of hers. Imagine that! You could have knocked me over with a feather.

"What I do," I told her, "doesn't mean what it means to people when you do something."

I learned a little trick of hers as she was leaving. She went around choosing hors d'oeuvres she liked and had them wrapped to go. "I'll arrive too late to get any food," she explained. "Besides, I get so tired of all those chicken dinners." I helped her collect her snack, and out she went from that place to catch the plane for Albany.

After six years of court battles, John Henry won a $3.5 million libel verdict, later reduced to $550,000, against Hartnett and AWARE, Inc. The suit cost him his CBS job, but his victory ended the pernicious practice of blacklisting in the entertainment industry. He settled on his east Texas farm, tending poultry, fishing a well-stocked trout pond, preparing lectures for colleges and commentary for National Public Radio. He is, by his own account, "choppin' in high cotton."

Early in 1958, the Atomic Energy Commission sponsored a conference on thorium at Brookhaven National Laboratory, the first time that the scientists working on the element had assembled since Manhattan Project days. "During the war, as you have probably heard," wrote the conference coordinator, "code names were used for various materials of importance to the Manhattan Project. Uranium was Tuballoy; Uranium 235 was Oralloy; Thorium was Myrnaloy. I thought you might enjoy meeting the men who referred constantly to Myrnaloy throughout the war. I know they would enjoy meeting the real Myrna Loy."

My husband and I were invited to be guests of honor at dinner on the night of the conference. Since thorium, called the "peaceful project," was considered the most benign radioactive material—at least they thought so then—we accepted without feeling too hypocritical. Before dinner we even donned great big boots and all that protective regalia to see the atomic reactor, the cosmotron, and several projects in progress. It was fascinating, awesome, a bit frightening, particularly when we went through the detector on the way out. No bells rang, nothing. We were clean.

Howland had agreed to accompany me, but things were very shaky between us. I don't like to make excuses for myself. I'm coming out of this too good, as it is. Howland was a marvelous, brilliant man, yet it's true that men of his generation were brought up to expect their wives to be like their mothers: they ran households; they were pillars of the community; they did not have careers. Although his mother was a divine lady, who went to college when few women did, she came from a rigid New England background. Their ancestral home in New Bedford had a widow's walk, where generations of women watched and waited for their men to return from whaling trips. That was the tradition Howland came from, a stoic, stiff-upper-lip, show-no-emotion tradition of women waiting.

Oh, I thought at the beginning, this man isn't going to be like that; this won't happen to me. Well, it did. He wasn't terribly conscious of it; he couldn't quite express it. It was a sort of unspoken dissatisfaction. I tried to fight it, curtailing picture work, relinquishing UNESCO. I hesitated when the U.N. asked me to narrate *The Long Road*, its first television film on the status of women, including the slave trade in the Middle East, which seemed rather appropriate to my situation. But I did it. I finally realized that you can't stop being what you are. You can't disown a lifetime of commitment and responsibility.

So many women in the profession had difficulty keeping marriages going unless they quit or found subservient husbands—managers, handmaidens, whatever they called it. Most of the male stars whose marriages have lasted married women who maybe were starlets but never became stars; they just gave up after marrying. It was hard for a man to tolerate the activities of a woman who wasn't there when they woke up—she'd gone to the studio. Most actresses of my generation will agree with me. Ours is a very demanding business; any business is if you are a woman who wants to express herself.

It's going to be easier now for young people to get along. They are beginning to share responsibilities. A woman isn't expected to have a profession and still run a household by herself. Men will wash dishes and change diapers now. Men will do a lot of things around the house that they wouldn't have been caught dead doing in my day; that was not their work, that was woman's work. I'm just talking in generalities—

I don't like to pin anything down; otherwise, the blame is put on every-body but me, and that's not fair. I'm sure I wasn't a perfect person; I had my faults and problems. Who can judge when you get into char-acter? You think that was the reason—well, maybe that wasn't the rea-son, maybe there were other reasons that you don't comprehend. How does anybody really know why a combination doesn't work?

You know the problem with Howland and Myrna? proposes Elsie Jensen Brock, the AAUN's West Coast director. *He married her because to him she was a pinup girl. She was Hollywood. She was glamorous. She was somebody to show off. He was the typical State Department employee, well educated, brilliant, and able, but he was a stuffed shirt. Now, that was his great weakness. He had this Rhodes Scholar type of personal ego that goes with some of those boys. They are a little better than anybody else because they've got that scholarship.*

He didn't recognize that Myrna had brains—or else he didn't want to know. I told him once in no uncertain terms: "You must recognize Myrna's capacity. She may not talk your language, but she knows *and has certain principles that she lives by and they are very important. She has come a long, long way from the little woman who was a pinup girl." He answered, "You're saying that because she's your friend." I said, "Oh, no, you're my friend, too, and you have your weaknesses and she has hers, but you can't look down on people because they haven't had your education. You just can't do that to anybody." I couldn't unbend him.*

There were many times when he took her to UNESCO *meetings and his nose was out of joint because they fussed over her and not him. Myrna earned that. She read a great deal and studied. She knew what she was talking about. But I'm sure Howland's ego was hurt at times like that, and it added to the difficulty and strained relationships. People can't sometimes take it. They have to have somebody who is, shall we say, Hollywood image and nothing else. There mustn't be any brains.*

Hoping, I suppose, that distance might resuscitate my marriage, I re-turned to Hollywood. Dore Schary asked me to appear in a film of Nathanael West's *Miss Lonelyhearts*, which Montgomery Clift and Robert

Ryan had agreed to do for a fraction of their usual fees because they believed in it. I agreed because I believed in Dore, a close friend, who would write and produce it. As for the project itself, I questioned the attempt to film a movie in which the main character is actually a Christ figure. It could only be done as a bizarre sort of fantasy, which general audiences were not ready for in 1959. Monty Clift always said that it should never have been released as a commercial film; he thought it would have done well in art houses. Still, we all had great affection for that picture.

When Dore mentioned that Monty Clift was "thrilled" by the prospect of appearing with me, I considered it mere gallantry. When I reached the Goldwyn studio, however, it proved to be an understatement. By the time I arrived, the poor boy was falling apart, anticipating my reaction to his flowers of welcome. He had been up most of the previous night planning those flowers and composing a sweet note to go with them. That's what an intense kind of person he was.

Monty was a great talent, whose acting I had always admired. He had extraordinary instincts. I had a scene with Bob Ryan that didn't work—it was beautifully written; there was just too much of it. I brought it to Monty's dressing room, where we often lunched together. "Something's wrong with this scene," I told him. "It won't play this way." He took a pencil and just starting striking out words, like a surgeon removing his hundredth appendix. His cutting saved that scene and strengthened my impact. His observations about the script were always astute and correct. He would have made a great director, which eventually he wanted to be. "Would you ever direct yourself?" I once asked him. "Are you kidding?" he replied. "As a director, I simply wouldn't put up with all that crap from me."

Monty was having problems then. He was full of all kinds of problems, many of them imaginary. He had been seeing psychiatrists several days a week for years, depending on such drugs as Nembutal and Doriden, and drinking excessively. I never really knew if there was an actual physical illness, although his doctor kept giving him "staph" shots. He had been smashed up in a terrible automobile accident. God knows what that had done to him and what they had to do to put him back together.

We responded to each other immediately, perhaps because he was so vulnerable under his social veneer and I saw so much of myself in that contradiction. I helped to nurse him through *Lonelyhearts,* as did Maureen Stapleton, who made an auspicious début in the picture, and Nancy Walker, a close friend of his from New York. Monty inspired the maternal instincts of the women around him. You wanted to protect him. He was really terribly timid underneath it all. Yet, if he was sure of you, he could be a bit of a rascal. He used his keen intuition and sensitivity to his advantage. He knew how to get to you.

"I've always wanted to work with you," Bob Ryan complained gallantly, "and now that I am, I hardly see you. You're too busy taking care of Monty." This was true, but I adored Bob and considered him a brilliant, giving actor. Our scenes in *Lonelyhearts* are among my best in any picture. I discovered how warm and intelligent Bob was in New York, where he and his wife gave marvelous dinner parties. We were all New York people, Bob, Monty, Maureen, and I, and wasted no time getting out of Hollywood after *Lonelyhearts.*

Absence, it seemed, did nothing for my marriage. It had been one of those things: you keep working at something a long time, and finally, forget it. After eight years together, Howland and I announced our separation.

This woman needs so much warmth, Estelle Linzer observes. She needs something more than warmth, and that's communication. If it's the telephone or ringing the doorbell or anything. I know her needs, which I don't have that strongly. She is not the unflappable character she played in the movies. She has to touch some way. And I never saw Howland reach out for anything unless he needed it.

She was mortally hurt when the marriage broke up, because she knew it was her last chance to make the kind of life she had started with Arthur—love and marriage, home and career. Howland's pursuits were so important to her, but he just didn't give Myrna what she needed so badly at that time. She needed attention, love, and affection, a pat on the back once in a while about her career. It was a crucial time for Myrna. I don't care how close your women friends are, if you're intimately involved with a man, that man has to be the answer for you, and he wasn't.

So she finally walked out, which is Myrna's pattern. She picks up her clothes and she goes. She took a small apartment at the

Volney, a residence hotel at Seventy-fourth and Madison. I re-member how lonely and bereft she was after the breakup. She became very withdrawn. I think she was really terribly hurt that he didn't seem to care. She didn't want to talk about it. She didn't want to go to the theater or the movies or anything like that. She was getting over an illness, a psychic illness.

I left the apartment to Howland and moved into the Volney, the hotel on which Dorothy Parker based her play *Ladies of the Corridor*. And who should spot me in the lobby right away but Dottie herself? "Myrna," she called, "don't tell me you're living here. How wonderful! We'll have great fudge and pillow-fight evenings."

We didn't make fudge, but we had some great evenings, especially when Lillian Hellman, an old friend of Dottie's, would join us. Dash-iell Hammett, Lillian's longtime companion, was seriously ill on Cape Cod. She urged Dottie to come up there and help care for him. "Now that she has him," Dottie snapped, "she doesn't know what to do with him." Dottie went to Hollywood instead, while Lillian, Dash's inspira-tion for Nora Charles, kept solitary vigil over her dying lover.

I would see Lillian occasionally over the years, the last time at a dinner in her honor shortly before she herself died. She looked around the room and observed rather wistfully, "I don't see too many friends here . . . Oh, Myrna . . . Myrna's here." She approached me effu-sively, inviting me to "come and have tea." But her mood changed abruptly when Jules Feiffer, to whom she was rather attached, greeted me with a warm embrace. The look she gave me would have cowed Attila the Hun. Lillian could be difficult.

The columns featured my impending divorce and conjured a fifth marriage, to Montgomery Clift. One of his biographers supposedly claimed that friends of mine thought that I wanted to marry Monty. Although the biographer thanks me in her book, I don't remember ever speaking to that woman, not a word. There was always great affection between Monty and me, but he was fifteen years younger. He saw me as a sup-portive friend, I'm sure; a mother figure, perhaps, to lean upon. If he romanticized in his mind an affair between us, it was only to impress others. One night at dinner, he kept trying to give S. J. Perelman the impression that we were living together, which didn't fool that humorist for a minute. Monty never really believed it, either. Maintaining that image was important to him, because he could never quite settle for homosexuality. He wanted men but loved women, a contradiction that tormented him. He couldn't accept it. It was a tragedy.

I saw in Monty a gifted man who was deteriorating; someone for whom I cared who needed taking care of. There were nights when I literally had to carry him out of Jimmy's LaGrange or other places we patronized. Once at Dinty Moore's, while I was telling Maureen Stapleton a story about Gable, Monty crawled up on the table and began shouting nonsense to the room at large. He would not be upstaged. But he made you forget the excesses. He was a stimulating person, an illuminating companion. We saw a lot of theater together, which he invariably enhanced with his astute observations, and he gave delightful, celebrity-populated dinner parties at his home.

That's where I finally met Marlene Dietrich. Can you believe that we had never crossed paths during all our years in Hollywood? Everyone always says, "Well, she's a hausfrau." She's anything but. She's a very glamorous lady with a lot of charm, although she spent most of that evening telling me how the transparent dress she wore in her concerts was constructed. She detailed the entire process bead by bead—the net, and how this went on, that went on, and how she supervised the lighting in order to enhance every facet. "My God," Monty whispered, "how many beads can she describe?" But her infinite attention to herself and to the mechanics of the business fascinated me. "Never mind," I told him. "That's why she's so terrific-looking."

Monty could be funny, delightfully wicked, and very lovable. He was like a child in many ways, full of dreams and ideas and faith in my capabilities. He longed to do Colette's *Chéri* opposite me as the mistress, which he insisted I was born to play. He wanted to direct me as Lady Macbeth and to do *Hamlet*, with Peter Finch as the king and me as the queen. "Can you imagine Gertrude with that wonderful nose?" he asked. Being as intelligent as he was, I'm sure by this time he realized that these were pipe dreams impossible to achieve. As a young man, he had shone with curiosity and fervor. There had been no one more in charge of himself. If there was an exhibit somewhere, a performance he wanted to see, he would hop a train and go to Philadelphia, Washington, Boston, anyplace something illuminating might be. He had assembled a magnificent library, with which he had educated himself very well, but he wasn't using it much by the time I knew him.

He was not well; there was no question about it. A disintegration was taking place that alarmed his friends. He was surrounded by people who loved him, people gathering around. His old friend Kevin Mc-Carthy still dropped in occasionally. Nancy Walker and Roddy Mc-Dowall were steadfast. Libby Holman, who had been close for years, faded in and out of the picture. In fact, the columns kept insisting that Monty was switching from Myrna Loy back to Libby Holman and vice versa, completely missing the point.

Monty sought support from most of his friends. With Libby Holman it was more a case of mutual leaning. He responded to frailty in women. When he made *The Misfits* with Marilyn Monroe, he adored her and identified with her, maintaining that they were birds of a feather. I suppose, in their tremulous ways, they were. Libby was tougher, but she was no bulwark.

She had been a singer before marrying an heir to the Reynolds tobacco fortune. We used to joke about "Moanin' Low," a torch song she introduced on Broadway, because people fooled around with it in the thirties, transposing "Moanin' Low" into "Myrna Loy." When her husband died mysteriously, they suspected her. She had nothing to do with it, I'm sure, but the dreadful rumors ultimately destroyed her. She might have survived if she had concentrated on reviving her career rather than wallowing in her inherited money and self-pity. She was a bad influence on Monty in regard to drink and drugs. She had too much money, which does bad things to a person, sometimes, just as not having enough does. Money can be destructive when people depend on it and don't get out and do something. Libby married again, a very nice man, who made her happy for a while. Then she lost a son in a skiing accident. I didn't see her toward the end of her life; I wasn't in New York when she killed herself.

Elizabeth Taylor, a more positive influence, remained faithful to Monty from the time they did *A Place in the Sun* together, in 1951, until he died. I admire Elizabeth. I haven't spent much time with her—we're seldom in the same town long enough—but I know her and how kind she is, how loyal. I saw her for the first time in the M-G-M makeup department when she was going to school out on the back lot and making *National Velvet*. She was just a little girl then, but I had never seen anything so beautiful in my life.

She helped Monty through *Raintree County* after his accident, through *Suddenly Last Summer,* and fought to get him for *Reflections in a Golden Eye.* He was a risk then, drinking and prone to production-halting illnesses. No company would insure him, so Elizabeth, ignoring the great financial risk, made herself liable for his insurance. Unfortunately, Monty died before filming began, a heart attack at forty-five. What a terrible loss! He had so much potential, but he just couldn't manage it. Everything got to him. He needed a few more layers of skin to cope with this mad world.

Roddy McDowall, whom I'd met through Monty, became a refreshing companion after my divorce. Roddy has a talent for friendship. He wears himself out sometimes sending postcards, calling, finding new and exciting things to do. One night, he dragged me to Julius Monk's Upstairs at the Downstairs to hear a new singer. She sang an hour of Cole Porter at midnight and she was sensational, like a French chanteuse with a murmury voice and a piquant face. "Let's get Noel over here," I suggested. Noel Coward was preparing *Look After Lulu* for Broadway and in need of a leading lady. "This is the girl for him." When we brought him the following night, he was properly captivated and signed the girl for *Look After Lulu.* That's how Tammy Grimes got her start.

A great many people love Roddy. He works at it. He really cares. "From now on," I told him, "I'm going to give my strength or whatever I have to you, because you're a good man and you deserve it. I'll donate all that sort of thing to you." I was sick to death of neurotics waking me up in the middle of the night. If you have an at all sympathetic nature, you get caught by these people. Some of them are wonderful people and some are not—some of them merely indulge their neuroses. Judy Garland used to call me at all hours. I adored Judy—she could be bright and funny—but her nocturnal ramblings were beyond me. Compassion was never enough. Finally I had to tell her in no uncertain terms to stop calling. I even drifted away from Monty in the end. Many of his friends did. Ultimately you must protect yourself.

When Roddy lived in New York, we had fabulous evenings at his place—writers, directors, producers, actors, children of actors, dogs, all gobbling Halloween candy and jelly beans from great big jars and watching movies. He managed to find everything you ever did. Even the ones you'd rather forget. He played a devilish trick on me one night, luring me there and showing *The Mask of Fu Manchu,* the ghastly picture in which I play Boris Karloff's sadistic daughter. Roddy still calls me "Fu."

So many young actors who were becoming successful then came to Roddy's. Ben Gazzara courted Janice Rule there before they married. Tammy Grimes, after we discovered her, became a regular. There were evenings when Jason Robards or Christopher Plummer would behave outrageously and wait for me to be shocked. I disappointed them, although Tennessee Williams accomplished it inadvertently. As he sat beside me holding forth one evening, ashes from his cigarette ignited his trousers. "Get some water!" I shouted "Tennessee's on fire!" As we frantically doused him, the oblivious playwright, apparently lulled by the sound of his own voice, just kept on talking.

Richard Burton and Robert Goulet, who were appearing with Roddy in *Camelot*, were always there. Richard and his first wife, Sybil, who became great friends of mine, arrived one night with his Welsh brothers and sister in tow. They all sang together, and nobody sings like the Welsh. They were simply enchanting, like a choir of robust angels. Richard kept urging me to try Shakespeare, insisting I'd be a good Portia or Lady Macbeth. "Portia? No! I'm too old," I told him. "Lady Macbeth? Well, yes."

"You know, Myrna," Sybil volunteered, "across my little stretch of Welsh valley is a village, three or four streets with a chapel and a pub, that claims you. We all grew up believing that your people came from there."

"No! No!" Richard contradicted in that matchless voice. "She doesn't come from your valley. She comes from the valley around the corner from *my* village." Stanley Baker, who was present and had grown up with Sybil, sided with her, Richard's siblings sided with him, and Welsh hell broke loose.

"Well, Fu," Roddy said above the commotion, "I think that all along Wales people are claiming you."

Laurence Olivier swept me off my feet at one of those parties. A tremor ran through me when he took my hand and fixed those bottomless eyes on me. He actually sent shivers up my back—he's one of the sexiest men I've ever met. Merle Oberon was there that night, so adorable and charming. It was so interesting seeing her with Larry: the *Wuthering Heights* pair sitting side by side. Those were good days and we miss them terribly. Roddy provided a gathering place for people.

There were still ties to Hollywood: Mother was there; old friends; my incongruous saltbox house in Pacific Palisades. I liked going back to work at my old trade. But I had established vital patterns of living in New York and felt more at home, more productive there. If you're bored in New York, it's your own fault. Something's always happening. But in Hollywood, if you're no longer reigning, you simply don't matter. You're measured by the car you drive, the house you own, the gross of your last picture. What's that term they use now? The bottom line. During my M-G-M heyday, I would be deluged with flowers and telegrams the day shooting started. When I returned to 20th Century-Fox for *From the Terrace* early in 1960, my dressing room was bare. Noticing the tributes stacked in Paul Newman's dressing room, I realized that I was yesterday and he was today.

The reward came when I walked on the set. The crew welcomed me with an ovation. They had known me since I was a kid under contract to Fox thirty years before; they had all grown up with me. When Paul and I shot our scenes together, I'd hear, "Hi ya, Myrna. How are you?" or "Welcome home, Myrna." I'd look up and recognize old familiar faces manning the lights. They teased Paul mercilessly: "Hey, Myrna, who's that youngster you're working with?" or "Myrna, you givin' actin' lessons these days?" Paul took it in his stride. He was very sweet about it, displaying none of the cockiness of so many young stars. He gave me a lot to work from as his dissolute mother, a real departure for me. One scene—I'm sitting in front of the mirror telling him to go for his own good—is a stunner. Paul was already a pro.

Years later, when I was touring in *Don Juan in Hell*, we played a college town near New Orleans. Paul happened to be there shooting *The Drowning Pool*, so I went to see him that afternoon. I remember walking down a country road past every kid in town waiting to glimpse Paul Newman. When he saw me, he rushed over, threw his arms around me, and kissed me, elicting a collective swoon from those kids, who were probably wondering, who's that lucky old lady? We went off and talked until they called him back to work. "I can't come to the show," he said apologetically. "I have—"

"I know . . . I know. You don't have to tell me. You have an early call."

He smiled. "Is there anything I can do for you?"

"Yes. Tell me where I can get a good pecan pie." We laughed, he said he'd let me know, and I went back to my hotel. Half an hour later, a beautiful pecan pie arrived. That's Paul.

It wasn't a great time to make a Hollywood comeback, with the industry harried by strikes and production greatly curtailed. But before I finished *From the Terrace*, Ross Hunter signed me for *Midnight Lace* at Universal.

Myrna was my heroine, attests Ross Hunter. *She was the clone for the stars I used, chic even in dungarees. I owe my biggest breakthrough as a producer to her. I studied her comedies with William Powell. I ran eight of their pictures and got the idea of doing* Pillow Talk. *I modeled my stars on Powell and Loy: took Doris Day out of the kitchen; put Rock Hudson in tails. People said at the time that romantic comedy came of age with* Pillow Talk. *Well, if it's true, I can't take the credit. It was Powell and Loy.*

I had always wanted to work with Myrna, and the part of Doris Day's worldly aunt in Midnight Lace *made it possible. I've never worked with anybody who gave so much to a role. She made a good role excellent. And she always looked great. Every time I looked at her I glowed. Myrna cares—that's why she's a star. It's rare in this town that a star remains a star so long. She's a dependable friend, too, which is even rarer.*

She spread peace and humor all over the set. She was so supportive to Doris and me. Doris's big scene required prolonged hysteria, which was tough on her. She gave it her all, cried and cried, and no one seemed able to help her control it. She finally almost passed out, and we had to send her home. We would have lost a day's shooting if Myrna hadn't stepped in unflustered to do an unscheduled scene in one take. She was ready. That's a star!

Working for Ross Hunter was a joy; you could always be sure that he would give you the best. He has a thing about having fresh flowers on the set and real jewelry. Everything we wore was from Harry Winston. There were armed security guards on the set to keep an eye on it all. It was a beautiful production and Ross had showcased me with a witty sort of part, or so I thought. I was playing it as a nice woman who loved her niece, but it turned out that people suspected me. They thought I was working with Rex Harrison to knock Doris off. So everything I had tried to do with the part came to naught; all the little scenes I had with her apparently didn't mean a thing. That's the danger of being in a mystery. You're all suspect, no matter what you do. I still hadn't learned that, although I'd been in so many mysteries and played, rather auspiciously, the wife of a detective.

I have nothing but the best to say about Doris Day. She was wonderful to me, really lovely. She sent flowers when I started and remained friendly and attentive. As I've said, it's difficult when you start stepping down. You fight so hard to get to the top and then you realize it's time to gracefully give in a little. Doris, who was riding high then, never played the prima donna. I appreciated her attitude enormously.

The men were another story. Rex Harrison was in a strange kind of mood, no doubt because his wife, Kay Kendall, had died. He had very little time for me or anybody else, as far as I could tell; he did his job and that was it. John Gavin, whom Ross was trying to groom into another Rock Hudson, was a very handsome man who didn't quite have what it takes. I used to tease him about his right-wing proclivities. "You'd better be careful," I warned him. "You shouldn't be seen with me." He must have been careful—he rode Reagan's coattails right into an ambassadorship. That was the last time I saw Herbert Marshall, a most charming man, who had been part of the British crowd that came to my Hidden Valley house. Having lost a leg in World War I, he gave all those suave performances on a wooden one. You would never have known it, even in *Midnight Lace*, when he had became somewhat feeble. It was terribly sad to see, as it is with so many friends as one gets on. But I've lost a lot of young ones, too, who went before their time.

Ross had lured "Irene" out of semi-retirement to do the clothes for Doris and me. Having practically discovered her for my personal wardrobe years before, I was surprised and delighted. She had gone to Bullocks Wilshire after I had used her, then to M-G-M, where she became the top designer after Adrian left in the early forties. Irene had married Cedric Gibbons's brother, who had taken me out occasionally, so we were going to have lunch and catch up. The next thing I hear, she has jumped out of the window of some building in Hollywood. I had no inkling she was so distraught. Someone said she had been drinking, but I wasn't aware of it. Awful, just awful! She was so gifted, so talented, but obviously it wasn't enough.

After completing *Midnight Lace*, I finally went to Juárez for a quickie divorce from Howland. We had been separated for nearly two years, so quickie was hardly the word—painless might be more to the point. I had waited and hoped until I was numb.

What a relief to get back to New York and another Presidential campaign! I wasn't too keen on Jack Kennedy in 1960. Supporting him meant pulling away from my commitment to Adlai, who was for a long time the archenemy of the Kennedys—not of Jack, particularly, but certainly of the Kennedys' position in the Democratic Party. I kept plugging away for Adlai until he himself put a stop to it. "I heard what you said about 1960, even if I was far away," he wrote to me from Illinois. "Thanks!—my good and loyal friend—but no! no! no! Let's make a deal—you make pictures (I love 'em) and I'll practice law—or play with my grandchildren!" And, despite a halfhearted bid for renomination in 1960, he really meant it.

I'm capable of having a fixed position and yet being able to change. That seems like a paradox, and it is. But my principles don't change. What changes is the pragmatic aspect. Although my politics have tended to be idealistic, I'm from rugged pioneer stock and dead-on practical. In other words, Nixon was running against Kennedy and I didn't want Nixon to win. I have been one of his staunch non-supporters since he ran against Helen Gahagan Douglas in California and Mrs. Roosevelt asked me to help raise money and votes to stop him. Too bad it didn't—permanently. I would have done anything to keep him out.

Many Stevenson supporters, I discovered, would not let go. Universal's head of publicity in New York, Alice Lee Boatwright, with whom I publicized *Midnight Lace*, underscored that dilemma. On the way home from *Luncheon at Sardi's*, Arlene Francis's radio show, Boaty approached the subject of politics: "Last time, I worked with a strong, vocal group of women, the nucleus of 'Broadway for Stevenson.' But we're disenchanted that he hasn't gotten the nomination, heartbroken that we don't have him as our candidate. We're not going to work with Jack Kennedy."

I was stunned. "You can't do that. You'll give the election to Nixon. Why don't you let me meet with these women? Get them together one evening and I'll talk to them." Actually, as a member of the New York State Democratic Committee, my job after Kennedy's nomination was to reconcile such splinter groups.

Barbara Handman and Phyllis Newman, the fearless leaders, assembled their forces, including Betty Comden, Isabel Haliburton, Amy Greene, Eleanor Bissinger, Rosie Tobias, and Ellen Madison. Many of them would become my friends, but that night they were hard nuts to crack, idolizing Adlai, suspicious of Jack Kennedy and his forebears. Diminutive Amy, sprawled on a sofa, snarled at me, "Can you promise that Adlai will get Secretary of State if Kennedy wins?"

"I can't make promises like that," I told her, although the Kennedy people *had* promised that in exchange for his support. Those women made it extremely tough for me. I talked until I was blue in the face, trying to make some sense of the situation. I didn't exactly put a gun to their heads, but I startled them: "Do you want Nixon? All right then, you do just what you're planning to do and you'll get him." I gave them his background in vivid detail: his attack on Helen Gahagan Douglas; his manipulation of the Red scare. Finally, long after midnight, little Amy called for a vote. They came through, every one of them, and worked like little dogs after that.

Bobbie Handman, a front-runner in reform politics, even helped to organize a final event to seduce diehard Stevensonians. We took over the Morosco Theatre, where *The Best Man* was playing, to present "Adlai for Broadway." The curtain went up and there stood Eleanor Roosevelt, Governor Lehman, Tallulah Bankhead, Henry Fonda, Lauren Bacall, and on and on. James Thurber introduced Mort Sahl, who introduced Adlai, who reiterated that he would not run and urged everyone to join him in supporting Kennedy.

I worked damn hard for Kennedy, traveling, making speeches, supporting him all the way. His staff said I got Syracuse for him almost single-handedly, which isn't far from the truth. I covered every inch of that city. I had experienced several Presidential campaigns, but none so intense. It was the nature of the man: hell-bent on winning, he had little time for anything else. He was a strange man. During all the months we campaigned shoulder to shoulder, I could never get him to respond to me, which was partly due to my own reserve. I can't pursue people if they don't meet me halfway.

Once, when he reached New York after a round of campaign

speeches, his throat was irritated and he worried about losing his voice. While sharing yet another dais at yet another political luncheon, this one at the Waldorf, I mentioned a wonderful throat specialist whom theater people used. "If your trouble persists," I told him, "I'll arrange for him to see you." Jack thanked me curtly and walked away. There was never a word beyond the minimum, never an attempt to be friendly. Jackie, on the other hand, had the ability to communicate with people on a personal level. She seemed aware of what people were doing in the campaign and had the grace to show her appreciation. She always made time for polite small talk, which her husband seemed unable or unwilling to do. Jackie was most pleasant and communicative; in fact, when we meet she still is.

Part of my problem with Jack Kennedy was a suggestion in his manner that he considered the kitchen or the bedchamber to be a woman's province. He had some of that Irish-Catholic macho indoctrination. With his men friends, his cronies, he could be congenial enough, and when he performed, when those cameras rolled, he was terrific. We shared many a platform while he made speeches and, believe me, he exuded charm, almost a theatrical charm. When he was up there selling something, he was irresistible. I remember going to the garment district with him for a tremendous rally and he absolutely mesmerized them. They went crazy. He was bright and attractive and he used his sense of humor cleverly. More to the point, he was beginning to espouse the right ideas.

I will always be grateful to him for including me in his National Conference on Constitutional Rights and American Freedom. Generally I had been invited to U.N.-related events, but Jack or his aides perceived my commitment to civil rights. My participation in the conference, chaired by that fighting liberal Hubert Humphrey, would lead to my long involvement with the NCDH (National Committee Against Discrimination in Housing).

That conference, scheduled by the Kennedy forces one month before the election, established the candidate as a serious proponent of civil rights—an example of brilliant campaign strategy used to the maximum. After attending the closing session at the Park Sheraton, the Kennedys led a motorcade to a big rally in Harlem, where bleachers had been erected for conference participants. He and Jackie absolutely captivated the crowds. They were young and beautiful and rich. They said the right things and promised the best things. They were unbeatable.

Mrs. Roosevelt, Governor Lehman, and I shared a car that day. On the way back, an aide asked if we could possibly stop at Kennedy headquarters in what had become known as Spanish Harlem. "We're in trouble there," he explained. "Many of these people aren't going to vote. They can't read English and don't understand how important it is."

"Yes," Mrs. R. said without hesitation. "Of course we'll stop."

The car pulled up to a storefront, where a vast crowd was milling around. This was considered a dangerous area at the time, but we never even thought about it. Mrs. R. jumped out of the car, with the rest of us close behind. They had no place for us to stand to make speeches. All they could produce were two little beige folding chairs. Mrs. Roosevelt climbed up on one, Governor Lehman on the other, and I stood between them waiting to catch the first one that fell. That was their platform. They stood there and spoke to the people. I'll never forget how they responded to her. "She is like a piece of alabaster," Eugene McCarthy said of her at that point in her life; "all the rough parts have been smoothed out and what you are seeing now is the pure thing itself." She was really a charismatic person. Something drew you to her, perhaps that quality of alabaster honed by her dedication and commitment. She couldn't stop; if there was a job to do, she had to do it.

Kennedy made his last campaign appearance at a rally in New Jersey, and I was with him up until the very last minute. We flew all over Long Island, then over to New Jersey on a final swing, arriving late for the rally. A mob of avid supporters almost trampled us to death as we got out of the car. I lost one of my shoes. When we walked in, the whole place went wild. That was Sunday. The election was on Tuesday. So we campaigned together until he returned to Boston for Election Day; still I never got to know him. But who cares? He won!

There was a big snowstorm on January 19th, the day before the Inauguration and the Inaugural Ball. My plane was the last allowed to land in Washington. A beau of mine, George Kogel, a Kennedy volunteer from a family of Kings Point builders, was my escort. Estelle Linzer and a friend of hers made it a foursome. We never saw a Kennedy the night of the ball, but we got tangled up in their motorcade on the way. It was a festive and crowded political bash. Every Democrat with a white tie was there. Hubert Humphrey made a big fuss over us. I loved that man and always regret that the right time never came for him to be President. That night he kept introducing me to his sisters, and at one point spilled champagne all over my dress. It was a beautiful dress, but I didn't care—Senator Humphrey could do that if he wanted to. "Your trip to Washington must have been exciting," my mother wrote. "Our new President is living up to his promises, so I hope people in general stand by him. Did you see where young girls want to have their noses changed to look like Jackie's? Several papers say there hasn't been such a scramble for new noses since the youngsters wanted *yours!*"

On February 7th, I received a polite note from Evelyn Lincoln, Kennedy's secretary, acknowledging my "efforts on his behalf." I am certainly not vain enough to think that the newly elected President had nothing better to do than to thank me himself, but, God knows, those who contributed money rather than time got theirs. I never really felt that he recalled or cared about what I done when he no longer needed me. However, the important thing was his performance as President. During his first year in office, considering the narrow margin of victory, he did remarkably well with Congress, getting more support for his programs than he ever expected.

During that tragically brief term, he or his staff did include me in a White House reception commemorating the Centennial of the Emancipation Proclamation. I felt honored to be among some of the nation's most prominent blacks, and applauded the President for observing the occasion—not a usual gesture then. Later, they invited me to a full-blown White House dinner for King Hassan II of Morocco, with engraved menus, a glittering guest list, and a performance of *Brigadoon* in the East Room. Afterward, with his disarming public demeanor, the President introduced its author, Alan Jay Lerner, with whom he had attended Choate and Harvard. "We went to school together," our host quipped, "and no one thought either one of us would amount to anything." Jackie looked radiant, which I told her. She was her usual charming, open self, very excited about their new farm in Middleburg, Virginia. "I don't know when it will be ready," she remarked, "but I'm hoping we can move in before the hunting season this fall." But even on this happy occasion I couldn't get the President to respond. I remember going up to him to say something and he just walked on by. He was looking for the King of Morocco, I guess. That was in March of 1963. I wouldn't get another chance.

10

THE CLASSIC

Mr. President, it is not common to find an actress or actor who is a true classic—someone who excels in every role and who is able to conquer the fickleness of movie fans. Myrna Loy, however, is one of those classics. —SENATOR HOWARD METZENBAUM, Congressional Record, 1981

After one of my "Support Kennedy!" gatherings during the 1960 campaign, Boaty Boatwright and I dined at The Running Footman. We had become close friends while publicizing *Midnight Lace* and campaigning for Kennedy, but I never imagined she could change my life with an idle question.

"Why don't you do some theater?" she began.

"I think the time has passed for me to do it," I hedged. "My agent's always getting scripts for me, but I've never felt I would be a stage actress. I don't have the training. All my life I've been working in films."

"Suppose you did summer stock to start off?"

"Well, that's part of the problem. People keep saying, 'You mustn't do stock. You're a big star. You'll lose face.' But how can I learn what works on stage unless I go out and do it before audiences?"

"We'll find a play you like, surround you with people who'd take care of you. Why not let me look into it, at least?"

I gave tentative assent, hoping she would forget all about it, because, frankly, I was scared to death. Irresistible offers kept coming—Lindsay and Crouse actually wrote *State of the Union* with me in mind—but I always managed to resist. Only once, a year before Boaty's attempt, did I relent, and for no less a tempter than Noel Coward. That experience nearly kept me off the stage forever.

I had known Noel from his occasional visits to Hollywood over the years. There were a few friends he would see—Cary Grant, among them—and he always visited my sets, claiming that he liked to watch me work. We had never quite managed to work together, though, so I was delighted when he called me at the Volney. "Myrna," he declared, "I have a play you'd be wonderful for." He sent over the script of *South Sea Bubble* with the two men who produced his plays worldwide. They wanted to tour it first, then bring it to Broadway. They were no fools— they knew I had a few things to learn. "I'll consider it," I told them, and agreed to read for Noel later that week. Roddy McDowall, sensing my apprehension, offered to read with me.

We went down to some theater where Noel, fresh from the dentist and riddled with novocaine, was waiting impatiently. I walked out on that stage to read lines for the first time in my career and "Master," as he was called, began firing orders at me. "Now, Myrna," he kept saying, "one thing you must do in the theatah is project." Then I would read a few more words of dialogue and that crisp voice would ring out again. "Now, Myrna, it is essential in the theatah to be heard." Roddy tried to cue me, but Noel kept interrupting with his one-sided litany. You must do this "in the theatah," you must do that "in the theatah." Noel was a great gentleman, but when it same to his profession he pulled no punches. He just kept hammering away until I was completely discouraged. I decided then and there that the theatah was not for me.

My bout with the Master did not harm our friendship. Whenever he came to New York, I would be swept into an inevitable rush of parties and openings. I was also elected—along with his friends and assistants, Graham Payn and Cole Lesley, and a few other intimates— to keep vigil at Sardi's or at his East Fifty-fourth Street apartment after his own plays opened. He would face those deathwatches with a blasé, sociable veneer, while that nasty little voice inside kept repeating, "It isn't going to work." Often, during the fifties and sixties, it didn't.

The publicity and advance sale for *Sail Away*, Noel's first musical in years, were heartening enough to warrant optimism and a gala opening. The Sardis, grateful for a new Noel Coward play and hopeful for the usual long run, gave the party afterward themselves. Noel, as he loved to do, populated his table with actresses: Marlene Dietrich, Margaret Leighton, Dorothy Dickson, Elaine Stritch, the star of *Sail Away*, and myself. Despite his fame and worldly aura, Noel remained charmingly star-struck, and in his mind's eye his "little lot," as he referred to us that evening, were forever caught in our primes.

Delighted with the opening performance and the party, he called it a "real Noel Coward night." But it was hardly a real Noel Coward play. It was charming but old-fashioned, and beneath his bravado one sensed defensiveness, a questioning of his powers, as the tepid notices came in. Fortunately, neither his self-esteem nor his output was diminished for long. Our deathwatches continued throughout the sixties with *The Girl Who Came to Supper* and *High Spirits*, culminating in a revival of *Private Lives*, which prompted the critics to place the Master in the pantheon of twentieth-century playwrights. Noel, considering it his due, wore his laurels willingly.

Two genuine "Noel Coward nights" highlighted his last visits to New York. In February, 1970, Earl Blackwell turned Raffles into Sir Noel's Pub to celebrate his recent knighthood. Huddled around tiny tables, each designated by the title of a Coward play, were the Lunts, Dorothy and Dick Rodgers, Mary and Doug Fairbanks, Jr., and Adele Astaire. The guest of honor, slightly bent but beaming, his wit flashing as ever, held court at a banquette flanked by Beatrice Lillie and Cary Grant. Early in the evening, Graham Payn sent a note over: "Myrna, we're in trouble. Bea has fled. Will you please come over and sit with Master?" Poor Bea! She was having problems, probably some form of Alzheimer's disease, and walked out on her old friend.

I'm glad to say I knew Bea in her prime. When we were both working in Hollywood and living at Château Marmont, we would go over to Musso Frank's for dinner and talk the night away. On New Year's Eve, we attended a string of Beverly Hills parties, including Reggie Gardiner's, before winding up on the "wrong side of the tracks" at Robert Clary's. In his lovely little house on the other side of Olympic Boulevard, a bunch of young performers, dominated by Kaye Ballard, strutted their stuff. Not to be outdone, Bea pulled out some of her private repertoire, which was, to put it mildly, risqué. Delivering song after song with her inimitable brand of surprised wickedness, she had us in hysterics, begging for more. Bea was in heaven, a performer to her fingertips, having the time of her life.

That wonderful New Year's Eve came back to me as I replaced her beside Noel at Raffles. Cary didn't man the other side for long—he went off to be with his young daughter, whom he absolutely adored. Sir Noel, delighted with his knighthood, told with great relish how it happened. The Queen Mother invited him to lunch at Clarence House, then sent down word that she was indisposed and hoped he could "make do with two stand-ins." Her daughters, Queen Elizabeth and Princess Margaret, appeared and, over lunch, asked if he would accept the honor. And high time, too, I say! But charmingly done.

It made him very happy. He played the piano and sang his songs at the party. It was all kind of *gemütlich*, with Jules Stein, Kay Thompson, and Richard Harris joining the impromptu entertainment, and Peggy Wood tearfully singing "I'll See You Again," Noel's most popular song, which she had introduced in *Bitter Sweet* forty years before.

Our last "Noel Coward night" came in January, 1973, at a gala invitational performance of *Oh, Coward!*, in honor of the author. After that delightful rendering of his words and music, brilliantly devised by Roderick Cook, the Master himself responded to a standing ovation. "I like the songs," he observed crisply. "The songs are great."

The next day at Roddy McDowall's, Noel had some amusing things to say about the gala. He had escorted Marlene Dietrich, who had been solicitous and very sweet on the way to the theater. He wasn't well and Marlene was going to take care of him. When they reached the New Theatre, there was a steep stairway to negotiate. As they started down, with Marlene guiding him, lights came on and the crowd applauded. Marlene, who apparently wasn't doing too well herself, began posing and leaning on Noel. "It was a most terrifying descent," he said, "feeling for those steps while Marlene clung to me, pulling me over. I nearly broke my neck."

As he saw me home after Roddy's luncheon, we chatted in the back seat. "There's something absurd about this whole thing," I said. "In all these years, although you've written so many things that were just right for me, I've never done one of your plays. When Metro made *Private Lives*, I was too young, my career was too young."

"And when I tried to get you over to England for *Blithe Spirit*," he added, "they wouldn't let you go. The war was on and they were afraid of losing you." I didn't mention that I might have done *South Sea Bubble* if he'd been a bit more patient.

"There's only one thing left for me," I decided, "the mother in *Hay Fever*."

"You're too young to do *Hay Fever!*" he snapped. I was well into my sixties, for God's sake, but that was Noel being gallant.

When we arrived, although he was then very frail, he got out of the car to pass me into my lobby. He clasped my hands and looked into my eyes as we parted. "Myrna, dear," he said clearly, "you have never played a false note." It was a hell of a compliment from the Master. I ran upstairs and wrote it down.

He left the next day for his house in Jamaica. He died there two months later. His plays, his songs, his embodiment of crisp elegance will never die.

My discouraging reading for Noel in 1959 had decided me against doing "theatah." But I had not bargained for Boaty Boatwright's persistence. She had got through to Edie Van Cleve, my agent at William Morris, which was an accomplishment in itself. "What is it you're calling about?" asked Edie, who could be very formidable.

"I'm calling about Myrna Loy doing summer stock," Boaty explained.

"Oh, my dear," Edie protested, "I've been turning down scripts for Miss Loy for years. Established producers offer her marvelous parts. Why on earth do you think she would do this for you?"

"Because," Boaty blurted out, "I'm a really good Democrat." Edie laughed and told her to come on over.

From there began "the great swindle," as I called it, the conspiracy to get me on the stage. Boaty, without telling me, proceeded to assemble a workable package. Wynn Handman, a fine director and acting teacher, the husband of another Kennedy campaigner, agreed to direct and coach me. Eleanor Bissinger, yet another political ally and one of the Lebenthal & Co. family, backed the project. Bill Barnes, who had been Tennessee Williams's agent, signed on as advance man. When Otto Preminger offered him a very good job that summer, Billy told him, "Only if I can start in September. I couldn't leave this." They were all so loyal and protective, those wonderful swindlers.

Armed with the rights to Leslie Stevens's *Marriage-Go-Round*, which Claudette Colbert and Charles Boyer had just done on Broadway, Boaty went to Edie Van Cleve. "This is it!" she declared. "Can you deliver Myrna?" I really didn't know what was happening. I tried to worm out by demanding a co-star of Boyer's stature, and Robby Lantz, Roddy McDowall's agent, countered with Claude Dauphin, another client of his. Robby, who had been in on the swindle, asked to represent me at that time. I was delighted. He's one of the most civilized men around. For an agent, everyone says, he has a great sense of humor. He got me out of my William Morris contract, and has remained my agent, protector, and, along with his wife, Shirlee, friend.

There I was, framed by friends, with no visible means of escape. Wynn Handman began coming over to my apartment three or four days a week. We'd sit at the table by the windows overlooking the city and he would talk about stage acting. We went through the script; then he broke it down and had me do the speeches. Subtly he introduced a very different medium, carefully nurturing me for this crucial step. When we moved to his studio to give me more feeling of the stage, a little distance, I panicked. "I can't do this," I groaned. "It's beyond me." The swindlers said that Claude Dauphin was on his way over from Paris, which wasn't true, so that I couldn't back out. My reluctance was not motivated by fear alone. Other obligations did not dissolve in the face of a theatrical career.

When I appeared on one of those radio interview shows at that time, listeners phoned in questions ranging from "How's Asta?" to "Should Communist China be admitted to the U.N.?" I had a foot in both worlds and intended to keep it that way. I flew to Huntsville, Alabama, to help launch the Madison County Democratic Women's Division as keynote speaker at a luncheon for Congressman Bob Jones. I flew to Boston to represent the U.S. Committee for Refugees in a program arranged by its Massachusetts affiliate. As an appointee to the National Advisory Council of the AAUN, I gave "moral support" and all that entailed—hosting a U.N. tour for ABC Television's *Expedition, New York*, for instance—while serving as communications consultant.

My appointment as co-chairman of the Advisory Council of the National Committee Against Discrimination in Housing (NCDH), which comprised thirty-three organizations advocating civil rights, represented an even more time-consuming responsibility. The frustration and despair of people trapped in ghettos lead to anger and violence unless we act to bring about change. One way to achieve it is through open housing, which remains one of the most crucial issues of our time. I always felt that if I had to go to battle for it, I could—and I did, when the Real Estate Boards of Manhattan, Brooklyn, and the Bronx opposed amending the city's anti-discrimination laws.

During a five-hour public hearing, after haranguing the City Council's General Welfare Committee on domestic issues, I added that discrimination at home was affecting our foreign relations. From my UNESCO experience, I knew that housing discrimination was felt keenly by U.N. personnel—from delegates to clerks. "Just one discriminatory act, just one closed door," I explained, "can have serious repercussions in all our negotiations." The media response was fantastic. Because of this other image of me, the newspapers, which might have buried the hearings, gave them headline coverage. We even made the *Daily News!* The amendments passed unanimously. All I can say is, thank God for *The Thin Man!*

A week later, I flew to Laconia, New Hampshire, to make my stage début. Bette Davis called before I left, said, "Now look, this is what you've got to be prepared for," and listed pointers for physical and mental survival on the road. Fortunately, Leone Rossen, my secretary, came from California to help. She started for Laconia before me in a station wagon loaded down with my luggage and costumes. Leone would tour with me several times before getting fed up. It was rough on her, particularly all the driving between theaters. I wouldn't drive. It took too much of my energy—and I needed every bit!

We had only a week to rehearse on the stage of the Lakes Region Playhouse, a converted barn on Lake Winnipesaukee. Accustomed to the precision of a Hollywood set, I needed the security of my props being exactly in place. In a summer-stock situation, however, you don't have entirely seasoned professionals. Most of them are apprentices, stagestruck teenagers who volunteer in order to learn. They are zealous and solicitous, to be sure, but they are kids. I used to walk around and check for protruding nails and other hazards before every performance. Theater actors tend to be more relaxed about such things, particularly in rehearsal, although Claude Dauphin always sat on stage for twenty minutes before curtain time. That was part of his discipline. I was lucky to have Claude. Whenever I did anything remotely right, he would say, "Well . . . it took me twenty-five years to learn that," which wasn't true—he was born with that timing. He was just building me up.

By opening night, Wynn had imparted those technical things that one can learn only from a stage director. Laughter, for example. "I don't know about you," Claude teased in rehearsal, "but I know where all my laughs come in." He had gone over the script with his friend

Charles Boyer. In films we don't stop for laughs; they do it in the cutting later on. But on stage, if a laugh is coming up, you stop stark-still, wait for it to break, and as it's breaking like a wave, you move in with a louder voice to pick up the play. You must also learn to open yourself up to both sides. You must project, as Noel had impatiently emphasized. I always had used natural tones on the screen. I never pushed. My everyday kind of truth was very usable in front of a camera, but it's hard to maintain subtle shading when you think you're shouting. The need to become real in stage terms felt dishonest to me. At rehearsal, Wynn would stand out in the theater, calling, "Myrna, I can't hear you."

"I'm shouting," I'd call back. "I will not go beyond this."

"Well, you're not doing a stage performance."

He persisted into opening week. He'd come backstage between acts, pop his head into my dressing room, and whisper, "You're still not doing it, Myrna."

"But I'm shouting."

"Just take my word for it—I'll tell you when you hit it right." Around the third or fourth performance, I hit it. When you do that on stage, it's like breaking the sound barrier. All of a sudden it feels right, because you're in tune with the way it wants to be. It no longer feels dishonest, but, rather, honest in terms of what the theater demands.

The tour was a huge success, attests Boaty Boatwright. *We broke house records all along the sterling circuit, the deluxe New England summer theaters. That package was fantastically expensive. Those theaters paid more than they had ever paid for summer stock, but they made more. Everyone was wild with the glee of this great star selling out. I never made so much money in my life. Wynn made a lot of money, Myrna and Claude made a lot of money, Ellie Bissinger doubled her investment, and we all had a wonderful time.*

It was a joyous entry into theater for Myrna, but tough. She'd never lived like that. "On safari," Claude called it. Some of those places were really primitive, and she's a perfectionist, overseeing everything, following a strict routine. She has to have her nap. She has to have her dinner. She has to know where to get her breakfast. There was a lot of handholding. But she endured it and never lost her vitality. It was extraordinary to watch her come on stage every night and come alive. When she made her entrance, there was always enormous applause followed by whispers: "Is it Myrna Loy? It really is! Yes, look at her! She hasn't got a day older." That face doesn't change. Her hair is always red. She's always impeccably groomed. Then, across the footlights, she serves that subtle combination of graciousness and a certain ironic attitude toward life in her slight smile.

It was incredible how those women would come up to Myrna afterward and want to touch her. After years of idolizing her screen image, they wanted to be sure she was real. She was extraordinarily gracious to them in the old-fashioned manner. She stood there patiently night after night, signing autographs, chatting with them, having pictures taken with them. It was just a bunch of baloney to me, but my God, she did it and it helped next time she came into town.

When we hit Westport, people started coming up from New York to take a look. They had to add three extra performances. Alan Pakula saw it that weekend and decided he wanted Myrna for his planned Broadway production of There Must Be a Pony! *I think Mike Nichols saw her there and got the idea to use her as the mother in* Barefoot in the Park. *She turned down the role in the original Broadway production, but headed the national company for years. So, an idle question at dinner one night opened a whole new career for Myrna Loy.*

After returning from safari, I conducted a press conference at the National Housing Center, along with Algernon Black and Charles Abrams, NCDH chairman and president, respectively. We released copies of a statement urging President Kennedy to fulfill his campaign pledge to eliminate racial discrimination in federal housing programs. Despite the passing of the Housing Act of 1961, we had uncovered massive evidence that eighty percent of federally sponsored public housing was operated on a segregated basis. Making the benefits of the Housing Act available to all, regardless of race, creed, or national origin, depended on executive action by the man who had involved me in the NCDH in the first place. He never got the chance. It would require seven more years of struggle before his successor signed the Civil Rights Act of 1968.

A concurrent battle involved the John Birch Society's attempt to discredit the AAUN. We were always under siege from some extreme right-wing group. When I appeared on a radio show once in the Midwest, these poor fools had been set up by the Birchers to keep calling in with the same questions: "Didn't all the money collected for UNICEF go to the Soviet Union?" As I very carefully answered the question each time, the host looked at me and shook his head: "I can't believe this." I said, "Well, believe it!" They never let up on us, but their concentrated campaign in 1961 particularly disturbed Mrs. Roosevelt. She wondered—this is an example of her modesty—if I might invite people influential in the arts to dine at her house and discuss solutions to the problem. As if they wouldn't have come for her!

I called on some old reliables: Jules Feiffer, John Hersey, Paul Newman, and Joanne Woodward. Otto Preminger also accepted. He was one of those people I'd known for a long, long time but not well. He had a reputation for being very difficult, but he came to Mrs. Roosevelt's and that's to his credit. Dick Gregory came in huffing and puffing after a delayed flight from Chicago. I have never seen anyone in such a state: he revered Mrs. Roosevelt and this invitation had come out of the blue. It was a delight to behold his excitement.

The cook prepared a nice dinner, although our hostess was hardly a gourmet. She was very indifferent to food—it was the discussion afterward that concerned her. She explained the situation between the Birchers and the AAUN and asked what could be done in the area of communications to offset the groundless attacks. The guests were prepared with constructive suggestions; she was interested and receptive. Alas, little came of it, because she was beginning to fail.

She tried to keep active, but seemed very frail at her last AAUN meeting in 1962. I sent her a little handkerchief for her seventy-eighth birthday on October 11th. "You were more than good to think of me," she wrote, "and I cannot tell you how deeply I appreciate your good wishes." But Maureen Core, her secretary, had to sign the typed note for her.

Less than a month later she died.

Adlai Stevenson eulogized her at the Cathedral Church of St. John the Divine. "She would rather light a candle than curse the darkness," he movingly observed, "and her glow has warmed the world." As chairman of the Eleanor Roosevelt Memorial Foundation, he asked me to join the National Council. "I would be honored if in such a way I can help you carry on the work of that dear and remarkable lady," I replied, words that hardly expressed the depth of my feelings.

Despite right-wing attacks and political skulduggery, the AAUN proudly celebrated its fortieth anniversary in the fall of 1963. I shared the dais in the Pierre's Grand Ballroom with John Roosevelt; U Thant, Secretary-General of the U.N.; Herman Steinkraus, president of the AAUN; Clark Eichelberger, its founder; and others dedicated to maintaining peace in a troubled world. My speech that evening, which recalled working with the AAUN in California and meeting Jan Masaryk, brought fifteen years of involvement full circle.

Two other long-cherished goals came to fruition that fall. We launched a successful campaign for a stronger Fair Housing Law in New York State and held a Founders' Reception for the American Place Theatre. While coaching me for my stage début, Wynn Handman shared his dreams of a place where American writers could experience theater, a creative environment where they could develop regardless of commerciality. Today there are several theaters doing new plays by American writers, but non-profit theater hardly existed twenty-five years ago. Excited by the idea, I encouraged Wynn to proceed, which income from our *Marriage-Go-Round* tour gave him the wherewithal to do. When the Reverend Sidney Lanier, then presiding at the very established St. Thomas's Episcopal Church, heard Wynn talking so religiously about the writer as prophet changing society, it inspired him. Sidney sought a church that could be a mission to the arts by housing such a theater. He found it in St. Clement's Episcopal Church, a moribund Gothic structure in Hell's Kitchen. They started incorporating some very exciting things into the church service, and over a two-year period the American Place Theatre crystallized.

By the time of the Founders' Reception, on November 21, 1963, Tennessee Williams and several others had joined Wynn, Sidney, and me on the board of directors, and dozens of influential people had become founders and advisers. Ronald and Marietta Tree hosted the reception in their big house on East Seventy-ninth Street. Robert Penn Warren and Lionel Abel read from their poetry. William Goyen read a prose passage from his work. I read Gertrude Stein's piece about Alfred Stieglitz, whose phrase "an American place" had inspired Wynn. The highlight of the evening was Robert Lowell's reading of his poems. Wynn was planning to open the theater with *The Old Glory*, Lowell's adaptation of Melville's *Benito Cereno*, which every Broadway producer had turned down. We all left the reception in great spirits.

Something unforeseen shattered our spirits the following day. President Kennedy was assassinated. So what could be called the first official performance of the American Place Theatre at St. Clement's was a memorial service led by Sidney Lanier two days later. We were all in a state of shock, but were thankful to be able to do something. Many of those involved with establishing the theater attended. People did not want to be alone.

I read Emily Dickinson's "After great pain a formal feeling comes—/ The nerves sit ceremonious like tombs . . . ," which is so beautiful and true. Robert Lowell sat beside me, even more shy and withdrawn than usual. He was not a man for conversation; working, he was more articulate. But he stood when his turn came and movingly recited a Scottish ballad about Lord Murray, a gallant soldier. Tennessee Williams read a poem by Stephen Spender, made all the more touching because Tennessee stood shivering at the altar, clutching his heavy overcoat to himself. The room wasn't cold. He was just so deeply affected by the tragedy.

After the service, we were downstairs having rolls and coffee when the news came that Lee Harvey Oswald, the alleged perpetrator, had been shot. "We have to go back upstairs," Sidney said. So we went upstairs and he did another service for Oswald, which I considered most remarkable.

We walked over to Downey's afterward. Tennessee, who disappeared without a word between services, had beat us to it. Still shivering in his coat, he huddled there by himself getting drunk. Deciding that was precisely the thing to be doing on that drastic day, we joined him and quickly caught up.

A year later, after becoming a non-profit corporation and getting some grants and contributions, we opened the theater, as planned, with *The Old Glory*. It was hailed as a landmark theatrical event. Those early years in the little Gothic church in Hell's Kitchen were highlighted by productions of William Alfred's *Hogan's Goat* and the works of young writers like Ronald Ribman, Anne Sexton, Ed Bullins, Joyce Carol Oates, Steven Tesich, and Ronald Milner. We presented Sam Shepard's first full-length play. It's frightening when I think of the number of plays we did. The actors we launched include Dustin Hoffman, Faye Dunaway, Roscoe Lee Browne, Cliff Gorman, Frank Langella, Michael Douglas, and Philip Anglim.

I loved that ramshackle place, better even than the fine new theater built for us in 1971 at Forty-sixth and Sixth—thanks to the Lindsay administration's offer to allow increased rental space to builders who incorporated theaters into their new skyscrapers. We honored Mayor Lindsay for his contribution to the performing arts, but the new theater has been a mixed blessing. Our maintenance costs are astronomical. Corporations and foundations give money, then say, "All right, now make it on your own!" We are an experimental theater—perhaps every fifth play will make money, perhaps it won't. But we've discovered a lot of very gifted people along the way and elevated the American theater.

So far, Wynn has managed to stay true to his dream and keep it afloat, but right now we are in a life-or-death struggle. It's difficult to do avant-garde theater in a conservative atmosphere; there's just no support for it. Our early years were a time of experimentation and innovation, of communities being heard from and uncharted waters being tested. Nowadays people are infatuated with tradition, so Wynn has presented a popular side with an American Humor Series, which has been very well received. The plays make people laugh and we help the maintenance without compromising.

I draw great support from Myrna at board meetings, observes Wynn Handman, where some of the other trustees tend to be very pragmatic and say, "Why don't we do it this way?" Their way. She will speak up and save me from disagreements, because I often get very upset and rant on about our goals and the theater's integrity. It's often quite hostile, but there is Myrna with that maturity and wisdom and that commitment to me personally and to the idea of the theater. She understands and shares my need to be pure and keep the integrity of the institution. She is a person who loves very deeply, who feels very deeply, who is very spiritual—so much so that everyone knows it, even those who you don't think have much sensitivity. They know that, because she just has it. They listen to her. She carries a lot of weight, and you have to respect her. It's amazing that she spent all those years in Hollywood, when Hollywood was Hollywood, without having been brainwashed. It doesn't seem to have altered her at all. She draws on her roots in Montana, her heritage. She has the American spirit in the very best sense.

In the spring of 1964, Saint Subber, the producer of *Barefoot in the Park*, approached Robby Lantz about having me do the national tour. I read the script, saw Millie Natwick in the role on Broadway, and accepted with relief. The role of the widowed mother of the bride was a godsend, considering the general run of film roles being offered to women of my age. It had reached the point where I wondered what screenwriters had against us.

I didn't have to audition for *Barefoot* or for any play I've done—so far. It was Neil Simon's first hit as a playwright and Mike Nichols's directorial breakthrough, so they wanted a "name" to ensure its success on the road. Fortunately, I was well seasoned by that time. The summer following my stage début, I returned to the sterling circuit in a pre-Broadway tryout of *There Must Be a Pony!* Jim Kirkwood, Jr., had adapted the play from his novel about himself and his actress mother, Lila Lee. We started in Ogunquit, Maine, with high hopes and a Broadway opening scheduled for October at the Cort.

Things began to deteriorate as we neared New York. Out-of-town critics attacked me and the play. There was still that hangover from films; they were punishing me for having been a movie star. No matter how much you work—and I worked very hard—the tendency is to make it difficult for you, particularly if you have the temerity to aim for Broadway. There's no question that the role was a departure for me. Lila, as depicted by her son, had a drinking problem, a flamboyant temperament, and a mean streak. The kind of vulnerability that made her palatable was hardly my forte. Besides, I had to deal with a live baby leopard that kept growing as we toured and became extremely jealous when I addressed anyone else on stage.

Jim, intimidated by the critics, started changing his play. He's a perfectionist, as his marvelous book for *A Chorus Line* attests, but I don't think that many of the changes were as effective as his original script. And he's so quick the actors couldn't catch up with him. Another problem was that Alan Pakula, our producer, spent much of the time in Hollywood producing his second picture, *To Kill a Mockingbird*.

As I recall, another producer got into it and I began hearing rumors that he wanted to replace me with Kim Stanley. Apparently, Alan and Jim objected and never did anything about it. *There Must Be a Pony!* closed on the road after a profitable summer and didn't resurface until Elizabeth Taylor did it on television last year. It wasn't a very pleasant experience for me, but it helped to prepare me for *Barefoot in the Park*.

We rehearsed at the Biltmore Theatre while the Broadway production was still selling out there. People were lined up waiting to buy tickets. I had signed with the stipulation that Mike Nichols would direct the national company. Although his reputation as a director rested on *Barefoot* at that point, I had seen him work with Elaine May and knew how witty and smart and quick he was. That intimidated me a tiny bit, and I think it was mutual—both he and Neil Simon knew all about my career—but all that dissolved quickly in the atmosphere of work. Neil attended every rehearsal—watching, observing everything, but never interfering. He's too professional for that. If he had ideas or opinions, which he often did, he discussed them with Mike Nichols later.

Mike's wonderful to watch. His methods are so subtle and deft, his sense of timing perfect. He claimed that his only problem with me was in the attempt to make me look like a frumpy widow who's given up on life. "God damn it, Myrna," he would groan, "it's impossible to dress you down!" We finally accomplished it with one of those fake beaver coats, a sort of funny hat, and a pair of galoshes. Playing that role was an exercise for me, because I had to handle my own laughs and everybody else's. That play is so full of laughs that you hardly finish with one before there's another. Mike made some changes in direction for me, which I still use whenever I do *Barefoot*. I have the script with his original staging. It's so precious.

Mike raved about the "wonderful kids" who would play the newlyweds. They hadn't done that much as yet, but he was terribly excited to have found two such talented young actors to send out on the road. I couldn't have agreed more. One of them was Richard Benjamin. The other was Joan Van Ark. Dick is a wildly talented man, who is now realizing his ambition to direct—he used to observe Mike so closely at rehearsals. And Joanie, bless her heart, is coming into her own. There were times when I could have killed her. "For God's sake," I'd plead, "stop running—stop doing so much!" She did a lot of television, which

Dick didn't do. He was able to land the big parts earlier than she was; now she's getting a lot of attention. They were wonderful to work with. From the beginning, that was a joy.

The national tour opened on July 25, 1964, in Central City, Colorado. We flew from New York to Denver, where buses waited to take us up to the opera house. I'll never forget riding along with Neil beside me and Mike across the aisle gaping at the West; these two urbanites had never seen its like. Mike used to tell about his first hungry days in New York: going to Automats, getting cups of hot water, pouring in ketchup to make tomato soup. One felt that Neil, on the other hand, had been well taken care of by his family. But New York was their bailiwick, and their reaction to Colorado was something to behold. The West often scares New Yorkers because it's so vast and open. There are no barriers; it goes on and on. "This is my country," I reminded them as we left the plains for the mountains. "This is where I come from."

"I can't believe it," Neil muttered, spellbound by the Rockies.

We launched our tour amid great celebrations at the Central City Opera House. A note from President Johnson reached me there. "I was told about the wonderful work you have been doing," he wrote, "and I just wanted to thank you. I am grateful for the time and talent you are giving to the cause." Actually, I had been unable to do as much for him as I had for Jack Kennedy, but I continued to campaign along the way whenever possible to ensure his election in '64. I opposed escalating the war he had inherited, but held high hopes for that crusty Texan as a domestic-affairs President. His thoughtful note was a nice send-off as we descended the Rockies and headed for the Midwest. We didn't know then that we would be touring with tremendous success for two and a half years.

The railways weren't interested in us; they wanted freight, not people. But traveling by car or bus gave me a chance to see parts of the country I'd only glimpsed from the air. What a joy to encounter it town by town, city by city, and to grow more proud of it with every mile. It delighted me to play cities like Louisville, St. Paul, and Columbus and to realize that there are no "rural" audiences anymore. They were sharp and responsive everywhere. I was amazed by the number of people— conservative people, people who were children practically when I was up there—who came backstage just to stand there and stare at me. They would ask about Bill Powell and Asta—everybody remembers that dog. Why, he made *The New York Times* crossword puzzle long before I did! Often the men would look at me and ask, "May I kiss you?" You could see that they had carried this fantasy all those years. "Of course you may," I'd say, and then their wives would kiss me, too. I've probably saved more marriages because of Nora Charles!

When we were somewhere north of Kansas City, Harry Truman's secretary called me from Independence. "The President wants you to see his library," she explained, "and he wants to see you." It meant getting up at six, then driving back to open that night in Kansas City, but I accepted with pleasure. In this world of here today, gone tomorrow, it was an honor to be remembered by the former President.

I was taken on a tour of the library, which was interesting and modest, suitable to the man who built it. He hadn't wanted a memorial to himself, but to the Presidency. He had gathered memorabilia of all the great men and small who had held the office. "I like nothing better than to have a bunch of kids come in," he told me when I joined him in his office. "I go out and talk to them, explain things to them."

He seemed well enough, despite a recent fall, which I suspected might have been a stroke. He wasn't incapacitated, merely slowed down, but far from the dynamic scrapper I had known in Washington. There was a certain amount of sadness in him. Seeing that he needed a boost, I tried to think of things that would cheer him: "Oh, I can't tell you how much we miss you in Washington. I told Dean Acheson recently that all the tall men have left the city." And they had. They've never come back, either. There might have been a few during the Kennedy administration, but it's not the same. I did most of the talking that day and he just ate it up, pleased that people hadn't forgotten him. Although he had stepped down voluntarily, the aftermath of power and service leaves one a little forlorn.

I asked about Bess, which always pleased him. "Oh, she's fine"— he smiled—"still full of piss and vinegar." I was sorry not to see her, but I had to get back for the performance.

"I wish you could come and see the play," I said.

"Unfortunately, that would wreck my routine. I go to bed early and get up early. I come into the office every day, you know," he added proudly, and I could see how much that library meant to him. It virtually sustained him after politics. That was a long day for me, but it was wonderful to see him and to find him happy, at least, with what he had brought there.

For the first time since Hollywood's paleolithic age, when I danced at Grauman's, that tour put me back there on the stage. I arrived on Christmas Day and gaped at the new pavilion of the Music Center as I whirled by in a taxi on my way from the airport to a family reunion at my mother's house. Countless friends visited the Huntington Hartford Theatre during the run. Bill Powell kept sending American Beauty roses, but never came to see me. Finally, I called to ask why. "I'm so deaf I'd have to sit right in the front row to hear anything at all," he explained. "Everybody would see me and cause unholy commotion, which I'm sure you don't want. . . ."

"All right," I allowed, "but I'm coming down to Palm Springs right away." I bearded the lion in his den. He had cut himself off from the business, but I think he missed it.

I continued to see Bill whenever I visited Palm Springs, where Betty and Bob Black had also retired. Our old give-and-take survived. "What on earth do you do with yourself down here?" I asked.

"I do my weeds," he replied.

"For God's sake, Bill, you don't know one weed from another."

"Well, it beats playing Elvis Presley's grandfather!" Bill knew when to get out.

"How are you?" I asked, several visits later.

"I'm doing all right for a hundred-year-old man," Bill quipped. I laughed because he was only in his seventies then, but the joke wore thin as he passed ninety.

When he died, at ninety-one, I was one of the first people Mousie called. For weeks afterward, friends wrote and telephoned condolences, as if I had lost a husband. Well, our screen partnership lasted thirteen years through fourteen pictures, longer than any of my marriages. To this day, forty years after our last appearance together, people consider us a couple. I never enjoyed work more than with Bill. He was a brilliant actor, a delightful companion, a great friend, and, above all, a true gentleman, with those often attributed but seldom possessed qualities: great style, class, breeding. There's nobody like him. There's never going to be anybody quite like him. I miss him more than I can say.

You couldn't get into or out of the stage door when I played the

Huntington Hartford. There were always great hordes of people waiting, many of them youngsters with movie books under their arms. When they're that young and want my autograph, I'm highly flattered. The Myrna Loy Fan Club was still going strong with those hard-core followers who seem to build their lives around favorite stars. They are a curious breed, journeying out to Hollywood in search of their idols, often settling there to live out their lives, and searching still—for those idols, perhaps, for youth, dreams. Who knows? I always gave them autographs and whatever time I could spare. It's the least an actor can do. They are the ones who buy tickets and keep you up there.

We were booked into the Blackstone Theatre, in Chicago, for four months and stayed for nearly a year. It was a marvelous run. People came from all over—even relatives' and friends from Montana made it to the Blackstone. When Adlai Stevenson, on a whirlwind tour, passed through to dedicate a statue, he called to say that he wanted to see the show and come backstage afterward. I was delighted. The last occasion we'd spent any time together was at one of Mary Lasker's Christmas parties before my tour started. Mary, who always placed her money and influence behind worthy causes, had gathered some very powerful people that night. But, much to the chagrin of the other ladies present, Adlai spent most of his time with me. "You'll never be asked there again," quipped my escort, Bennett Korn.

There was still quite a group of powerful and beautiful women stalking Adlai, although many things hadn't worked out for him politically and personally. He had backed Kennedy and what did he get for it? They made him Permanent U.S. Representative to the U.N., which was merely one of those sops. He did a tremendous job, but if he couldn't be President, he should have been Secretary of State. He became disheartened, giving the impression to those who knew him that he didn't value himself anymore. He became something of a social butterfly, eating on the town.

"You can't reach around me," he said when we embraced backstage. "I'm getting too fat." I didn't respond. "I know it," he added defensively. "I'm eating too much and smoking too much and I know all about it."

"Well," I asked, "what are you going to do about it?"

"Probably nothing," he replied.

Although he had been warned about his heart, he continued on his tour after Chicago. He went to London, where, only a few weeks later, he suddenly died.

I will never forget walking into that theater for the matinée after hearing the news. I'd never before had to play while bearing such a burden. They had my understudy there. They had everyone ready to pick up the pieces if I wasn't able to go on. Dick Benjamin, Joanie Van Ark, and my leading man, Sandor Szabo, were fantastic. If I made a mistake or dropped a line, they would pick it up. When I first went out and people were laughing, I wondered, What are they laughing about? That was my first reaction: Why am I making them laugh? In the second act, I thought, Well, Adlai's wit was one of his great gifts, his ability to make people laugh. That realization made it bearable, somehow, and enabled me to finish the show.

The stage seems big at first, but it really isn't. The audience sees everything. As I've said, actors in a comedy, if they're behaving themselves, stand stark-still during one another's laugh lines. The minute there's a distraction, the eye of the audience follows it and the laugh dies. Judging by my experiences with Ina Claire and Clifton Webb, scene-stealing had been common practice in their day. It isn't anymore, thank goodness. Certainly I never stood for it in my companies. I seldom had to, because they were all so well disciplined. We didn't have any problems in *Barefoot* until we had to change some of the company in Chicago and Christina Crawford appeared.

After a year on the road, Dick and Joanie came to me like fledglings ready to leave the nest: "We want to try our hands at Hollywood." I didn't want them to go, but they were too talented to keep back. "You're absolutely right," I said; "this is the time to do it!" It was like a family breaking up. Meanwhile, Neil made another resounding smash on Broadway with *The Odd Couple*. The people in charge took my stage manager and several others away from me; they had another hit that would go on for years, and there was no way of knowing how long we'd run. As it turned out, I played Chicago for forty-nine weeks and kept going from there.

They sent Harvey Medlinski, Mike's assistant, to stage-manage and to rehearse the replacements. Christina Crawford arrived with him to take over the role of my daughter. The idea of Joan's daughter playing the role delighted me, until I discovered how recalcitrant this child was.

I've never known anybody else like her—ever. Her stubbornness was really unbelievable. She would not do a single thing that anyone told her to do. You'd go out there on the stage and you couldn't find her. One thing an actor needs to know is exactly where people are on the stage; Christina completely disregarded her blocking, throwing the rest of us off. Harvey let her get away with it, which baffled me. He was a marvelous man, a professional, who had always been reliable.

"Harvey," I pleaded, "we've never done it this way. We have Mike's script."

"Well," he'd say, "try it another way." I didn't know then that they were hatching a big romance. I don't blame Harvey. He was a victim. Eventually he married Christina—a short marriage.

I sent an SOS to Dick Benjamin, who was directing the London production of *Barefoot:* "Stop by on your way to Hollywood. I need you." He worked with her, but couldn't do anything with her—absolutely nothing! She was going to do it her way. It was self-defeating and sad, because the girl had potential. When she finally played the part, they gave her a good review, which only made things worse for the rest of us. The cast was really in a state of panic. In desperation, I sent for Robby Lantz, who flew to Chicago, saw the show, and called Neil Simon. Neil flew out from New York the next day. "Now, look," he said to me before the performance, "you're just upset because you never had a situation like this. You've never had to work with replacements before."

"Yes," I said. "I've been fortunate in that respect. But why don't you go out and take a look before we talk?"

Neil came back after the show. "I apologize, Myrna," he said. "It won't do."

They fired Christina, for which, of course, she always blamed me. I did everything to help her and make it work. I gave her every opportunity. She had three directors. But this was a young woman with an incredible attitude. I've never seen anything like her determination to be something that she wasn't. She wanted to be Joan Crawford. I think that's the basis of the book she wrote afterward and everything else. I saw what her mind created, the fantasy world she lived in, when Joan came through Chicago on one of her Pepsi-Cola junkets.

"Is your mother coming to the play?" I asked.

"Of course not!" Christina snapped. "She wouldn't come to the play."

"What do you mean she wouldn't come?" I snapped back. "We're old friends. We've known each other forever, and I would certainly think she'd want to see you perform."

"No," insisted Christina, "and it's a good thing, too. If she came, she'd have to make a Joan Crawford entrance. She'd wait until the curtain went up before she came in and they'd have to turn up the houselights as she walked down the aisle. The audience would applaud her, and she'd curtsy, as if she were the star of the show, before sitting down—"

"Nonsense!" I said, interrupting her almost trance-like recitation. "Your mother would never do a thing like that. She's too professional." But Christina had dreamed that up, and to me it sounded like the creation of a girl who envied her mother, grew to hate her, and wanted to destroy her.

Joan didn't attend the play—they probably weren't speaking at that point. What would you do with a problem child like that? *I* wanted to beat the hell out of that girl after only one rehearsal!

Joan and I had remained friends since our first meeting on *Pretty Ladies*, in 1925—as much as you can be friends when you're working in pictures. We'd meet on the run at the studio or chat at parties, although Joan didn't do much partygoing. In fact, I did much more, thanks to my social husbands. You can't socialize and carry the workloads that we did during our M-G-M heydays. But we were always friends; it was the kind of friendship, set in the early years, that stayed. Joan kept up a fabulous correspondence, writing long letters—particularly at Christmastime—to the people she liked. She remembered anniversaries and milestones in the lives of her friends. She never forgot names, dates, or obligations.

After her last husband, Alfred Steele, died, she would call frequently and we'd talk for hours or lunch together. She was lonely and wanted to work, but acceptable film offers were few and far between for women of our age. I tried to get her to go into the theater. "It's wonderfully fulfilling when you can handle it," I told her. "You'd love it." The idea terrified her. She could have done it—she was a fine actress, a great actress, but she never felt confident about her ability. "I envy you like mad," she told me. "You've latched on to the secret of growing old gracefully—and usefully." That touched and somewhat saddened me, because Joan was implying that she hadn't.

"And what about you?" I replied. "Look what you've done and continue to do." It wasn't generally known, but she was really working as Pepsi's international spokesperson to repay the debts incurred by her husband as the company's president. She dismissed all that. Joan wasn't the bravura character of her more sensational movies, but thanks to the power of film, the creations of her daughter, and the gossipmongers of Hollywood, she will be remembered that way.

I'm not suggesting that Joan was the girl next door. There was something gloriously absurd in her devotion to the duties of stardom. Lunching with her was always an event; she still did everything in style. We could never go out in a taxi. Heaven forbid! Joan would hire a limousine to pick us up and bring us home. That's a bit much for me—I travel in taxis, and if I wouldn't get mobbed, I'd take buses. Joan is criticized for such things, for having to be a star, but she's not the only one. When Jean-Pierre Aumont and I were doing *Barefoot* in dinner theater recently, he recalled dining with Marlene Dietrich before coming over from Paris: "We dined right across the street from her apartment, but she insisted that we take a limousine. So the driver took us around the block. She just liked the idea of the chauffeur opening the car door for her."

It is vanity to a great extent, but also it's fear. Even now, I can go to the theater, and if I can't get a cab right away, the professional autograph hounds will grab me—say, at Sardi's—and pursue me. I saw those people nearly crush Marilyn Monroe to death at the opening of one of her pictures, and they're still around. It's terrifying when they start breaking down the barriers. You're afraid to look left or right for fear of instigating something.

The last time I saw Joan, she picked me up to lunch at "21." "I've been grounded," she told me. "My doctors won't let me fly anymore." She had heard the bad news about having cancer, I suppose, although she didn't specify. If she had, she was taking it well; she was gay and funny and we had a marvelous time with Florence Kriendler, a friend of hers, whose husband co-owned "21." When I complained about the age spots on my arms, Joan said, "Oh, my doctor is giving me some wonderful lotion for those. Come back with me to the apartment and I'll give you the prescription." That was typical of Joan, always helpful, always generous in little ways and in bigger ones, too.

We went back to her vast, all-white apartment after lunch and she had her secretary get the prescription and told me where to buy the lotion. "Of course, you know what's just as good?" Joan added. "Horse pee!" That just laid me out. We both started giggling, as we had when we were hopeful chorus girls fifty years before. She wanted me to stay, but it was late and I had another engagement that evening. I regretted leaving, because I never saw my old friend again.

Joan became a recluse, not bedridden, but apartment-bound, with very few people around her. She would answer the phone pretending to be her secretary in order to avoid talking to people. But when we spoke, she remained cheerful, never self-pitying, and never mentioned the cancer. I had no idea how ill she was. It was the most tragic, awful thing. The day she died I had a note on my pad: "Call Joan."

A month after Joan's death, in 1977, the Academy arranged a celebration of her life and career to honor her and to dispel the melancholy and unkind things written about her when she died. Christina appeared, uninvited, with her husband, and later claimed that I snubbed her, which wasn't true. She did not manage to mar that unique tribute, which engendered an extraordinary range of people and an overwhelming outpouring of affection. It was the first time that the entire industry—from all the major guilds and unions right down to Malone's Studio Cleaners—came together to honor one of its own. It wasn't given by the greats, but by the hairdressers, the wardrobe and makeup people, all the studio workers to whom Joan had always been so kind. I presided, in their name, along with John Wayne, Robert Young, Joan's godson Jack Jones, and Steven Spielberg, who had made his directorial début on a television show starring Joan. "She treated me like I knew what I was doing, and I didn't," he recalled. "I loved her for that." We strove for a kind of coffee-klatsch atmosphere. George Cukor was in charge, so anybody who dared begin with "It gives me great pleasure"— out!

After all the upheavals and departures, I needed a stage manager who was also a strong director to put *Barefoot* back in shape. "If we could get Burry Fredrik to come out," asked Saint Subber, "would you like that?" I would, and she did. An accomplished director and producer, Burry spruced up the show for the remainder of the Chicago run and stayed on during a month in Philadelphia and an unexpected run in Washington. Since the original company had played a four-week tryout in the capital, the producers were not sure that we would draw.

We filled the National Theatre for the entire summer, a big, smashing hit! It surprised everyone.

You must discipline yourself when you're on the road, but, with so many friends in Washington, I went about a good deal. The Democratic senators from Montana, Mike Mansfield and Lee Metcalf, gave a luncheon for me in the Senate dining room.

The Metcalfs, during my stay, guided me on an edifying tour of the Capitol. I returned the favor with some long-distance campaigning when Lee ran for reelection against a conservative backed by the same Anaconda mining interests that my mother fought for years.

Lady Bird Johnson, always charming and genuinely concerned with essential issues, invited me to tea at the White House. The President, that hard-nosed Texan who was soft as molasses with me, asked me back for the unveiling of Elizabeth Shoumatoff's portrait of President Roosevelt. That moving event held particular significance for me; clasped in F.D.R.'s hand, symbolizing his ideals, was the Atlantic Charter, which he had been off signing one of the days I breathlessly reached the White House to meet him. "Few men in history have served freedom so effectively and so nobly as he did, both in our own land and around the world," quoth L.B.J., who venerated him and longed, under less heroic circumstances, alas, to emulate him.

After more than two arduous but fulfilling years, the national tour ended on that high note in Washington. "It is impossible for me to put into words how wonderful it has been to have you starring in *Barefoot*," wrote Saint Subber; whereupon he did so, beautifully. And well he might have—he could have retired on the profits! Saint set out to find a play for us to do on Broadway, and after rejecting a few possibilities here, we flew to London to look at Alan Ayckbourn's *Relatively Speaking*. It certainly had a wonderful part for me, and Peter Bridge, the English producer, was anxious for us to do it. When we returned, however, Saint decided that it wouldn't work without alterations in this country; Ayckbourn's difficult, there's no question about it, and he hadn't been done here yet. Saint, usually a man of taste, began fussing around with the play prior to a scheduled Broadway opening.

Meanwhile, I concentrated on my NCDH duties. I was dismayed but not surprised when Congress tabled the Civil Rights Bill in 1966. It had amazed me during the Washington run to see more people lobbying against it than for it. I hit the road to campaign against the "nameless fear" that obstructed such legislation. "This nameless fear is irrational," I told the National Conference on Educational Radio, in Racine, Wisconsin. "It's based on an economic fallacy that fair-housing laws automatically make property values go down."

In Los Angeles, I addressed the opening session of the NCDH Regional Conference and testified before the Governor's Commission on the Rumford Act. That controversial open-housing law was nullified in 1964 by the passage of Proposition 14, then reinstated when the California Supreme Court ruled Proposition 14 unconstitutional. The U.S. Supreme Court had agreed to review the decision, and it was essential to voice support of the Rumford Act, particularly since Governor-elect Ronald Reagan, not surprisingly, supported Proposition 14. "I represent an element of my profession which is opposed to some of the philosophy of other members of my profession," I began at the hearing, before contradicting the opinions of Mr. Reagan, whose election I had opposed. Fortunately, especially since our survey of 778 Los Angeles County landlords found fifty-seven percent of them admitting to barring blacks, the U.S. Supreme Court upheld the Rumford Act—another step toward the passing of a national civil rights act.

It would take another year of fighting, but on April 12, 1968, President Johnson signed the Civil Rights Act into law. I wasn't able to be there, but he sent me a pen with which it had been signed. Two months later, the Supreme Court reinforced that legislation by upholding a Reconstruction Era civil rights law that prohibited racial discrimination in all sales and rentals of property. Nevertheless, the work of the NCDH is far from finished. Now we must overcome the many subtle ways used to circumvent those laws.

When L.B.J. astutely decided not to seek re-election, I could not in good faith support Vice-President Humphrey. I had admired Hubert for years as a fighting liberal, but he'd lost credibility during his Vice-Presidency with his support of the war in Vietnam. He ultimately redeemed himself, and I can't help pondering now how different our world might be if Hubert Humphrey had won. We'd certainly have some noble social legislation on the books rather than the blot of Watergate. In 1967, however, I sought a compatible candidate with the strength to oppose my longtime nemesis.

A light appeared on the horizon in the person of Senator Eugene McCarthy, although few considered him a contender when I joined his

Arts and Letters Committee. Before approaching McCarthy, we had asked Bobby Kennedy to carry the anti-war banner into the primaries. He turned us down, fearing that a loss would kill his political future. Eugene McCarthy was no stranger to me. I had admired him since the days of "McCarthy's marauders" in Congress, when he pushed through some farsighted social legislation and initiated the kind of civil rights reform later introduced by Kennedy and passed by Johnson. I remembered the speech that he made in Chicago the last time Stevenson ran. "Don't reject this man!" McCarthy had pleaded, which is what I came to feel about McCarthy himself in 1968: another intellectual, to be sure, a poet; but also a former baseball player, full of energy and ideas.

I became deeply involved in the McCarthy campaign, canvassing several primary states alongside those wonderful kids from the universities. They approached the campaign trail with plenty of enthusiasm and little pocket money. They were so full of peanut butter I'd take them out to dinner to make sure they got a good meal. It was very exciting, this youth movement, but it went deeper than that. Beyond the idealism and almost theatrical zeal was a real wish to understand and to make a better world from that understanding. As rebels in search of a cause, they had marched, marched everywhere in protest. McCarthy became the catalyst that united them and consolidated their goals. He inspired them with his disdain for hoary political clichés, yet he sought to inform them rather than to ignite them. He exercised a parental responsibility toward them and they responded by shaving their beards, pulling back their hair, and keeping "clean for Gene." He showed them how to work within the system. It was called "the children's crusade"—at first with derision, when Al Lowenstein advanced his concept of student power; then, when McCarthy began to win, with admiration and respect.

It was not then a question of the mindless radicalization and blatant violence that followed. But it *was* rebellion, and a good thing, too. That is better than the apathy we had after the war and into the flaccid fifties (and seem to have again now). I had lived through the Joe McCarthy era. It was a loathsome time—especially the silence. Thank God the young people of the sixties did not want to be silent anymore!

They were surprised at first to find me on their side, considering me a reactionary because of all those Bill Powell pictures, perhaps, with the grand sets and money coming from nowhere. "She was in the original *Ben-Hur* before my parents were born!" one of them scoffed. But I think they eventually changed their minds. "She's old enough to be my grandmother," another admitted, "and I'm more tired than she is." I still hear from those kids. They invite me to their weddings, send announcements when their children are born. We shared a glorious crusade.

After McCarthy's extraordinary showing in the New Hampshire primary, the Kennedy forces sniffed blood and decided to go out for the kill themselves, insinuating that McCarthy had been merely a stalking horse. "I have made no concessions to anyone," Gene stated dryly. "I haven't sought out any other candidate. I haven't been approached by anyone, except that three-o'clock-in-the-morning visit I had in Green Bay, Wisconsin, by Senator Kennedy of Massachusetts, at which nothing happened except that we discussed the St. Patrick's Day parade in Boston. I thought it was rather unfair of him to come at three o'clock in the morning when one's life processes are supposed to be at their lowest point. But having resisted him that night, or at least to the point when nothing was even suggested, I think I will be strong enough to resist anyone or any proposal from now through Chicago."

The implication of that nocturnal visit, stated or not, was "Pass it over; Bobby wants it!" And, implication or not, Gene had responded clearly: "You can all just get the hell out of here! I want my night's sleep."

We redoubled our efforts in the remaining primaries, particularly in Indiana, after the national office of Citizens for Kennedy issued a brochure distorting McCarthy's legislative voting record. Ultimately disavowed by the Kennedy camp, but widely circulated by them nevertheless, those misstatements overshadowed the Indiana campaign but not the campaigners. Paul Newman joined me there for some heavy participation. At first, he had been reluctant to get involved. Bobbie Handman, chairperson of the Arts and Letters Committee, would phone him every night and he would make excuses. Bobbie persisted, but happened to miss a night. The next day his wife, Joanne Woodward, phoned her. "Keep on calling!" she urged. Paul finally relented: "I'm driving from Boston to New York. I'll go up and see what's happening in New Hampshire." After that he never left the campaign. That was another unique aspect of the McCarthy crusade. Never before had so many actors, writers, and artists of all kinds dedicated themselves so openly and constructively to a candidate.

We would leave our hotel in Indianapolis early in the morning and go our separate ways on long, long treks. Paul covered the state in a camper, with his beer in the back. Indiana campaigners took me for miles, from town to town. As we drove from Wabash to Peru, the redbud was in bloom and everything looked fresh and welcoming. I'm a country girl at heart, I remember thinking. Unfortunately, we lost in Indiana; then Kennedy won a clear-cut victory in Nebraska.

We rallied for the more decisive encounters in Oregon and California. I flew into every nook and cranny of Oregon with those wonderful cowboy pilots: just two of them up front, me in back, usually, sailing over the magnificent mountains. I felt rather safe in those little planes; they could land anywhere, even on the water if necessary. It would have been quite another story if we had hit any storms, but they watched the weather carefully. Not that I had any alternative. There was no other way to meet my statewide schedule of interviews, receptions, speeches, luncheons, and dinners. I shared so many meals with so many civic groups and political organizations that Eleanor Roosevelt's wistful complaint haunted me: "I get so tired of all those chicken dinners."

I shared many a platform with various Kennedys, who have a marvelous way of rallying when one of them runs. Wherever they went, camera crews hovered with state-of-the-art equipment on their backs: Bobby's personal cameramen. They just followed him around. And sure enough, you would see it on the news that night. We didn't have the money for that kind of coverage, nor would it have suited Gene's relaxed, self-possessed manner. In fact, Kennedy's "single-minded pursuit of power," as The New York Times put it, actually alienated many voters. McCarthy's Oregon victory made him a serious contender for the nomination.

We faced California with optimism and boundless energy. I spoke everywhere, from picnics in Long Beach to evangelical temples in Watts. On primary night, we gathered at McCarthy headquarters in the Grand Ballroom of the Beverly Hilton to watch election coverage on television. They showed Bobby speaking at his headquarters at the Ambassador. The cameras followed him as he exited by a back door. Then we heard a shot.

Oh, it was just chaos. It was unbelievable. I will never forget that night as long as I live. Our kids didn't know how to deal with it. They were shocked and confused, feeling guilty because they were McCarthy supporters. "You have nothing to feel guilty about," I kept repeating. "It isn't our fault." I remember everybody wandering somnambulistically around. Robert Lowell, whom Gene called his "whimsical campaign adviser," seemed shell-shocked when he came up to me and suggested getting something to eat. "I've got problems here," I told him. "I'll join you later." But I never did. I was too busy with my kids, comforting them, feeding them, getting their parents on the phone so they could make contact. I felt a great responsibility for those idealistic youngsters who were following McCarthy, trying to work within the system. I feared that the result of Bobby Kennedy's mindless murder would be cynicism and withdrawal.

Gene himself was in a state of shock. He walked silently to his room and we did not see him again. He left early the next morning. Bobby's death did something very definite to him—it changed something. I remember the look of utter bewilderment he gave me as he went to his room that fateful night. It has taken him a long time to get over it. In fact, I don't think he's over it yet.

We had been hoping that Bobby would come into the New York primary with all he had available to him, because we were going to beat him. Steve Smith admits that. We had planned a big rally at Lewisohn Stadium, near Harlem, to celebrate McCarthy's splendid civil rights record, but the candidate did not want to appear; he considered it inappropriate to campaign after Bobby's death. They kept calling me from headquarters: "Do you know where he is? We're afraid he won't show up." We begged him. We set a time and waited and at the very last minute he appeared—briefly. He said a few words and left me and a few others to carry on. I was proud of our recovery, because we really delivered his civil rights history to the black community. I saved that script for years.

I made reservations for the Democratic Convention in Chicago, but filming kept me in Hollywood. It's probably a good thing—they would have slapped me in jail, I'm sure. That is one thing I've missed so far, but who knows? The way things are going, I may end up there yet. I think Nixon would have liked to put me away, and I wouldn't have blamed him if he had, frankly. But I'd go smiling defiantly, like those heroic suffragettes.

Gene wrote to me on August 23rd: "Before leaving for Chicago, I want to tell you how much I appreciate all the effort you have given to my campaign. . . ." It was as if he didn't expect to return. He became even more disheartened by the bloody confrontations between the police and the demonstrators in the streets of Chicago. To reduce tensions, he considered withdrawing his name from nomination; then, fearing an adverse effect if he appeared to be running away, he stayed in. He did not have a chance in hell at that point. Obviously all the party mechanisms were against him. Humphrey got the nomination and Nixon ultimately got the Presidency.

It was overcast on Capitol Hill the day after the election. "It is a day for visiting the sick and burying the dead," observed Eugene McCarthy. "It's gray everywhere—all over the land."

The script that kept me from the convention, *The April Fools*, seemed promising after eight years of refusing unsuitable film roles. Good parts were few and far between, especially if you were not predisposed to playing mentally deranged killers and spending hours in the makeup department being turned into such witches. I would much rather be remembered as sexy and witty and soignée. It's demeaning to think that elderly actresses can only play psychotic killers or cannibalistic mothers. We're still full of life and energy. We still have a lot of joy to give moviegoers if we can get the roles.

The April Fools, a romantic fairy tale with underlying social criticism, offered just such a role on paper. Charles Boyer and I played long-married eccentrics whose happiness convinces Jack Lemmon and Catherine Deneuve to chuck their mundane, materialistic lives and run off together. Charles and Jack greeted me with flowers and kisses at Studio Center in the Valley—publicity, to be sure, but charming, nonetheless. I had known Charles for years, but, excepting a Lux Radio Theater version of *Appointment for Love* in 1942, had never acted with him. He was always charming, of course, exactly the way he was on the screen, but more dignified and intellectual. He took great pride in having started a French library in California. I think it was with Arthur that I used to dine at the Boyers' house—it was as far back as that. But my first inkling of Charles's potential as a great screen lover went even farther back.

I was returning from a compulsory elocution lesson on the back lot during my first days at M-G-M, when this gorgeous man passed me. I immediately asked someone about him and discovered that he was on the lot dubbing our pictures for the French-speaking market. "My God, he's spectacular!" I exclaimed. "Why doesn't somebody do something about him?" The next thing I knew, somebody had.

I knew Charles for so long, but it seems I really didn't know him at all. His life ended in terrible tragedy. His only son killed himself playing Russian roulette—one of those crazy kids! Charles was in France at the time, which added guilt for not being there to his sorrow. Then, of course, Charles and his wife, Pat Paterson, were very close. When she died, I guess he couldn't take it; he killed himself two days later. I never would have believed that he could do such a thing. I tell you, it bowled me over, but Jack Lemmon said afterward that the son's death had broken him. He never recovered.

There's something unique about Jack Lemmon. He is the kind of actor I understand and admire. He is also the kind of person who is always entertaining with a sort of desperate intensity that so many great performers possess. I remember a party at Billy Wilder's out in Malibu where Jack played and sang practically non-stop all evening. He has that intrinsic need to perform. On the set he was delightful; so was Catherine Deneuve, lovely and scared to death in her first American picture. But something happened at the end of *April Fools*. They began cutting, and Charles and I were the main casualties. It was badly edited, really chopped up terribly after the producers decided to emphasize a chase sequence. Poor Charles ended up with less film than I did. Everybody wondered what the devil Myrna Loy was doing in that picture.

In order to make *Relatively Speaking* palatable to the American taste, Saint Subber brought in Muriel Resnik to rework Alan Ayckbourn's play for a scheduled fall opening. She changed the locale from London to Philadelphia, among other things, and through no fault of hers the play began losing its integrity. After months of frustrating but comic transatlantic communication between producers and playwrights, Ayckbourn quite rightly said, "Take it away from them! They can't have it!" So despite the fact that Ray Milland, who would have been marvelous, was scheduled to co-star, the Broadway production was canceled. Years later, I resurrected it, waded through its difficulties, and, by God, it worked! It became wonderfully funny and very successful for me in summer stock and dinner theater.

I like comedy. It is my talent. But little is being done in films in my vein—certainly not with me in mind, at any rate. The older you get, of course, the less you can expect that material will be written especially for you, particularly when you have repeatedly curtailed your career for marriage and other commitments. There are young people in the business who don't know Myrna Loy from Adam. Recently, some commercial producer wanted me to audition for a voice-over. In a pig's eye! That is what you are up against these days. So much for "living legends."

Theatrical films are generally more specialized nowadays. It is the television movies that approximate what Hollywood used to make in subject matter and popular appeal. Despite all the brilliant new technology, though, they are not realizing their potential. There is no time in television. Those in charge ask you to do the part on Tuesday. You get the script on Wednesday. Thursday you're on a plane, and Friday you're on the set. It all seems so haphazard. The quality of television could improve tremendously if they just took a little more time from conception to post-production.

But if you have to work for a living, as I must, what are you to do? You just have to take a part with possibilities and make something of it. I was discussing this with Loretta Young recently. "Well, if you want to work," she said, "you have to work the way you do. You have to get blood out of a turnip. Bette Davis has done it at times, and other times she hasn't done it. Helen Hayes—I've seen her do it. I guess you do it on your own. I don't know. I just won't get up in the morning."

She is lucky she doesn't have to; otherwise, you must keep trying to get blood from a turnip. *The Elevator,* a better-than-average television movie, gave me the role of a lonely older woman who creates harmless fantasies to fill her life. That role was witty. It wasn't written that way—just the outside of it—but it worked. Fortunately, we had a congenial cast—Roddy McDowall, Teresa Wright, Jim Farentino, among them—because we were thrown together for days of filming in the actual elevator of a Los Angeles office building. You need a sense of humor to do that. We just laughed a lot and somehow got through it—very close, very tired, and very scared that the overcrowded elevator would plunge to the basement.

Do Not Fold, Spindle, or Mutilate is memorable because I worked with Helen Hayes, Sylvia Sidney, and Mildred Natwick. I had probably the dullest part, playing Helen's sister, but Sylvia was marvelous, and you can imagine Millie fluttering and fainting, and Helen—you can't ask for anything more. We all got along so well and laughed so much.

It is a misconception that actresses don't work well together. We were old enough and wise enough to relax and play with each other rather than try to upstage each other, so the show was tremendously easy and pure fun in the making.

I've known Helen for years. It was she, along with her husband, Charlie MacArthur, and Ben Hecht, who once pretended to sign me for a film to vex Louis B. Mayer. Helen's a great lady, a good sport, and, first and foremost, a professional. We took the same flight from New York to Los Angeles to do that show. The first thing I knew, she came up and said, "Myrna, it's you! Let's run our lines." So, except for a bit of conversation at mealtime, we ran lines all the way to California.

Death Takes a Holiday gave me a chance to work with Melvyn Douglas again in something we could chew on. Mel and I became friends at M-G-M and stayed friends through the years. "At first, I thought it would be exciting working with all those glamorous ladies," Mel told me, "but after I got into a picture, it was just another day at the factory. You're the only one from that period I really still enjoy seeing as a friend." We didn't see each other all the time, but it remained a warm relationship. We dined together every night while filming, which gave us a chance to catch up. I even brought my former maid, Theresa Penn, who, as I've said, adored Mel, out to the studio to see him after all that time. She nearly died of joy.

When you get two people together who really know their stuff, everything seems to come so easily and so right. It's like falling off a log, just as it was with Hank Fonda not too long ago. It is amazing what comes out on screen: there is a reality. Mel and I have some lovely moments just here and there in *Death Takes a Holiday*. We filmed the last of them way up on the hill at Universal, where, on that childhood visit, I had seen William Farnum shootin' it out. Mel was in the midst of a moving speech, doing it beautifully, when suddenly we heard a studio tour guide bellowing, "And this is Rock Hudson's dressing room . . ." The travelogue persisted throughout our gentle scene. "O.K.!" Mel roared when we finished. "I've had it!" He stomped off the set and flew back to New York on the next plane without doing his dubs. Universal had to send someone after him to record them, which delighted me. It is really such an insult to actors to work under those circumstances.

Theater, understandably, became my primary source of income and professional fulfillment. We opened a national tour of *Dear Love* at the

Alley Theatre, in Houston. That touching two-character play was based on the correspondence of Elizabeth Barrett and Robert Browning, by Jerome Kilty, who also played Browning. We didn't break box-office records, but response as we toured was heartening. "Until yesterday," wrote a woman from a Phoenix trailer park, "I had never seen a live play with real actors—and I am 58! But *Dear Love* made up for everything I may have missed through the years." Another fan, who waited at the stage door each night with stills for me to autograph, claimed to have seen all of my pictures. When I asked about *Dear Love*, she made excuses for not having seen it, indicating that it was too highbrow. "Highbrow?" I replied. "Why, didn't you know that Elizabeth Barrett was a drug addict?" The woman stared at me in amazement. "Imagine! A drug addict!" she exclaimed. "I must see that play!" Can you believe that? And the woman was over eighty. For somewhat related reasons, we never brought *Dear Love* to Broadway.

I played Doña Ana in a national tour of *Don Juan in Hell*, directed by John Houseman. He would take the crosstown bus from Juilliard, where he was teaching, and stroll down York Avenue to my apartment to coach me. Recalling Agnes Moorehead's rather austere Doña Ana in John's previous production, I questioned my suitability. "I want a female in this role," John explained, "a real woman. She has all the tricks. That's why I want you to play it." John proceeded to read the piece aloud, illuminating its subtleties for me, exposing so much of Shaw's essence in our stimulating sessions.

We flew out to California, where John rehearsed me with Ricardo Montalban, Edward Mulhare, and Kurt Kasznar before opening at the University of Arizona. It was called a Concert Tour. We played some theaters, but mostly concert halls and university auditoriums. And we filled them—just the four of us with four stools, mikes, and music stands for our scripts. We never actually used the scripts in performance—you were in trouble if you lost your place without having memorized it— but having them on stage served to keep Shaw out there with us. It is a fascinating piece to perform. You keep finding new things in it. The students we played to found Shaw's foresight, as I do, uncanny. He blasts our ways of life, pointing out the destructive genius of man, showing how his death is in his weapons. We should have done a performance for Ronald Reagan.

Ricardo Montalban's Don Juan was fabulous. He is one of our finest actors, but he has been forced to play oversexed Latinos for most of his career. For some reason—prejudice, I suppose—a Latin man always gets typed. Now Ricardo is a big success in television. He is very happy about it and I am happy for him; but, come on, he's better than that! Edward Mulhare made a superb Devil—he possessed all the charm and wit for that part. Kurt Kasznar, a wonderfully comedic Captain, also played nursemaid to me. I lost my watch. Kurt bought me a watch. I lost my hat. Kurt bought me a hat. During long, bumpy bus rides between towns, he would play Lena Horne records and dance, sing, and carry on up and down the aisle. We had a wonderful time.

The four of us never had a harsh word on that tour, and we played 158 cities in six months: one-night stands; traveling by bus—"Load at nine-fifteen! Leave at nine-forty-five!"—eating greasy food at truck stops; barely making the curtain, without dinner or anything; just arriving, changing into our evening wear, and there we were! After the show, no place to eat, so maybe a can of beans and some soda crackers in your hotel room; go to bed; next morning pay the bill and the same routine. Our only contretemps came in Florida, when we found cockroaches in our beds. I tried to make light of it and Ricardo hit the ceiling. Otherwise, no bugs and no problems.

In this day and age, Ricardo Montalban relates, one works with people who achieve success very quickly because of television, which breeds instant stars who disappear instantly. And while they are instant stars you sometimes see behavior that leaves much to be desired in professionalism, dedication, and love of your craft. It was so thoroughly refreshing to see someone like Myrna, with her professional background, bear up under this incredibly grueling tour without a single complaint. She was always cheerful and solicitous, always smiling and always on stage, like the Rock of Gibraltar, giving a wonderful performance. "You don't want too much comfort," she said when I complained about our dressing rooms. "So much concentration is necessary. As long as I have a place for my clothes, a good light . . . A good cell is all I want." She was a marvelous example to me.

I made my belated Broadway début, after several near-misses, in an all-star revival of Clare Boothe Luce's *The Women*. It was the first thing that really seemed right for me, although I don't condone Clare's rather cruel view of our sex. She wrote it aeons before women's lib, of course, as a satire about utterly male-dependent women with nothing to do but tear each other's lives apart. The feminists were up in arms about the revival, but seeing women behave that way helps to explain why we have a women's movement. There are no men in the play. All they do is talk about men. It shows the predicament of leisure-class women when they considered that working was beneath them. They were all caught in the man-trap notion of the thirties, when a husband meant a meal ticket. Today, I suppose, you'd call them jet-setters. Alexis Smith, who brilliantly played the worst of them, says of their current counterparts: "They fly off in jet planes, and get involved in charities. They mistake activity for creativity." I know them, but keep away from them. I have always been liberated insofar as I have always worked.

We rehearsed in a ballroom way up on West End Avenue. It was a difficult show to coordinate, with so many important actresses doing relatively small parts and with mechanized sets by Oliver Smith that were hell to negotiate. "Ladies," our director, Morton Da Costa, began, "we have seven or twelve or twenty stars, and so we'll behave as if there's no star. We're professionals getting a play on, and that's the way we'll do it." I must say, that is the way everyone behaved. There were no harsh words, no temperament. Bitchery on stage notwithstanding, that company of forty-four women worked as a team. And we won the seldom given Outer Critics Circle Award for Ensemble Acting to prove it. Alexis, whom I've known for years, is a lovely person and a hard, disciplined worker. She would lie flat on her back during rehearsal breaks and do kicks to keep her body in shape. She certainly accomplished it. It's gorgeous! Jan Miner, whom I recommended for the Countess, and Kim Hunter, a longtime political ally, are superb actresses and good friends. Rhonda Fleming, who came East to make her stage début, Dorothy Loudon, and Lainie Kazan turned out to be marvelous comediennes and people.

During tryouts in Philadelphia, we would all go out after the show and someone from every newspaper would be snooping around, looking for gossip. "Everybody invites me to dinner," our publicist, Shirley Herz, maintained. "They all think, Oh, she's going to have stories! But there's nothing to tell. You all get along too disgustingly well." We disappointed a lot of people, even after the authoress arrived. Kim, who played my daughter, was wary and protective. "Mrs. Luce had little to say to me," she remarked at a party following the first preview. "I guess she doesn't consider me or Myrna her favorite people. We're quite liberal, and, as you know, Mrs. Luce is very, very conservative." Actually, I've known Clare on and off for a long time, and we've always teased each other about our political differences. "We have opposite points of view about most things," she says. "We don't agree on many things, but we've been friends for years." That's the way she puts it.

Clare attended the last few rehearsals and she was there in Philadelphia, very excited about her play being revived, always ladylike and polite, seemingly happy with all of us. She never overtly interfered—not when I was around, anyway! She'd have had a lot of nerve to have said anything to us about our performances; Teek, as Morton Da Costa was called, would never have condoned it. Clare made the mistake of telling poor Rhonda that she would write some new lines for her, not intending to do so. It was merely a kind of social move, but Teek suffered for it. "Rhonda is at me every minute about those lines," he complained. "She calls me at the most unfortunate times. Invariably—I think she has antennae—she gets me off the john!" Finally, he exploded: "Thanks to you, Rhonda, for Chrissakes, I haven't had one good bowel movement since this thing started!" In desperation, he wrote the lines himself.

A bigger crisis came before we left Philadelphia: Teek and Clare conferred and apparently decided that Crystal, the husband-stealing salesgirl, should be blonde, as written. Clare wanted a blonde, so Teek had hired Lainie Kazan with the stipulation that she would wear a wig. Lainie agreed, then resisted—with good reason. She is a zaftig, exotic brunette, who could never be the blonde type. "I feel like a guy in drag in a blonde wig," she groaned. There was a struggle and Lainie was fired. I can't honestly say that Clare convinced them to do it—you never really know the basis of such conflicts. You only know that someone with tears in her eyes is being replaced. That was a terrible blow to Lainie, who had previously suffered some other career setbacks. Jan and I literally held her up to get her through that tense and difficult situation. She survived and prospered, but at the time it was like losing a member of the family.

We had full houses and good reviews in Philadelphia. If we had stayed on the road, which I wanted to do, we would have made enough money to stay open on Broadway. But our young producers were so thrilled by the out-of-town response that we came in before we should have. Our New York reviews were good enough and the show generated endless publicity. We got World Series coverage by challenging the all-male cast of *The Changing Room* to a baseball game in Central Park during the Broadway Show League season. Alexis offered to run for me. "I'll run for myself!" I snapped, and, by God, I drove in two runs with an infield single and scored myself. *The Women* won, with the help of our opponents, 85–3. We also had the benefit of the authoress's solicitude. Clare constantly came to the theater and gave Shirley Herz pointers on how to get the most publicity for the show. Alas, none of it worked. We opened at the Forty-sixth Street Theatre at the end of April and did not have a chance to build an audience for it before the summer doldrums closed us. They couldn't meet the $65,000-a-week operating cost, even after we took salary cuts to keep it going.

The wailing that went on after our last performance! I'll never forget Dorothy Loudon weeping, but, thank heavens, she got her big break soon afterward in *Annie*. Having been so close, it is traumatic when suddenly you are torn apart. You experience that in pictures, as well, but without quite the same intensity. There is something more intimate and structured about doing a play. You go through hell getting it organized and rehearsed and ready for opening night. You are together and working out something that's very difficult. You all share the same burden and the same exhilaration. There is a tremendous bond backstage before an opening. The trust is extraordinary. I think that's why people become actors.

My romantic life, so to speak, has not been entirely eclipsed by work. You go on having crushes until you die. I'm not going to tell you who they are—I wouldn't dare. Maybe they don't last long, but that part of you doesn't just turn off.

It works the other way as well, although often it's the screen image that gets 'em. Peter Sellers, who claimed to have always "dreamed" of knowing me, finally arranged a meeting. He took me to Peter Duchin's opening at the Maisonette, where he was rather shy and as full of wonder about my career as any fan. He even asked for an autographed picture.

Billy Rose wanted something more tangible. When we were introduced at Sardi's one evening, he took out a little gold pen to jot down my phone number. We dined together once or twice, as I recall; then he asked me out to his island estate off Norwalk for what was supposed to be a weekend houseparty. Well, it was just the two of us, and that diminutive, rather unattractive man got romantic. I wasn't quite sure how to handle his advances, until their ineffectuality started me laughing. That inadvertently did the trick. Billy retreated and never bothered me again.

There were beaus and there were escorts. George Kogel, whom I have mentioned, was a serious beau until I realized that making the inevitable compromises again was beyond me. George Oppenheimer, who co-wrote *Libeled Lady* among other notable scripts at M-G-M, became a stimulating escort when he returned East as *Newsday*'s theatre critic. We attended "second nights" together for years. After divorcing my fourth husband, however, I have resisted cohabitation. Not that I regret my marriages—only that they didn't work. Each of my husbands brought me so much life, so many aspects of the world that might have eluded me. Arthur made his contribution; Gene made his; Howland and even John Hertz made theirs. But I don't look back and mourn their loss, because so many things afterward were just as terrific. Companionship, yes, you do miss that. I am not the lone-wolf type of woman, I am not that self-sufficient; I like having a man around. But it's too difficult, the responsibility. I don't care to put up with anyone else. I wasn't very good at it when I was younger, and now . . . No, I will go to bed alone, with my hair in curlers and plugs in my ears. I have not been married for a long time now. I probably won't be again, but who can say? Perhaps I will be married two weeks from now. Somebody may knock on the door and I will open it and . . . Who knows?

When you get to be as old as I am, it really is not that important. Children become important; the young people are important. It becomes an entirely different thing so far as your emotional makeup is concerned. I am fortunate to have young friends. They keep me young. They include me in their various projects, and when I am in trouble they are all there. There is a lovely story, untold until now, because I never talk about my two operations. Grandmother Johnson used to say that illness was not a fit topic for polite conversation, and in my business they bury you if you have the sniffles. I had one operation in 1975, another in 1979, when they were still plucking breasts like grapes. My surgery, the first time, was scheduled for seven-thirty in the morning, so Boaty Boatwright and Bobbie Handman arrived an hour beforehand to keep vigil. An emergency kept my doctor from getting to me on time, but those girls held their post tenaciously. At four in the afternoon, when they wheeled me out of intensive care, my sentries were still standing there. Boaty took one look at me—unconscious, my head wrapped turban-style—and began to cry. "Oh, my God!" she sobbed. "It's just like her death scene in *The Rains Came!*"

I did not dwell morbidly on the deleterious aftereffects of a mastectomy. I thought of my grandmothers crossing the plains and of my mother, who never faltered because of age or illness. I will never forget her in her eighties, sitting in the middle of her living room, defying the machines that were tearing down all the houses between hers and Wilshire Boulevard. She had been forced to sell to the city, but she would not budge until she got her money. There was never a choice for me. With those examples, I just have to keep going.

I idolize Auntie Myrna not because she's a famous actress but because of the way she is as a person, explains her stepgranddaughter Debbie Hornblow. *The thing that gets me consistently about her is that you just can't get the woman down. She survives and comes out of it with her chin up in the air. "I've gotten so much out of it," she told me when I thought about becoming an actress, "but I've had to sacrifice so much. You are the family I have. I don't have any of my own. The rewards are many, but the commitment has to be total and full." She's been through so much that could have defeated anyone a long time ago, but she gets up and she keeps on renewing herself. That to me is the most you can say about anyone.*

Bill Frye, a friend who produced some of my television movies, asked me to appear in *Airport 1975*, a sequel to Ross Hunter's blockbuster *Airport*. Bill called and listed the all-star cast. It sounded good to me, so I asked him to send the script. "Well, your part isn't really written yet," he said, "but you'd be working with Sid Caesar and could improvise." Working with Sid, whom I considered a brilliant performer, was incentive enough. I flew to Washington to film the takeoff at Dulles, then to Salt Lake International Airport for the hair-raising landing. We shot interiors in a collapsible plane built on a Universal sound stage.

That is where Sid and I did our scenes—or were supposed to do them. They wanted improvisation and it was not happening. He turned out be one of the most painfully shy people I have ever met. It is hard to believe of such an outgoing comedian, but I had to break through the incredible shyness of this man with sheer persistence. I'd storm into his trailer: "O.K., now, let's go! Let's do this scene!" I never really brought him out completely, but we managed to work out some funny things together. "Hey," I kidded Bill Frye, "you owe me scriptwriting fees."

I got on my high horse and turned down the role of Dora Charleston in *Murder by Death*, Neil Simon's send-up of the great movie detectives. It meant playing opposite David Niven, as Dick, in a prestigious all-star production at a terrific salary, but the script bristled with double entendre and such business as Dick goosing Dora. Furious that they expected me to demean a role that had contributed so much to my career, I complained to my friend Natalie Taylor. She, in turn, told Katherine De Mille. "I would encourage you to not only say 'No' but to make public your reasons," Katie wrote supportively. "Don't sell out!" Actually, I was overreacting. The finished film, with Maggie Smith in the role, turned out to be harmless. Even so, from a casting point of view, it would have been ridiculous to have Myrna Loy doing Myrna Loy.

A similar situation arose when a pharmaceutical giant offered me a fortune to tout its generic pain reliever on television. Easy money, I thought, and agreed to read the script. Well, it claimed to cure everything from migraine to rheumatism and arthritis. "It doesn't," I told them, "and I'm not going to lie about it." So much for spoofs and commercials and easy money. Compromise is never easy.

I am not sure how to define Black Comedy, except to say that it is comedy set in tragedy and very difficult to carry off. Several stars and producers had admired *The End*, Jerry Belson's irreverent story of a fatally ill man trying unsuccessfully to kill himself, but only one of them had the courage to tackle it. Burt Reynolds jumped in as director, star, and co-producer. It did not surprise me in the least. When people were sticking their noses in the air about his nude centerfold in *Cosmopolitan*, I howled and said, "I'll bet it's his little joke." I was dead right. "Why should women have to undress all the time?" he asked later. "Why not undress a man for a change?" So I had a certain amount of confidence in him when he called one day. "I want you for my mother," he declared. "You and Pat O'Brien have always been my ideal parents and he's already agreed to do the father."

Pat and I had just one scene, but Burt made the most of it on and off screen. At a huge, festive party to welcome us, Burt had the sound stage decorated with an enormous blowup from *Consolation Marriage* in 1931. As we posed for photographers beneath that glossy advertisement for gilded youth—Pat, a handsome young man; me, with the fabulous profile—Pat turned to me and said, "Myrna, you want to see my pacemaker?" I declined the offer, so he ripped his shirt open and went around showing it to everyone else. He was priceless, better than ever. Working together was not very different after forty-seven years, really, except we had been younger then.

At first, directing us had been intimidating to Burt. "How can I tell Myrna Loy what to do?" he asked me. "You've been in seven of my all-time favorite movies." Perhaps we tested him at the start, but he did not drop the ball and we soon gave ourselves to him completely. He is a very gifted director, full of ideas. He never wastes time, as so many fledglings do, because he does his homework. And he is such a delightful man to be with, witty and dear. He always calls when he visits New York: "Hello, Mom, this is your erstwhile son. When can we have dinner?"

In 1981, after vandals decapitated the statue of me as "Aspiration" at Venice High, Burt quietly—without even mentioning it to me—sent a generous check to aid William Van Orden's reconstruction.

I was a fan of Miss Loy long before I was her friend, Reynolds wrote to Acting Principal Dr. Charles Welsh. I hope the students of Venice High realize that the human being behind their symbol stands for the highest ideals on which this nation was founded and to which it continues to aspire. Long before it was fashionable and at a time when show-business personalities never allowed their beliefs to be communicated, Myrna Loy spoke out loudly and clearly for justice and equality and a dignified existence for every living person on the globe. Thousands of hours out of her life have been given to strengthening the causes in which she believes—including civil rights, fair housing, and the rights of individuals to follow their dreams. I wish both the faculty and

*the students at Venice High could know Myrna Loy personally,
as we have all benefited from her clear vision, strong beliefs, and
hard work.*

During a dinner party one night, Sidney Lumet mentioned that he had
always wanted to do a film with me. "Fine," I told him. "I'm just a
ring away."

Two years later, in June, 1978, he called me in Indianapolis, where
I was launching a tour of *Relatively Speaking*: "Myrna, I've got a part
for you at long last. Will you read the script?"

"I'd like to, but I'm touring until October."

"We start shooting in January, so there's no conflict. I'll send you
the script, or I'll come out there." I told him to send it, since I was due
in New York for an examination—this was before my second operation—and could see him then.

Just Tell Me What You Want, a biting satire about a brash tycoon
who wants to rule the world, held the best role I had been offered in
years. Stella Liberti, the tycoon's executive secretary, is one of those
peripheral people in the corporate world who wield enormous power.
She practically runs the show and narrates the film with asides to the
audience—much of which was cut in the final print. I met with Sidney
and Jay Presson Allen, who adapted the script from her novel, and said
I would love to do it.

We rehearsed for three weeks in a marvelous old Socialist club in
lower Manhattan where Sidney's father once had been a member. Sidney is one of the few film directors I have worked with who rehearse.
So did Willy Wyler—he rehearsed us for two weeks on the apartment
set before we shot *The Best Years of Our Lives*. It is like doing a play.
We were letter-perfect when filming started and Sidney had worked out
the angles and blocking. He is a very interesting director and a very
compulsive man, going all the time, wound up. When he is off on a
tangent, it is impossible to divert him to discuss a problem or a bit of
business. Fortunately, he is smaller than I am. One day in rehearsal,
after trying unsuccessfully to get his attention, I leaned over and pinned
him against the wall. "Now, you listen to me," I demanded. "I have
something to say to you." He listened.

Sidney loves location. They all think it is terrific nowadays, but it is
a hardship in many ways. We shot my opening scenes in a small office

at Warners' Rockefeller Center headquarters. As they tried to get close-ups of me at the desk, I looked up and saw the cameraman, his assistants, Sidney, and a few others huddled against the wall. "Take out the wall!" I ordered, which cracked them up, because in the studio you can remove the walls and push back the crew. That is one of the many benefits of the studio, where I prefer to work.

We started on location in the silent days, shooting out at Malibu or Griffith Park. Then came sound, requiring completely enclosed cameras. Next the sound stage and the technology to go with it were developed. The great artistry of the movies, it seems to me, is in creating whole worlds within the studio. We had two blocks of a New York street out on the M-G-M back lot that looked more real than the real thing, although they were merely false fronts. That was the magic of Hollywood. Now moviemakers go out on location and think they are innovating.

Sidney suspected that Alan King, known primarily as a stand-up comedian, was a good actor. Alan proved him right with his strong and funny performance as the ruthless tycoon. I could scarcely keep a straight face in many of our scenes together, particularly when he kept confessing his lifelong infatuation. "My fantasy as a young man was to be Nick Charles to your Nora," he admitted, which was not unusual for a man of his generation. Alan, however, actually wanted to do something about it. We never got beyond calling each other "Nick" and "Nora," but his wife used to come around just to make sure. Let me tell you, that man wishes he were a lot older.

Ali MacGraw does a nice job as Alan's current mistress, but the critics continue to punish her for having been a model. Scared to death when we started the picture, she really believed that she would not get through it. That appalling tennis picture she made for her ex-husband, Robert Evans, had weakened her career and her confidence. "I have my return flight to California, just in case," she told me.

"Cut that out," I said sharply. "I don't want to hear you say that again." I kept bolstering her up and we became good friends. That is one of the nicest girls who ever lived. Sidney worked very hard with her. He drove her crazy. She said he used to come in and say, "Now laugh. Now cry. Now do this or that . . . ," which is impossible for an actress. But whatever he did, it worked. She does good work in that film.

I consider *Just Tell Me What You Want* a hilarious parable of our time, but Warner Brothers killed it. They just do not know how to handle pictures out there anymore. They're so scared—they want to make money, money, money; the money is the only thing that interests them. If a picture fails to start raking in millions its first day out, forget it. They pulled it in New York after only two weeks. "Where's that picture?" people kept asking. "Call Warner Brothers and ask them," I pointedly replied.

After reuniting Alan and Ali in the last shot of the picture, I walk away humming "Isn't It Romantic?" It occurred to me that I had appeared in the film for which Rodgers and Hart had written that song nearly fifty years before. Such intimations of continuity prevailed after my second operation, thoughts of where I had been, where I was going. I curtailed picture work without, at first, bemoaning this great, glamorous profession where you get up at five-thirty in the morning. Can you imagine anyone being that insane? But we are. I am not complaining. I survived, but a lot of people don't. I have had a rewarding life—of course, you can't have everything. But then, you don't need everything. I have had the fulfillment of a career and, in lieu of lasting marriage or my own progeny, I have devoted friends and their children and the memory of extraordinary people who have touched my life. There are so many exceptional people in the world if you just look around. There isn't a day in my life that I don't meet or hear from an old friend.

You meet Hollywood colleagues in New York years later and it becomes a different relationship: old friends, attests Maureen O'Sullivan. *Myrna's a true friend. She has that quality of understanding what things mean to you. You don't have to explain. When my son, a sculptor, had his first exhibition, I called Myrna. She was there battling the crowds. When I received an award from the Sculptors' Society for services rendered, I called Myrna. She drove to Brooklyn with me, a long way to go for a friend, but we had so many laughs on the way and she got a standing ovation when they introduced her. When my daughter Stephanie Farrow was contemplating an acting career, I sent her to Myrna. "You know, Mother," Stephanie said afterward, "she made me feel I really could be an actress."*

Old acquaintances popped up in the strangest places. One day some years ago, I was starting across Fifth Avenue when somebody grabbed my arm. I looked up to see Oscar Levant's unmistakable face as he escorted me to the other side. "That was wonderful," he said when we reached the curb. "Let's go back and do it again."

Averell Harriman, a longtime political ally, turned up beside me at a theatrical tribute for Franklin Delano Roosevelt, another former New York governor. Only for F.D.R. would Averell have consented to make his Broadway début at the age of ninety.

A new ally appeared in the person of Charles A. Lindbergh, although our politics had never been particularly compatible. The Lone Eagle made a rare public appearance to co-host a reception and news conference benefiting the University of Montana's Lubrecht Experimental Forest. Montanans remain loyal to their state and its university, and I more so, having acquired alumna privileges as a recipient of the university's honorary Order of the Grizzly. Publicity-shy Lindbergh, a Montanan only by association, since his son operated a ranch abutting the forest, made the ultimate sacrifice for the state and the cause of conservation. Philanthropy, nevertheless, had its limits. When he grew impatient with the questions of newsmen, he walked off muttering, "That's enough for now," and left me holding the bag.

When Arnold Weissberger and Milton Goldman, two theatrical men-about-town, escorted Paulette Goddard and me to a Martha Graham gala at the Metropolitan Opera House, we dressed—Polly to the nines, as usual, with those fabulous jewels. She looks great and she is rich. She had recently become Erich Remarque's widow. Polly always looks out for herself. At intermission, we sauntered to the bar, feeling rather elegant. And why not? "Look at this!" Polly gasped. "Everybody else is wearing jeans!"

When Joan Bennett's daughters gave a surprise party for her at Sardi's, Dede, her daughter by her first marriage, who is a friend of mine, included me. (I always seem to fit in with the children.) At a time when the children of celebrities are writing cruel books about them, it was refreshing to see that expression of love and gratitude. They even assembled a little film retrospective in which, coincidentally, I appeared in a shot from our 1931 potboiler, *Hush Money*. No one deserves such a loving tribute more than Joanie. Not only is she a wonderful mother but she was the burden-bearer of the Bennett family. Her sisters were never any help in dealing with the eccentricities of their talented but alcoholic father; Connie was always playing cards and Barbara had neurological problems. Joanie was forever picking up the pieces. Then, her husband, Walter Wanger, spent all of his money and most of hers on that misadventure called *Joan of Arc*, and thanked Joan by shooting her agent in a jealous rage. But she pulled herself out of that and started doing theater and television to give her girls the very best. I have always thought Joanie was something.

Near the end of the Dallas run of *Relatively Speaking*, Greer Garson appeared backstage with an exquisite carrying case of perfume from Gucci. I was bowled over by her gracious gesture. I never knew her terribly well in Hollywood, but closer friends often did far less when I hit their bailiwicks. Greer apologized for not having seen the play sooner and entertaining me properly: "Buddy has had a heart attack and I've been frantic." A few weeks later, while still nursing her husband, *Greer* had a heart attack! Fortunately, she has recovered and seems better than ever. Things are not always so heartening. After one of Ilka Chase's marvelous luncheons in New York, she sent me her latest book. Before I could even thank her, Ilka was gone. It happens too often these days. So many friends have gone since we started this book, so many, many friends.

I returned to M-G-M in 1981, my first visit since finishing *Song of the Thin Man* in 1947. George Cukor, Sam Marx, and David Chasman, then vice-president in charge of production, hosted a luncheon for me in the little executive's alcove of the commissary. Cary Grant, along with Frank Rosenfelt and David Begelman, stopped by after the board meeting at which M-G-M purchased United Artists. Cary, a member of the board, decided that my visit had brought them luck. It did not last. M-G-M has hit hard times since then, and now Ted Turner seems to be chopping it up for firewood. Cary looked marvelous that day. It was the first time we had met since he had taken another young wife. "Congratulations, you old fool," I chided, grabbing a bicep. "Solid as a rock," I observed. And he remained so, vigorous and fit, until we suddenly lost him last year.

After lunch, the director of publicity took me on a brief tour of the lot. We rode in a sort of fancy golf cart through valleys between sound stages and other studio buildings, one of which has since been named for me. Occasionally, costumed chorus girls strolled by from the set of a Steve Martin picture they were filming. I thought of Lucille Le Sueur and Myrna Williams walking that street dressed as snowflakes for *Pretty Ladies*. It reassured me to see the old place alive. I had avoided going back for fear it would be a shambles.

Not that I am particularly sentimental about M-G-M or those so-called good old days. Why is everyone so infatuated with the past? I am interested in "now," not in the thirties or forties. And these days they are trying to bring back the fifties—the dreariest decade of them all. At a "Fabulous Forties" benefit for Phoenix House, a drug-rehabilitation center, someone asked me to tell the fifteen hundred guests why the forties were so fabulous. "First," I began, "we had a war; then there was the atom bomb; and to top off the decade, we had Joe McCarthy on a rampage to find Communists under all our beds." The past always looks better in retrospect, but those of us who lived through those decades should try to remember what difficult times they were. Something must be terribly wrong with today to make so many people yearn for the past. But the danger in escaping to the past is that we will never move forward; we will be too busy dwelling on the imagined glories of earlier decades.

I think Myrna's great gift is complete adjustment to now being the only time there really is, speculates Tammy Grimes. Sometimes I project myself into the future. I think: My God! I really am going to grow old like everybody else. What a tragedy! I haven't done nearly enough! It comforts me then to think about someone like Myrna. That is the way to live. She is ageless. This lady has no regrets. She never gripes about anything. She comes in celebration and it's very natural for her. She's never on. She's just there in that complete sense, with all the cloaks of this life of hers. She must have been living that way when she was very young, because she remembers all these things and wants to share them with us. It has nothing to do with ego. She is carrying her life and the gifts of her life with her.

Whenever I sit down for any length of time, something inside my head starts nagging at me. I have got to keep on the go, keep working. I have been working since I was seventeen, and I am certainly not prepared to quit yet. The chance to play Henry Fonda's wife in *Summer Solstice* ended my convalescence. It was merely a sixty-minute teleplay, but Hank liked the script. "It's a lovely story about the survival of a marriage," he told me. "It's a mature love story which ought to be told." As soon as I accepted, I immediately felt better than I had in ages.

We filmed on Cape Cod in autumn of 1980, along twisting roads and deserted beaches edged by pine trees and bayberry bushes and sea grass beginning to blanch. Hank and I were great friends politically. He was one of the stalwarts; whenever I needed him, he was there. Never having worked with him, however, I was wary. So was he. But working together was like a poem. We have the same approach to acting— to be as real as possible, which he certainly is. He gave me what I wanted. Few of them did in sixty years and a hundred and twenty-four films.

Although ABC later bought *Summer Solstice*—the first time a major network had ever purchased a drama made by a local station—WCVB-TV in Boston produced it. Their crew approached us like legends at first, even Ralph Rosenbloom, one of our foremost film editors, who had lately turned to directing. "I never knew what a martini was till I saw *The Thin Man*," he confessed. "I was a poor kid from Brooklyn during the Depression, watching this sophisticated woman up there on the screen. Now I'm *working* with you!" When filming started, we stopped being legends and became actors.

In the last scene, shot out of sequence, my character has died on the beach. As the husband cradles her lifeless body, a large hat covers her face. To relieve me of a tedious chore, Hank suggested that my stand-in could do it, since my face would not show. "All I need's a sack of flour," he insisted.

"Well, here's your sack of flour," I countered, dropping into his lap. I could not cheat. The stand-in was a different shape. The scene was too intimate. It would not have been fair to Hank or the script.

The final day's filming, our most intimate and touching exchange, took place in an old shingled house high above Ballston Beach in Truro. Our stand-ins stretched on the bed. The civilians who owned the house watched in terror as the denim swarm wreaked ordered pandemonium upon the premises. When all was ready, Hank and I replaced the stand-ins. After a flurry of makeup and wardrobe people, Ralph ordered and the assistant mouthed, "Roll 'em!" We played the scene, but the sound mixer complained that gels on the windows were flapping and people were milling around on the porch. The scene rolled again, Hank and I quietly sustaining our intimacy without benefit of visible methods. One of the crew asked how we managed without the ritualistic preparations indulged in by so many younger actors.

"I always watch them and I laugh at them," Hank said. "It amuses me and it's so ridiculous to me."

"We don't have to go through all the motions that those kids do," I added. "We didn't start acting yesterday, you know."

Following the third and final take, the thirty-one-year-old author, Bill Phillips, approached us in tears. "I didn't really understand what I was writing," he told us, "until I heard you say the lines."

There were still a few more shots without dialogue to complete on the porch. It was cold and windy. Many young staffers took shelter inside while the shots were set up. We waited on the porch. Hank, gazing longingly down at the beach where men were casting for striped bass, spoke of early days on the Cape with the University Players. I recalled fishing with my stepson off Malibu. After shooting us rocking on the long porch, they determined that they had enough to wrap up the show a day under schedule. Someone noted the speed with which our scenes were completed, crediting our professionalism. "And new tricks," I added, referring to the technological advances that fascinate me. Stars and, occasionally, directors are talked about, but think of the people and technology involved! Even this little company that they got together in Boston was fantastic.

I got such a bang out of doing that show—it was like a shot of adrenaline. Hank felt the same. His pacemaker notwithstanding, he loved to work. "I would rather be working than not working," he declared, "even when it's tough."

"That will go on with both of us," I said. "We'll be like that until we drop in our tracks." It is a strange thing about acting. There are those who are in it for money or one reason or another, but most actors who are really actors, who really care about their profession, feel that way. Hank was indefatigable. He even tried out a play in Connecticut shortly afterward. I went out to see it and he was marvelous. But *Summer Solstice* would be his last film—and mine to date.

Hank's death knocked me for a loop. I consoled myself with the realization that he could never have endured being an invalid. When we flew from Cape Cod back to New York, he wanted to keep going.

"Let's go out and party," he urged. "We've got to celebrate the end of our picture." That is what we always did in Hollywood. It was in his blood. His wife, Shirlee, and I were exhausted from traveling and tending to him, particularly Shirlee, who managed to carry more luggage than a mule team. I begged off, but he dragged Shirlee out somewhere and she told me later that she fell asleep in her plate. Hank wanted to howl, and that was that. The day he died, *Entertainment Tonight* called me about doing a tribute: "You want me to do *what?*" I broke down crying and hung up.

You cannot say that I am entirely unscathed by the wages of celebrity and public exposure, but I was raised with a set of values that neutralized the negative aspects. This business about "unless you're rich, you ain't nobody" was always foreign to me. I have hauled in a lot of money. I have spent a lot of money. It does not matter. My father wasn't rich, but he was an honest man. After he died, nearly every fraternal organization in the state honored him. It struck me then that the important thing for my life was to have ideals—education, for instance, and I do not mean the ivory-towered kind—and to have goals that do not necessarily shine the way gold does. Of course, gold seems to be power, but it can be power for good. The Prophet Mohammed said if you have two loaves of bread, sell one and buy hyacinths. Artists, I fancy, are the purveyors of hyacinths. That is an enormous responsibility.

If you live long enough and fight hard enough, a sense of comforting continuity comes. I think I can say, without sounding too presumptuous, that something came of my work for peace, freedom, and justice, even in the face of our present administration. Ronald Reagan has lived up to my expectations, which were not very great; he did, after all, tell us everything he was going to do beforehand. And I had inklings before that, not only in Hollywood but in Chicago, after dining with his conservative in-laws, the Loyal Davises. When they began reviling Adlai Stevenson and his humanitarian policies, I stood up from their table, scornfully surveyed that gathering of plutocrats, and headed straight for the door. It was a short jump from the views expressed there to the patio politics of their son-in-law. It didn't surprise me. Still, especially after the Iran-contra affair, this galloping pragmatism infesting the land is terrifying. Can you imagine how all of us who worked for years with Mrs. Roosevelt for her social programs feel now to see them wiped off the map? Yet the inspiration derived from her deeds—from her very being—prevails. We still celebrate her birthday every year—not her death, her birth. A dwindling group of friends and AAUN colleagues—Clark Eichelberger, Estelle Linzer, Joe and Trude Lash, Curtis Roosevelt, her grandson—has gathered over the years in the U.N. garden by the stone bench that bears Adlai's tribute to her: "She would rather light a candle than curse the darkness, and her glow has warmed the world." We take flowers and put them down there and talk about her. That is all. Oh, could we use Eleanor Roosevelt now! I often think, What would she do? I know she would not just sit back.

The United Nations and its humanitarian agencies also face hard times now, with Reagan bent on cutting their funding. That is what happens in the United Nations. You go through these phases and then things straighten out. The concept of world peace and the will to uplift mankind will persevere. Their resilience was underscored for me by the eightieth-birthday celebration for Clark Eichelberger, my AAUN mentor, which benefited another U.N.-related project—the Commission to Study the Organization of Peace. A farewell tribute to U Thant, after his decade of benign but forceful leadership as U.N. Secretary-General, reaffirmed the credibility of the individual within the organization. And my own small contribution was recognized when I helped, as a member of the National Commission for Adult Literacy, to launch UNESCO's fund-raising drive to combat world illiteracy. During the ceremony, UNESCO officials surprised me with its Silver Medallion for my years of service. While reciting the preamble to the U.N. Charter at the annual U.N. Ambassadors' Dinner recently, I looked around and realized I was on the same dais in the Waldorf ballroom where my involvement began forty years ago. Continuity.

It is difficult for an American to imagine, but freedom, too, needs reaffirmation. This was brought home yet again when Justice Douglas's widow asked me to participate in a benefit for the William O. Douglas Inquiry into the State of Individual Freedom, which provides a forum for debate on freedom-related issues. The Shuberts donated the Broadway Theatre and Bobbie Handman devised an extraordinary program: actors read the Constitution, while six judges sat on stage interpolating and Henry Fonda read Justice Douglas's applicable decisions. People were hanging on the edge of their seats, because the Constitution builds phrase by phrase, creating dramatic tension.

I read the Fourth Amendment; Melvyn Douglas read the Sixth. When

Helen Gahagan Douglas appeared on stage to read the Fifth Amendment, everyone in that full house cheered wildly. They knew how ill she was and what that amendment meant to her. Since Watergate, there had even been bumper stickers saying, "Don't blame us: We voted for Helen Gahagan Douglas!" I stood in the wings with tears streaming down my face as they honored my comrade-at-arms.

Now we are fighting the Moral Majority, with its implications of McCarthyism and Fascism, and its mass-media Elmer Gantrys influencing the electorate. I joined People for the American Way, the countergroup established by Norman Lear. It is not political. It is based on protecting our liberty. Norman called not long ago and asked me to outline the dangers of the Moral Majority to various suburban political organizations "as someone who's been there." Continuity.

In the pursuit of justice, my NCDH duties still include raising funds and making speeches in the ongoing battle to open the suburbs to minority workers who get jobs but not housing in adjacent areas. Enlightened as we are, we still condone exploitation, unemployment, and discrimination. We even get tired of having them pointed out to us. The example of men like Frank S. Horne, Lena's uncle, who was dean of the open-housing movement, reminds us that such inequities do not vanish without effort. While presiding at the NCDH's Twentieth Anniversary Dinner, I joined in a special tribute to this rare man—a poet, a teacher, a fighter, and a star by which I set my course in the NCDH. "It were enough to possess beauty and charm," Dr. Horne wrote to me shortly before his death, "but your interest and work help keep many of us believing in Concord bridge. You have added delight to conviction." Those words are more representative of his generous spirit than of my worthiness, but you can imagine what they mean to me coming from such a man.

When the magazine W printed an interview expressing my political views, Senator Howard Metzenbaum took note. He read the article into the *Congressional Record*, describing me as "a woman who has the courage to stand up for her convictions." Well, I was raised to do that by pioneers who valued such attributes. I could ask for no greater tribute. Whenever I bemoan the current fate of those convictions, I am comforted by the knowledge that others will perpetuate them. After all, according to Robert Browning, whose consort I once played, ". . . a man's reach should exceed his grasp, or what's a heaven for?"

INDEX